150
.A769
the
2005

the
theorem

a complete answer to
human behavior

Douglas M. Arone

D1453289

23 PLEASANT STREET
BRUNSWICK, ME 04011-2295

Copyright © 2005 O Books
O Books is an imprint of The Bothy, John Hunt Publishing Ltd.,
Deershot Lodge, Park Lane, Ropley, Hants, SO24 0BE, UK
office@johnhunt-publishing.com
www.O-books.net

Distribution in:
UK
Orca Book Services
orders@orcabookservices.co.uk
Tel: 01202 665432 Fax: 01202 666219 Int. code (44)

USA AND CANADA
NBN
custserv@nbnbooks.com
Tel: 1 800 462 6420 Fax: 1 800 338 4550

AUSTRALIA
Brumby Books
sales@brumbybooks.com
Tel: 61 3 9761 5535 Fax: 61 3 9761 7095

NEW ZEALAND
Peaceful Living
books@peaceful-living.co.nz
Tel: 64 09 921 6222 Fax: 64 09 921 6220

SINGAPORE
STP
davidbuckland@tlp.com.sg
Tel: 65 6276 Fax: 65 6276 7119

SOUTH AFRICA
Alternative Books
altbook@global.co.za
Tel: 27 011 792 7730 Fax: 27 011 972 7787

Text: © 2005 Douglas M. Arone

Design: BookDesign™, London

ISBN 1 905047 10 X

All rights reserved. Except for brief quotations in critical
articles or reviews, no part of this book may be reproduced in
any manner without prior written permission from the
publishers.

The rights of Douglas M. Arone as author has been asserted in
accordance with the Copyright, Designs and Patents Act 1988.

A CIP catalogue record for this book is available from the
British Library.

Printed in the USA by Maple-Vail Manufacturing Group

the
theorem

a complete answer to
human behavior

Douglas M. Arone

BOOKS

WINCHESTER UK
NEW YORK USA

*This work is dedicated to all those
throughout the history of humankind who
have searched for these answers to Human
Behavior, but have fallen short...*

ACKNOWLEDGMENTS

The Essential: To my wife, Karin M.M. Bartels-Arone. To my sons, Nicholas, Calvin, and Julian, who suffered the life of an artist with dignity and pride unprecedented. To Dawn M. Deibert who was there at the time of the initial discovery, Ma and Pa Bartels, and Ron Bartels.

The Guides: Mel Calmes, Susan Thompson, Ron Ashliman, Hugh Beaton, and Tunde.

Everyone Else: And certainly, there is no chronology of importance here. Kathy Bunker, Mrs. Erskine, Elizabeth and George Stearns, Charlotte and Roy Royster, the memory of Timothy Centeno, Wiley and Marlene Ramey, my Brother, and all the others whom I am sure I will remember tomorrow that have helped bring this important discovery and work to publication, and of course, to John.

It is to these individuals that may fade upon numerous reprints and editions on this page throughout the course of history, yet, whose assistance and influence are forever immortalized in the mind of this author.

C O N T E N T S

INTRODUCTION

Arguably, the genius of any great discovery lies in its originality — a fresh idea that is set to challenge traditional modes of thinking while advancing man's march along the path of progress. The work before us fits neatly into these criteria, and it's all the more remarkable for the manner in which it came into being. It is a case of monumental irony that a man who once aspired to be in the ranks of great writers such as Tolstoy, James Joyce, and Honore Balzac — among many others — should "stumble upon" one of the most important scientific discoveries of our time. And, yet, it was not merely an accidental find, but rather the outcome of a deep yearning which, when fulfilled, had all the qualities of an inspirational experience — the kind that speaks of a contact with something greater than oneself and leaves its subject feeling profoundly humble and utterly helpless.

The author's dream for several years was to find a satisfying psychological theory that he could then apply to the hero of a novel that he one day would write. An admirable skill of successful writers is their ability to arouse in the reader some degree of identification with the different characters of their work — the ability that is the result of a keen awareness of what we would refer to as human nature. One, therefore, understands the author's motivations. Not satisfied with any of the available theories — including that of Freud himself — he sought to discover his own. Like a hermit withdrawing from virtually all worldly contact, he set about his lonely quest. As is often the case, there were many disappointing leads, and several times he was tempted to give up his search and succumb to the lure of the mundane — take a regular job, as is the lot of many, and provide for his family. If he managed to fight off his doubts concerning the worthiness of his efforts, one can only imagine it's because he had crossed that indefinable line in the journey of discovery where the goal as yet is beyond reach. However, within the seeker is a conviction that it is attainable.

His breakthrough came one evening as he sat working in the front room in his lonely apartment, contemplating an approaching thunderstorm. The author had seen many storms before as they are commonplace in the part of the country to which he had retreated for his work. However, for some reason, he took particular notice of this one. Awestruck by the display of nature's glory before him, he seemed transfixed by the power of this storm that nevertheless threatened to engulf him. Soon, the entire sky and horizon were transformed by an intense red glow that added grandeur to an already fascinating picture. The air was charged with static electricity that caused the lights in his apartment to flicker on and off in a feeble effort to mimic the flashes of lightning occurring outside. Suddenly, everything came together in what had become his jumbled mind of ideas. At that moment he was struck by the realization that the essential aspects of man's nature — the ebbs and flows of our emotions and feelings, our motivations and reasons — have their origin in life in the womb. Far from the idea that the human fetus is cocooned from the cares and woes of existence, our first experience of fear, joy, and sorrow actually precedes our birth. This, in a nutshell, is what this book is set to tell the world.

The discovery itself was made well over ten years ago and if it's taken that long to present it in the form before us, then it's taken that long for the author to overcome intense doubts about the validity of his findings, doubts about his credentials to present them, and doubts about his own importance in the "scheme of things". Important as the discovery itself promised to be, it was, nevertheless, more than what the author had expected. With no relevant educational experience in the natural sciences, the task that lay ahead of him was to find a way to convince a skeptical audience that he had something new to add to the body of knowledge about human behavior that already exists.

And so, anticipating a hostile reception from the world — particularly the scientific community — there were many occasions when he felt inclined to do nothing. Yet, he could not dismiss as a fanciful notion what came to him that evening. It became imperative that he conducted his own study in various fields, including neurobiology, neuroimmunology, neuroanatomy, neurochemistry, and immunology — to mention but a few. The aim was to find results of established research that would support the model of human behavior that he sought to develop with his discovery. It is an undeniable fact that he has accomplished his task with exceptional brilliance.

Nevertheless, one can expect murmurs of disagreements with some of the bold claims made here. The idea of fetal consciousness is bound to be unsettling for many and should perhaps provoke the most reaction. However, the definition of consciousness will vary depending on the ideological orientation of the individual from whom an answer is sought. In a clinical sense, consciousness is the state in which the particular human organism is able to perceive and respond to his or her environment in a purposeful and meaningful manner. This definition presupposes that the parts of the brain that are responsible for the wakeful alert state function optimally. We would have no difficulty in accepting the fact that a newborn baby is conscious. The next question then would be: does any one particular event — for instance, expulsion from the womb, or severing the umbilical cord — confer this consciousness? It seems more likely that a newborn's consciousness is an attribute that has preceded its birth, and is the outcome of the developmental process in which nerve cells in the brain and other parts of the body are being formed as part of that development. Some of these cells specialize and begin to function as sense organs able to respond to the changes within the growing fetus and in the environment that is the uterus, while others function as efferent organs able to react to these changes. The inference, therefore, is that the emergence of human consciousness corresponds to the growth and development of the human fetus — a seamless process that makes it near impossible to define the moment of its "beginning." At any rate, we are now being confronted with the fact of newborn babies who — born several weeks before the world expected them — are nevertheless of fetal age.

The bigger question for us, therefore, maybe: what is the nature of this consciousness? The position of the author is to assert that it is capable of generating the preverbal thought process that underlies our emotions and behaviors. Acknowledging that requires the satisfaction of logic and reason to be convinced. We must, nevertheless, recognize that these are purely human attributes, and need not be projected to nature's remit to create. What we like to see as nature's reasons may, in fact, be its methods and while we may ask endlessly, why? What we often discover is how. Thus, whatever objections we may have about the idea of fetal consciousness, and the necessity or value of its distress, nature is decidedly proud of its accomplishments. We may find no rational and cerebral reason to raise young, nevertheless, we do it with ardor and passion. As we ponder these and other thoughts, it is worth remembering that it was never the author's object or aim to prove fetal consciousness. What he came to realize is that the foundation of human emotions and behavior is formed during intrauterine development — in what he has termed the "first fear" and "euphoric" cycles. It is the reader who recognizes that he or she is being led to his or her own conclusion of fetal consciousness.

The work itself reads like a detective novel — the only hint perhaps of the author's original ambition — and one cannot help but be intrigued, if not persuaded, by the evidence presented. Yet, much of the strength of the work lies in the sense one feels while reading it, that the events so aptly articulated resonate with ones own experience. In a sense it "feels true." A good point comes in the illustration of what happens as we sleep and dream. Whatever else we may have learned or believed about sleep, we are here given to realize that one of the essential aspects of dreams is the feeling state underlying them. Thus, we have fear as one underlying emotion, which produces nightmare on one hand and joy on the other, from which our "sweet dreams" —

leaving us with a warm fuzzy feeling — are derived. Perhaps it is obvious enough; however, very few of us would have recognized before now that these feelings — states — occur in a cyclical fashion every night so that in the first half of our sleep period, the fearful dreams predominate, and in the second half, it is the sweet dreams that we have more of. Then we are made to see how this cycle recapitulates what we experienced as fetuses in our mother's womb. And, just in case we require proof, the author guides us through the example of mania in the condition "Bipolar Disorder" (or, the more colloquial, "manic-depression") to an elegant display of this sleep model. Finally, for the first time, we can truly understand why in spite of the fact that while dreaming we often perceive the events in our dreams as "real," we very quickly forget the details upon awakening.

The book is awash with examples from the field of mental illness for it is the symptoms of various mental disorders that we are confronted with, the reality of the fetal experiences, that this work is about. We do recognize that symptoms of mental illness in many respects are exaggerations of normal experience and therefore lend themselves to the study and understanding of human behavior. The reader is therefore not to be put off by the examples from the field. This is by no means a textbook of psychopathology and one may anticipate it arousing discussion and debate in as disparate settings as a doctor's lounge, a hairdressing salon, a bar, and a church vestry.

This brings us to a brief discussion on the implication of these findings. What is presented before us is no ordinary finding and it seems unlikely that, in the usual empirical methods of scientific research, anyone would have come up with the picture of intrauterine life that the author discloses here. History presents us with other instances of apparent chance discoveries, which then lead to significant changes in the way humanity thinks and conducts its business of living. One is left to wonder, therefore, if it is just a mere coincidence that at the time when man is "advancing" to the point of utilizing what a human organism is in its earliest phase of development for research, we should be confronted with these fresh insights. Given the nature of the discovery process, the question may be asked; why now? No doubt, religious leaders and thinkers, psychologists, philosophers, sociologists, and scientific researchers will want to examine closely the contents of this work. These fresh discoveries may support already established positions in these fields, or may cause new ground to be explored. In the least we are given an opportunity to re-examine our position on the importance of life in the womb. Not that this importance has ever been in doubt, but it takes a certain degree of attention and focus paid to it so that a new level of awareness comes into being, and with that a change in attitude.

No one would ever think today that it is short of criminal or insane to offer a newborn up to a god (or God) in sacrifice. Yet, in the history of mankind, such events have taken place and were considered normal and necessary. The result of the change — in spite of the many possible reasons for it — is a newer understanding and acceptance of the humanity of a newborn such that we do identify with it and find abhorrent any thought that it be killed for any reason.

Today, the battle rages between those who believe that human life begins at birth and those who believe that it begins at some arbitrary moment in the developmental process in the womb when it is considered viable — i.e., able to survive outside the womb. (In the latter case we see a progressive shift to a younger age of the fetus as the technology advances to permit improved support of existence outside the womb.) The problem may lie however in the question itself: "When does life begin"? We see it as an impossible question and we trip on ourselves whenever we attempt to provide an answer to it. Life does not begin, life simply is. No one has yet been born of a corpse, and while a man may die a few moments after he causes a woman to conceive, his seed in her is his living cell, a distillation of his characteristics, experience, and attributes, which ensures a continuation — albeit transformed — of what he had been. The same is true of the woman — and perhaps even more so. To be alive is evidence that one's mother was alive, at least until the moment of one's birth, and so each one is a continuation of his or her mother's existence. Metaphorically, it is like an endless relay race in which each new generation of parents passes a baton to each of their offspring who, therefore, become co-opted into the race. Without digressing too far into the realm of the esoteric, it is easy to see that, strictly speaking, each and every one of us is ageless — a symbol of the dictum: "life without end." This is as true for us as it is for every life form we run into in our wanderings.

A particularly interesting observation of the human experience of being is that having seemingly had no part to play in the circumstances that brought together the two people who are one's parents, one, nevertheless, has no doubt as to the inevitability of one's existence. Thus, we need not struggle to find some definable moment in the intrauterine phase of human development in order to feel capable of granting or according the "occupant" human status, value, or importance. Our own personal sense of these qualities thus makes us inviolable and establishes the same in every phase of intrauterine development.

This work also brings to light another essential aspect of the developmental process that we undergo during the life in the womb and underscores a psychological truth. The author suggests that primary in the experience of the developing fetus is its knowledge of the reality of its mother — an experience that precedes the acquisition of the language to describe it and precedes the development of a mental image of her. A child is born knowing it is to be with someone. What this tells us is that a basic element of our reality is that we exist in relation to another. Vital to every aspect of the health of the newborn is the quality of the relationship between it and its mother — this is nature's standards, not merely a man-made ideal. We discover here that nature assumes an optimal period of close interaction between the newborn and its mother for about two years,

This position challenges our modern-day view of child-rearing practices, but those women, who are inclined to work soon after the birth of their child, need not feel under attack. One well understands that as a matter of expediency, a mother may not be in a position to fulfill nature's obligation for her in respect of tending to her newborn in these times. The fact of the matter, however, is that nature did not anticipate modernity — we have to take responsibility for this. From a sociological point of view, an optimistic potential outcome of the new knowledge that this work brings is a re-establishment of the pre-eminence of motherhood and, therefore, parenthood in the collective life experience that we call society. This may well take several decades, but when it does happen, it will represent an advance in our level of understanding about us.

It is pertinent to add that the author is mindful of the potential for this work to be misappropriated by one particular interest group or another — such that he may be seen as the mouthpiece of such groups or of having political motivations. These reservations nonetheless, many will agree that these findings are too important to be stifled out of these considerations. Each reader is able to make his or her own interpretation of what is contained here and one may hope that it leads to the emergence of a greater understanding of, and respect for, human existence.

Leaving aside these philosophical observations, we note other interesting insights about our day-to-day experience, which are derived from these revelations. Here, we refer to the effects of the "memory block," which inhibit the process of learning in the uterus. One is inclined to think that this phenomenon continues to operate in adult life — especially where our feelings are concerned. How often does it occur that we find our conviction change depending on our mood, and whatever mood we are in, we scant recognize ourselves in the experience of the previous mood state? This, so that, for instance, the same person we love without reservation at certain times, we also hate with utmost certainty at other times? And the wisdom of holding our tongue is that we soon forget the person we became in our moment of anger and hatefulness. However, with our words, we may make what is but a passing phase permanent. Perhaps the enduring nature of this work will become evident as certain features described in the book begin to creep into our colloquial language — when a wife is able to dismiss her husband's occasional outbursts with: "Oh, you are just back in your 'first fear cycle.'"

However, more important, it should help define the future direction of research so that more can be accomplished in our quest for a more universal experience of a happy existence on this massive ball of rock, soil, water, and vegetation spinning endlessly in space with inhabitants who must forever cope with the lingering sense that they have been taken for a ride — not knowing by whom, and never knowing why.

B. Abolade MD; MRCP (UK)
Montgomery, Alabama.

PART ONE

THE MODEL

CHAPTER ONE

THE TWO CYCLES

It all starts with a lie. It is doubtful that it is Nature's intention we remember it as a lie. It is doubtful that it is Nature's intention that we remember it at all, however, we do, and its impact lasts a lifetime. The lie colors our world, defines the extremes of our morality, imprisons men and fascinates us to no end. It holds such a power, that while we strive for truth, we cannot help but be intrigued by the power of a lie. Yet, it all starts out as nothing more than a necessary aspect of our development. Yes, without the lie, there would be no deception, no mystery, no trickery, no illusion, no fraud, no double-dealing, and no untruths. Yes, without the lie the world would be a perfect place. It would be perfect indeed; perfectly dull and perfectly colorless. For there would also be no creativity, no fantasy and… no imagination!

There would even be worse consequences than no imagination, if this aspect of our development did not exist. Without this deception inherent in our earliest origins there would be no reproduction of the human species. Therefore, without the lie there would be no human species. Indeed, the lie is powerful. The schizophrenic sees through the lie, the autistic never experiences it, and everyone else lives and was trained by it.

The lie actually starts out as a deception. The deception starts out as a misinterpretation. The misinterpretation starts out as an important aspect of our development. It is a simple misinterpretation, a misread of environmental cues. What is amazing about this misinterpretation is where and when it takes place. The misinterpretation occurs at a time and place where we were most vulnerable. In this place we were imprisoned not only by the lie, however, also by Nature herself. And, it was all for our own good.

The misinterpretation of environmental cues occurs in a very unique environment indeed. The misinterpretation begins in the womb. The misinterpretation occurs to the fetus, from the early stages of its development. The misinterpretation is due to a function of the developing fetal brain. This function is responsible for blocking the short-term memory of the conscious fetus. This will be explained later in this chapter.

To understand this fetal misinterpretation of cues is to understand the origins of human behavior. And to understand the origins of human behavior is to possess the keys to the answers that mankind has struggled to understand since the beginning of its existence.

Before you can understand what this fetal misinterpretation is, it is necessary to understand a little about its life and the environment in which it lives. To understand this, it is first necessary to understand a little about the economy and efficiency of Nature, especially in the development of the human species. And, the development of the human species begins with the development of the human fetus. This is exactly where the journey to the answers begins.

In the womb, the fetus realizes two cycles of development. The first of the two cycles occurs when its mother is resting or sleeping, primarily at night. This cycle will be defined as the "First Fear Cycle of Development." This is an extremely painful, unpleasant and horrific cycle of development for the fetus to experience. During this cycle the fetal activity level is high. While it may occasionally sleep, passing out from exhaustion, throughout most of the cycle the fetus remains awake, alert and active.

The second cycle the fetus experiences, is very much in contrast of the first. During this cycle the environment for the fetus is very pleasant, in fact it is extremely pleasant. This cycle will be defined as the "Euphoric Cycle of Development." This cycle occurs primarily during the day or when the mother is awake and active. During this developmental cycle the fetus is less active. In the Euphoric Cycle the fetus spends most of its time resting, sleeping, relaxing and growing.

In the following two chapters both of these developmental cycles will be explained in detail. One of the most fascinating aspects of these developmental cycles is how Nature alternates the fetal activity level with that of its mother. In other words, so as not to overburden the mother, who is already sustaining two lives in one body, Nature minimizes the impact of this burden. When the fetus is active, the mother is not. When the mother is active, the fetus is not. This is only the first of the many aspects of the economy of Nature you will realize throughout this book. While this sounds very simple and obvious, by these two cycles of alternating development, Nature goes to great lengths to ensure this economy is achieved.

It is important to realize that these two cycles vary many times throughout a twenty-four hour period, and for each pregnancy, due to the mother's sleep-wake cycle. To make this model understandable, it is necessary to simplify. Therefore the focus will be on two specific cycles of development occurring during two specific periods of time. The First Fear Cycle of Development will occur at night, when the mother is resting or sleeping. The Euphoric Cycle of Development occurs during the day, when the mother is active.

Now, the origin of the lie, the fetal misinterpretation, originates from its exposure to these two cycles in the womb. It is not the cycles themselves, however, it is the altered perception of the fetus that causes it to misread or misinterpret the environmental cues in each cycle. This altered perception is due to the fact that the fetal short-term memory is blocked. This misinterpretation will be fully explained in the third chapter. For now, what we are going to focus on is the blocked short-term memory of the fetus.

To ensure that the fetus conforms, in the most effective manner, to each of these two developmental cycles, Nature prohibits or blocks the short-term memory of the fetus. How this affects the fetus is, while in one cycle it cannot remember or anticipate the existence of the other cycle. For example, when the fetus is in the Euphoric Cycle it cannot remember the existence of the First Fear Cycle of Development. It believes that the cycle it is in, that it will remain there indefinitely. It is very similar to a state of amnesia that the fetus experiences. The purpose of the blocking of the fetal short-term memory will be explained in later chapters.

The blocking of the fetal short-term memory will be defined as "Memory Block." The Memory Block is a neural function with widespread involvement of the limbic system of the fetal brain. Do not be concerned about terms such as limbic system. If you are interested in a more detailed description of the areas involved with the fetal Memory Block, you can check the Neural Notes in the appendix. If not, forget it. For, this is nothing more than a part of the fetal brain. Indeed, it is not necessary to understand this term to understand The Theorem.

Memory Block, however, is one term that you will need to know, its definition will therefore be repeated throughout the book, including here. The Memory Block is a function of the developing fetal brain that blocks the short-term memory.

CHAPTER TWO

THE EUPHORIC CYCLE OF DEVELOPMENT

The Euphoric Cycle of Development is the least involved of the two developmental cycles that the fetus realizes in the womb. This, however, does not mean that it is insignificant. The purpose of the Euphoric Cycle is to reduce fetal activity. This is important for two major reasons.

The first and most obvious reason is that the cycle occurs when the mother is moving, awake, and utilizing energy for her own subsistence and survival. Indeed, the energy involved in sustaining two lives in one body is enormous. Nature's first concern, as you will see throughout The Theorem, is the mother. If she should perish, two lives would be lost.

The second reason that intrauterine activity should be reduced is the rest, the healing, and the growth of the fetus. The fetus has spent much of the previous night, as you will see in the next chapter, in a state of high activity. By the time the morning arrives and its mother begins moving about her daily tasks, the fetus is physically and mentally exhausted. Lack of an organized demanding developmental cycle will give the developing fetal body and brain time to heal, rest and most importantly to grow.

Neurochemical Manipulation of the Fetus

Life in the womb is a very painful experience for the fetus. To maintain fetal consciousness, during a period of such rapid physical and neural development, is almost an impossible task. In fact, it would be an impossible task for Nature to accomplish, without the utilization of large amounts of pain killing neurochemicals circulating throughout the developing fetal brain. There are numerous pain killing neurochemicals, however, for the purpose of simplification, we will group them all into one. Therefore all pain killing neurochemicals in the developing fetal brain will be defined as dopamine. For a more detailed explanation of the neurochemicals involved in this process see the Neural Notes in the appendix.

So, throughout the book the entire group of pain killing neurochemicals will be called dopamine. While we are not so much interested in the neural aspects of this neurotransmitter, we are interested in the effects it has on fetal behavior. While dopamine serves many purposes in the development of the human fetus, we are only interested in one. Indeed, we are interested in the dopamine flow through the pleasure and reward pathways of the developing fetal brain.

So, what does this mean? It means that dopamine makes life in the womb tolerable for the fetus. It means that life, for the fetus, is so painful in the womb that dopamine makes it livable. It means that without dopamine the pain the fetus would realize would be so intense that it would simply leave the womb; no matter what stage of development it was in. Dopamine in the womb equals life. It is that important.

Now, this brings us back to the definition of this section, which is "Neurochemical Manipulation of the Fetus." What this simply means, is that to keep the fetus from leaving a painful situation such as consciousness in the womb during its own development, Nature neurochemically, which means dopamine, manipulates, which means provides for, the fetus with high levels of this pain killing neurochemical, so that it will not leave the womb. Therefore, by flooding the pleasure and reward pathways or centers of the fetal brain with pain relieving neurochemicals, such as dopamine, this makes life in the womb tolerable.

The next question to be answered then would be what are the reward and pleasure pathways or centers of the developing fetal brain? While there is a neurobiological explanation for this, it is not necessary to elaborate on them here. Just think of it as exactly what it says. Think of it as a receiving area of pleasure. When the dopamine flows through these areas, these pleasure and reward pathways; the pain of fetal life disappears. You could actually say that Nature drugs the fetus. This of course, is exactly what occurs.

This neurochemical manipulation takes place in both cycles. It is Nature's primary tool; which is utilized to essentially train the fetus. Nature trains the fetus to do exactly what it wants it to do, which in the Euphoric Cycle of Development, is very little.

Fetal State in the Euphoric Cycle

The way Nature trains the fetus to do very little in the Euphoric Cycle of Development is by providing large volumes of dopamine to the pleasure and rewards pathways of the fetal brain. This decreases the motivation of the fetus to move, for as you will see, during the First Fear Cycle of Development, the dopamine will be reduced and the fetus will have to generate its own dopamine flow. In this Euphoric Cycle, however, the dopamine is provided freely, large amounts of it. The fetus, essentially bounces around in a pool of dopamine as its mother walks and moves about. This, of course, is exactly how the dopamine is released to the fetus. The more its mother moves around, the larger the release of the dopamine is to the developing fetal brain, and therefore the more pleasurable life in the womb is for the fetus. Therefore, a direct relationship exists between the movement of the mother and the pleasure of the fetus. While there are limits to this, in general, the more its mother is moving, the more the dopamine will flow and the more pleasurable life is for the fetus.

Through this large flow of dopamine the fetus will respond in many ways. In addition to its reduced movement, it will smile, relax, sleep and generally realize a pleasurable, euphoric mental state. It will listen to its mother's voice as she talks to others. It is a noisy cycle, full of movement, as the fetus bounces, rocks and floods with the rhythm of its mother's movement. More than anything it will rest and grow. This is the pinnacle of life in the womb for the fetus.

The best part about the Euphoric Cycle, though, because of the Memory Block, is that the fetus believes this cycle will go on forever. Indeed, the fetus believes life in the womb will always be as pleasurable as this. This is important; the Memory Block serves a vital purpose in this cycle of development. It allows the fetus to fully relax and enjoy the rest it has earned. If it were not for the Memory Block it is doubtful the fetus would relax. This is because it would be anticipating the horrific First Fear Cycle that awaited it within a few hours.

Fetal Perception of its Environment

Standing outside the womb, looking at a pregnant woman, we have a fixed perception. This perception is based upon knowledge that inside the woman is a fetus, an unborn child that is completely dependent upon its mother. The fetus inside the womb, however, does not share this perspective. Due to its high level of consciousness, which will be explained in the following chapter, the fetus believes its world revolves around itself. The fetus, later as an infant and then as a child does not outgrow this perspective. Indeed, most children believe the world revolves around them, as well.

In both cycles, as you will see, the fetus believes that it is responsible for the environment it is in. Therefore, in the Euphoric Cycle, it believes that the pleasure it realizes is partially due to its own control. When its mother is talking, moving about and active, the fetus believes it is somehow, partially, responsible for this. This gives the fetus a heightened sense of confidence. It believes it is in control of its environment, its mother included, and this environment is pleasurable.

The Memory Block plays a large part in this belief. For, if the fetus could remember or anticipate that in a few hours, the environment it is currently in will worsen regardless of what it does, it would begin to understand that its mother's movements are completely independent of its control. Due to the Memory Block though, the fetus believes the conditions in the womb will always remain as they are; which is exactly the way it wants them to be, and that it is in control of this.

This fetal perception will become even clearer, in the next chapter, as you realize how it develops in relation to the First Fear Cycle. While this ends the chapter on the Euphoric Cycle, developmental aspects of this cycle will be mentioned throughout the book.

CHAPTER THREE

THE FIRST FEAR CYCLE OF DEVELOPMENT

Defining Fetal Consciousness

Before we can begin this exiting journey into what is the single aspect of human development that separates mankind above all other species of Nature, it is necessary to define just how conscious the fetus is in the womb. While this may sound as a bold step, as you will see later, what the fetus is capable of in this chapter is only the beginning.

The fetus in the womb is conscious. This consciousness is very similar to that of a newborn. Indeed, there is very little difference between the neural make-up of an advanced fetus and that of the newborn infant. While there is a specific date as to when this consciousness of the fetus develops; I will not reveal it here. It will not be revealed here for a very good reason, and that is, it would divert attention away from what is important in this work on human behavior and would instead, focus on what society has deemed important for their collective personal reasons. This may disillusion those who felt that when the fetus begins the process of labor, some how it is sprinkled with "the magic dust of consciousness." Unfortunately, this is not how it works at all.

Indeed, the fetus is completely conscious. While the consciousness certainly exists, it is a limited consciousness: just as the infant's consciousness is limited. The sole limitation of the fetal consciousness is the intentional suppression of its short-term memory. As you have seen earlier, Nature wants to prohibit learning in the womb; this is a primary purpose of the Memory Block. Indeed, the womb is no place for the fetus to learn, as you will see in Part Two of this book. Yes, the Memory Block that prohibits fetal learning by blocking short-term memory is so important to human development that Nature is willing to put the mother, her most valued gender, at risk to maintain it. This risk is due to the complex neurobiological mechanisms responsible for the Memory Block, as they suppress the mother's immune system. All you need to know now, however, is that it is very important that the fetus does not learn in the womb.

Misinterpretation of Environmental Cues

What is important to fetal development, however, is that the fetus misinterprets the cues to the changes during both of these developmental cycles. Now you will see just how important the Memory Block is to fetal development. Again, the lack of short-term memory causes the fetus to misinterpret cues of the intrauterine environment.

The misinterpretations occur in reaction to a simple conditioned response. The definition of conditioned response is not really important here. All that you need to realize is that every time the mother lies down or goes to sleep, the intrauterine environment, or the conditions in the womb, changes for the fetus. What happens is that the dopamine to the reward pathways or pleasure centers of the fetal brain decreases substantially. In other words, the fetus realizes a tremendous amount of pain. In response to this pain the fetus kicks, punches and desperately moves about. This kicking, punching, and movement, then, in return increase its own flow of dopamine to these pleasure or reward pathways. So, while before when the mother was moving about, it received the flow of dopamine from her, now however, the fetus must generate its own movement to realize this. Therefore, over time this becomes a conditioned response. Every time the dopamine is reduced the fetus kicks and punches, causing the dopamine to increase again. Since you know what causes the dopamine to be reduced is the lying down or sleeping of the mother, you therefore also know that when the mother lies down or sleeps that the fetus will be begin to kick or move about in pain. This movement will then, itself, increase the dopamine flow to the fetus.

Not only do you now know this, however, almost any woman who has ever been pregnant can tell you the same thing, as well. For most pregnant women realize that when they lie down to go to sleep the fetus becomes more active. What these pregnant women do not know, however, is that this movement is in response to pain, and the fetus is kicking and punching out in order to increase its dopamine flow.

If you think about it, there is nothing really spectacular about this, a conditioned response to changes in the intrauterine environment. Indeed, if this were any other mammal, a conditioned response would be hardly even remarkable. The problem with that statement, however, is this is not just any other mammal. It is the human fetus with a very small body, but a very large, developed brain.

This large brain is thinking all the time, it is not only thinking, however, it is drawing assumptions and conclusions from this very simple animal model of conditioned response. And the first assumption it will make will be an incorrect one. It is important to remember, before we continue, that this misinterpretation is intentionally established by Nature, specific for the human species. What causes the fetus to make this misinterpretation is the Memory Block. Because the fetus cannot remember what happened ten minutes before, never mind what happened yesterday morning, it believes that every event or change, which occurs in the womb, is original.

The first misinterpretation the fetus makes in response to the intrauterine environment is this. Because the dopamine is reduced and the pain is increased and because its mother and therefore the womb are slowing, it believes that she and therefore it itself, are in the process of dying. Now this makes sense if you remember that the fetus has nothing to gage these changes against. It does not know that its mother is simply lying down to go to sleep and will wake up in the morning. Because of the Memory Block it cannot remember this, believing this is the first time this slowing of the womb has occurred. This judgment is made within seconds.

The second misinterpretation the fetus makes is based on the first. Here the fetus believes that its conditioned response, the kicking, punching, and moving about is actually saving its mother's life and therefore its own. This makes sense as well, because by kicking, punching, and moving about the fetus is actually decreasing the amount of pain it is in. And because half of the fetal perception of death is based on an increase of pain, anything it can do to reduce that pain will reduce its' belief that it is dying. Therefore, the fetus believes that as long as it keeps kicking and punching about, its mother and therefore itself, will remain alive. The fetus faces a very big problem with this, however, for it simply cannot continue to kick and punch out for very long, as it tires easily. This all is explained later in this chapter.

For, now all you need to realize is that every time the mother lies down or goes to sleep the fetus misinterprets the changes in the intrauterine environment as the beginning of the death of its mother and therefore itself. In addition to this, the fetus misinterprets its conditioned response to the dopamine reduction and believes that its kicking, punching, and moving about is actually saving both of their lives.

Now, as if this was not enough to mislead the fetus into believing that its mother and itself are in the process of dying, Nature provides another event to even further reassure this belief. It is the initiation of independent fetal breathing. For simplicity and throughout the remainder of the book the initiation of independent fetal breathing will be defined as a "fetal apnea." The apnea is the most painful event the fetus will experience. What happens during a fetal apnea is that, for a short period of time, the oxygen supply to the fetus is cut off. In response to this, the fetal lungs expand and contract. Again, this is a very painful event. Now, Nature has a very good reason for these fetal apneas, which will be explained later in this chapter. For now, what we are focused on is the fetal interpretation of this apnea. Of course, you could imagine if suddenly your oxygen supply were cut off, what the first thought that entered your mind would be. It is the same for the fetus, for now, it is essentially convinced that its mother and therefore it also is in the process of dying.

This group of events that the fetus experiences when the mother is lying down or sleeping and the fetal response to it will be defined as the First Fear. There is much more to this developmental cycle as you will see, therefore cumulatively, it will be defined as the First Fear Cycle of Development.

Remember, if it were not for the Memory Block, the fetus would never misinterpret these cues. It would simply realize a painful cycle, knowing that the mother was only sleeping, and that neither her, nor it was in any danger of dying.

Before we go back to the womb to join the fetus in this horrific cycle, it is important to remember two things. The first is that the fetus believes that every time the womb slows down, from the mother lying down or sleeping, that its mother and therefore itself are in the process of dying. The second is that the fetus believes that its kicking and punching out is saving both of their lives.

Fetal Response to the Developmental Cycle

What you are about to read is a description of the First Fear Cycle of Development. In this section you will learn how the fetus, which misinterprets the intrauterine cues, now attempts to save its dying mother and therefore its own life. You will understand how, when it physically fails to save what it believes is its dying mother, who is only sleeping, what the fetal response is to this failure. Finally, you will understand what the purpose is to the multiple aspects of this developmental cycle.

From the relaxed state of the Euphoric Cycle the fetus is shocked and startled out of its resting cycle into a condition of high alert. The mother is lying down; the First Fear Cycle of Development has begun. The fetus has been here before; however, it remembers little or nothing of it. It misreads the cues, as expected, its mother and therefore it also is dying. Of this it is certain. Her heartbeat has decreased and death is imminent. Breathing is now restricted, as the fetus suffers apnea after apnea. The dopamine that once flowed freely through the developing fetal brain now diminishes, making every movement painful. The fetus must escape, or at least arouse its dying mother.

In desperation with what little air is available to its expanding lungs, the fetus kicks and punches out, attempting to gain some response, some movement, and some reassurance that its only fear is not occurring. While the fetus kicks with all its might, its mother feels little effect. This is because the pathways that carry the information from the neurons in the brain to the muscles are not fully myelinated, or developed. While the command for kicking and punching is there, the delivery is slow and blunted. The mother as she lies down feels the fetus moving slowly, maybe kicking gently or turning. As it is Nature's way, the mother is oblivious to the suffering of the fetus, which believes that they are both dying. All that is occurring, however, is that the mother is lying down, to go to sleep.

Back inside the womb, the fetus is exhausted. It has only been minutes since the mother began lying down, however, for the fetus it seems as if it has been there forever. Because of the Memory Block, it believes this cycle, which to it is a cycle of pain and death, will go on forever.

Everything that occurs during this cycle has a specific developmental purpose. A major purpose of the Memory Block is to allow the fetus to respond immediately to changes in the intrauterine environment. The fetal response from the relaxed state of the Euphoric Cycle to the tensed flexion state of the First Fear Cycle of Development occurs within seconds. This quick change in the fetal state develops important reflexes and muscles. These reflexes will save the life of the fetus during the long process of labor, which it will shortly undertake. The apneas expand the fetal lungs preparing it for life outside the womb. It is those critical first few breaths that will determine whether the baby will live or die.

Finally, back inside the womb, the fetus realizes a movement from the mother as she turns on her side. The fetus has accomplished its goal; the mother is still alive. The dopamine, while dramatically reduced, flows a little more freely to the reward pathways and pleasure centers of the fetal brain. The reprieve quickly ends, however, as its mother settles back into a deep cycle of sleep. The cycle of pain for the fetus continues. The fetus kicks and punches out again, with its ineffective movements, until exhaustion finally consumes it. With no other choice it gives up and waits to die, as its mother's heart beat slows again, a sure sign that death is near. It will be a long night for the developing fetus and there will be much time for it to experiment. Every experiment the fetus makes in the womb, however, is not an experiment at all. Instead it is all part of a carefully crafted plan by

Nature to ensure that every minute the mother is sleeping will be utilized fully for development of the fetus.

Experimentation by the Fetus and Developmental Consequences

Yes, it will be a long night for the fetus. There will be many hours spent in silence, in a world where silence means death and sound means life. It will spend many hours throughout the night with its ear close to the walls of the womb, listening. It will place its ear close to the wall to listen for a sound, any sound. For sound is hope, it is its only hope to disbelieve what it believes to be true, which is its mother and therefore it itself is not dying. Sound is hope; sound is life for the fetus. First and foremost, the fetus is listening to its mother's heartbeat. It will spend many hours listening to the bass of her heartbeat. The fetus will become hopeful when her heart rate increases; as this signals that she could still be alive and it will become desperate when the rate decreases, as this surely signals death. In addition to the bass of its mother's heartbeat the fetus will listen for sounds outside the womb. Here it will listen for anything constant, as it will provide some reassurance to disprove its fear. The listening serves an important developmental purpose as well. For, the contrast between the bass of the mother's heartbeat and sounds outside the womb, differentiate the tones and program the neurons of the auditory cortex of the developing fetal brain. Even more significant than auditory development, however, is that the connection is made. Sound equals life: silence equals death. This connection will have profound effects on every aspect of life; long after the fetus has left the womb.

Another experiment, which comes out of necessity, is the exploration of the fingers and toes. After a few minutes the fetus is exhausted from its kicking and punching, the First Fear Cycle of Development, however, continues all night. The fetus must find a way to wake its dying mother without using up such a large amount of energy. The movement of the arms and legs requires too much blood and therefore too much energy. Instead, the fetus begins to explore with its fingers and toes, always with the same goal, to save its dying mother and therefore its own life. The fetus now moves its fingers around the womb trying to gain a response from its mother, who is now unresponsive during her deepest stages of sleep. The fetus does not give up; however, it continues moving its hands and fingers touching the intrauterine walls, trying to create a response. Nature, however, has safeguarded the womb. This is for a very good reason. The reason is that the fetus could injure its mother by causing internal damage with its probing fingers and toes. How Nature does this is one of the most efficient and miraculous aspects of fetal development.

To keep the fetus from ripping into the intrauterine walls, Nature leaves the fetal fingers undeveloped. Because the intrauterine walls are warm and the fingertips are not fully developed, every time the fetus touches them it realizes a hot or burning response to the sensory areas of the cortex of the fetal brain. This burning or painful response serves two important purposes. The first and most obvious is it prohibits the fetus from touching for a long period of time the intrauterine walls. More importantly this painful response prevents the fetus from grabbing the walls and causing severe internal injury to its mother.

The second purpose of this burning response the fetus realizes shows the efficiency of Nature in using every aspect of this developmental cycle to its fullest potential. What this means is that because intrauterine walls are warm, in addition as protection for the mother, Nature efficiently uses them for development. To understand this, you must remember that the short-term memory of the fetus is blocked. So, while it will touch the walls with its fingers and quickly withdraw them, when it realizes a hot or burning sensation, it will quickly forget that it ever happened. Therefore a few minutes later, once it has forgotten the burning response it will try it once more. Again, it will touch the warm intrauterine walls and again, it will realize a painful or burning response. Again, the fetus will withdraw its hands and fingers from the walls and again, within a few minutes the fetus will forget the entire event occurred. Now, this process will continue all throughout the night. The fetus will touch in order to arouse what it believes to be its dying mother, then realize the painful sensation and withdraw. What is so amazing about this process is that it is exactly what Nature wants to occur. For, every time the fetus realizes this painful burning in the sensory nerves of the finger, the sensory neurons in the brain are being encoded with that response. Now, Nature has two reasons that it wants these sensory neurons encoded while the fetus is still in the womb. The first is a process of labor itself. When the fetus finally does leave the womb, its path will be essentially mapped out. The body temperature of its mother will determine this mapping of the route the fetus should take. This of course means that the cooler areas of the birth canal will not burn the fetal fingers; this will serve as a guide or pathway to direct the fetus in the proper direction, thus causing minimal internal damage to its mother. Yes, Nature leaves very little to chance, very little is instinctual here, everything works together in perfect unison, little chance will be taken in order to ensure that the fetus completes the process of labor successfully and that its mother is not harmed in the process. The second and most obvious reason is that this coded sensory information will, later in life, protect the flesh of the individual's fingers from injury due to burning. This coding is just another important aspect made possible by the Memory Block. It is also testament to the efficiency of Nature, using every aspect of the First Fear Cycle for developmental purposes.

Olfactory Development — the Sense of Smell

While in most mammals the olfactory system is utilized primarily for the detection of pheromones, for the process of mating, in the human species Nature uses it for something more important, development in the womb itself. Because the intrauterine environment is not a visual experience, Nature uses the fetal olfactory system or sense of smell to signal changes in the intrauterine environment, from the Euphoric Cycle to the First Fear Cycle of Development. Here is how it works. Remember, earlier in this chapter you realized that when the mother slows down, the dopamine is reduced to the fetus, this in return prompts the fetus to kick and punch out in order to increase the dopamine flow to its reward pathways. The olfactory system is essential in this process. One of the major ways in which the fetus realizes a reduction in dopamine is through the olfactory neurons, which then reduce the dopamine to its rewards pathways and pleasure centers, when these changes in movement by the mother occur. In other words, every time the mother lies down or goes to sleep, the dopamine to the reward pathways and pleasure centers is reduced.

There is much more to this, to the importance of olfactory or sense of smell development in the womb for the fetus. To understand this, it is important to remember that the First Fear Cycle usually occurs at night when the mother is sleeping. During this time the intrauterine environment slows down all of its processes dramatically. One way in which this slow-down affects the fetus is in regard to the flushing and filtering of its own waste products. The fetus is consumed in its own waste products during the First Fear Cycle; from this it realizes the smells of pungent odors and foul smells to the fetal olfactory system. This is unlike the sweet smells that consumed the fetal olfactory system during the Euphoric Cycle, which occurred when the intrauterine environment was moving and its mother's high activity level increase the flushing and filtering of these waste products.

Now, while it may sound like nothing extraordinary, with Nature using both cycles for olfactory development; as you will see later and throughout The Theorem, however, little is of more importance. For now, what it is essential to understand is that the fetus smells pungent and foul odors during the First Fear Cycle and smells sweet or fresh odors during the Euphoric Cycle. Just like sound, a life long connection is made between the fetal experience and its initial sensory development. Indeed, for the fetus this nightly environment of the normal decay of the intrauterine environment will forever be associated with death.

Fetal Dopamine-Seeking Behavior

Throughout the long hours of the night, deep into the First Fear Cycle of Development, another very important developmental event occurs. The mother is now sound asleep, the fetus is sure that she is in the process of dying. It has done everything to try and relieve this fear. It has listened with its' ear close to the intrauterine walls for sound, some hope and believe that its' worst fears are not coming true. The sound of its mother's heartbeat slowing as she enters a deeper sleep cycle tell the fetus something different, indeed she is dying. The fetus has tried everything, it has kicked and punched trying to gain a response and save her life, it has failed. It has touched the walls to try and revive her, however, this has failed too. All there is for the fetus to do now is wait to die.

At least the fetus will not have to die in so much pain. For it has found an easier way, than the kicking and punching, to receive dopamine. Through trial and error the fetus finds its finger or thumb. Into its undeveloped mouth it goes. What is happening is one of the miracles of Nature and of the First Fear Cycle of Development is beginning.

Because the fetal mouth is not fully developed, any suction it applies to its finger will result in an increase in dopamine to the pleasure and reward centers of its developing brain. More specifically, what is occurring is that the fetal brain is not only realizing a net increase in dopamine, however, in addition, the dopamine, which is circulating throughout the brain, is utilized more efficiently in these reward pathways and pleasure centers within the brain. It is a process where the fetus guides the dopamine to where it is most effective. This sucking of its' finger or thumb then makes life in this horrific cycle a little more tolerable.

Nature, of course, has a very important reason for this. It is the connection that is made between this horrific situation and a release of dopamine. This connection, alone, will determine whether the fetus as an infant survives. After birth, the infant will not want to take any of the mother's bodily fluids. The infant will associate the milk from the mother's breast as containing the death and decay it is now consumed in as a fetus. Remember as a fetus, the infant was force-fed for nine months. The infant will have no comprehension or understanding as to the importance of food. The only chance that Nature has to get the infant to eat will be the dopamine-seeking behavior it develops in the womb.

This is how it works. In the womb during the First Fear Cycle, the fetus, quite by accident, begins sucking its fingers and thumb. These are very similar in size to the mother's nipple. When the dopamine decreases during the First Fear Cycle, the fetus must find other ways to increase it. The most potent dopamine release the typical fetus can realize is by the sucking of its fingers and thumb. Over time the fetus and later the infant will develop a conditioned response to pain. Every time they are in a situation of fear or pain they will reach for their fingers or thumb. Outside the womb, Nature expects the infant to realize situations of fear and pain. Instead of the infant sucking the fingers to gain a dopamine increase to the reward pathways of its developing brain, it is Nature's goal to have it reach, or assisted in reaching for its mother's nipple. If all Nature's training has been correct this will occur. Therefore, when the infant begins to nurse it is only interested in the dopamine from the sucking of the nipple. Again, the infant will have no interest in food whatsoever. If the infant does not take the nipple, nine months that Nature has invested will be for nothing. It is one, if not the most important aspect of intrauterine development.

Changes towards the End of the Pregnancy

Day after day, night after night, these two cycles continue throughout the pregnancy. During the day when its mother is active the fetus experiences the Euphoric Cycle of Development. Its developing brain is consumed with dopamine, as it listens to its mother's voice, smells sweet smells, smiles, rests and grows. All this is due to the high levels of dopamine it realizes. During this cycle the fetus is oblivious to the existence of any other cycle. It believes it has always been and will always remain in this moving, rocking and dopamine filled environment. It cannot remember the other cycle because of the Memory Block.

Every night when the mother lies down to go to sleep the fetus is shocked and startled when it is thrown into the other cycle of development. The fetus has entered the First Fear Cycle of Development. Through a series of misinterpretations the fetus believes its mother and therefore itself are in the process of dying. It kicks and punches out in an attempt to save its mother's life and therefore its own. The pain of its own development increases as the dopamine flow decreases. Instead of the sweet smells of the Euphoric Cycle, the womb is now filled with pungent odors and foul smells of its own bodily waste. Throughout the long night the fetus experiences the most painful of the apneas. During this, it loses its oxygen supply. This reassures it that its mother and therefore it itself are in the process of dying. It does everything it can to arouse, what it believes to be its dying mother, who is only sleeping. Nothing, however, works. Finally, the fetus awaits death, in pain and exhaustion. Because of the Memory Block, it believes that this cycle will last forever, as it cannot remember the existence of the other. It believes life in the womb has always been and will always be this way.

This is the life of the fetus throughout most of the pregnancy. It spends its time divided by two opposite developmental states. One is pleasurable the other is painful. Day after day, night after night, it lives life: fluctuating between these two extreme conditions and cycles of development.

Towards the end of the pregnancy conditions for the fetus begin to change. By now, the fetus has experienced these two cycles hundreds of times. Most of the developmental aspects of each cycle have reached their fruition. It is time, for Nature to signal the fetus that it is time to leave, as important development awaits it outside the womb.

The fetus has been well trained for the journey it will soon undertake. Due to the Memory Block, the fetus has spent months quickly responding to the changes in the intrauterine environment. This, in addition to its conformity to the conditioned response, has developed quick reflexes for the fetus. These will be vital for adapting to changes in the birth canal during labor. Due to the months of the fetal kicking and punching, the muscles in its arms and legs are well developed and strong. These muscles in the arms and especially the legs will push the fetus through the birth canal. The fetal heart is well conditioned, from the exhaustive aspects and conditioning, which occurred during this nightly cycle. The apneas have served their purpose, in regards to labor, as well. Night after night, the fetus went without oxygen for variable periods of time. This depletion of oxygen will occur again throughout the long process of labor. With its strong heart and lungs, the fetus should survive the marathon of a journey that is labor. Indeed, Nature has prepared the fetus to leave the womb in almost every way. Soon it will be time for it to go. There is only one problem. The fetus does not want to go.

Resultant Emotional Development

The question of why the fetus does not want to leave the womb brings us to another aspect of fetal development altogether. This area of development is resultant of the physical development that occurs to the fetus during the two cycles. For as you will see, the fetus experiences emotional, as well as, physical development during both cycles. This, of course, is due to the high state of consciousness the fetus realizes throughout the pregnancy. Because it was conscious, thinking and feeling, this physical development resulted in emotional development. Now, some of this emotional development is intentional, established by Nature for purposes such as the eventual reproduction of the species, which will be explained in later chapters. Other emotional development, however, is not intentional at all. Instead, it is only a necessary consequence of the physical development. In a way it is a tradeoff; for Nature to generate emotional development that would be necessary for the eventual reproduction of the human species, she enabled the fetus an advanced consciousness. As a tradeoff, other emotional development occurred that had little developmental value whatsoever. We will examine both aspects, with the developing fetus, as it nears the end of the pregnancy.

Much of this resultant emotional development occurs due to the Memory Block, which blocks the short-term memory of the fetus; this leads to fetal misinterpretations of the intrauterine environment. By now you are well aware of these misinterpretations. By believing its mother and therefore it itself is dying and that its kicking and punching keeps her alive, over a period of time, a relationship develops between the fetus and its mother. This relationship is distorted, based on the two misinterpretations by the fetus. In other words, the fetus believes that it is its job to keep its mother and therefore itself alive. The fetal emotional state is then directly influenced by its ability to obtain this goal. This is an example of one misinterpretation escalating up into another. The fetus believes that its mother is dying, it is saving her life, and now, it is the job of the fetus to continue to save her life and therefore its own. While the fetal focus is still on preserving its life, the relationship is expanding. While it realizes its dependence on its mother, it begins to believe that the dependence is mutual.

This evolution in fetal reasoning is understandable. Because the fetus believes that it has been keeping her alive for many months, it also believes that if it were to leave, she would die. This will be covered more in detail later in this chapter. What is important to realize now, is that the emotional range the fetus experiences varies with each cycle. The entire emotional range is based on the fetal believe that it is in control of saving both, its mother's and therefore its own life. For example, during the First Fear Cycle when it cannot wake its dying mother, in addition to the physical experience of pain, it will also realize anger, frustration and of course sadness. Because it is failing at its only job it will also be consumed with the sense of worthlessness.

The Memory Block intensifies the emotional reaction the fetus realizes in each cycle. For example, during the First Fear Cycle of Development when conditions are bad and the fetus believes that its mother and it itself are in the process of dying, the fetus will realize a sense of hopelessness. This is directly due to the Memory Block. In other words, whatever conditions the fetus experiences, it believes that condition will remain indefinitely. So, if it is unable to save its dying mother, which is actually only to wake her up, it believes this inability will continue forever. It does not know that in a few hours, when its mother wakes up that conditions will improve dramatically. The fetus simply does not know what is around the corner. The hopelessness is intensified, because no matter what the fetus does, at that moment, it is not able to generate a response. Because of the Memory Block there is no sense of time. There is no knowledge of the past or the future. Therefore every experience, whether good or bad, is projected indefinitely.

The Memory Block affects the fetal emotion of experience during the Euphoric Cycle of Development as well. The criteria for the emotional experience are the same as that for the First Fear Cycle of Development. In both cycles the fetus believes that it is responsible for saving its mother's life. Therefore when it is successful at accomplishing, what it believes to be its primary responsibility, a sense of overconfidence will consume it. It believes that because it can accomplish this goal, it can accomplish anything. It also believes that it will always be able to accomplish anything. It is very much like there are two walls that insulate the fetal emotions. These walls limit understanding of any change or variation. This intensifies or exaggerates every emotional reaction. These walls are caused by the Memory Block which blocks short-term memory and this memory is not exempt from emotional experience. So, while in the Euphoric Cycle it believes that the happiness, joy and euphoria will last forever, in the First Fear Cycle it believes the sadness, worthlessness and in many ways the hopelessness will last forever as well.

While the emotional reactions, as a result of physical development, will have life long implications, there is also a more immediate purpose for them. When in each cycle the fetal face will respond to the emotional state it experiences. For example, when in the First Fear Cycle, in response to pain, the face will grimace, frown and scowl; this will contract the facial muscles. In contrast, during the Euphoric Cycle, in response to its elated state, the face will expand from smiling and happiness. These two contrasting emotional ranges condition the facial muscles. This tightening, then loosening, strengthens the face. These facial muscles will be important during the process of labor. This is because, during the process of labor, the fetal face will make direct contact with the birth canal. These facial muscles, the strength or weakness of, may very well make the determination of whether the fetus can move itself effectively through the canal or not. This is just another example of how Nature takes no chances with the human fetus, using every aspect of the developmental cycles for the primary purpose of enabling a safe delivery out of the womb.

Towards the end of the pregnancy, the fetal emotional reactions begin to intensify and evolve into a more complex response. To understand this, it is first necessary to realize how Nature signals the fetus that it is time to leave.

The fetus is growing, rapidly. While the size of the body and the brain of the fetus are growing, the resources to sustain it remain fixed. One of the most important resources is space for the fetus to move. The fetus is essentially becoming cramped within the space that is allocated for it. Another resource that remains fixed, while the fetus continues to grow is dopamine. While the dopamine available to the fetus, to its reward pathways and pleasure centers, does not decrease, the fetus will realize a net reduction nonetheless. In other words, the ever-expanding fetal brain is in need of more dopamine than before, to gain the same effect. This net reduction to the rewards and pleasure pathways of the fetal brain makes life in the womb almost intolerable for the fetus. The fetus feels the pain of its own development like it never had before. All the conditions that the high levels of dopamine once masked, the fetus now feels.

The fetus is now in constant pain, especially during the First Fear Cycle of Development. With the decreased dopamine the effects of the fetal apneas intensify. The kicking and punching, to save its dying mother's life, are too painful to execute. The limited space makes movement prohibitive. The nutrients provided by its mother are not enough to sustain the growing fetus. As the fetal body grows, so do its waste products. Now, during the First Fear Cycle the fetus is constantly surrounded by what it perceives to be the smell of death and decay. The large fetal brain is putting pressure on its skull, causing constant head pain for the fetus. The decreased dopamine, more than before, is enabling the fetus to feel the effects of its developing dermatome or skin; this creates an itch that is impossible for the fetus to ignore. The sucking of its fingers or thumb fails to generate enough dopamine to withstand the pain that consumes the fetus.

Even during the Euphoric Cycle, the pleasure is reduced. While the dopamine still flows much more freely, than during the First Fear Cycle, in both cycles the fetus feels the effect of its growth.

This deterioration of the intrauterine environment affects the male even more than the female fetus. In fact, every aspect of the First Fear Cycle of Development is more intense for the male than for the female fetus. While this is true throughout the entire pregnancy, the differences are more obvious towards the end. This is because, female hormones that reduce or dilute the painful effect of the First Fear Cycle, protect the female fetus. These female hormones offset some of the effects of the decreased dopamine and dilute some of the deterioration towards the end of the pregnancy. Indeed, for the male the decision to go will be much easier than for the female fetus.

Nature wants both genders to go, however. Their time in the womb will soon be over. Most of Nature's work, the neural programming and organization, which are systematically guided by both cycles, have reached its end. If they stay too much longer they could not only risk their own lives, but their mother's as well.

The fetus, however, does not see things this way. In fact, they see things as quite the opposite. Oh, the fetus has thought about leaving before, to this there is little doubt. There are two major problems with this idea, however.

The first problem is the process of labor itself. The fetus knows which way to get out of the womb; however, to go that way would mean that it would have to enter areas that are warm, and therefore hot to the touch. This is Nature's way to prevent, or at least discourage a premature attempt at labor. So for the fetus to leave, it would have to take a chance on entering a burning or hot environment. Of course, this is not going to happen, however, again, this is fetal perception.

The second problem is much more involved, and in many ways, more prohibitive. This second reason also brings us back to the resultant emotional development that occurs in the womb. As you already know, the fetus has been kicking and punching every night in an attempt to save its dying mother and therefore its own life. You also already know, that the fetus believes that it is its job to save its dying mother's life and that its emotional state is directly influenced by its perceived success or failure at this goal. This belief of its mother's dependence contributes substantially into the decision making process at the end of pregnancy. The second reason that makes the fetal decision difficult is guilt.

Now remember, the fetus believes that it alone is responsible for saving its mother's life. The fetus therefore believes that without it being in the womb, on a nightly basis, to save her life, she would die. Yes, to leave its mother behind would be a guaranteed death sentence for her. Through all these months, the fetus has experienced both extremes of the human condition, encapsulated inside the mother. This is all the fetus knows. A bond has developed, while it is a backward bond, due to the fetal misinterpretation of the environmental cues, it is a bond nonetheless. In other words, how a mother feels about her fetus and baby is the exact same way that the fetus feels about its mother. What this means is that a mother, throughout the nine months of pregnancy nurtures, feels responsible and makes a commitment to the life of the fetus. Well, for the fetus it is the same thing. It believes, due to misinterpretation from the Memory Block, that it is responsible for saving its mother's life for almost nine months. The fetus also believes that it has made a commitment to its mother. If it were to leave, no matter how bad the conditions become, it would be breaking that commitment. To get some perspective on just how difficult this decision to go is for the fetus to make, it is necessary to look outside the womb, and back at the mother. The decision the fetus makes to leave, would be, in many ways, similar to a decision a mother would make if she would decide to put her newborn up for adoption, for this would be the breaking of a nine month commitment between mother and child. While there are many differences between the emotional level of an adult and that of a fetus or child, the decision is very serious nonetheless. As you will see in later chapters, it is this severe misinterpretation of the fetal role within the pregnancy that will define the basis for the emotional capacity throughout its entire life. This is also the origin of guilt.

The fetus therefore begins to get angry at the way conditions have deteriorated. It is not angry with its mother, not at all. The fetus becomes angry at itself, for what it has been thinking, during the last few weeks of pregnancy, as the intrauterine conditions continue to deteriorate. Yes, the fetus simply cannot believe that the idea of leaving its mother alone to die has consumed its thoughts for the past few weeks. The emotion that consumes the fetus during the end of pregnancy is guilt. Guilt moves the fetus like no other emotion ever had throughout the pregnancy. It cannot accept that it is capable of such a selfish thought. After all, it has worked so hard to keep her alive, night after night, month after month, and now, to just leave should be unthinkable, yet the thought lingers. Yes, it is guilt, the desire not to leave its mother alone to die, that, more than dopamine or any neurochemical, keeps the fetus from leaving.

For the female fetus this guilt is especially severe. It tears her apart inside. Remember, for her the First Fear Cycle was never as strong as for the male. She was provided with protective female hormones that diluted the intensity of the dopamine withdrawal and the conditioned response. So, even as conditions deteriorate she has no desire to leave. Her main problem is that she is growing. She is growing too large for the womb. Yes, if she could just stop growing; then she would never leave. Indeed, she would stay forever, saving its mother's life on a nightly basis. She will therefore hesitate, pausing through every step of the final days in the womb.

For the male fetus, when he decides to go, finally, he will leave without hesitation. This, however, is a ways off.

Hopelessness, while a constant emotion experienced throughout the nightly cycle of the First Fear, intensifies towards the end of the pregnancy. The fetus has tried almost everything to get the conditions in the womb to improve. Yet, they only seem to get worse instead. This, of course, is exactly what Nature wants the fetus to realize. The conditions are going to deteriorate even further, for it is time to leave. The feelings of worthlessness grow as well. Towards the end of pregnancy, the fetus has very little belief in its ability to save its dying mother's life, as the deterioration of conditions further validate its primary fear.

Labor Contractions

As the conditions deteriorate, the fetus realizes it must take some action. While it is consumed with guilt, it also begins to question whether its mother appreciates its efforts. Besides itself there is no one else it can blame. It begins to believe that its mother is taking up too much of the resources available. The fetus simply cannot stand the pain from the reduced dopamine to its reward or pleasure pathways and the resultant increase in the intensity of the First Fear Cycle. Not only does the fetus believe that it is in charge of saving its mother's life, however, that she knows it as well. It will send a clear signal to its mother, letting her know that while it does not want to leave, it will leave if conditions do not improve.

The plan is simple. The fetus will bluff leaving. It does not want to go, if it did, it would have already been gone. No, what the fetus is aiming for here is the improvement of conditions. It believes that by showing its mother it is serious about leaving, which it is not, that she will realize her dependence on it. This will obviously cause her to improve conditions in the womb and then the fetus could erase these horrible thoughts about leaving, which guilt prohibits it from doing. Again, it is a simple plan and the fetus believes it will work.

One night, during the First Fear Cycle, the fetus carries out its plan. It is important to realize here why this usually occurs at night. Every night, during the First Fear Cycle of Development, the conditions in the womb, as you have seen, deteriorate. The dopamine decreases and the pain level increases. This is also why labor most often begins in the evening or at night. So one night, the fetus begins movement towards the birth canal. Its mother realizes labor pains or contractions. She is ecstatic, although in pain. Her husband rushes her to the hospital. After examination, the doctor assures her that this is a false alarm. He tells her that it will probably be a few days yet, before the baby comes, maybe even a week. Now, the doctor does not know why it will be a few days still, he has simply seen it a thousand times in his long career. In some cases, the fetus, which bluffs, may go to far and actually break its mother's water, setting off a cascade of unstoppable events. Not this fetus, however, as it is careful.

Back in the womb, the fetus is exhausted, but realizes a sense of accomplishment. It waits for conditions to improve. It is certain they will. It waits, and waits and waits. To its surprise, however, conditions do not improve at all. In fact, they become progressively worse. The fetus is shocked; it believes its mother just has no idea how important it is in saving her life. Does she not know that she will die immediately if it were to leave? Again, the hopelessness, guilt and worthlessness — as it ponders for the first time that it may actually have to go. It feels rejected, unappreciated and to some extend unwanted. It is also starting, in a small way, to believe that by staying in the womb, it could be part of the problem. These final days of pregnancy are very confusing times for the fetus.

One of the reasons for the confusion is Nature herself. Towards the end of the pregnancy, Nature initiates changes between the fetus and its mother. Earlier you realized the relationship between the fetal Memory Block and its mother's immune system. This relationship being that the fetal Memory Block suppresses its mother's immune system. Because of this, Nature takes precautions in order to ensure the mother's immune health, during the process of and period directly after labor. The process of labor may be difficult and long, the mother may sustain injuries incurred during a difficult delivery. The mother is Nature's priority. For as you will see in later chapters, if the mother were to die, even after childbirth, there is a very good chance the infant would not survive. Because of this and that the majority of the developmental aspects in the womb have been accomplished; towards the end of the pregnancy Nature lifts slightly the neurobiological function of the fetal Memory Block.

In many cases, the slight lifting of the Memory Block is hardly noticeable to the fetus in the womb. In others, as you will see in the final chapter of the book, it is more substantial. In general, however, this slight lifting will confuse fetal emotions. One of the most obvious results is that the fetus will not be able to follow the developmental aspects of each cycle as effectively as before. For example, at the end of the pregnancy, with the slight lifting of the Memory Block the fetus will not fully relax during the Euphoric Cycle. In other words, because it is allowed a very slight increase in short-term memory, it has an idea of the existence of one cycle while in another. So the fetus, towards the end of the pregnancy while in the Euphoric Cycle, will not be allowed the complete blissful euphoria it once experienced. This is because it will be anticipating or at least expecting the existence of another condition besides the one it currently is experiencing. To say that the fetus anticipates the existence of the First Fear Cycle while in the Euphoric Cycle would not be correct, at least in most cases. The timing, onset and intensity of each cycle will still be masked. However, the very expectation that another condition exists, will only confuse the initial fetal misinterpretations that it has been led to believe are correct, for many months. Now, this is very important and will be covered in much more detail in the final chapter of the book. For now, it is important to realize that the fetus will not be as relaxed or rested in the Euphoric Cycle. This only adds to the general deterioration of the fetal environment during the last few days of the pregnancy.

Indeed, Nature is pointing in every direction to the fetus that it is time to leave. Now in some cases, even after all these signs and cues pointing in the direction of leaving, the fetus will remain stubborn and still refuse to leave the womb. This fetus may try one last plan to generate a change and improvement in the conditions of the deteriorating womb. This final plan is created out of desperation. This is what occurs. At night, during the First Fear Cycle, when its mother is in the process of dying, which is only sleeping, the fetus simply does nothing to save her life, and therefore its own. This is how desperate the fetus has become. It believes that by allowing its mother to transiently experience death that she may respond by improving conditions. Of course, this does not work either, as its mother simply continues sleeping, until finally, unable to withstand the decrease in dopamine the fetus generates its own movement and therefore dopamine increase.

Labor

Out of plans, out of hope and out of threats, the fetus for the first time plans to do what it never wanted to do. It will have to leave. The conditions have increasingly grown worse. It has no choice. Yet, what a choice it is. Leaving its mother alone to die will be the most difficult decision it will most likely make in its entire life, and it is made even before it can talk! So, in one night, during the First Fear Cycle, when the nightly cycle of death begins, the fetus chooses to leave. The fetus, heartbroken with regrets and consumed with guilt about leaving its mother alone to die, begins the process of labor. Reluctantly, it leaves the hopeless situation behind.

If Nature has accomplished every developmental goal, the fetus will complete labor and its evolution into infancy successfully. It will make it down the dark tunnel of birth and into the bright light of life successfully.

However, what is this? Confusion will consume the infant's face the moment it adjust its eyes to the bright lights. Yes, you can look in a thousand newborns, no a million, at the very second they hear its mother's voice talking or they look at her face. Ninety-eight percent of the time the look on the infant's face will be the same. The first emotion the infant experiences, in life outside the womb, is confusion and then shock. No, the infant is not in shock because it is in a bright room, full of strange people. No, it is not this at all. The infant is in shock, surprised and stunned that its mother is still alive. It simply cannot believe that this is happening. To see her and to hear her voice, defies everything Nature has taught it for nine months. Of course, the infant will never forgive Nature for this deception, however, we will get to that in later chapters. For now, the moment the infant looks into its mother's eyes, a bond is renewed that in most cases will never be broken. Indeed, it is a moment of love.

It will take the infant a few years to overcome the trauma of this bizarre series of events, and they will spend much longer trying to make sense out of all that has happened.

Neuronal Programming

While the fetus has left the womb to begin the experience of infancy in a new world, its past will never be far behind. In fact, they will be carrying the entire experience on their shoulders for a long time. As every single aspect of every single event in both cycles, including their birth was encoded or programmed into developing fetal neurons. Every apnea, every punch, every kick, every touch and every response to that touch, was all recorded. Every second of the Euphoric Cycle, every smile and every noise listened to, were all recorded. Even the fetal heart rate was recorded. Every emotion and reflex of every single aspect of both cycles was recorded in the developing fetal neurons. Not a second was missed.

As you will see in the following chapters, millions of these neurons in the infant's brain will be eliminated. Others will be reprogrammed and still others reinforced. Those remaining will form the infant, child and adult subconscious. These two developmental cycles, life in the womb, will then in the subconscious influence every conscious thought, in every waking hour for the rest of the individual's life. During their deepest sleep, these neurons will rise again and fire uninhibited. Indeed, as you will see, Nature will utilize these developmental cycles in ways that are almost unimaginable. While the journey for the fetus has ended, the journey to the answers to human behavior has just begun.

CHAPTER FOUR

INFANCY

Yes, it is love at first sight for both, the newborn infant and its mother. Far from innocent however, the newborn infant has already experienced the most horrific event it might ever experience, and has already made the most difficult decision it may ever be forced to make. The newborn is a hero! It has struggled nightly, for months, with death and has arisen victorious! This heroic day will be saluted every year. Yet, the birthday will never mean what it means to the infant right now.

When the fetus left the womb, it took a chance. It took a chance against all common logic and now the results are favorable. Its mother is still alive. It is a confusing situation the infant finds itself born into.

The first priority of the newborn infant is its mother. It will use its newly discovered senses, the eyes, to watch her at every minute. After all, she should begin the process of dying any minute. This is what the fetus was taught, and what the newborn infant still believes to be true. Yes, maybe there was a mistake. Its mother should have died when it left the womb, but maybe, somehow, she is strong enough to hold on a few hours, however, no longer.

The newborn wants to watch her, wants to hear her, and wants to know that she is alive. After all, if she dies, it will stop breathing and begin dying as well. Of course this is not true, however, the newborn infant believes it is, for in the womb it was conditioned to experience the intense, painful apneas when she was sleeping. The fetus believed they were both dying, instead. The newborn will pay very close attention to her at every minute. This will be especially true at night, for this is when the First Fear Cycle of Development occurred. Now the Memory Block, which slightly lifted towards the end of pregnancy, lifts more every day. The infant can begin to make subtle connections. It begins noticing patterns. It notices not only patterns about the present, however about the past as well. The first pattern about its past it will notice is that every night its mother will begin the process of dying and therefore it will too.

The entire goal of the newborn during the first few weeks will be to make sure it keeps its mother alive at night. This, of course, only means to keep her awake. While it will be a minor inconvenience for its exhausted mother; to the newborn infant, it still believes it is a matter of live and death. The newborn infant will do anything to keep its mother awake, alive, at night. It will kick, cry, fuss, and anything else it can do as long as its mother stays awake. It wants to see her eyes open, throughout the night, at all cost.

Patterns of Infant Behavior

To understand the behavior of infants, it is only necessary to understand the two cycles of development they realized in the womb. It is actually very simple. Infant behavior is not that complex at all. Anything that reminds them of the First Fear Cycle of Development, they will dislike. On the other hand, anything that reminds them or directly mimics the Euphoric Cycle of Development, they will like. For example, negative things that remind them of the First Fear Cycle will include; darkness, quiet, stillness, restricted movement, its mother sleeping, and dirty diapers. This will all be intensified during the night. This they will like, things that remind them of the Euphoric Cycle will include; rocking, gentle bouncing, cleanliness, unrestricted movement, and hearing the awake mother's voice.

To understand why this is, all you must remember is that every event of the First Fear and Euphoric Cycle of Development is programmed into the neurons that are consuming every thought of the infant. As you will see in the next chapter, Nature has a very specific plan for these neurons, however, for now, they are dominating the infant's thought. Now, we will go to the likes and dislikes and see how directly they mimic each cycle.

The infant will enjoy anything that reminds them of, or mimics their experience in the Euphoric Cycle. Rocking is the most obvious. Rocking is exactly what the fetus experienced during the Euphoric Cycle, as its mother walked around, the fetus, in the womb, rocked gently back and forth. This rocking motion generated an increased dopamine release to the pleasure and reward pathways of the fetal developing brain. Whether or not the infant realizes an increase in dopamine from this rocking motion, like the fetus did, is irrelevant, for the association is made and it will last a lifetime. Any other type of movement, as long as it is controlled and preferably rhythmic, will provide the same enjoyment. Anything from rolling in a stroller back and forth, to a jump swing that the infant can bounce up and down upon, to a gentle bounce on a parent's knee, will do the trick. Again, the key is controlled, rhythmic movement that will directly mimic their experience in the womb during this desired cycle. This will be the first showing of what will be a lifelong attempt to mimic the movement of the Euphoric Cycle and obtain that illusive dopamine that once flowed so freely. While it will begin with rocking by its mother, it will evolve into dancing and bicycles, then a societal love for everything that vibrates and moves from motorcycles to rhythmic movement of the automobile. In the end, full circle, it will come back to the rocking chair of the elderly, as they spend their final days, as they did their first, mimicking the Euphoric Cycle. This love of movement will be stronger for the male, as both cycles in the womb were stronger for him. The individual's entire life will continue to be shaped and molded by the short nine months in the womb, as the influence is forever locked in the subconscious, influencing every thought and motivating every action. As you will see later, Nature has something much more important in mind for this rocking movement in regards to the proliferation of the human species.

The infant will like cleanliness. It will like cleanliness, only in regard to its own human waste; this will be explained in the next section thoroughly. The infant will like anything that can generate movement. It will like a wind up toy that makes noise, a rattle it can shake, a mobile above the crib. This is important, because they can constantly see or generate noise and movement; this reassures them that they are not in the process of dying. The infant will shake the rattle especially when its mother is not around, as this is when the association of the First Fear Cycle is at its worst. Because the Memory Block is still strong, the infant will have to repeat this process, to reassure itself, every few minutes. In fact, by observing an infant with a rattle you can quickly judge the time lapse of its partially blocked memory. The self-generation of noise or movement is the most important developmental aspect of early infancy. For the first time they can begin to control what once controlled them so severely. You will see this again, this attempt of infantile control over the First Fear Cycle, later in this chapter under "The origins of speech."

The final two situations that an infant will like have to do directly with its mother. As you have realized earlier, the first priority of the infant is its mother. Indeed, it could put up with all the things that it dislikes, experiencing very little movement or sound, as long as it sees its mother all the time, with open eyes and preferably moving. After all, the other things are only mimicry and she is the real thing, the source of the infant's ongoing concern. The infant believes that if something happens to its mother, something bad will happen to itself as well. This thought consumes the infant from morning until it finally passes out from exhaustion. For the infant still believes that she can die at any minute and that it will soon follow. And who can blame it, as this is exactly what it was lead to believe for many months in the womb.

Things that the infant will not like will include darkness. While darkness prevailed in both cycles, the infant associates darkness with restricted vision and vulnerability. The infant will tolerate darkness as long as factors from the Euphoric Cycle, such as movement are present, if not, it will just remind it too much of the First Fear Cycle. Stillness was the condition in the womb during the First Fear Cycle, late at night when its mother was sleeping. Of course, the fetus misinterpreted this as death, which by now is well established.

In the womb, stillness and silence represented death to its mother and to itself, this was the fetal perception. The infant will want to be free to move around. In the womb, especially at the end of pregnancy, movement was obviously restricted. While the infant might be all right in the crib, it must be able to create movements in some way, so as to reassure it that it is not in the process of dying. It will need to remind itself every couple of minutes that it is not dying. This is because the Memory Block is still very strong, short-term memory is very limited and therefore, the infant forgets quickly. There is a very obvious reason the infant dislikes its mother sleeping. At night, during the First Fear Cycle, the fetus misinterpreted her sleeping for her death and therefore its own. It will dislike any mimicry of that cycle.

While a wet or dirty diaper may seem unimportant, it is actually one of the most telling of the conditions listed above. In fact, Nature will use this model for many things, including, as you will see later, gender identity and human reproduction. It all begins in the womb, with the association of the two cycles and with olfactory development. During the First Fear Cycle, in the long hours of the night, the fetal bodily waste products are not flushed as frequently throughout the intrauterine environment. Nature, economical and efficient, utilizes these conditions for olfactory development (sense of smell) and resultant neuronal programming. A connection is made between the development of the fetus experiences, which is olfactory, and the condition the fetus realizes at that time, which is unpleasant. The olfactory development of pungent odors and foul smells just happens to be what is available to Nature, when the mother is sleeping. Therefore, the olfactory development is the coding of pungent and foul odors of its own bodily waste. The fetal condition, as you have seen in the last chapter, is painful and horrific as it tries to save its mother's and its own life. After birth, the association will be, from infancy throughout its entire life, of human waste to this painful and horrific cycle in the womb. Human waste will, therefore, represent the death and decay of the womb that the infant, as did the fetus, will not want to be associated with. The neurons, encoded with all these events, are dominating the infant's thoughts. Therefore, an infant with wet or dirty diapers will cry, however, not for the reasons commonly believed. While a wet or dirty diaper maybe inconvenient to the infant and irritating to the skin, this is not the primary reason that they will be unhappy or cry. No, it is much more important than this, as they believe the longer they remain in their own waste, the more likely that they are back in the First Fear Cycle and the more likely its mother and therefore itself will begin dying. You will see this negative association many times throughout the book; again this is one of Nature's most effective developmental tools, with the human species.

It is important to realize that if Nature somehow chose to program sweet smells for the olfactory development during the First Fear Cycle, the individual's aversion to those sweet smells would be equally as strong. It is all the association, and in this case the association is negative, because the olfactory development occurs during the First Fear Cycle.

While the newborn has evolved from a fetus into infancy, life in the womb can be viewed by its behavior in many ways. One of the most obvious ways this quickly becomes apparent, is when a parent attempts to sooth a crying infant. As long as the infant is being rocked, it is usually quiet and will fall asleep, however, as soon as the rocking stops it often wakes up crying. The reason for this can be best explained in the context of an automobile ride, for this is one of the most obvious windows from which we can view the two cycles, and their transitions in the womb.

Anyone who has traveled with an infant on an automobile trip can attest to the following. The vibration and movement of the car will usually rock the infant into a deep sleep. However, when the car comes to a stop, often the infant will wake up. Now, they will not always cry, however, there is something that you can almost always notice on their face, it is a look of startle and fear. To understand why this is, it is helpful to return to the Euphoric Cycle. When its mother was moving during her active time, then lies down to rest or to sleep, the fetus was thrown from a very pleasurable Euphoric Cycle into the horrific First Fear Cycle. Because of the Memory Block, the fetus had no idea it was coming. It had no idea that the Euphoric Cycle would ever end. So when it entered the First Fear Cycle, as its mother lies down, it was as if the first time it ever happened. It was as if the bottom dropped out of its world. It went from a relaxed, drugged, sleepy state into a state where it had to fight for its life. This, of course, is exactly what Nature wanted, as it was the simplest and most efficient way to develop fetal reflexes. As you know by now, these reflexes were essential for saving the fetal life during labor. This, of course, is exactly what the changes in the speed of the automobile are mimicking, the rapid transition from the relaxed Euphoric Cycle to the alert startle of the First Fear Cycle. So when the infant wakes up, it will be abruptly, again expecting to fight for its life. Of course, this does not necessary mean, that only infants will experience this phenomena, children and adults may wake up startled from this transition as well. While an adult may justify this fear by looking out at the road, or to connect it to the fear of an accident, this is not the base reason. This is because, as you will see, many of the neurons encoded with this event will remain with the individual forever.

The Origins of Speech

The single aspect that motivates the human species to communicate vocally is the First Fear Cycle of Development. While a very complex explanation is necessary, from this origin to the cumulative progression that finalizes in the process of talking, it will be explained as simply as possible.

To understand why we, as a species, talk and verbally communicate, we must first return to the long hours of the night during, the First Fear Cycle of Development. During this time, after hours upon hours of battling to save its mother's and therefore its own life, the fetus was exhausted. Its mother was in her deepest sleep at this time. The fetus, however, would not give up. While it was too tired, too exhausted to even move a finger in an attempt to initiate a response, it still had hope. It had hopes that somehow, someway it was wrong. The only sliver of hope for the exhausted fetus was sound.

In the womb, during the First Fear Cycle, sound was not only hope. In the womb sound was life itself. Sound was everything, if the fetus could just hear a different sound, from one it had heard a second before, then it could disbelieve this horrible misinterpretation that Nature had lead it to believe it was true. Its mother's heartbeat was slowing. The fetus always interpreted this as her dying. Through the long hours of the night, it would listen for changes in that heartbeat. If it could hear a subtle increase then this was hope. If, with ear so close to the intrauterine wall that it realized a mild burning sensation, it could pick up a unique sound, then this was hope. Through its mother's long sleep cycle, sound was all that kept the fetus going. Sound was everything. This, of course, served a very important purpose in the development of fetal hearing. This was, as you have already seen, critical in the differentiation of sounds, which were programmed into the auditory cortex.

In the womb, the connection is made. It is the connection that will outlast the fetal stay in the womb. It is the connection that will last a lifetime. The connection is between sound and life, silence and death. This connection or association is programmed into the developing fetal neurons, which will evolve, after a few modifications, into the subconscious of the infant, child and adult. The subconscious will be explained in detail in a later chapter.

To the infant this connection is well established. The infant wants to hear sound, preferably its mother's voice. This will offset the fear that she is dying. The problem with noise, however, is that it is not always available. Indeed, there are times when its mother is simply silent. The infant learns quickly that the most effective way to generate a consistent supply of sound is by creating it on its own. When the neurons, encoded with the First Fear Cycle, fire and influence the infant's thoughts with the belief that its mother and therefore itself is dying, sound will offset this belief. With the Memory Block still strong, still partially blocking the infant's short-term memory, it will have to continually create sound, as it forgets, almost as quickly as it makes it.

It begins with crying. While crying offers a physiological relief to pain, it also creates sound. The infant, as it ages, realizes crying does not always gain the most effective response. It begins to make sounds, to mimic others. Through trial and error, it finds words. It would not do any of this, if each time it generated sound, that it was not offsetting the initial fear that dominates its conscious and subconscious thoughts. It is the quickest way, the most effective way to respond to the fear of silence that meant death for its mother and therefore to itself. As you will see in the chapter on "The Subconscious", these same neurons, encoded with that fear, influence the neural pattern and therefore, human behavior in ways that hardly seem imaginable.

There are two other factors that enhance this initial motivation. The first factor is the Euphoric Cycle. Everything the infant associates with the Euphoric Cycle is positive. When you look at the behavior of the pregnant mother, during the fetal Euphoric Cycle, you realize not only was she moving around, but often talking as well. One thing is for certain, in most cases at least, she was talking more and listening to other voices during the day or when she was active than during her deepest sleep. The Euphoric Cycle was full of noise. The infant not only likes movement that mimics the Euphoric Cycle, but sound as well. By mimicking this sound, which was generated by its mother, during the Euphoric Cycle, the infant reproduces its experience in that cycle, much as the same way the rocking or rhythmic movement does.

The final aspect, for motivation of speech, is control of environment. This is a powerful motivator as well. The first aspect of the infant's environment it wants to control is its mother. As you have already seen, it wants to know that she is alive at all times. By crying, it can almost magically make her appear. This is very powerful. This reinforces the other two motivations of the generation of sound.

As time goes on, crying will lose its effectiveness, communication through the verbal connection of words will be necessary. As the infant grows older, evolving into childhood, and finally, later, as an adult, the core motivations for speech and talking will remain the same. What is important to realize, is that each time an adult, child or infant talks, the core motivation for speech will remain the same, this being to generate sound, which in and of itself offsets the First Fear Cycle, that in the silence, their mother and therefore they themselves are in the process of dying. It is literally true, that the reason people talk; is to hear themselves talk.

To hear our self making sounds is the primary motivator of speech. The primary motivator of making sounds is to offset the fear of dying. This fear was realized in the womb, as a fetus during the First Fear Cycle of Development. This fear is encoded into the neurons that form our subconscious and therefore influence every conscious thought that in turn influence our action, which in this case is to talk. While the second of the two reasons; mimicry of the Euphoric Cycle and control of our environment, are important reasons, without the first we would not talk. Indeed, as you will see in Part Two of this book, without the initial experience of the First Fear Cycle of Development altered, there would be little or no motivation to speak at all.

CHAPTER FIVE

FIRST FEAR NOT RELIEVED

After birth, it is Nature's intention to eliminate many of the neurons encoded with the events of the First Fear and Euphoric Cycles, from the developing infant's brain. While there are many purposes for this, here we will focus on the major reasons.

The most obvious reason is that many aspects of the First Fear and Euphoric Cycles of Development are not necessary for the infant's life and life in general, outside the womb. The developmental cycles in the womb have served one of their major purposes. The fetus has evolved safely into infancy. Therefore, there is no need for the infant to live outside the womb, consumed with a neural pattern that is essential for life and development inside. Indeed, the birth of the infant was a major purpose, as you have seen, of the First Fear and Euphoric Cycles of Development. As you will see later in this chapter, an excess of these neurons, encoded with the events of the two cycles, will simply hinder the development of the infant.

Another important reason to eliminate many of these neurons encoded, or programmed during the First Fear and Euphoric Cycles are the needs and the demands of the actual neurons themselves. These neurons were programmed at a time of rapid neural development. Therefore, their demands for neurochemicals such as dopamine are very high. As you have realized, in the womb, dopamine played a very critical role in the neurochemical manipulation and subsequent development of the fetus. Outside the womb, however, a major purpose of this neurochemical manipulation has concluded, this being the conformity of the activity level in the womb during each cycle of development. Again, there are many neurochemicals essential during intrauterine development that will not be explained here. What is important to understand is that these neurons programmed in the womb, will have a higher demand for the neurochemicals used in their encoding or programming than those developed after birth.

Another very important reason to eliminate the neurons encoded with the events of the two cycles in the womb is the consequent Memory Block that is encoded with them. As in each of these neurons, programmed with the events of the First Fear and Euphoric Cycles of Development, the Memory Block, which was essential for the conformity to each cycle, was encoded into them as well. Therefore, by eliminating these fetal neurons, much of the Memory Block will be eliminated as well. This will then partially reduce the blockage of the infant's short-term memory and they can begin the important process of learning.

An even more important reason to eliminate the fetal neurons encoded with both cycles and the Memory Block is the immune system. Just as the fetal Memory Block partially suppressed its mother's immune system, the same Memory Block will now suppress the infant's immune system, as well. In other words, the infant essentially inherits the suppression of its immune system from its mother. This suppression is conveyed by the Memory Block, which is programmed into these fetal neurons, encoded with the two cycles in the womb. Now, Nature has a very important purpose for this suppression, which will be discussed later in this chapter. For now, it is only important to realize, that with the elimination of each of these neurons encoded with the First Fear and Euphoric Cycles of Development, the Memory Block is eliminated as well. By eliminating the Memory Block, its suppression of the infant's immune system is eliminated as well. Therefore, by eliminating the neurons encoded with the two cycles of development in the womb, the suppression of the immune system is reduced.

This reduction in immune suppression will be realized in obvious ways for the infant. This may save the infant's life as its untested immune system builds up immunities to various harmful exposures.

Neural Elimination, Reprogramming and Reinforcement

Of course, not all of the neurons encoded with the events of the First Fear and Euphoric Cycles will be eliminated. In fact, there are three possibilities that await these fetal neurons encoded with the two cycles of development. The first, as you have already seen, is elimination. The second possibility is reprogramming. Here, these fetal neurons will be reprogrammed or modified, either partially or fully, with experiences the infant realizes outside the womb. We will not spend very much time on this option, as a very technical explanation would be required and it is not essential for the model of human behavior. The third option or possibility is reinforcement. This is the most important option in respect to human behavior. This will be explained in detail later in this chapter. Briefly, reinforcement is dependent on environmental factors outside the womb.

To accomplish this reorganization of the neural pattern of the infant, Nature provides a "window" of time, in which this can be accomplished. After this "window" is closed, the changes in the fate or make up of these neurons can still occur, however, the changes are much slower, if they occur at all. While the length that this "window" is open varies for each infant, it is usually the first two years of life, with a heavy emphasis on the first six months. Again, the fate or make up of these neurons can be decided well into the seventh or eight year, or even longer, however, after these first two years, this critical period that this "window" is open, it is not likely that major changes will occur. So, it is safe to say, that by two years of age, a large portion of the neural pattern, the direction it will take in regards to the neurons encoded with the First Fear and Euphoric Cycles of Development, is already established. As you will see throughout the book, these first two years, this critical period, will be very important in establishing the overall outcome of the individual.

During the first two years, this "window" that Nature provides for the process of neuronal elimination, reprogramming and reinforcement is defined as a period of neuronal plasticity. While this is a technical term, its definition is accurate of its description. What this essentially means is that these fetal neurons encoded with the two cycles of development are plastic or flexible. They are flexible to change. As you will realize later, these changes are almost completely guided by the infant's environment.

What Determines the Neuron's Fate?

Now then, the big question of course is, what factors determine whether the neuron becomes eliminated, reprogrammed or reinforced? The answer is quite simple. It is the infant's environment. More specifically than this even, it is the infant's environment in regards to the two developmental cycles, it experienced in the womb. Look at it as a matching game. If any factors outside the womb mimic any factors inside the womb or the fetal perception inside the womb, the neuron will remain, in this case, becoming reinforced. Unfortunately, as you will see, it is a matching game that no infant wants to play

To understand what this all means, all we need to do is to go back and look at the likes and dislikes of the infant in the last chapter. We will tie both chapters together with a simple example.

We will use an example of a male infant that is ten months old. We will call him Johnny. Inside Johnny's developing infant brain, millions of neurons encoded with the events of the First Fear and Euphoric Cycles of Development are actively waiting the neural reprogramming, that you have just been introduced to. Now, unfortunately for Johnny, his early childhood is not very good in regards to his final neural development. Johnny lies in his crib all day and cries for his mother. His mother is too preoccupied with other affairs and never comes. Now, inside Johnny's developing brain a myriad of events is occurring. Every time Johnny cries for his mother and she does not come, another neuron (or maybe one thousand neurons!) of the First Fear Cycle of Development is reinforced. So, Johnny's thoughts that leads to the reinforcement of the neuron are, "My mother is not here, therefore she is dead and I will die soon." This connects to the fetal perception of dependence. This is the same reason the fetus kicked and punched through the long hours of the night trying to save its mother's and therefore its own life. The fetus believed if its mother were to die, which of course was only sleeping, that it was in the process of dying as well. These events are well established, being repeated over and over again, night after night, in the womb, during the First Fear Cycle of Development. These events were all recorded or encoded into the developing fetal neurons in Johnny's brain, by reenacting this fear or reinforcing it, the neurons encoded with the First Fear Cycle, are now reinforced as well. This is exactly what happens every time Johnny's mother does not come.

Now, if every time Johnny cries, his mother comes running into the room, the opposite is going to occur. Without the necessary reinforcement, these neurons are too fragile or plastic to remain. They will then be eliminated or available for reprogramming. Here, Johnny realizes his mother is not dead and therefore he will not die. Again, without a partial or full duplication of the initial fetal fear, the neuron will not be reinforced.

Johnny's mother, however, does not come in the room. In fact, there is little movement or noise in his little dark room. Now, what is important to realize, is that not only is the belief, that his mother and therefore himself is in the process of death, going to be reinforced, however, everything else encoded in that neuron containing the First Fear Cycle of Development will be reinforced as well. For example, the fetal kicking, punching and trying to regain a response from its dying mother, the fetal emotional state, and the Memory Block, are all included in those neurons. These events were all grouped into one or more neurons that will now, most likely, remain forever in Johnny's subconscious.

In addition to the events themselves, these fetal neurons will have other consequences for the boy as well. Because they are encoded with the Memory Block, he will realize additional suppression on his immune system. As you remember, there is a direct relationship between the Memory Block and the individual's immune system. The more Memory Block remaining the stronger the suppression on the individual's immune system will be. And because encoded in each neuron of the First Fear and Euphoric Cycles of intrauterine development is the Memory Block and because he has so many of these neurons remaining, he will realize this strong suppression on his immune system.

In addition to this, there will be other neurobiological implications as well. Because these neurons were developed at a time of high dopamine and other neurochemical utilization, which was in the womb, these neurons will have a higher demand for those neurochemicals. Later in life, not only will the boy realize a deficit of these neurochemicals circulating through his bloodstream, but also, as you will see, the neural mechanisms responsible for producing these neurochemicals will not, over a long period of time, be able to continue to offset this initial imbalance.

The key to these neurons' survival is reinforcement. Without reinforcement many of these neurons programmed in the womb are not strong enough to survive. In this case, Johnny's environment, by mimicking directly the fetal perception encoded in the neurons, provides the reinforcement. This is just the beginning, as you will see, of Johnny's problems he will encounter throughout his life, as he will likely realize the condition of First Fear Not Relieved. This will be explained in more detail later in this chapter and throughout the book.

Duplication of Fetal Neurons

It is important to clarify something here. Nature intends for many of the neurons containing the First Fear and Euphoric Cycles of Development to remain permanently. These neurons, as you will see, will form the individual's subconscious. Because the two cycles of development occurred night after night in the womb, for months at a time, many of these neurons encoded with these developmental events were duplicated. In other words, essentially the same or very similar developmental aspects are encoded into millions of developing fetal neurons. It is therefore, Nature's purpose during this period of plasticity to eliminate or reprogram many of these duplicated neurons.

Therefore, no matter how advantageous the infant's environment is, in regards to elimination and reprogramming of these fetal neurons, there is never any chance that all or even the majority of them will realize this fate. As Nature has many intended purposes for these neurons and the developmental events they represent.

Fate of Euphoric Cycle Neurons

A large part of "Part One" of the book will focus on the negative aspects of the condition of First Fear Not Relieved. Like the neurons encoded with the First Fear Cycle of Development, the neurons encoded with the Euphoric Cycle of Development are subject to the same criteria concerning elimination, reprogramming and reinforcement. Like the neurons of the First Fear Cycle, this period of plasticity extends throughout the first two years of life. Like the neurons of the First Fear Cycle, those of the Euphoric Cycle can be reinforced by environmental factors outside the womb, which mimic conditions or perceptions inside the womb. For example, if an infant realizes an environment full of movement, the neurons encoded with the Euphoric Cycle of Development will be reinforced. Unlike the neurons encoded with the First Fear Cycle, an excess of reinforced neurons encoded with the Euphoric Cycle do not hold the same negative developmental aspects.

An excess of remaining neurons encoded with the Euphoric Cycle is responsible for a single disorder, manic depression, which will be explained later in the book. In contrast, an excess of remaining neurons encoded with the First Fear Cycle is responsible for numerous disorders and behavioral implications; therefore, the focus here will be on the condition of First Fear Not Relieved. This is not to say that we will leave the Euphoric Cycle of Development behind. This is not the case at all. Indeed, the Euphoric Cycle of Development is an essential aspect of human behavior, just not with the same implications or magnitude of the other cycle. Developmental aspects in which the Euphoric Cycle is important include the purpose of sleep and reproduction.

Therefore, while an excess of neurons reinforced is of consequence to the individual, those of the Euphoric Cycle are not as severe. The focus then will be on the condition of First Fear Not Relieved.

Defining First Fear not Relieved

While the remainder of "Part One" of the book is partially devoted to the condition of First Fear Not Relieved and the term is essentially self-defining through the material, a brief summary of the definition here will be helpful. As you have seen, if enough neurons encoded with the First Fear Cycle of Development are not eliminated or reprogrammed, but reinforced instead, the infant will realize a series of detrimental effects. This condition will be defined as "First Fear Not Relieved."

This condition is caused by environmental factors realized by the infant, during the first few years of life. First Fear Not Relieved is caused by one or more environmental factors that fail to meet Nature's minimum criteria for the development of the human infant. These specific environmental factors will be discussed later in this chapter. In general, this condition is realized when the environment the infant experiences outside the womb in any way mimics the fetal experience or perception inside the womb. This matching of conditions generates a chain of neurobiological events, which causes the neurons encoded with the First Fear Cycle of Development to become reinforced, and therefore remaining.

Because it was never Nature's intention that such large bodies of developmental neurons remain, the infant will realize an imbalance in its neural pattern. This is a lifetime condition, which grows with the infant into childhood and their adult years. Even in old age, this imbalance remains.

The effects of this imbalance on the individual and their life are widespread. There are immune, mental and behavior implications to this imbalance. These will be explained throughout "Part One" of the book. First Fear Not Relieved is not a single disorder, however, a condition responsible for the majority of disorders of human behavior.

So what does this all mean? It quite simply means that if the infant realizes a less than favorable environment, during their first few years, they will realize a lifetime of problems. Favorable conditions being defined here as conditions that are established by Nature for the satisfactory reproduction of the species. This will be explained more thoroughly at the end of this chapter, for, as you will see, Nature essentially prunes or eliminates the human species at two important stages of development. The first occurs during the fetal stage, the second was intended to take place during infancy. All of this, this chain of events, takes place due to the reinforcement of the developmental neurons encoded with the First Fear Cycle of Development. So, as you will see, the first few years of life are extremely important and any deviation from Nature's intended purpose will initiate a lifetime of implications. In general, this lifetime of implications will force the individual to live life outside the womb heavily influenced by neurons that were programmed, and intended for developmental cycles inside the womb.

Conditions Responsible for First Fear not Relieved

The following is a list of environmental conditions the infant realizes that leads to the condition of First Fear Not Relieved. Before the list is given, however, there are some important factors concerning it that need to be explained.

The first aspect is the list itself. This is not a complete list of environmental factors that lead to this condition. While there are countless other factors, only the most obvious and major reasons will be given here.

The second aspect is the importance of each singular environmental factor in relation to the condition of First Fear Not Relieved. What this means is that a single factor may lead to the condition or it may take a group of factors to initiate it. Each individual infant is unique; its intrauterine environment was unique; and therefore, the amount of factors necessary to realize the condition of First Fear Not Relieved will be unique as well. What we are talking about is the obtaining of a threshold. When a certain number or repetition of a singular environmental factor is obtained, the condition of First Fear Not Relieved will be realized.

The third aspect that is important to recognize, before we get into the list of environmental conditions, is the infant's mother herself. This list of environmental conditions is heavily burdened upon the infant's mother. While this may seem unbalanced, this imbalance should be kept in perspective. The burden realized, should be taken in context to the gift received. Indeed, the gift of creating life is the greatest bestowed upon a species. The gender chosen to receive that gift is the female. Therefore, it should not be surprising that the largest burden or responsibility is placed upon that gender. This list should be viewed in relation to neurobiological factors and should not be misread through societal implications.

On the other hand, the results of the failures of environmental factors are heavily burdened upon the male infant, in contrast to the female infant. This imbalance is due to the differences of the intrauterine environment between the male and female fetus. Because the First Fear Cycle of Developmental was stronger for the male than the female, any deviation from the normal elimination and reprogramming of neurons will result in more severe repercussions. Indeed, if something goes wrong within the female infant's environment the damage may very well be manageable: however, when something goes wrong within the male infant's environment, it will go terribly wrong with more obvious implications.

The following, then, is a list of environmental factors experienced by the infant that will lead to First Fear Not Relieved. Each factor will be briefly discussed in relation to the reason of its importance.

Death of the Mother

This, of course, will be the most obvious environmental factor leading to the condition of First Fear Not Relieved. The actual physical death of the mother would therefore justify the fetal perception and misinterpretation that its mother, once it left the womb would die. Because of the dependence it realized in the womb, it would believe that its death would soon follow. This would reinforce the neurons encoded with the First Fear Cycle of Development. While earlier you realized that the amount of environmental factors responsible for the development of this condition, vary with each individual; in this case, this single factor alone would be enough.

Prolonged Illness of the Mother

While this would not be as dramatic for the infant as its mother's actual, physical death, it would be substantial nonetheless. The infant would interpret the illness in two ways. The first would be her restricted movement. If a long period of bed rest would be required the infant would interpret this lack of movement, being her same state during the First Fear Cycle, as her position during her death. The second reason is the infant would interpret the smell of its mother, the smell of any illness, as that of the smell of death and decay that occurred during the First Fear Cycle in the womb. This would lead to the reinforcement of the neurons encoded with the First Fear Cycle of Development.

Prolonged Absence of the Mother

If for any reason the mother is separated from the infant, for a long period of time, this will reinforce the infant's fear that when it left the womb its mother would die. By reinforcing this fear, the neurons encoded with the developmental cycle will be reinforced as well. So, the question becomes, what defines a prolonged absence? Again, this will vary with the individual infant, this variation is to be based on the fetal intrauterine environment and any combination of other factors provided here. One thing is certain, however, this absence will be especially weighted at night. As this is when the First Fear Cycle of Development occurred and when the infant's anticipation of its mother's death will reach its climax.

In general, this prolonged absence refers to a period of time, rather than a scheduled routine, in other words, a period of weeks or months in contrast to a period of minutes or hours. Not only is this prolonged absence weighted at night, but on the age of the infant as well. As with many of these factors listed, the most impact will be realized within the first six months.

Any Form of Abuse by the Mother, Father or Others

Here, we see the first environmental factor involving someone besides its mother. Because the First Fear Cycle of Development was painful for the fetus, any mimicking of that pain will lead to reinforcement of these neurons and therefore, the condition of First Fear Not Relieved. Again, this will be heavily weighted during the first six months of the infant's life. Remember, behind the fear of its mother's death is the fetal fear of the death of itself. Any reinforcement of that fear alone will reinforce the neurons of the developmental cycle. Like the death of the mother, this factor alone would most likely be enough to initiate the condition of First Fear Not Relieved.

Physical Abuse to the Mother

This is also a very strong environmental factor that will likely lead to the condition of First Fear Not Relieved. Whether the abuse is by the father, a stranger or others, the infant's fear reinforces the fetal fear that its mother and therefore it itself is in the process of dying. While all physical abuse to its mother will affect the infant, obviously a pattern of abuse will have more impact.

Dirty Environment

The definition of dirty, here, is in relation to the infant's olfactory or sense of smell. If an infant is left too long, and not changed, its diaper wet or dirty, this would reinforce the neurons encoded with the First Fear Cycle, as this was the cycle of development in which Nature chose to program pungent or foul odors into the fetal olfactory cortex. This association, outside the womb, of pungent or foul odors will reinforce the neurons of the First Fear Cycle of Development.

While dirty diapers would be the most obvious exposure the infant would have to foul or pungent odors, it does not necessarily mean it could be the only one. For example, if the pungent or foul odors consumed, on a daily basis from the infant's immediate environment, from a factory, farm, chemical or even sewage plant, this could trigger a reinforcement of these neurons as well.

Lack of Movement — Restricted Movement

If the infant is disabled or injured at an early age, especially the first six months, this prohibits freedom to generate their own movement; this could reinforce neurons encoded with the First Fear Cycle as well. The reason here is that, while fetal movement in the womb was restricted, the conditioned response of the First Fear Cycle was kicking, punching and moving about. If, as an infant, this were restricted, it would eliminate the ability to respond to the perceived death of its mother and therefore itself; thus reinforcing the vulnerability and therefore the First Fear Cycle.

Lack of Holding by the Mother

While looked upon as an emotional reason, this has a neurobiological basis as well. It is actually an extension of absence of the mother or any related inattention. By the mother holding the infant, it realizes she is alive and in control. By the infant realizing its mother is in control physically of the infant: this allows the infant to start the beginning of the process of disbelieving the initial misinterpretation that it perceived in the womb. This misinterpretation was that the fetus was responsible for keeping its mother alive. By allowing the infant to begin the process of disbelief of the initial deception or misinterpretation, this alone will eliminate millions of neurons encoded with the First Fear Cycle of Development. Therefore, if the holding is not available and the perceived control is not transferred to its mother, this mimics the fetal perception of the First Fear Cycle, when the fetus was responsible for saving her life and therefore its own, thus, reinforcing the neurons.

Generally Poor Conditions

The definition of poor here refers to improper care of the infant by its mother. While not a specific environmental factor, this is a combination of any of the factors listed above. In general, a lack of basic care such as feeding, changing, holding or exposure to negative environmental factors, could cause reinforcement of the neurons encoded with the First Fear Cycle of Development.

Too Strong First Fear cycle

In some cases, the amount of neurons, encoded with the First Fear Cycle, in the developing infant's brain will simply be too large to eliminate or reprogram. Therefore, under the most ideal environmental circumstances, the condition of First Fear Not Relieved will be realized.

This imbalance of the relationship between the neurons encoded with the First Fear Cycle and the ability of environmental factors during infancy to eliminate or reprogram them would originate within the pregnancy itself. What this means is that in each pregnancy, Nature anticipates, through a neurobiological process within the mother, a sleep-wake pattern. If this pattern exceeds a certain threshold, an imbalance of developmental cycles will occur. For example, if a pregnant mother were to be restricted in her movement and the First Fear Cycle of Development could not down-regulate in response to this change of activity level, the fetus could experience too strong of a First Fear Cycle. Now, in most cases, if this down-regulation does not occur, this would result in problems for the fetus, outside the scope of the developmental cycles. In some other cases, however, the fetus could survive the pregnancy essentially unaffected. The effect, then, would be realized later during infancy, as environmental factors could not obtain a balance with the amount of First Fear Cycle neurons remaining.

Lack of Father — Female Infant

It is not to say that the father does not play an important role in the development of the male infant. This would be far from accurate to say. He does not, however, represent a specific neurobiological environmental factor as he does with the female infant. Indeed, only with the female infant, can his presence and attention to his infant daughter directly affect the elimination of neurons encoded with the First Fear Cycle of Development. How this exactly works will not be explained here. Instead, it will be covered, in detail, in the chapter on "Boys and Girls" under "Lack of Father and the Effect on the Female."

What is important to realize here — is that the neurobiological role of the father, as an environmental factor, in relation to the female infant, does not occur until she realizes her own gender identity. The presence, as you will see, of a father is not enough; however, to be an environmental factor he must be supportive of the female infant. Again, this environmental condition will be explained in detail in the chapter on "Boys and Girls."

Premature Birth

This requires special explanation in relation to the condition of First Fear Not Relieved. Theoretically, an infant who was delivered prematurely should have less exposure to the First Fear Cycle of Development. Therefore, theoretically, the infant should have a lower number of neurons encoded with the First Fear Cycle. Therefore, theoretically, the infant should have no trouble avoiding the condition of First Fear Not Relieved, as environmental conditions should far outweigh the amount of neurons encoded with the cycle. In fact, this is far from common. The problem is the reason for the premature birth in the first place. For example, if its mother were ill or unable to sustain the pregnancy to completion, this would carry over to a factor responsible for First Fear Not Relieved. This would be because the mother would most likely, for the very reason she could not sustain the pregnancy, contribute to the environmental factor of First Fear Not Relieved.

Another case, in which a similar situation could occur, would be if the fetus initiated labor, from an intense First Fear Cycle, due to its mother's own dopamine-seeking behavior. In other words, if the mother were to take dopamine-enhancing drugs, such as cocaine, this reduces the dopamine available for the fetus. The fetus, therefore unable to withstand the intense First Fear Cycle, simply leaves the womb prematurely. In this case, the infant would have less exposure to the First Fear Cycle and therefore, a lower number of neurons encoded with the developmental cycles. The problem again, would be the environment the infant was born into. As it would be unlikely that such an addict or even occasional drug-user would provide an environment that would at least not have one or multiple factors for the condition First Fear Not Relieved. In both cases, the factors that generate the premature labor will hinder the elimination and reprogramming of the neurons encoded with the First Fear Cycle, no matter how limited their number.

Another reason that the fetus that is born prematurely will not likely avoid the condition of First Fear Not Relieved is the likelihood of complications the newborn infant may realize immediately after birth. This will be especially true in developed nations where advanced medical care is available. For example, if the newborn infant were put into an incubator or other device for its own survivability, this factor alone would likely cause the condition of First Fear Not Relieved. As immediately after birth this belief that its mother is dead will be reinforced, thus reinforcing the neurons encoded with the First Fear Cycle.

This concludes the list of conditions for First Fear Not Relieved. Again, there are many other smaller factors that can lead to this condition. In fact, almost anything within the infant's environment, such as less sun light than normal, can mimic conditions in the womb. This, then, can lead to the ultimate reinforcement of the neurons encoded with the First Fear Cycle of Development. It is important to realize, it is all about obtaining a balance. If this balance is not achieved, as you will see in the next section of this chapter, there will be repercussions.

In the next chapter on "The Subconscious", you will realize what happens to the neurons encoded with both cycles of development that remain after this initial period of reorganization. They will be utilized in everything from the behaviors of eating to reproduction.

Initial Effects of First Fear not Relieved

While a complete explanation on First Fear Not Relieved is provided in Chapter nine "First Fear Not Relieved — The Individual," we will briefly look at a summary of the effects of the condition on the infant here. The infant who realizes the condition of First Fear Not Relieved will have a difficult time, not only in life, but also, in surviving infancy. Historically, with the exception of the last hundred years in developed nations, this has been the case. As it still is the case in many undeveloped nations today. There is a very important purpose for this, which will be discussed at the end of this chapter. What we are concerned with here is the reason the infant with this condition will have a difficult time with survival.

The infant who realizes the condition First Fear Not Relieved will realize immediate neurobiological and physical implications from this condition. Within the infant's developing brain, while the elimination and reprogramming events are taking place, the effects of the condition are already beginning to show signs. This infant whose neurons are encoded with the First Fear Cycle are not being eliminated or reprogrammed, but are reinforced instead. The first sign this condition will show has to do with the infant's immune system. Remember, encoded in every single neuron of the First Fear Cycle of Development is the Memory Block. The Memory Block, in turn, suppresses the immune system. This infant simply has too many neurons encoded with the First Fear Cycle of Development remaining. Therefore, the infant has too much Memory Block remaining, resulting in a severely suppressed immune system. While all infants, as they go through this period of neural reprogramming, experience a suppressed immune system, for this infant it will be especially severe. This will leave the infant with First Fear Not Relieved, even more susceptible to infections and illness. It will also have a much more difficult time fighting an infection. Again, less than a hundred years ago, this, in most cases, would have been too much for the infant and it would simply not survive. In today's advanced society, however, with the administration of penicillin and other drugs, this infant will likely be fine.

The infant's immune system is not a static entity, however. In other words, it is not just going to give up and let the infant die. It will fight back, and in the case of the infant with First Fear Not Relieved, it will fight back very hard. Indeed, with multiple assaults against the infant's immune system, it will fight back; attacking almost anything that even resembles a harmful substance. This, as you will see, will become a problem in itself. This is the process of up-regulation by the immune system. In this process the infant's immune system becomes hypersensitive. This hypersensitive immune system will result in allergies for the infant, fighting substances that are not normally harmful at all. The infant may become allergic to dust mites, pollen, and household pets and may even show early signs of asthma. What is even worse, the infant may even develop an allergy to its own mother's milk. As you will see later, assuming the infant survives, this will only be the beginning of their problems.

Another problem the infant with this condition will realize is the very neural function that suppresses the immune system, the Memory Block. The Memory Block, encoded into each neuron of the First Fear Cycle of Development, blocks the short-term memory of the infant, just as it did for the fetus. Therefore, the infant with this condition will have a more severely blocked short-term memory, a shorter attention span and difficulty in learning. While many of the effects of an increased amount of Memory Block will not show up until childhood, still milestones of development will be delayed.

The effects of First Fear Not Relieved, as you have seen, will be exaggerated for the male infant in comparison to the female infant. This is because, for the male fetus the First Fear Cycle of Development was more severe. Because of this increased severity of the First Fear Cycle, the male fetus realized more of the Memory Block. This was because the stronger the First Fear Cycle of Development was, the more of the Memory Block that was necessary to mask the existence of one developmental cycle from the other. And this was all encoded into the developing fetal neurons. Therefore, these neurons will suppress the male's immune system more than the female's. It is a simple equation; the stronger the First Fear Cycle, the more of the Memory Block that is necessary. The more Memory Block, the more the immune system is suppressed. The male infant, with First Fear Not Relieved, will therefore, have an especially difficult time. As you will see in a later chapter, the infant with First Fear Not Relieved will also realize a very high risk for Sudden Infant Death Syndrome.

Nature's Pruning of the Human Species

The question then becomes, why would Nature do this to the infant? After investing over nine months on the infant, burdening the mother and possibly putting her life at risk, why would Nature, by suppressing the infant's immune system, put it at such a risk? The answer here is actually quite simple, the reason for the answer, however, is not.

The answer is that this is Nature's method of pruning the human species. As you realized earlier, Nature picks two major time periods to eliminate or prune the human species. The first is in the womb. In many cases the First Fear Cycle of Development is simply too much for the fetus and it will die. If the First Fear Cycle of Development is not strong enough, the fetus will die during labor. The second period of time for elimination or pruning is not as simple. For whatever reason, Nature directly ties the survivability of the infant to the presence of its healthy mother, involved and around the infant all the time. Nature, it seems, has no purpose for the infant without its healthy mother nearby.

The reason Nature has done this could be one of many. Remember, Nature's model of the human species is an old one, millions of years old. It is possible that it had to do with the food supply of primitive Homo Sapiens. It could also be that, as you will see, the reproduction of the human species is reliant on psychological, rather than strictly neurobiological factors. It could be for many reasons. One thing is certain though, whatever the reason is, it was intentional. For, it is very clear, that if too many of the neurons encoded with the First Fear Cycle remain in the developing infant's brain, these neurons act as a trigger by suppressing the infant's immune system. This trigger, especially in undeveloped nations and historically worldwide, puts the infant at a high risk for death.

While in advanced nations today, this is unlikely to occur, this does not mean that the infant will not realize a lifetime of repercussions from an environmental failure during the first few years of its life. In fact, an infant that survives, which in the perspective of Nature, was never intended to survive, sets off a cascade of events that five hundred years ago would likely never have taken place. This is true, not only for the individual, however, for the society in which it lives as well. It will forever change and redefine the world in which it enters. As you will see, it will spend its life trying to regain a balance that was lost or was never achieved during infancy. When enough of these infants survive, as is the case today, the entire societal focus is redefined, and it itself begins to try and regain a balance that was once lost or never achieved.

CHAPTER SIX

THE SUBCONSCIOUS

Yes, as you will see, very few of the individual's thoughts are completely original. Every thought a person makes is influenced by the particle of another thought, which in turn is nothing more than a neuron encoded with the two cycles of development they experienced as a fetus in the womb.

Once the important process of neural elimination, reprogramming and reinforcement has taken place, a more permanent neural pattern of the brain begins to emerge. Now, this pattern is continually changing, however, for simplicity we will look at it in a fixed state, at a time when the major changes have already occurred.

After the neurons encoded with the First Fear and Euphoric Cycles of Development have been reorganized during infancy — the remaining neurons form the individual's subconscious — all that this means, is that every thought processed in the individual's conscious state is partially influenced by the remaining neurons encoded with either the First Fear Cycle or Euphoric Cycle of Development. Once the initial reorganization has occurred, these neurons become located in deep layers of the cerebral cortex. Upon every action, every thought and every motivation, these neurons are activated or fired. All this means that their influence is realized.

These neurons, encoded with the First Fear and Euphoric Cycles, do not fire completely, however. They only are partially activated, only partially fired. A better term for this partial activation of the neurons encoded with the First Fear Cycle or the Euphoric Cycle is, inhibited. The reason that these neurons only partially fired, in an inhibited manner, is that Nature does not want the individual who is awake, living, completely back in the womb. This would not be effective at all. What is effective, however, is having important developmental information, influencing every thought, not consuming it.

This inhibited, or partially firing neuron, now influences other neurons that are not so deeply rooted in the brain. These neurons, those encoded with the First Fear and Euphoric Cycles influence; are more towards the surface. The deep neurons, the developmental neurons, influence the surface neurons, which are programmed with events that occur during the individual's daily life. Therefore, the influence of the two developmental cycles is never far behind. Again, every thought, action and motivation is influenced by a preprogrammed thought, action and motivation. This preprogramming was carefully guided by Nature for the fetus in the womb. Nature has many purposes for this; an example here will show this purpose more effectively.

We will use the example of Bobby, a six-year-old boy. Bobby is in the kitchen with his mother, she is cooking dinner. Now, Bobby is playing close to the stove, too close for his mother's comfort. His mother tells him, "Bobby, don't play so close to the stove, I don't want you to burn yourself." Bobby reacts to this command in a certain way. While listening to his mother, those neurons encoded with the First Fear Cycle of Development are influencing his thoughts and therefore the processing of the command his mother makes. One aspect of the First Fear Cycle of Development that is encoded into these neurons is the burning or painful sensation Bobby felt as a fetus in the womb. Remember, every time the fetus touched the intrauterine walls, it realized a burning sensation on its undeveloped fingertips. The purpose of this was to not only keep the fetus from internally injuring its mother, however, also served the purpose of encoding the sensory neurons and the sensory nerves of the developing fetus, with this sensation. These neurons are now influencing Bobby's processing, reaction and ultimate response to information realized in his conscious state. In this case, it is a command by his mother to move away from the stove. His response is, "Okay Mom," as he realizes that he does not desire to re-experience the painful or burning sensation he once did. Of course, in two minutes, he will forget all of this and likely move closer to the stove again. This is because, along with the developmental information encoded in those neurons, that he needed to pull up in order to respond, they also contain the Memory Block, which blocked the short-term memory of the fetus and is now blocking Bobby's short-term memory as he responded. Without the prior developmental exposure, Bobby would have to burn his hands first to realize what this meant. If he, by some chance, forgot that he burned his hands, he would have to re-experience it all over again. However, with these developmental neurons, constantly influencing every thought, there is a basis for the experience.

Therefore, it is important to realize, that when the individual is awake, each thought realized is influenced by the two developmental cycles. This structures the individual's thoughts in accordance to Nature's intentions for the human species.

Of course, the individuals with the condition of First Fear Not Relieved will realize even more of an influence from their fetal experience in the womb. While the difference will not be detectable in their neural pattern, it certainly will be in their behavior. This does not mean that their development is any better or more effective than the individual without this condition, as many of the neurons remaining were duplicates.

Neurons of the First Fear and Euphoric Cycles during Sleep

While the neurons encoded with the First Fear and Euphoric Cycles of Development only partially fire, or fire inhibited during the day, during the individual's sleep, this changes dramatically. During their deepest or slow wave sleep, the neurons encoded with these two cycles of development fire uninhibited or fire completely, exerting their full influence on the thoughts of the individual. Of course, this influence will not be realized directly, as the individual is sound asleep. Now, there is a very important developmental purpose for this, which will be explained in the chapter on "Sleep and Dreams." In short, the images of these two developmental cycles then transfer over to a stage of lighter or REM sleep and mix with images from the individual's every day life, thus further strengthening the influence of these two developmental cycles. For now, however, it is only important to know that the neurons encoded with the First Fear and Euphoric Cycles of Development fire partially or inhibited during the awake states, and during the individual's deepest or slow wave sleep fire fully or uninhibited.

How the Developmental Neurons Motivate Behavior

While in many ways the human brain is very complex, in others, however, it is very simple. This simplicity is especially true in regards to the motivation of human behavior. As you now know, the neurons encoded with the two cycles of development form the subconscious. From the subconscious, the neurons encoded with these developmental cycles, influence every thought and action. Not only that, however, they also influence every motivation an individual undertakes.

Every time something is experienced, whether it is an auditory, visual, olfactory or other sensory experience, this pulls up a group of neurons from one or the other cycles of development. If the experience mimics the Euphoric Cycle, it is positive. If it mimics the First Fear Cycle, it is negative. While there are limitations to the second part of this statement, such as in some cases, if a situation mimics the First Fear Cycle it can be positive, this occurs when the individual takes action to negate it. This will be explained later. In general, however, if the experience mimics the Euphoric Cycle it will be positive and the experiences that mimic the First Fear Cycle will be negative.

The individual will then be obviously motivated to avoid experiences with negative associations and gravitate towards experiences of this more positive nature. Therefore, throughout an individual's life and their motivations will be centered on this essential quest to surround themselves with associations that mimic the Euphoric Cycle. We will go back to Bobby, for an example.

Now, Bobby is out shopping with his mother. In front of the store, he spots a machine, shaped like a giant toy car. He begs his mother for a quarter, to put into the machine so that he can go for a ride. She finally gives in. Bobby puts the quarter into the machine of the giant toy car, sits on it and begins his ride. The ride begins; back and forth it goes, not very far or not very fast, vibrating all the time. Now, to an adult this may seem like a waste of money, however, to Bobby it is not that at all. Because for three minutes, or as long as the ride last, Bobby is back in the Euphoric Cycle. The car is rocking and vibrating, just like he was in the womb when his mother was walking around. Indeed, Bobby is in paradise once again, in the place were dopamine flowed freely and no pain was felt at all.

The ride is now over for Bobby. He begs his mother for just one more ride. Bobby's mom picks him up and puts him into the shopping cart. Bobby does not mind this, because mom pushing him in the cart will also mimic the Euphoric Cycle. Bobby asks if on the way out he could maybe ride the giant toy car one more time. His mom's reply is this: "Maybe if you are good in the store, as long as you don't tell your dad, you know we are short on money." No, dad does not go for such foolish amusement as this. What Bobby's mother does not understand is that dad will spend almost one third of their income on trying to mimic the Euphoric Cycle. First, there is a car payment, maybe two, and then there is dad's off-road motorcycle. Add dad's beer and cigarettes to the list and it equals a whole one third of their monthly income. All of these things directly mimic the movement and vibration of the Euphoric Cycle or increase the dopamine flow to dad's reward pathways of his brain, which was his exact fetal experience during the Euphoric Cycle. Indeed, in comparison to his dad, Bobby's mimicry of the Euphoric Cycle is cheap.

Every time Bobby, or any other individual is exposed to something, to an experience that mimics the Euphoric Cycle, all the remaining neurons encoded with that cycle fire, while inhibited, influencing every thought. Indeed, coloring, decorating every perception with happiness, joy from the painless elevated experience of the Euphoric Cycle. An entire ray of positive emotions consumes them. In one word, they are happy.

Later in the day, Bobby gets into trouble. He has done something wrong. As punishment mom makes Bobby go sit in a room alone, in a corner with his head facing towards the wall. She tells him that he must sit still. The room is quiet. Bobby is totally alone. This, of course, pulls up the influence of all those neurons of the First Fear Cycle of Development. As late at night, as a fetus, when Bobby's mother was sleeping, deep into the First Fear Cycle, the womb was very quiet. Bobby, as a fetus misinterpreted that when his mother was sleeping, she was in the process of dying. During the First Fear Cycle the dopamine flow was reduced, and in the silent womb sound meant life and silence meant death. Now, in contrast to riding the toy car in the Euphoric Cycle, Bobby is stuck back into the cycle of death, the First Fear Cycle of Development. In this room he cannot see his mother, the neurons that are influencing his thoughts tell him that therefore she is in the process of dying and that he will die soon. In this room there is little sound, he cannot even do what Nature conditioned him to do, which was to move when the environment became still. This movement would at least increase the dopamine flow to the reward pathways of his brain. So now, all the negative e.notions are pulled up with this association. He is even trapped in a room, which very much mimics being trapped in the womb. He will avoid any situation that mimics the First Fear Cycle whenever possible. Bobby will keep acting up when in that room, for he is trying one thing, like the infant who cries for its mother, Bobby's whole purpose is to offset or negate those First Fear neurons, he wants to hear his mother's voice. He would prefer to hear her happy voice, however, even yelling at him will do. In his subconscious, those neurons encoded with the First Fear Cycle, want to know that she is still alive, so that he will remain alive.

This is exactly what motivates human behavior. Every individual wants to mimic the Euphoric Cycle in some way. Every individual also wants to avoid mimicking the fetal perception or experience of the First Fear Cycle of Development, as with each cycle brings up the range of emotions experienced during that event. It cannot be escaped. It is the foundation of every thought. It is the foundation of the subconscious. It is the subconscious itself. The subconscious is nothing more than a recording of fetal experience in one of the two cycles, with each association a recording is pulled up. From the moment of our birth, to the moment of our death, it is essentially the same recording. No matter how high man climbs, no matter how far away from the earth he goes, he will forever be grounded by Nature, as it influences every single thought.

The two cycles of development do not only form our subconscious. These two cycles also forever alter the way in which we see the world outside the womb. It is always two. It is always one condition in contrast to another. We see the world in two; there is right and wrong, good and bad, happy and sad, goodness and evil, up and down, heaven and hell, ying and yang. The list is endless. While outside the womb there are a hundred conditions between two extremes, however, our thoughts, our perceptions, our pleasures and our pains will forever be shaped by the simple number two. It is always one condition bounced off the extreme of another. This all started with two simple opposite cycles of development, one of pleasure and one of pain. It is how the brain is formed, develops and, ultimately, responds to the world outside the womb.

CHAPTER SEVEN

BOYS AND GIRLS

The intrauterine experience continues to exert a very strong influence on children. In fact, watching an infant will allow you to view the dynamics of the two cycles they experienced in the womb; this being, they enjoy activities that mimic the Euphoric Cycle and dislike situations that mimic those realized during the First Fear Cycle, it is not until childhood, however, that you can begin to view the dramatic impact that these short nine months before birth has on their lives. More than this, however, is that while watching a child, with the comprehension of Nature's intentions at hand, you begin to realize the impact their experience before birth will have on the rest of their life. Indeed, many of the themes that consume their adult years, in relation to the two cycles of development, begin to show the first signs during childhood.

Before we begin to view this exiting development, we will briefly check upon the neurobiological process of those who have successfully completed infancy. While the major neurobiological changes, the elimination, reprogramming and reinforcement of neurons encoded with the two cycles of development, have long since reached their peak, by the time of childhood, these events continue at a slower pace. One of the results of this is that the Memory Block, which suppressed the child's immune system, has been reduced. While the child will still realize illness more frequently than the adult, the stability over the immune suppression during infancy is obvious.

This net reduction of neurons encoded with the Memory Block will translate into other changes for the child as well. With the blockage of the short-term memory reduced, this allows the important process of learning to accelerate. Of course, the child's developing brain is still consumed much more than the adults with the neurons encoded with the two cycles of development and their resultant Memory Block. This causes them to forget things quickly and reduces their attention span. This effect is exaggerated any time the child is in a situation that in any way mimics life inside the womb. For example, a child on a very long automobile trip, or even a short one, can demonstrate this point clearly. The automobile ride mimics the Euphoric Cycle of Development. On a long trip, however, even the mimicry of this pleasurable cycle cannot save a child from boredom, as their attention span remains short. They want to be constantly entertained. They want to get to whatever place the parents are taking them, as soon as possible. Because of this they will often ask, "How long until we get there?" One of the parents will tell them how long it will be. Then, five minutes later the child will repeat the same question all over again, "How long until we get there?" While this may be frustrating for the parents, it is a very telling event in regards to the amount of Memory Block encoded in the developmental neurons of the two cycles, which are still, even in childhood, dominating their conscious thoughts. While as an infant their short-term memory may have been from thirty to sixty seconds, now in childhood it may extend from five minutes to a much longer period. It all depends on numerous factors, including how many of the neurons encoded with the First Fear and Euphoric Cycles of Development were eliminated during infancy. What is important to realize is that because the child is in a situation that mimics the intrauterine experience, the Memory Block and other aspects of that experience will exert a stronger influence. The child asks a question, and then forgets five minutes later; that they ever asked it in the first place, this is all due to the Memory Block. When confronted with this the child will often act surprised, then subtly embarrassed, as it becomes obvious that they honestly forgot the passage of time between the two questions, which itself is another result of the Memory Block. Now, the same child at home playing a game that requires concentration and short-term memory might do exceedingly well. This is because a game does not mimic, in any way, life in the womb and their intrauterine experience.

Children Going to School

The introduction of school, even pre-school or kindergarten can be a dramatic event for children, especially for the male child. This is assuming the child has not realized any previous severe separation from its mother; this first separation can be traumatic. This is because the child's neural pattern is still dominated by the neurons encoded with both cycles of the intrauterine development, separation will therefore, immediately pull up neurons encoded with the First Fear Cycle. Once its mother is no longer visible, the child, especially the male, will fear the worst. The child reasons, subconsciously, after all she may be in a process of dying. This would mean to the child, if she dies its death would quickly follow. This will be especially true if an environmental cue reinforces these fears. For example, if a child should hear a siren from an ambulance, police or fire vehicle, their subconscious assumes the worst. To them, this coincidental cue is a sign that something has happened to their mother, believing they will die quickly there after. Now, in some cases, the response to this environmental cue will be so overwhelming that the fear will enter their conscious thoughts, not even remaining subordinate in their subconscious. This will be especially true if its mother does not show up at the expected time, or at night under the supervision of a baby-sitter. The reason that this affect will be worse at night is, of course, because that is when the First Fear Cycle occurred in the womb.

Indeed, the distant siren of an ambulance will override all other sounds for the concerned child, when its mother is not there.

Upon children's first exposure to the classroom and the regime of school, the differences between each gender's intrauterine experiences, become immediately obvious. The First Fear Cycle of Development was much stronger and more intense for the male fetus. The end result of this was that much more Memory Block was necessary to mask one cycle from the other. In school this increased amount of Memory Block, contained in the neurons of the male's subconscious, quickly becomes apparent. Because of this increased Memory Block, the male child will have a much more difficult time concentrating and therefore learning in contrast to the female child. Indeed for girls, having less Memory Block means a much easier time learning than for the boys. Where the girls will be organized in their thoughts and motivations, boys will be easily distracted and suffer a shorter attention span. While there will be exceptions to this, due to environmental factors, in most cases girls will have an easier time during their first few years of school, as the trauma from the intrauterine experience will remain much longer for boys than girls.

The restriction of movement, required in a classroom setting, will be especially severe for the boys. This is because, while its mother was not moving very much during the First Fear Cycle of Development, the fetus, especially the male, certainly was. The male fetus was kicking, punching, turning and twisting all in attempt to save what it believed was its dying mother, who was only sleeping. The neurons encoded with the First Fear Cycle of Development are simply full of movement. This movement is especially centered on its legs, fingers and hands, as these were the most utilized areas during this active cycle. While the young boy's brain is taking commands from his teacher, as she tells him to sit still, the movements encoded in these neurons, which dominate his subconscious, are difficult to suppress.

These neurons encoded with movement are constantly firing, busting out of his subconscious into his conscious actions. Therefore, not only does concentration take extra energy to obtain, however, also sitting still takes extra energy to accomplish.

Indeed, the boy is a little slow getting out of the gate. It is understandable when you realize that the trauma and development he experienced, as a fetus in the womb during the First Fear Cycle, is much more severe than the girl experienced, as a fetus during this cycle. While boys are slow to start, it is a long race and they will catch up eventually.

The Origin of the Lie

Before we get into the individual behaviors of each gender, there is one aspect of children's behavior that we will address here. It is the lie. Yes, we will return to the lie once again. The child by now will arrive at times in their young life when situations will arise that in many ways mimic their final days in the womb, the last days of pregnancy. In other words: a situation with no perceived positive outcome.

If you remember, the fetus, during its last days in the womb, was essentially stuck in a "no win" situation. It was faced with the dilemma that was impossible to resolve. The conditions in the womb were deteriorating rapidly. Life was becoming unbearably painful. To leave, was to possibly face death; to stay, however, would mean certain death. Again, remember that the fetal perception of death was limited to the comprehension of pain, and the pain the fetus realized during these final days was immense. Then, there was the situation with its mother, for the fetus believed that by its kicking and moving it was keeping her alive. If it were to leave, she would die. To the fetus then, whatever decision it made would result in consequences that were not desirable.

When the fetus finally decided to leave, it expected to leave behind its mother who certainly would die. She did not die however, as the infant's first expression will attest to its surprise. Indeed, the fetus expected the worst to happen and it did not happen. To understand how this event will ultimately affect the child's decision making, we must first return to the child's infancy.

While the infant is lying in its crib, during the long day, making sounds and touching its blanket, it is also doing something else very important. It is thinking. It is thinking and trying to figure out this riddle of what happened to it. Now, it has been waiting, lying in its crib and waiting for its mother to die. It has waited for not only hours and days, however, but for weeks and months. Yet, every time it cries, its mother comes running to reduce or offset its fear. The infant simply cannot figure this out. While the strong Memory Block leaves its memory very cloudy, its thoughts, however, are very clear. While it cannot figure out the whole puzzle, it does know this; when it left the womb it believed it was leaving its mother alone to die. She should have died; everything it was lead to believe, told it this. In fact, it so much believed that she should have died that it misinterpreted its mother's reaction, the pain she underwent during labor as the process of her death. It also knows that before it left the womb, it was faced with an impossible situation, and then, later, after birth, realized the outcome of that impossible situation was more positive than it ever could have imagined. The infant also realizes that all of this was due to this deception by some force, some seemingly magical force that it had no control over. This is a very powerful conclusion for the infant to make. It is also a very common conclusion, one that is the very origin of our capacity to lie and it is all made subconsciously. More than that, it is a very powerful lesson that it was taught. The lesson was this; when faced with a situation of impossible odds, when it looks like nothing will work out, wait for this magical force to change it and make it all work out right.

Now, as a child stuck in a situation that they cannot win or the odds do not look in their favor, they will wait for this magical force to make everything all right. The problem with this type of wishful-ness, however, is that it does not often come true. While childhood is full of wonder, imagination and creativity it is very short on deception by some magical force. Therefore, when faced with a situation that they cannot possibly win, like that previously experienced during its final days in the womb, they wait for the magic power of deception to come and make everything all right. They wait and wait, however, this magical force never comes. So, while they hold out as long as they can, in the end they simply settle for mimicking it. Thus, the child creates or invents the deception themselves and do this with the best intentions. This is very important to realize, for the child truly believes when they create a deception or lie, that something very good will come out of a bad situation. The motivation behind it is pure. Initially, in deception there is no ill intent or negative motivation. They expect a miracle, like their mother remaining alive when she should have died.

So, if a child breaks something or finds themselves in a situation that they cannot get out of, one that mimics the difficult situation they realized during their final days in the womb, full of impossible odds, a "no win" situation where every angle they turn is another bad consequence, they will do as they were trained, essentially by Nature to do. They will create their own magical deception and lie. Again, they will do this only with the best of intentions.

Now, this behavior is usually totally unacceptable to the child's parents. They tell the child that lying is bad, lying is wrong. They may even punish the child. To the child, however, these are only words and occasional actions, for the child has experienced a completely different reality altogether. After all, who can blame them? Who can blame a child for lying? What they were taught was not a broken lamp or a homework assignment; it was a life and death issue. They were trained through their misinterpretation; the intentional misinterpretation by Nature that deception was the only way to save its mother's life and therefore its own. This is as big as it gets. So the words of mom and dad, and even their actions are dwarfed by a child's perception of the power of deception and the lie, as they experienced as a fetus, proof that it can save their life. No matter what their parents, or even society tells them it will forever be dwarfed by this initial experience that is engrained, encoded in the neurons of their subconscious.

What the child will learn, however, about the lie from its parents, is that it should save them for only very bad situations. Childhood is essentially a process of becoming trained to discriminate when to lie and when the truth will yield better results, as the capacity to lie is engrained in every individual's subconscious; this is an integral part of the human species. For when things get bad, very bad and in any way mimic the decisions the individual, as a fetus made during the final days in the womb, they will do as they witnessed Nature do and that is to deceive and therefore ultimately lie.

Of course, many people lie to protect another person, or to not emotionally hurt somebody else. This makes perfect sense when you realize that many of the fetal intentions during the end of the pregnancy where related to the same purpose. The fetus believed that if it left, its mother would be hurt and therefore, dying. As you have already seen, the only way out of this situation, and to protect its mother was through the ultimate outcome of deception. Therefore, it comes very natural for the individual, when situations that mimic this arise, to react in the same manner.

Also, it is important to realize that encoded in the same neuronal base as the final days of life in the womb and therefore, the final deception realized, after birth, is guilt. The fetus felt guilt towards leaving its mother alone to die. Therefore, when an individual lies, which is nothing more then the summation of this neuronal base, guilt will likely be included in the individual's emotional response. In other words, guilt by itself has nothing to do with the process of lying; it is only that the witnessing of deception originates at the same time that the fetus was consumed with guilt: that guilt will often trail, throughout one's life, the process of the lie.

Boys

There are some major themes that reflect the intrauterine experience, which dominate the childhood of a young boy. Many of these themes can be easily identified from watching his behavior. From the toys he plays with, to his relationship with Nature, these themes occur and reoccur consistently and predictably.

Toys

A major theme of a young boy's life is escaping from the world of death and decay that he left behind in the womb. During infancy the male infant was enabled less-restricted movement, however, this is not enough. In childhood he wants to get away, as quick as he can from the horrific events, the First Fear Cycle of Development, that occurred to him in the womb. While boys are still dependent upon their mothers, subconsciously, they dream of getting away from the death and decay they believe she has inside her, as fast as they can. Never again, do they want to be trapped in such a horrific place. This motivation dominates their subconscious from morning until night. Never again, do they want to fight that invisible enemy that was attempting to kill their mother and therefore themselves. Not only do they never want to go back, but also they want to make sure they are free to escape should a situation similar ever develop.

The first tool to escape they will usually choose is a car. While it is only a toy car it represents escape and freedom. While a toy car that looks fast is preferable, any car will do. With that toy car in hand, they will show their world exactly why it interests them. With one hand they will start the car from a fixed point and then move it as fast as they can across the carpet, floor or pavement, often vocalizing a zooming sound with their voice. If the car moves at the speed desired, a smile consumes their face, as it has served its purpose. Speed is the key and quickness of escape. This is because of what is consuming their subconscious. In their subconscious is the fear of being stuck once again in the First Fear Cycle of Development, the event that once entrapped them so brutally. Every time the young boy races that car along the floor they are reassuring themselves, those neurons encoded with the First Fear Cycle that they are now free, no longer chained to that horrific event in that horrific place.

While a toy car is the usual choice, any object that signifies a quick escape will serve the same symbolic purpose for the young boy. A plane or space ship will also do the trick. The best thing about a toy plane is that not only does it fly fast, but also high above the ground. This is important as a plane can fly high above the death and decay of the womb, of Nature and the earth itself. In many ways, this is the first sign of the child's desire to flee Nature. This theme will be explained later in this chapter.

Some toys serve a dual symbolic purpose for young boys. A good example of this is the fire engine, or fire truck. Yes, what young boy's childhood would be complete without a fire engine? The first purpose the fire engine serves is that because it has wheels it can provide a handy form of escape. While it is not fast, it does not have to be. This is because, the fire engine has the ability to accomplish a very important task and this is the second reason. To understand this, we must return to the final days the fetus experienced in the womb. One of Nature's safeguards to keep the fetus from prematurely leaving the womb was the burning and painful response it realized when it touched the areas, not only of the intrauterine walls, however, of the birth canal as well. Indeed, to the fetus the birth canal was essentially a field of fire that they would have to cross before ever leaving the womb. Nature's idea here was to time the maturity of the fetal dermatome with the timing of delivery. In other words, if the dermatome and sensory neurons were not fully developed, the fetus would realize a burning, hot and painful sensation every time it touched areas of the mother's body, the intrauterine environment that were warmer than others. Even when this maturity was reached, the fetus still realized an uncomfortable response. In many ways, to the fetus, hot and prohibitive areas surrounded life in the womb. Burning up, when it initiated birth was a very large fetal fear.

Now, outside the womb, the young boy finds a handy toy that empowers him. Indeed, nothing elevates him above this fear more than the fire engine. With its hoses, and the promise of cool water flowing from the truck he can disprove his fetal fears encoded in the neurons of his subconscious. With the fire truck in hand he can, at least symbolically, control what once controlled him. Of course, the only thing more exciting than a fire engine for a young boy is a visit to the fire station. There is no place most young boys would rather be. The fire station symbolizes the pinnacle of safety from the horrific hot environment he endured for nine months. A fire man himself; well he is a type of God for a young boy. Here is a man, who has the power to rescue him from that horrific, hot environment if it should ever consume him again. Indeed, to strive to become a fireman is a lofty and noble goal. It will be a popular career choice for a young boy, when asked what he wants to be when he grows up. Of course, most boys, as their neural pattern changes and matures, will outgrow this childhood fascination. For others, however, this fear remains strong and will ultimately guide their choice in careers.

Not only was the womb a hot horrific place for the male fetus to endure, however, a very violent place as well. For the male, the First Fear Cycle of Development was much more violent than for the female fetus, as it realized a diluted First Fear Cycle due to the protective female hormones. For the male fetus, it punched, kicked and tried to initiate a response from its dying mother, who was only sleeping, in a much more aggressive manner. The male fetus did this, because the drop in dopamine levels from the Euphoric Cycle to the First Fear Cycle affected it more severely. The pain it experienced was much greater than the female's. This difference in intrauterine environment will ultimately determine the difference in physical development, facial features and overall differentiation of genders. For the male fetus, however, this only translated into a more violent horrific environment. While the young boy's subconscious has not identified exactly who it was that attacked its mother and therefore itself, on a nightly basis, the young boy fears, even outside the womb, it could attack again, at any time. The young boy will therefore gravitate towards toys that offer protection from this invisible enemy. A toy army tank or jeep cannot only escape from this horrific environment, however, can also fight back should complications in this flight arise. Yes, loaded with guns, bazookas and the latest military hardware, these toys provide hours of fascination for the male child. Again and again, he will envision imaginary battles, where he is victorious. Each time he plays with this toy, he is disproving the neurons encoded with the First Fear Cycle that dominate the fears of his subconscious.

Toys to combat the violence he once experienced will not be limited to tanks and jeeps, however. A toy gun is a great symbolic defense against the First Fear Cycle of Development. The best part about a toy gun is that he can carry it around with him, thus providing a constant reassurance against neurons encoded with that memory. He will play cops and robbers, Cowboys and Indians, and good guys and bad guys, against his brothers and sisters, his friends, neighbors and parents. Even though he is told not to, he will shoot invisible bullets, toy darts, plastic BBs at anyone he feels is an adversary at the moment. The importance here is his search for identification of an enemy.

Young boys will also be fascinated with other aspects of their intrauterine experience. In addition to holes, they will also be interested in sewer drains, caves and tunnels. This will be especially true if water is flowing through or to them. They will want to know where the holes, caves, sewer drains and tunnels, lead to. They hope that by answering this, they can answer the even more pressing question, which is encoded in the neurons of their subconscious. This question is, "What happened to them during their brief nine months in the womb?" After all, they may find a secret escape hatch, as they once did in the womb.

The Importance of Cartoons and Videogames

Childhood for the male is not only about protection or fleeing from the invisible enemy; it is also about trying to figure out what happened to him in the womb. Unlike the infant, however, the child has more tools to accomplish this inquiry. The clue to this can be found in what interest them. The cartoon is an almost perfect example. It is usually short, accounting for the high remaining amount of Memory Block and the resultant short attention span of the child. It is the content, however, of the cartoon that is so accurate in portraying the fetal perception of life in the womb.

In a cartoon, there will usually be a main character, often a rabbit, duck, coyote, mouse, cat, or even a person. Through the course of the cartoon this comical character will be confronted, again and again, with physical insults and punishments, such as a rock falling on their head, a canon firing at them or dynamite exploding. All of these things should kill the cartoon character. Yet, they survive. This repetition does not happen only once during the cartoon, but three, four or even ten times. Now, the cartoon character falls off a cliff. Now, the cartoon character has a rock falling on its head. Now, without a single scratch, it survives the explosion of dynamite! Boom! Now, it gets catapulted into space, and then falls down to earth on its head. Over and over again this happens, throughout the cartoon while the character is injured, by the next frame it is completely restored, undamaged. Now to an adult this is ridiculous, this is not reality, who would watch this? The answer is, of course, is the child. To them, it is powerful; it is so powerful that they will get up early on a Saturday morning to watch it. Why? The answer, of course, is obvious as the cartoon directly mimics the fetal perception of the two cycles in the womb. Every night, it was deceived into believing that its mother was dying. It kicked, punched and fought a loosing battle to save her life. Then in the morning, as she woke up and the Euphoric Cycle began, she was completely restored to perfect health. This event, these two cycles, this dying then reappearing, happened to the fetus night after night, over and over again, for months at the time. The child who watches this cartoon is attempting to come to an understanding, in their subconscious of what happened to them in the womb. If the child can find something that makes sense to them, because it mimics life in the womb, they can begin to understand the bizarre experience they have realized. Cartoons accomplish this perfectly, as every time the child sees the character appear, face death, then reappear unharmed, the neurons encoded with the First Fear and Euphoric Cycles are being sorted out in their subconscious. Eventually, this repetition will become boring, as they age, however, it has served its important purpose. These violent cartoons will obviously be much more popular with boys than girls as it directly mimics their intrauterine experience more accurately.

While cartoons of multiple life themes help the male child make sense of his intrauterine experience, this therapeutic medium is somewhat outdated. In other words, today's children have an interactive medium, where they can get the same form of relief. Enter the videogame. Now, videogames represent the fetal intrauterine experience in three important ways. The first is the use of the fingers in controlling the videogames. During the long hours of the night in the First Fear Cycle of Development, the fetus was exhausted from all the kicking and punching, yet, it still tried to gain a response from what it believed to be its dying mother. Unable to exert the energy necessary to kick and punch any longer, the only movement it could still generate was the use of its hands and fingers. In the womb, the fetus attempted to control something much larger than it by the use of its fingers. Outside the womb, as a child with a videogame, it is the same principle. By the sole use of its fingers, they can control something much larger than themselves, which sets the stage for the next two representations of life in the womb for videogames.

Then, there is the theme of attack. This is the popular theme for many videogames. Here, it does not matter if space ships, aliens, monkeys, gangsters or giant birds are attacking the player. This is because it is the same indefinable enemy that is attacking the child, which attacked the fetus in the womb. Now, however, the child can fight back. They will spend hours and hours defending themselves, and destroying the enemy of any particular game. What they are actually destroying is the faceless monster that they fought night after night in the womb, the one that try to kill their mother and therefore themselves. It is the same faceless monster that is dominating their subconscious, in the remaining neurons encoded with the First Fear Cycle of Development. Now, this same faceless monster will show up, again and again, throughout the boy's life. It will be the same monster hiding under his bed, outside his window or inside his closet that prevents him from sleeping at night. It will be the bad guy in the police drama and the monster in the horror movies. Here, however, it is not faceless at all; it is the videogame opponent that he, if his skill level is high enough, can conquer. In some ways, by conquering the videogame opponent, he is conquering the fear encoded in his subconscious.

The final parallel of videogames to life in the womb is the same one provided by cartoons. This is the attainment of multiple lives. Instead of the cartoon character, here it is the videogame player himself. Just like in the cartoon, the player can be killed often, only to reappear fully unharmed. The player is not only entitled to one life during a game, but often many. Again, to an adult, whose neural pattern has evolved and matured; this concept of multiple lives is not only unrealistic, but also ridiculous. To a child, however, who has just experienced, in the womb, this theme of multiple lives by its mother, it is closer to reality than imaginable, as every night its mother, while sleeping, appeared to be dying to the fetus, in the morning she was suddenly restored back to life. Every time the boy plays the videogame and his character dies, then reappears, his subconscious is reassured that, "Yes, this is exactly how it happened." Understanding this initial deception that occurred in the womb is one of the most significant puzzles that consume not only the infant's but the child's subconscious as well. After all, how does a child make sense of his mother dying night after night then waking up unharmed and healthy as ever? Then, when he left the womb he expected his mother to be dead, however, she remained alive. Again, to a child, especially a boy, there is no way to understand this, therefore, all he can do is to find a medium such as cartoons or videogames that express or connect to this bizarre experience. While this all may seem like make belief, however, based on the fetal perception and the intentional misinterpretation, due to the Memory Block, created by Nature, this was very close to the child's reality.

Another way in which boys attempt to deal with their intrauterine experience is attachment to superheroes. And who can blame them for this? Indeed, during the nightly fight with death, who could have not used a superhero for a little help? While the infants who survive their fetal experience are heroes themselves, there is always a need for additional support. It was a horrific environment the fetus realized each night as its mother was lying down to go to sleep, thus, beginning the First Fear Cycle of Development. It was a nightly fight against death itself. This was especially true; the fight was especially dramatic for the male fetus. It only made sense then, that since these events are still consuming the young boy's subconscious, he will gravitate towards superheroes. Like the intrauterine environment the boy realized as a fetus, a good superhero will change or transform. This transformation, of course, will mimic the transformation of the womb itself during the two cycles. The superhero at one moment can be simply a normal person, however, when things get bad he can then become a super person, capable of unbelievable feats, like saving the world. Now, if we look at the fetal perception, we will realize exactly why the young boy can relate to these superhero characters and to this theme. The fetus believed that it was saving its own world. Its world was the womb and its mother. Also, during the Euphoric Cycle, there was little for the fetus to do, but to enjoy life. For the superhero this would represent his normal status. When the intrauterine environment changed, however, the fetus would be forced to save its mother, which is its world. Here, the superhero has an ability to change from a normal person to a super person. This transformation occurs when things get bad, as when the cycles changed in the womb for the fetus from the Euphoric Cycle into that of the First Fear Cycle. Of course, it helps if not only the superhero transforms, like the two cycles in the womb did, but also they should live or have their hideout in a structure that resembles the womb, such as a cave. With this formula in hand, many a successful superhero series have been launched. The reason they are popular is for one simple reason, this is, of course, because they touch on an experience that every viewer or reader has experienced. This experience is life in the womb, the two cycles of development and the process of birth itself, and the child is, chronologically, very close to these events. All these shows, stories or books relate to the individual's subconscious, which is exactly where the neurons encoded with the memory of these two cycles of intrauterine development are contained.

Space as an Escape from Nature

Some superheroes live in even a better place than one that mimics the womb. Some superheroes come from outer space itself. This will begin the boy's and the entire human species' fascination with space. The reason is quite simple. In space, there is no death and decay, because there is no Nature.

By the time the young boy reaches childhood, he begins to identify who he thinks is responsible for the events that occurred to him in the womb. He begins to believe that it was Nature herself. While he is not sure, he has a pretty good idea that it was Nature who imprisoned him, deceived him and made him foolishly kick and punch for nine long months to save his dying mother's life, when she was only sleeping. Now, this is a very important realization for the young boy to make. It is so important that it will be covered in detail later in the chapter and throughout the book. For now, it is only important to realize that once a boy connects Nature to the events he experienced as a fetus in the womb, he will look for ways to not only escape the womb, such as fast toy cars and planes, but from Nature itself. Space, of course, is the perfect escape from Nature. It is the final frontier from the death and decay upon the earth. It is another dream for a boy. When he grows up, he may want to become an astronaut or live in space. After all, if there is no Nature in space, then there will be no apneas, no dying mother and no perceived death at all. There will be no deception and no pain. All of this is, of course, encoded into the neurons of the boy's subconscious. Therefore, if a superhero comes from space, he must know the secrets of how to beat Nature and this planet of death and decay.

It is important to realize that while the young boy will eventually outgrow the need to watch cartoons or play videogames and believe in superheroes, his interest in themes that represent his experience of life in the womb and fighting the First Fear Cycle will never leave him. Instead, they will simply evolve. As he grows older and into adulthood, the entertainment medium that will draw his interest will still focus on these themes, as the remaining neurons encoded with the memory of life in the womb form his subconscious.

A good example of the evolution in this theme would be a common space adventure movie. What often occurs in these movies is that the main characters have to leave a planet or a ship that is about to explode. At the end of this type of movie, the hero must leave, however, often stays too long for sentimental reasons, such as saving another person. Then just before the spaceship or planet explodes, the hero gets out safely. This is nothing more than a re-enactment of the fetal experience during the final days of pregnancy. The womb, like the planet, is deteriorating rapidly. The fetus knows it has to leave, like the hero in the movie, however wants to stay to save its mother's life. Then at the last minute the fetus escapes the womb, which is the dying planet or spaceship in the movie, just in time. Indeed, the fetus realized that its mother, like the hero in the movie with the planet or spaceship, was dying and that it must leave. Everyone who watches this movie knows that the hero should leave sooner than he does; however, they empathize with him for staying longer. This empathy is based on the fact that everyone who has watched the movie has experienced the same emotions, because they realized an almost identical event, being life in the womb and birth itself.

There is something even more telling of the fetal intrauterine experience that commonly occurs in these space adventures or any adventure movies. Often, at the end of these space movies; after the planet or ship has blown up, a minor character that appeared to be lost in the explosion suddenly turns up alive. This, of course, mimics the exact surprise the infant experienced when it believed, after birth, that its mother should have been dead, however, was alive after all. Remember, the fetus believed that it was keeping its mother alive. If it left; it believed she would die. Therefore, when the infant realized she was alive, it was pleasantly surprised; this theme of surprised survival is always popular with an audience.

While we could go on and on interpreting movie themes in terms of life in the womb, as the most popular movies will always contain the most accurate components and reenactments of this experience; it is not necessary. These themes, the themes of leaving a dying planet or surprised survival or slaying a monster or arresting or shooting a bad guy, are all themes based on the First Fear Cycle or life in the womb in general. All that is important to realize here is that these movies or themes exist because they mimic the common experience that every individual born has undertaken. This experience is permanently etched into the subconscious of everyone and while the experience itself has eluded detection, the symbolic re-enactment of it has not.

Magic and Deception

In addition to the lie, boys will be interested in other forms of deception and even magic. After all, it was a major theme of life in the womb for the fetus and the neurons encoded with the memory of that life still dominate the young boy's subconscious. Therefore, magic will often be a fascination. To see an object appear then disappear again, directly mimics the fetal perception of the two cycles in the womb. In one moment the fetus was kicking and trying to save its mother's life, then the next, when the Euphoric Cycle began, magically she was not dying at all. Within minutes the fetus had completely forgotten the existence of the other cycle. Indeed the intrauterine experience and the Memory Block itself were Nature's "slight of hand."

Games of deception will also be popular with children, especially boys. Even, "hide and seek" is deeply entrenched in the intrauterine experience. When one child looks for the other, the child has vanished, then, suddenly reappears only minutes later. This deception mimics what happened in the womb. In one minute the intrauterine environment was pleasurable, during the Euphoric Cycle. The next minute, the Euphoric Cycle like the child in the game vanishes. In the next moment a horrific environment consumes the fetus as the First Fear Cycle begins. Halloween is a special day that has its true roots deep within the intrauterine experience. Here a child can have essentially two identities at once. They can be themselves and also simultaneously be dressed up as someone or something different altogether. Often a child will pick a costume, which is very symbolic of the intrauterine experience. For example, they might want to dress up as a creature that would be a manifestation of the First Fear Cycle of Development. In other words, on Halloween night, the faceless monster that consumed the fetus and now consumes the child's subconscious now has a face. This face will be a ghost or a goblin, a monster, vampire or other ghoul. By the child becoming this faceless monster, they are empowering themselves as they begin to disbelieve the horror they once experienced. The mimicry of these ghouls, this manifestation of the First Fear Cycle will usually be undertaken by older children, who are well on their way to disbelieving the validity of their fears, as they move away from the fetal experience. For younger children, they will be more likely to dress up as a symbolic object or person that can control or slay the faceless monster they encountered, during the First Fear Cycle. This is because; at a younger age the belief in that fear is much stronger, as they are closer to the actual events in the womb themselves. A popular costume that would represent this symbolic power would be a superhero.

Even the concept of the "haunted house" mimics life in the womb for the fetus. Here a child must face a re-enactment of the First Fear Cycle. They must walk through a dark hall or house filled with scary noises and objects. Here, like the womb it is dark. Like the womb, during the First Fear Cycle, it is very scary. When a child successfully accomplishes walking through a haunted house, the process is very therapeutic. Revisiting and surviving mimicry of the First Fear Cycle essentially disproves the neurons in their subconscious, for a short period of time. In addition, the entire intrauterine experience is put into perspective and therefore, the fear involved becomes somewhat diluted. Of course, very young children will not usually want to get near a haunted house. This is because, again, they are simply too close in age to the actual events in the womb itself.

Boys' Perception of Girls

Boys do not only see their mothers as containing the capacity to generate the death and decay they experienced as a fetus in the womb inside of them, they also believe little girls have this capacity as well. In other words, boys, in general, will associate the death and decay they experienced in the womb, with little girls. Subconsciously, they reason that after all they are the same gender. Therefore, they are not eager to associate with any aspect of what once entrapped them in a horrific environment for nine months. The young boys often term the death and decay that they are certain young girls contain as "cooties." They also believe girls contain "germs." If you ask a young boy what "cooties" means, it is unlikely that you will get a straight answer. In his subconscious, however, it is very clear. It is the olfactory development or development of sense of smell that occurred during the First Fear

Cycle. It is the olfactory coding of pungent and foul odors, including fetal waste products that consumed the womb during the long hours of the night as its mother slept, during the First Fear Cycle of Development. These smells signaled the coming of the cycle of perceived death in the womb of its mother and therefore of itself. Upon this olfactory signal the fetus was essentially forced to kick and punch in order to save its mother's life. The smell of death and decay was the catalyst that brought about all these horrific events. It is the same death and decay the young boy symbolically escapes every time he races that toy car across the floor. It is the same death and decay that he wants to go to space to escape. And now, it is the same death and decay that the boy believes is inside the young girl. Boys will not only often tease little girls about it, however, they will create, "boys only clubs" where girls are not allowed.

Of course, this will all change within a few years. Indeed, it is a major irony of human behavior, as in less than ten years, as the boy's neural pattern matures, he may very well fight his best friend over the same girl they, together, locked out of their club. Yes, right around the corner, a day will come when he cannot get contaminated enough by those "cooties". This is still a while off however, for at six or seven years old, he is still too close to the actual events in the womb itself. At this young age, the boy's subconscious is still consumed by too many neurons encoded with the events of the First Fear Cycle of Development.

Boys' Relationship with Nature

The inevitable conclusion the boy draws, in his subconscious, concerning events that occurred to him in the womb, is that it was Nature after all who was responsible. Nature alone was responsible for all the horror and the deception he experienced in the womb. After all, who else could it have been? It certainly was not his mother, for she too was a victim to the death that consumed both mother and fetus every night. No, the child figures that it must have been Nature alone who was responsible for all that happened.

This realization alone, in the end, will be responsible for more forest cut down, more rivers dammed, animals hunted and environment destroyed than for reasons of money, greed, need, and ignorance, combined. Yes, the battle of man against Nature begins in the womb and mankind's first assault on her, begins during childhood. The desire for this battle is especially for the male as he, realized as a fetus, a much more violent and painful First Fear Cycle of Development.

Once the boy, subconsciously, realizes that it was Nature who entrapped him in the womb for nine months, made him fight for his life every night, and deceived him that his mother and therefore himself was in the process of dying, he is eager to seek revenge. Life in the womb: these difficult origins are something his subconscious will never forget, as the neurons encoded with the memory of these events influence every thought and therefore every motivation.

To deal with the immense power of Nature that entrapped them so mercilessly, boys will often try to control it, often destroying it in the process. For example, a boy might capture a bug and put it in a bottle. This of course mimics exactly what Nature did to him in the womb. Now it is doubtful that the boy has a conscious intention of leaving the bug in the bottle to die, however, when his mother calls him inside for dinner, it is likely this is exactly what will happen. Now, there is a very good reason for this, as subconsciously he wants to seek revenge on the entity to which the insect belongs. He wants to seek revenge on Nature for leaving him trapped in his mother to die. Indeed, he will give the bug in the bottle the same concern he feels Nature gave him.

Other ways at which boys will want to capture or control Nature include pulling the wings of moths, catching frogs and stepping on all the insects they can. Boys will catch fish and may even demonstrate an early interest in hunting. While he is told not to harm animals, he may do so, as it is all a fair game to a young boy to seek revenge against Nature.

There are other ways to control Nature besides killing or trapping it. Boys will often be interested in controlling dirt. Toys that control dirt will fascinate them such as cranes, trucks and bulldozers. Often, they will dig a hole, thus mimicking the womb, thus begin controlling its shape and outcome, by using toys especially designed for this purpose. Of course, every boy feels better off the ground, high above the death and decay of Nature. The perfect place to experience this is a tree house. In a tree house he not only above the death and decay, however, more importantly, by modifying a tree he is controlling or modifying Nature.

This, of course, is just the beginning, the earliest signs of the battle of mankind's contempt against Nature. Indeed, so obvious and so extreme is this battle that a complete chapter will be devoted to it later in the book.

Play That Mimics the Euphoric Cycle

Not all play that young boys undertake has its focus on the First Fear Cycle; other play that both boys and girls initiate, mimics the more positive Euphoric Cycle of Development. Nowhere else is this more obvious than at a typical children's playground.

The playground is a virtual re-enactment of the Euphoric Cycle. Movement is the key here. The child wants playground equipment that mimics their movement as a fetus realized during the Euphoric Cycle, when the dopamine to the reward pathways of their developing brain flowed freely. A swing accurately recreates this movement. Up and down in a controlled rhythmic movement is the promise of a playground swing. This, of course, is exactly the effect the fetus experienced as its mother walked around, thus creating the Euphoric Cycle. Swinging is essentially an exaggeration of the rocking, which soothe them as an infant, which itself recreated the fetal movement during this desirable cycle. There is something else that is important to mention about the child's desire to play on a playground swing.

What is occurring with the choice of a swing is that the further the child moves away from their actual experience in the womb and the Euphoric Cycle itself, the more exaggerated this rocking and rhythmic movement will have to become to obtain the same or similar effect it realized as a fetus. This is due to the aging of the individual and resultant maturation of the individual's neural pattern. Whereas, during infancy rocking by its mother would do the trick; now, during childhood that rocking movement will have to graduate into a swinging motion. Later in life this exaggeration will progress even further. The effect that was realized by movement on a bicycle will later be realized in an automobile. Later even an automobile will not produce this effect alone. To gain this effect the individual must drive fast in an automobile. Finally, it will take a roller coaster to recreate the same sensation for the young adult, as the infant realized by being rocked, which itself, again is nothing more than mimicry of the fetal experience during the Euphoric Cycle. Now, this progression will continue up until a fixed point in time. Usually, this occurs when the individual reaches middle age. At that time, the entire equation begins to reverse itself; this is a result of the maturing neural pattern. In other words, for a middle-aged woman like a young child, a roller coaster may be too fast. Both of them would prefer the gentler rhythm of a front porch swing. Finally, this mimicry of the Euphoric Cycle will come full circle during old age, to the rocking chair. This is because the neural pattern that inhibits the neurons encoded with the First Fear and Euphoric Cycles weakens as a normal part of aging. So what is beginning at the playground is one of the first steps of this progressive exaggeration.

A merry-go-round is another piece of playground equipment that promises a return to the movement, the child, as a fetus experienced during the Euphoric Cycle. Indeed, the dizzying sensation from spinning around, in every way, mimics the fetal experience during this positive cycle. Then, there are the little stationary plastic animals on giant coiled springs. Here a child can go back and forth, working hard to obtain that elusive dopamine release that once flowed so freely.

While not a traditional piece of playground equipment, a trampoline is the ultimate re-enactment of the fetal experience during the Euphoric Cycle. Yes, a child is lucky who has a trampoline, as kids will come from all over the neighborhood to jump on it. The trampoline is a guaranteed generator of smiles. You can almost see the euphoria on their small faces as they jump up and down. As its mother walked around, the fetus bounced up and down, their developing brain engulfed in a pool of dopamine. A pogo stick, jumping rope and the rocking horse, indeed the list can go on and on. All of these activities re-enact the same Euphoric Cycle.

Not all playground equipment mimics the Euphoric Cycle, some recreates an even more important experience, birth itself. It is the world of the giant slide. While to an adult the slide is far from giant, for the child, however, it seems enormous. For the child, there is much more involved with a simple playground slide than meets the eye. To master the slide, in many ways, is to master the memory of the child's own birth. It is easier said than done, however, for what playground is complete without watching the scared face of a small child at the top of the slide when they realize, they have bitten off more than they can chew, and they coyly attempt to step back down off the stairs they have just climbed? And who can blame them? After all the process of birth was terrifying at best! Yes, the first time down a slide they will need the reassuring hands of mom and dad to help them down. A slide mimics the falling sensation of birth; there is simply no other purpose for it. As the fetus initiated labor it began sliding down the birth canal on its journey to infancy. While the process of birth was not fast at all, to the fetus, the fall was very dramatic. After all its entire life, up until then, was lived in a very small area that was the womb. Now, to go sliding down the birth canal head first, this was the origin of the free fall itself!

The problem with the traditional slide, however, is that it is just not effective enough. No matter how many times the playground supervisor tells the boys to not go down head first, they still do it. This is a much more desired position, because this is exactly how most boys were born. Indeed, the rules of the playground and for the slide are great for those born in a breech position, however, not for the head first. This problem is solved, however, by updating this archaic tool of mimicry. Enter the water slide. Here kids can safely slide, head first, down a wet tube, which is almost the identical sensation as birth itself. It is important to realize that each time the child or individual re-enacts their birth, in this manner; they are disproving the First Fear Cycle neurons that form their subconscious. This, along with the movement that mimics the Euphoric Cycle, helps them master what influences their every thought and action.

The process of birth affected some individuals more dramatically. If these individuals live by the ocean they will gravitate toward surfing. In this sport, not only does the surfer realize the wet environment that is much like the womb, the weightlessness and falling sensation, and occasional tube ride inside a wave that mimics the birth canal itself, but they also get salt water in their mouth that mimics the saline that the fetus tasted during the long process of labor. In many ways, surfing more than any other hobby or sport, most directly reenacts the sensation and experience the fetus realized during the process of labor. Every time a surfer rides a wave, they are essentially overcoming the fear of birth encoded in the First Fear Cycle neurons of their subconscious. Of course, surfing is not the only hobby or activity that is a reenactment of birth. To overcome this fear, many individuals turn to everything from bungee jumping to parachuting out of airplanes. To some extent skiing, snowboarding and bobsledding serve the same purpose as well.

Boys' Emergence into Maturity and Reproductive Behavior

As boys leave childhood into adolescence and early adulthood, changes begin to occur in their relations with the female gender. This, of course, is necessary. After all, the male of the human species will ultimately be the initiator of sexual reproduction and the ultimate proliferation of the species. To Nature, besides survival, there is not a more important role that he will play. Indeed, there is nothing Nature focuses on more intently, with her model of intrauterine development, than the ultimate reproduction of the species.

Yes, the boy has a long ways to go, a complete evolution from believing the young girl has "cooties" to the point that he will want to reproduce the species through her. It will be a long and subtle journey; however, with billions as the proof, overall, it works very effectively.

Again, it is a subtle transformation that occurs over time within the neural pattern of the male that will ultimately lead him to the female gender. It is a transformation that takes place in terms of months and years, instead of with other mammals, where it often takes only minutes and days. This is because, for the human species Nature does not rely on the use of pheromones for reproduction, at least not exclusively. Pheromones are sexual attractants realized through the olfactory system or the sense of smell. For most mammals the process of reproduction is simple. When the female is ready for mating, she releases a scent. The male mammal smells it and the scent ultimately releases dopamine to its reward pathways. When he smells the scent or pheromone he comes running, ready to reproduce. Ten minutes after reproduction, these two mammals may or may not have much interest in each other, as it matters little to Nature, for the first step of proliferation of that mammalian species has been accomplished.

With the human species it is not that simple, however. Remember, the olfactory system in the human fetus was used for something almost equally as important. It was used for the initiation of the First Fear Cycle of Development, which taken in combination with the Euphoric Cycle represents the factors that, neurobiologically and behaviorally elevate mankind above all other species. Therefore, the exclusive use of pheromones for the human species' reproduction would not work at all. Now, this is not to say that the sense of smell will have nothing to do with mate selection within the human species, this is not true at all. It is just that smell is one of many other important developmental aspects that are utilized.

The most important change in boys' perception in girls is due to the gradual distance from the events the male experienced within the womb itself. In other words, year by year, as the boy ages and emerges into adolescence the memory of the events in the womb, especially the association of the death and decay with the female gender subordinate deeper into his subconscious. Therefore, the first reason is simply a matter of time itself.

The second aspect will be the age of the male adolescent's own mother. As the boy's mother ages he will seek a substitute symbol to help him disbelieve the neurons encoded with the First Fear Cycle, that dominate his subconscious. In other words, as an infant and young boy, by seeing its mother moving around and healthy, he realizes that not only will she not die but that he will not as well. This connection between the well being of his mother and his physical health and pain level is established in the womb, reinforced through his subconscious and finally, realized through his daily contact with his mother. This contact with his mother makes him feel better, while part of him does not want to become to close to her as he evolves from infancy into childhood, he also very much, at the same time, needs her presence to help disbelieve what is engrained in his subconscious. This, of course, is a deep connection between her health and his. Therefore, as she ages, experiencing the normal decay of this process, he will look for a substitute to reduce the First Fear Cycle neurons, which influence his every waking thought. This is because the adolescent cannot allow the thought of his mother's inevitable aging and death to enter from his subconscious to his conscious thoughts. It is important to realize here that very much for the male is at stake. This is because, as an infant or as a child, every time he sees his mother healthy and active, his neural pattern will change. When he disbelieves that she is in the process of dying, by seeing her in a healthy condition, the influence in his subconscious of the First Fear Cycle is reduced. By reducing the influence of this negative cycle, he is allowed an increase in the influence of the more positive Euphoric Cycle. It is very accurate to say, that when the infant or young boy sees his mother healthy, he gets or gains something from this. Now, as his mother ages, he will look for a substitute to realize this same gain, he once realized through her. In the future, when he associates with a healthy female, he will realize the same reduction of the influence of the negative First Fear Cycle neurons within his subconscious. This relationship between the female's health and the male's psychological well being, with the exception of the factors that initiate reproduction, is the strongest bond that keeps the male and female pair together. This bond is so strong that the pair will often stay involved together long after reproduction has occurred. An extreme example of this can be seen, in some cases, with older couples. Many times when the female dies first, the male will often follow within a few years.

The most important aspect of the boy's changing perception towards the female gender will be the maturity of his neural pattern in regards to his sleep-dream cycle. Indeed, one of the primary purposes of sleep, as you will realize in the next chapter, is the review of the two cycles of fetal development. The most important purpose of this review, that occurs during sleep, with the exception of aspects related to survival, is the review of developmental aspects related to reproduction. While a full understanding of this process will be gained in the next chapter, a brief overview here is necessary. In general, during the stage of slow wave sleep, the remaining neurons encoded with the two cycles of the intrauterine development fire uninhibited. What this means, is that the entire remaining neuronal base encoded with life in the womb fires completely uninhibited, thus, allowing the sleeper to review their entire experience, they realized as a fetus. During the next stage of sleep, which is a lighter sleep or REM sleep; this review and images of this review filter in, and mix with images of the sleeper's daily life. The mixing of images from these two stages of sleep produces dreams. Now, upon awakening, most of these dreams are not remembered by the sleeper, however, the influence on the individual's motivations, actions and therefore, behaviors are realized, nonetheless.

We will look at a fifteen-year-old boy as an example. At night, during slow wave sleep the boy reviews the events of the First Fear Cycle, the dying of his mother and the attempt to save her life. These images co-exist with the review of the Euphoric Cycle, the fetal rocking and moving, the pleasure realized from the high levels of dopamine flowing through the fetal reward pathways. Now, in light or REM sleep, these images connect with the female he either has seen or sees frequently. From this process of mixing these images of the two cycles and images from his waking state, he develops and realizes a motivation for his daily behavior. This motivation is created, specifically during REM sleep by the process of dreams. The image of a female of his daily life is mixed with a review of the First Fear Cycle, then the Euphoric Cycle. The motivation for the behavior of his daily life will be this; he will want to see this girl in a condition that mimics, not the First Fear Cycle, however, reenacting the Euphoric Cycle. Through his dream process, guided by the two cycles of intrauterine development, he will sort out the ultimate motivation. In his dream he will see her, alive and healthy and together with himself they will mimic his fetal experience during the Euphoric Cycle. In other words, he will dream about being as close to her as possible and re-enacting the rocking and rhythmic motion like he experienced as a fetus during the Euphoric Cycle. This re-enactment of course, is the process of sexual intercourse. This is also why this boy will realize an erection of his penis during this REM sleep and dream cycle. Sometimes, if the image of the dream is dramatic enough he will conclude the sexual act within his dream and reach a climax. Again, he will remember very little of these dreams, however, the influence, during his waking state, will be realized nonetheless.

The model of human sexual reproduction is actually quite simple. At night the boy, through the mixing of the images of the two intrauterine developmental cycles and of those of his daily life, in the sleep-dream process, he rehearses Nature's intentions for his motivation during his waking state. This intention, of course, is reproduction and Nature's ultimate goal of proliferation of the species. If you add the sleep-dream process to the reduction of the influence of the neurons encoded with the First Fear Cycle, when he is around a girl, it becomes easy to understand why a teenage boy is very motivated by girls. This, of course, is exactly Nature's intention.

The girls, of course, add to the enticement. For reasons you will realize in the next section of this chapter, girls often smell very much like the sweet smells that were programmed during the fetal Euphoric Cycle. This, subconsciously, promises the boy that he can disprove the belief that his mother and therefore himself is in the process of dying. This is because the girl has been substitute for the boy's mother. This association makes him feel better and changes his neural pattern temporarily. This temporary change reduces the negative influence from the neurons encoded with the First Fear Cycle and increases the positive influence of those neurons encoded with the Euphoric Cycle, both of which dominate his subconscious and therefore influence every thought.

Just associating with the girl is not enough for the boy, however; as he is eager to bring the relationship to the climax he rehearses every night during his sleep-dream cycle. This climax is, of course, sexual intercourse. The boy, typically, will be the aggressor, urging the girl on to reproduce or at least mimic reproduction through intercourse.

It is essential to Nature that the male ultimately initiates intercourse. Therefore, Nature has provided him with additional incentives to ensure that he accomplishes this task. In addition to the presence of the female, temporarily changing his neural pattern within his subconscious, he is also neurochemically rewarded once orgasm has been realized. Nature uses the tried and true method of neurochemical manipulation through dopamine to obtain this result. Once the male reaches orgasm, he will realize a temporary increase in the amount of dopamine that flows to his reward pathways. This increase in dopamine is intended to not only reward the male, however, but to further convince him that this is where he wants to be, back in the Euphoric Cycle. This, of course, takes place very quickly and on a subconscious level. Now, if you look back at the Euphoric Cycle, you see how, to the male the act of sexual intercourse, in almost every way, mimics the Euphoric Cycle. There is the rocking and rhythmic motion the fetus realized, there is the sweet smell, which was a part of olfactory programming during that cycle, there is the vaginal secretions of the female, and finally there is the high level, while only temporarily, of dopamine he realized as a fetus during that pleasurable cycle. It is important to know that the rocking and rhythmic motion, common with male penetration of the female, during intercourse serves a dual purpose. The first is to mimic the Euphoric Cycle. The second is penetration itself, as increased penetration and deepening of the male's penile thrust will increase the chances of fertilization of the female's egg, which essentially is the primary goal of Nature in the first place.

It is essential to realize, how easy it is for Nature to entice the male back to the female without the exclusive use of pheromones for this process. This task is accomplished somewhat easily, because the male originated from the female. All that Nature has done here is to establish or leave remnants of development unresolved in the male's subconscious. Then, he refuses these unresolved aspects during his sleep-dream process and ultimately seeks a female in which he can resolve these aspects of subconscious development upon. This will, ultimately, lead to intercourse and the resultant reproduction. Yes, for Nature the model of male reproductive behavior is quite simple.

What is not simple at all, however, is the female model. As you will see in the next section of this chapter, the accomplishment of sexual interest by the female gender towards the male gender is an exceedingly difficult task without the sole use of pheromones for enticement. Indeed, this is one of the most difficult tasks Nature faces with the human species. The reason this is so difficult, is that both male and female originate from the female. Therefore, while it is easy to lead the male back to his origins, it is extremely difficult to map the female towards a gender that she has no developmental exposure to in the womb, as this is the origin of all aspects of behavior. Not only is it a difficult task, however, also it is a fascinating one and one of Nature's most advanced accomplishments to date. As with the human species, unlike all others, reproduction is dominated by psychological and neurochemically manipulated factors.

Girls

Unlike boys, who see girls as having "cooties" inside of them or possessing the death and decay of the First Fear Cycle of Development, little girls do not share the same opinion of boys. Indeed, quite the opposite is true. The reason for this can best be understood by the little girl's choice in her primary toy. In fact, the young girl's selection and detachment to a doll is one of the most revealing symbols of what Nature has in store for her as she matures. To understand the young girl's interest in the doll, it is first necessary to return to life in the womb for the female fetus, especially the First Fear Cycle of Development.

Identification of the Death and Decay

During the long hours of the night, while its mother was sleeping, deep into the First Fear Cycle of Development, the intrauterine environment did not filter out the fetal bodily waste products. The fetus was essentially consumed within its own waste products and normal nightly decay of the intrauterine cycle. Nature, economically, used this time for olfactory development, programming olfactory neurons with foul and pungent odors. This olfactory programming by itself, developmentally, means very little. Where this aspect of olfactory development gains its importance is that it occurred during the painful and horrific First Fear Cycle of Development. Therefore, an association or connection is made between the negative change in the intrauterine environment and the coding of these pungent and foul odors. These odors, the fetal bodily waste products represent the death and decay of the intrauterine environment, which later in life becomes a very negative association.

You have already seen with the infant that the association of smelling its own bodily waste products reinforces the neurons encoded with the First Fear Cycle of Development. When an infant smells its own bodily waste, it believes that it is back in the First Fear Cycle and its mother and therefore it itself are in the process of dying. While, for the infant and child the association of bodily waste becomes a very negative one, to the female infant or young girl this negative association is much more severe. .

Once the young girl realizes that her gender is the same as her mother's, an intense fear sets in. The young girl believes and or fears that not only, is the death and decay she experienced as a fetus, contained inside her mother, however, it is inside her as well. If the young girl does not believe that she contains the death and decay inside of her yet, it is her fear that in the future this will consume her, just as it has consumed her mother. The belief of this young girl, then, is that she has the death and decay inside of her, including the pungent and foul odors, and she will face a live consumed by this death and decay. While this affects her in many ways, the most obvious is that she will not feel very good, not only about the belief in herself, however, in general, as her neural pattern shifts to the negative association of the First Fear Cycle of Development. And as you have seen in the chapter on "The Subconscious," one of the basic motivations of human behavior is to avoid the negative association related to this cycle and seek the positive associations that mimic the Euphoric Cycle. So, for the young girl this belief of the death and decay inside of her will be avoided at all costs.

Dolls

To offset the fear that she, like her mother, will face a future consumed with the death and decay inside of her, the young girl needs constant reassurance that this will not occur. Now ideally, as you will see later, it is Nature's intention that the young girl receives this reassurance from her father and, in most cases, this is exactly what occurs. What we are concentrated on here, however, is how her selection of a toy, specifically, demonstrates this fear and her intrauterine experience. The toy, more than all others, that will make a young girl happy, in most cases, is a doll. To offset the fear that the death and decay is inside of her, she will choose a doll. A doll is a symbol of a girl with no death and decay inside of her. This is for two major reasons. The first is because a doll is not alive and therefore, it cannot die. The most important reason, however, is because dolls, the popular ones at least, do not have reproductive organs, and therefore, can have none of the death and decay, which those organs represent. By this time in the young girl's life, she knows exactly, as do little boys, what areas of her mother's body are responsible for the death and decay. It is important here to reemphasize that all of this is occurring very much on a subconscious level for the child.

With the doll in hand, the little girl will dress and undress her, subconsciously checking and rechecking to make sure no death and decay has consumed the doll. In fact, every time the young girl sees the smooth plastic or porcelain pelvic area, free of reproductive organs, the little girl feels better. By checking and rechecking the doll and realizing it has no death and decay, her neural pattern shifts away from the negative association of the First Fear Cycle to the positive Euphoric Cycle in her subconscious. Indeed, the doll holds the promise that there is no death and decay inside of her. When the young girl chooses an older female doll, for example a doll that is representative of a girl in her teenage years, this gives the young girl hope that she can grow up and become, like the doll, a young adult female with no death and decay inside of her. Of course, if a young boy wants to enrage his little sister, he will simply get her doll dirty. This upsets the young girl, because now her doll is consumed with death and decay and no longer serves its symbolic role as effectively. Boys will also play with dolls, however, they will never be as popular as for girls. Most of the boys' dolls are focused on action figures or military personnel who fight the First Fear Cycle.

How big is this fear of death and decay for a young girl? You can answer the question for yourself when you walk down the doll aisle in a department store. The testament to the intensity of this fear is rows and rows of doll houses, doll clothes, doll carts, doll cars and, of course, hundreds of dolls, from dolls of little girls to dolls of young adult women.

While this may seem like a cruel trick Nature plays on the female, there is a very good purpose for it. This deception into leading her into believing that the death and decay is inside of her is quite necessary. As you will see without this belief, the female would have very little interest in the male at all. Reproduction between the sexes would simply not exist and therefore, the ultimate survivability of the human species would not occur. This will all be explained later in this chapter.

Influence of the Death and Decay on the Young Girl

Because of the fear that the death and decay is contained inside of her, the little girl will generally be much cleaner than her male counterpart. The young boy, subconsciously, knows that there is no womb inside of him nor will there ever be. Therefore, he knows he does not contain the death and decay inside of him. He can play in the dirt for hours, often carrying half of it home with him. He can play in the mud; fill his pockets full of rocks and soil and his face as well. It makes little difference to him.

To the young girl, however, this type of dirty play will be avoided, whenever possible. Because she cannot control the death and decay, and resultant foul odors she fears are inside of her, she works on her immediate surroundings instead. Subconsciously, she believes that if she can keep her face, hands and clothes clean, then, she can combat the death and decay from consuming her. In general, she will work; focusing on the cleanliness of her appearing, not for vanity however, to combat the death and decay that she subconsciously fears could consume her at any time. She will avoid anything that mimics the fetal exposure to death and decay inside the womb. Indeed, anything she feels with her fingers or sees that even remotely resembles what she felt during this horrific cycle will be avoided and termed, "yucky" or "gross". Slimy things that resemble the intrauterine environment, such as snails, worms, snakes and wet mud will be avoided as well. The reason she will avoid these things is that she fears similar sensations are inside of her, again subconsciously. And it is a great fear. When she sees these slimy things, her neural pattern, within her subconscious shifts and she realizes the negative association of the neurons encoded with the First Fear Cycle, rather than the association of the more positive Euphoric Cycle. Whereas young boys may want to control this slime, as it is a part of Nature that once controlled them.

Once the young girl has accepted her gender is the same as her mother's, she will often look to her for help. After all, what better teacher exists? For here is a woman that the young girl is sure has the death and decay inside of her, yet handles it all so very well. In fact, mom seems as if she is hardly affected by it at all. Yes, the young girl will often mimic her mother to learn how mom deals with a life of death and decay inside of her. The young girl will want to dress up like mom, put on lipstick and nail polish like mom and carry around a doll, like mom carried her. Once the young girl accepts that she too may have the death and decay inside of her, she will look to her mother for ways to help her mask it.

This is all simply in the beginning, however. Before it is all set and done, before the young girl reaches maturity and old age, a large part of her life will be spent trying to hide, disprove or fight the death and decay that she, subconsciously, fears is inside of her and surrounds her.

It may start out with a flowery smelling bubble bath, and then advance to a perfume, during adolescence.

Perfume is a very revealing product in relation to the young girl's intrauterine experience and the neural pattern, which influences her thoughts. By splashing perfume on herself, not only does she mask the foul odors she fears are inside of her, however, she also, now, has the scent that mimics the smell realized as a fetus during the olfactory development, which occurred in the Euphoric Cycle. During the Euphoric Cycle, Nature utilized the circulating and active intrauterine environment for coding of fetal olfactory neurons with sweet and fresh smells. By smelling the perfume that is on her body, which directly mimics this olfactory coding, the girl is surrounded with the association of the positive Euphoric Cycle. This changes her neural pattern, offsetting the negative association of the neurons encoded with the First Fear Cycle by the positive neurons encoded with the Euphoric Cycle, both of which dominate her subconscious.

Perfume is only one of the first steps, however, to mask the death and decay the girl fears. There will be lipstick, eyeliner, mascara, blush, foundation and other make-up to cover her face. This will make it unnatural, therefore containing no nature and therefore the most important aspect, containing no death and decay. Every time she puts on make-up, to cover the death and decay, this changes her neural pattern to a more positive association as well. There will be hair products, lotions, deodorants and other beauty aids. Indeed, billion dollar industries have been created and fed by the fear that consumes the female's subconscious, all of this in an attempt to conceal the death and decay.

The cleanliness the young girl shows in her environment will also evolve as she matures. Simply walk down the aisle in the grocery store entitled cleaning aids and you can begin to understand how this fear not only affects the young girl, however, an entire society as well. There are aids for cleaning sinks, bathtubs, toilets, counters, carpets, windows, laundry, furniture and floors. In her own house, like her mother's, she will clean, scrub and scour for hours upon hours, in order to keep the death and decay she fears inside her, away from her surroundings. Indeed, this one single aspect of intrauterine development will, ultimately, create one of the cleanest species and societies of Nature.

The "Tomboy" and Girls' Early Interest in Boys

Some young girls are clever, however. They refuse to give in. They refuse to give into the fact that the death and decay is inside of them. Indeed, they refuse to give into Nature altogether, by refusing their own gender. It is quite a clever move; they simply deny their female gender altogether. It is the earliest form of denial demonstrated by the human species. And who can blame them? After all the stakes are high, a lifetime of death and decay inside, who needs it? These girls are often referred to as "tomboys." They will dig in the dirt, climb trees and mimic almost all of the behaviors of the boys, who being of a different gender than themselves certainly have no death and decay inside of them. This refusal of identity usually occurs to young girls, who have a very difficult time accepting they are the same gender as their mother.

One obvious benefit for a young girl being a "tomboy" is that she often associates with many more boys than the more traditional young girl. While young boys see the girls as possessing the death and decay and should be avoided, the young girls do not see boys this way at all. In fact, young girls are actually very interested in boys. The association of boys makes a young girl feel better, as she surrounds herself with a more positive association. This will all be explained more in detail later in this chapter.

In most cases, the young girls will notice the boys much quicker than the other way around. Boys hold the promise of a life without death and decay and the young girls want to know everything about them, mostly how they pull this off. In the grammar school classrooms her eyes are often fixed on a favorite boy. On the playground, the young girls may literally chase a popular boy. Of course, over time this will change quite quickly.

Selection of Role Models and Entertainment

Young girls will also look outside her family for female role models that she is convinced do not posses the death and decay. Because these role models are displaced from their immediate access, the young girl is not willing to accept that this female shares the same biological qualities as them. It can start with young girls at a basketball game, carefully studying every move the cheerleader makes. While it may appear as if she is interested in the mechanics of the cheering and dancing, what is actually occurring is that by associating herself with these "living dolls," she feels better, thus, changing her neural pattern to a more positive association.

The young girl maybe interested in a popular female singer to the point of dressing like her and mimicking her actions and personality. Again, it is for the same reason, as up on a stage a female is elevated, above the death and decay of a typical female. This worship of an elevated female will often continue into adolescence.

The young girl is not as interested in cartoons as boys, where the mimicry of death occurs over and over again. Only for the character to be reborn minutes later. While this mimics exactly what happened to the mother of the female fetus in the womb, for girls watching this reenactment will hold little interest. This is because, the entire First Fear Cycle was not as strong and violent for the female as for the male fetus; therefore, young girls' interest in finding out what happened is not as intense as well. While young boys are interested in cartoon and characters that battle the invisible monsters of the First Fear Cycle, young girls would prefer to avoid this association altogether. Instead, they will focus on gravitating towards positive themes that mimic the Euphoric Cycle.

The young girl's choice of movies or cartoons will depict this. In a typical movie that appeals to a young girl, the following will occur. There is often a princess, who magically has no death and decay. She will be living high above Nature in a castle. Finally, a prince, who being a male has no death and decay inside of him, will take her away. Often the landscape will be filled with flowers, which, of course, smell exactly like the Euphoric Cycle. They may even fly away on a magical white horse. Of course, horses cannot fly and a princess has death and decay, however, the therapeutic purpose of the film has been accomplished.

Girls' Relationship with Nature

Because the young girl's intrauterine environment as a fetus was not as severe or harsh as for the male, she will not want to control Nature in the same manner as young boys. This is not to say that the young girl will not attempt to control Nature at all, it is just that she will undertake this task in a subtler manner. Instead, of blatantly controlling it through destruction, they will seek to control it through change or preservation. Where the male will want to tear down the trees, in most cases, the female will want to save them. The reason for this will be explained in detail in the chapter "Man versus Nature."

Change or transformation is a big theme of Nature that interest young girls. The process of a caterpillar changing into a butterfly, or butterflies in general may fascinate them. This transformation represents their subconscious desire to change from a girl to woman without the death and decay inside of them. While a caterpillar is crawling on the slimy ground, in the death and decay, it transforms itself into a butterfly that flies high above the death and decay. Like a doll that is a symbol of a girl or young woman with no death and decay, this evolution into a butterfly is a symbol of hope as well. While she will have little interest in the caterpillar, which represents the First Fear Cycle, she will be fascinated by the change and its new condition, after metamorphoses, once it reaches the stage of a butterfly, which represents the more beautiful Euphoric Cycle. In many ways, this is symbolic in regards to how she will live her life and make her choices. Because she cannot change the death and decay, she fears is inside of her, she will constantly seek associations of the positive Euphoric Cycle.

A flower or a rose may catch a young girl's interest as well. A flower serves two purposes. Not only does it change from a bud to a flower by blooming, which is a very positive aspect of Nature, however, the flower also smells very much like the sweet smells of the Euphoric Cycle. As this cycle was when sweet and fresh smells were encoded within the fetal olfactory neurons. Smelling a flower brings up a positive association, thus negating, temporarily, the fear of death and decay. Seeing a flower allows the young girl to see herself in a more positive light of Nature.

Girls will like many animals as well, as long as they are beautiful or cute. This again, is for the same reason of the positive association. By seeing a beautiful animal, the young girl can concentrate on the more pleasant aspects of Nature rather than an ugly animal that would focus on Nature's less attractive qualities, thus, reminding the girl, subconsciously, of her ultimate fear. As the fetal intrauterine environment was not as aggressive or violent for the female fetus as it was for the male fetus, the young girl will have little interest in aggressive animals. A fierce tiger, aggressive lion or growling bear will hold little of the girl's attention. Instead, she will be interested in more peaceful animals, especially if they are pretty.

Horses are often a favorite. Many times a young girl will collect plastic or porcelain horses. Like dolls they represent Nature without the death and decay. Subconsciously, when a girl collects plastic horses she is viewing Nature without death and decay. This is hope and promise to her in the future. Collection of this kind may not be outgrown as the young girl matures, as often middle-aged women enjoy collecting ceramic, porcelain or glass animals. For example, you may enter an elderly woman's house only to find yourself surrounded by hundreds of plastic, ceramic, porcelain, rock, and glass frogs. This serves the same purpose, as did the plastic horses for young girls. Each time the elderly woman sees those artificial animals with no death and decay, her neural pattern changes in her subconscious to a more positive influence. Indeed, if a porcelain animal is never alive, it can never die and therefore possesses no death and decay.

Girls' Emergence into Maturity and Reproductive Behavior

As you have seen, to get the male interested in the female, for Nature, was relatively simple. Because the male comes from the female, mapping out a route for him to take back to her was not only simple, however, also effective. To have the female come from the female and enable for any interest in the male, for Nature even, this was a Herculean task. You have also seen that Nature had to accomplish this difficult feat without cheating. In other words, she would not rely on the traditional mammalian model of pheromones enticement, as the human olfactory system was used for something else together.

Indeed, to use the two cycles of development in the womb, to encourage or at least allow the female to reproduce with the male, Nature would have to be very creative. If Nature failed, both genders would desire to return to where there origins began, which is, of course, the female. If this failure did occur, of course, there would be no mutual attraction between the genders and therefore, no reproduction. Without reproduction, there would be no species.

Nature would have to develop some method to get the female interested towards the gender, in which, in terms of intrauterine development the female had no previous exposure to. Nature had to somehow get the girl interested in the boy and more importantly the woman interested in the man. To find out how she did it, we will go step by step through the process.

The first step Nature had to accomplish in order to get the female interested in the male was to make sure the female was not interested in the female. While it sounds as if this should be easy, it was not at all. Remember, Nature only had exposure to the female, the intrauterine environment of its mother to work with. To accomplish this, Nature ensured an aversion to the female. And because the gender of the female fetus was the same as its mother's, this meant that Nature had to give her an aversion for herself as well. In other words, Nature essentially strips the female of her self-belief or self-esteem. It would be given back, conditionally, however, never completely. Nature accomplishes this, as you have seen, when the young girl realizes that her gender identity is the same as her mother's. The young girl then, subconsciously, believes that these foul odors, from the death and decay in the womb, are contained inside of her.

Therefore, for the female there is no actual escape from the womb, as there is for the male. This negative association of the First Fear Cycle is essentially inside of her. While the young girl is not sure of this, she has a pretty good idea subconsciously; that this is what has occurred.

As a young girl, the presence of her mother essentially reinforces this; you have seen how a doll gives the girl hope that she will grow up into a woman without death and decay.

For the second step, Nature would go outside of the womb. Once she led the female to believe that she has the death and decay inside of her, and therefore would not seek other females, as they all share the same condition, then Nature would substitute an object of attraction, which in this case occurs outside the womb. To do this Nature would use the male, preferably the girl's father. The father, for the female, has a very unique role. Once Nature has stripped the female of desire for other females, and therefore herself, it is Nature's intention that through exposure to her father the female would conditionally have her self-belief or self-esteem restored.

Here, you must forget about the existence of dolls altogether. This is because a doll was a variable that Nature never anticipated in the gender attraction and reproduction equation. With this in mind, the following is how Nature's intention for the female reproduction model is designed. In the womb, the female fetus realized the negative connection between the death and decay she experienced and the painful and horrific First Fear Cycle of Development. This is the same as for the male fetus. Outside the womb, once the young girl realizes that her gender is the same as her mother's, she begins to fear that the death and decay is inside of her, just as it is for her mother. This creates an aversion by the female towards other females. Included in this aversion is herself. This subconscious belief that the death and decay is inside of her, essentially strips the girl of her self-belief and self-esteem. The goal then, is to utilize the father as a symbol of disbelief that the death and decay is inside of the young girl. The idea here is that by association with this positive male, the father as a model, that later in life, she will seek male companionship to offset this fear that will continue to consume her subconscious. This seeking of companionship, in most cases, will be enough to allow reproduction to occur, as the male will be highly motivated and the aggressor to initiate this process.

Nature's use of the father for this purpose makes sense in many ways. After all, he is not the same gender as her mother; therefore, to the young girl he would have no death and decay inside of him. The idea then is that once the young girl realized that her gender is the same as her mother's, she would then, temporarily, avoid this negative association and gravitate towards her father. By being around her father, she could forget about the association with her mother, that association that she has the death and decay inside of her. Yes, the idea is that because the father has no death and decay inside of him, she would prefer to associate with him. In addition to this, the father would help her disbelief, by telling her that she was not only pretty, however, also smelled nice as well. This would then bring up the positive association of the Euphoric Cycle, enabling the young girl to feel even better, as her developing neural pattern shifts in her subconscious to this positive influence. The young girl in turn, would want to look pretty and smell nice to encourage this positive behavior from her father.

While this may sound like an unreliable model, to expect the father to compliment his young daughter, it is really not at all. The reason he would give these compliments is very reliable and this is, he truly believes it. Indeed, his daughter is very much like a doll. He believes that she certainly has no death and decay inside of her. While Nature made sure that this was her fear, the father does not see his daughter this way at all. Indeed, there is nothing non-genuine or manufactured in Nature's model. The father truly believes what he says, she is pretty, she smells good and in many ways she is perfect.

To understand this, you must realize that, this association with her makes him feel better. The more he watches her dancing, jumping around and just being a child in general, he feels better. For she symbolizes the female without the death and decay, this shifts his neural pattern away from the First Fear Cycle to the influence of the positive Euphoric Cycle. Therefore, it is a mutual relationship. By seeing a female, his daughter healthy, he associates the life and health of her with the life and health of himself. This, of course, all occurs on a subconscious level.

Nature's intention is then; when the young daughter grows older she will have a positive view on male companionship or at least association. As the father ages, the girl who is growing up as well, will seek a substitute for the positive association she realized with her father. It is important to reemphasize that a positive association with the male is all that is necessary, as he will do the rest. Indeed, the male, whether he is an adolescent or adult male is very eager to reproduce or at least mimic reproduction. The reasons for this have been explained earlier in this chapter. Therefore, the female may or may not have any interest in sexual contact; it is up to the male, from Nature's perspective, to initiate reproduction.

There are some obvious difficulties with Nature's model. Indeed, there will always be problems or deviations any time development for the sole purpose of reproduction occurs outside, instead of inside, the womb. While many aspects of the human species were experimental for Nature, this aspect is the most obvious. The most immediate problem is the reliability of the male or father. Indeed, historically, the male is a very unreliable variable. Not only is he often absent due to death from natural causes, but also there is another variable that was never entered in the initial equation. This variable, of course, was the absence of the father due to warfare. As you will see later in this chapter, the absence of the father from this reproduction equation substantially alters its effectiveness.

Another difficulty is that the father will misinterpret the model. In other words, if the positive association the father realizes by the presence of his daughter oversteps the naturally intended boundaries that exist within the family unit, the model will lose its effectiveness as well. Historically, this has been a serious flaw, as in these cases the father confuses or fails to identify his purpose, while important, is limited to encouragement and modeling and exceeds his natural boundaries and actually attempts to initiate reproduction with his daughter.

In most cases, however, these deviations do not occur and the model works flawlessly. Nature strips the female of her self-esteem and the male, conditionally through the father and eventually her mate, restores this self-esteem. With this even, there are problems. The problem is the male himself. Because Nature's model, of leading the male back to the female works so well, because his desire to initiate intercourse and the resultant reproduction is so strong, that he becomes a problem in the model. In other words, by late adolescence the female is essentially flooded by male attention. It seems every male is interested in this adolescent girl. This, for Nature is a problem. If the female gets too much self-esteem or positive association from the males, it is Nature's fear that she may turn to a female for association, or worst, yet not want to or not allow the male to initiate reproduction at all. This, of course, would result in the diminution of the species. Nature would have to solve this problem as well.

To solve this problem, Nature never lets it happen. In other words, to avoid the high level of self-esteem that results from the flood of male attention during late adolescence towards the female, years before, Nature ingeniously prevents the entire problem from occurring. Just about the time, the young girl starts to disbelieve that the death and decay is inside of her, about the same time that boys begin showing serious interest in her, she is confronted by the monthly menstrual cycle. This is Nature's way, at a time when her self-esteem is reaching a pinnacle, to strip her of it once again. During menstruation the girl is confronted with the fact that the death and decay is inside of her. By having the female experience this monthly cycle, she is physically reminded of the blood and odor that mimic the olfactory development, which occurred to her as a fetus during the First Fear Cycle of Development. Her worst fears as a young girl are now confirmed. Indeed, she has the death and decay inside of her. While consciously this is little more than an inconvenience, subconsciously however, it is devastating. This, of course, is exactly what Nature wants, indeed, the reproduction model is moving along perfectly.

Therefore, it is Nature's goal that by the time the girl reaches late adolescence; this flood of attention will be exactly what she needs to repair the damage to her self-belief and self-esteem that she suffered from the onset of her monthly menstrual cycle. This repaired self-esteem will only continue as long as she is near the male, this is the same as it was during her childhood with her father. Ideally, the late adolescent male will, symbolically, take the place of her father in his role of restoring the girl's self-esteem. He will shower her with compliments, and tell her that she smells nice and looks pretty, generally restoring her self-belief. The male is more than eager to assume this role. Indeed, he is led by his desire for the female from the moment he wakes up until he goes to sleep at night.

Nature takes reproduction of the human species very seriously, however. While the menstrual cycle should lead the female to this newfound replacement for her father, the problem with menstrual cycles is that they are not always predictable. Therefore, Nature has two other ways to ensure that the female allows this association with the male. The first is the subconscious itself. Like with the male, at the base of and influencing every thought of hers, are neurons encoded with the First Fear and Euphoric Cycles of Development. Indeed, almost every thought the female completes originates from the influence of the two cycles of intrauterine development. One of these cycles, the First Fear Cycle, reminds her of the negative association of the death and decay, she fears is inside of her.

The second aspect is the sleep-dream cycle. Like the males, she will review both developmental cycles during slow wave sleep, then, she will connect to images of her current life during light or REM sleep.

Events Leading up to Reproduction

Now if everything works like it is supposed to, Nature's model will culminate in intercourse, which will then generate reproduction. The male will want to associate as closely as possible to the female, for she is a symbol of a woman with very little death and decay inside of her. She smells sweet like the Euphoric Cycle. She is active like the Euphoric Cycle. Every time he is around her his neural pattern shifts within his subconscious to a more positive association. This makes him feel better. He wants to get as physically close to her as possible, entering the birth canal, with his sexual organ and he hopes they can mimic the Euphoric Cycle together. Once inside her, he will mimic the same experience he realized as a fetus in the Euphoric Cycle, he would rock back and forth. This will force a sexual climax and release of sperm. This rocking back and forth also deepens penetration, which ensures the sperm to reach the female's egg. If he has done his job properly, from the perspective of Nature, he will receive the desired dopamine rush to the reward pathways of his brain. In most cases, every step of the way he will be the aggressor, the initiator and the most persistent about initiating intercourse.

The female, on the other hand, will be more passive. With her reduced self-esteem, she will need the male to reassure her she is beautiful and smells good. He may even bring her a flower or rose, which is something in Nature, like she is and smells nice like she does. He may even take her dancing; this too mimics the Euphoric Cycle. This will bring the entire positive association together. Ultimately, she will allow him to attempt the mimicry of the Euphoric Cycle on her. She will not want to, at first; she will be scared, for she does not want him to know her secret. She does not want him to know what her subconscious, her menstruation and her sleep-dream cycle are telling her, that she has the death and decay inside of her. If he knows, it is her fear that she will be left alone, consumed with those neurons encoded with the First Fear Cycle dominating her thoughts. Yet, she does not want to reveal too much of herself to him both physically or emotionally; however, her fear of not giving into his desires, to lose him for that reason, will override all other fears, and she will submit.

Her interest in the male is not just association with him, because he is not the death and decay. This is not enough. She wants to see herself being desired, wanted and yearned for by the gender which is not the death and decay. She wants to be touched by him, held by him and reassured by him that she is not the death and decay.

When they, finally, join together for intercourse, it marks the culmination of preparation and planning that took place back in the womb. It is not only that, it is the success of an experiment that will lead to reproduction: of Nature's perfection displayed in unison between the two.

The fertilization of the female egg is a tricky affair, however. Nature has anticipated this as well. After all what if intercourse occurs, however, with no fertilization of the egg? Even worse than this for Nature would be if the female did not enjoy the experience and would never undertake it again. For it is unlikely that the female, unlike the male, will realize an orgasm during her first attempt and the resultant dopamine rush that accompanies it. In addition, the sexual act itself may very well have been painful to the female during her first experience. No, Nature needs to find a way to ensure that the female returns, or allows the male to continue to attempt reproduction upon her again.

The most obvious reason that would prompt the female to return for intercourse again and another attempt at reproduction would be the bond established between the male and female during the initial process. The second reason would be the male himself, as his realization of the temporary dopamine rush will encourage him to return again and again, thus, repeating the pleasurable experience he realized. Another reason that she may return is if she in fact realized an orgasm during her first attempt at intercourse, which in some cases may occur. If the female orgasm were reached, she would also realize the resultant temporary dopamine rush. If all these reasons fail to bring the female back for a second attempt, Nature has one final ploy to encourage her return.

To accomplish this last desperate attempt to entice the female to return, Nature will use the male and the well-utilized model of reduction of female self-belief or self-esteem. What happens here is that Nature will use the male to chip away, only temporarily at the female's fragile self-belief. Theoretically, this is a first, as Nature always utilized the male to restore the female's self-esteem. This is how it occurs. Immediately after intercourse, when the male has reached his sexual climax, once he has realized the dopamine rush, subconsciously, changes occur within his neural pattern. After this large amount of dopamine or dopamine rush has been realized into the reward pathways of the male's brain, a drop off occurs. In other words, the male reaches a peak of the flow of dopamine, and then it is reduced suddenly. Now, if you remember what this reaction signaled in the womb, you will realize what is about to occur. The female, who was once rocking and moving in a rhythmic movement, is now lying still.

This is the second mimicry of the First Fear Cycle. Now, what once was a positive association for the male quickly declines in perception into the First Fear Cycle of Development. So, what has happened is that everything that brought the male towards the female, to mimic the Euphoric Cycle and undertake intercourse, has just essentially been erased. The male, now, is suddenly confronted with a situation that in almost every way duplicates the worst association possible, the First Fear Cycle. This is due to the sudden drop off in dopamine, and the reduction in movement of the female. Now, like the young boy, the male's neural pattern shifts and suddenly he does not want to be trapped into the death and decay of the womb. In response to this now emerging neural pattern in his subconscious, he may move away from the female, only subtly or in extreme cases may want to exit the situation altogether.

Like many aspects of Nature, this neurobiological event that the male experiences, serves two purposes. The first is that Nature obviously does not want multiple intercourse sessions occurring, one right after another. This can only hinder the fertilization of the female precious egg, which is the entire goal of the process anyways. The second purpose deals with the female's response to this behavioral change within the male, after he has reached his orgasm.

The second purpose, in many ways, is Nature's final attempt to encourage the female to return for another attempt at intercourse. If all other methods fail, Nature will use the proven model of female rejection. It is how the female interprets this change in the male's behavior that can be so effective in the process of bonding and prompting her return. To understand this, it is important to see the perspective of the female after intercourse. Indeed, she is in a very vulnerable situation. In the first place, she was reluctant to expose, physically, too much of herself to the male. This was because she did not want him to know what she, subconsciously, believes to be true.

This is that she has the death and decay inside of her. Of course, it is too late for that now; as she lies naked and exposed, with these fears closes over her.

Therefore, she interprets this change in the post-intercourse behavior of the male to be a confirmation of her worst fears. Indeed, she feels he now knows that she has the death and decay inside of her. She feels he knows this and this is why he is behaving in this way. Now, this interplay is all happening, very subtly, on a subconscious level, but it is nonetheless effective. Eager to disprove that the death and decay is inside of her, it is Nature's intention that she returns, again and again, until this subtle rejection is not realized or until the fertilization of the egg and the beginning of the process of reproduction has been successful.

Pregnancy

Nature has new concerns about the male-female relationship when the female enters into pregnancy. The concern centers on the female's awareness and ability to conceive and create life, thus, mimicking Nature. Indeed, Nature's entire reproductive model could be lost, were the female to actually realize her dominance in natural selection that she has obtained. After all, it is true. There is no greater gift received by a gender than to produce life itself. If the female were to realize her role in Nature, then the lack of self-belief and the reduction of self-esteem as the cornerstone of the reproductive model would never work again. Indeed, if Nature were to allow the female to view the male in his true light, that as, in terms of natural selection, subordinate to the female, the possibility of the reproductive model which necessitates the primes of a lack of self-esteem of the female would not likely work again. In other words, if the female were allowed to see the male as less than her, in terms of natural gender selection, the likelihood of the female not believing in her self would be reduced. The net result of this would be a species, the human species, with only one offspring. If this were to occur, it is not likely that the human species would flourish.

Besides the reduction in offspring, if females were to realize this true subordinate role of the male, she may even at the vulnerable condition of pregnancy, find little purpose or value in his continued association. This is exactly what Nature does not want to occur, as the male's presence will be important, especially, if the newborn infant is a female, as the entire reproductive equation depends on him remaining in a patriarchal role, and not simply as a fertilizer of the female's egg. So, it is important, for the natural process that the male remains within this now expanding family unit. Therefore, even at the pinnacle of the female's achievement and at what should be the highest point of her self-esteem, Nature will initiate other methods to reduce the pregnant female's self-belief and self-esteem, thus, ensuring that she remains interested in remaining close to the male.

Besides the pregnancy, another reason the female will realize elevated self-belief and self-esteem during this time, is her lack of a monthly menstrual cycle. This was Nature's greatest tool to lead the female to, subconsciously, believe the negative association that the death and decay is inside of her, and therefore prompting her to seek out the male for positive association. Without this tool, typically utilized to guide the female to male association, Nature is left with only one. This is the sleep-dream cycle of the female.

While the mechanisms involved will be explained in the next chapter, in general, the pregnant female's dream content will be intensified and focused on the First Fear Cycle of Development. In addition to this, the recall of these dreams will be increased as well. In other words, to off set the lack of a menstrual cycle, Nature will intensify the female's dreams and recall, in regards to the death and decay. These dreams and this recall may even focus on the fetus and the soon to be newborn infant itself. During the stage of slow wave sleep, images of the death and decay are reviewed by the pregnant female sleeper; then during light and REM sleep, these images will connect to images from her daily life, which in most cases are focused on the pregnancy and the coming baby. She may recall dreams, such as having a baby that turns out not to be a baby at all. Or she may realize dreams, where the baby itself has some severe deformity, even though there is no practical base for this suspicion. She may even experience dreams, where her partner is unfaithful to her. The majority of the dream recall will focus on self-doubt and lack of self-belief in general. Again, a full discussion of the purpose of sleep and dreams will be provided in the next chapter. What is important to realize here, is that during the prime reproductive years for the female when Nature loses one tool such as the menstrual cycle, she will offset it with another such as an intensification of the sleep-dream cycle.

Indeed, it is a strange relationship Nature has with the female of the human species. On one hand, she is enabled the greatest gift to any gender, which is reproduction, elevating her high above the male. On the other hand, Nature chisels away at the female's self-esteem every chance available, leaving her, historically at least, somewhat submissive and subordinated to the male, all in the name of sexual attraction and the ultimate reproduction of the species.

Lack of Father and the Effect on the Female

What you have just read is how Nature's model of human reproduction is supposed to work and in most cases it does work just as planned. However, if the father or other male figure is not around to restore the female's self-esteem, some very profound changes occur, concerning the overall development of the female and ultimately the model of human reproduction.

This will be an environmental factor for First Fear Not Relieved for the female. Again, this is certainly not to say that the absence of the father or other male figure does not affect the male infant and child, because it certainly does affect them. It is just that the focus here is on the importance of the father or male figure for the female, and how his absence ultimately can affect the model of reproduction.

Because the lack of a father is an environmental factor for First Fear Not Relieved, should this occur, and the female realizes this condition, she would be subject to the same neurobiological implications explained in chapter five on "First Fear Not Relieved." It is also important to realize that the presence of a father alone does not necessarily negate this environmental factor for the female. If a father is not attentive to his daughter, or displays little or negative attention towards her, this can ultimately lead to the condition of First Fear Not Relieved.

While to almost all girls, dolls play an important role, to those without an encouraging male role model they may take on added importance. As you have seen, the doll is a symbol of a female without death and decay. As the young girl plays with the doll, she is constantly checking and rechecking to make sure she has no reproductive organs and therefore, no death and decay. This gives the young girl hope that she can grow up to become, like the doll, a female with no death and decay inside of her.

To the young girl without the supportive male role model, this symbol of no death and decay is all she has to offset the fear that Nature has imposed upon her. She may take a very early interest into boys as well. They too, like the doll, contain no death and decay inside of them. She may also be one of the girls that chase the boys around the playground. Indeed, she is desperate for confirmation, subconsciously, that there is no death and decay inside of her. Even with an exceptional and healthy mother these events will likely occur. This is one aspect of development that her mother cannot provide, for in the girl's subconscious, she realizes that her mother too contains this inside of her.

While she may be desperate for attention from males, in most cases, what occurs is that the young girl finds a substitute for the male reassurance. In other words, instead of finding encouragement from the male, as was Nature's intention, she begins to believe in associations of objects that contain no death and decay inside of them and will erase or offset this fear. In addition, she will spend a great deal of time masking the death and decay that she fears is inside of her. She will do this earlier and with greater intensity than the female who realizes a supportive male role model or father.

The girl, without a supportive male role model or father, may be the first in school to use make-up on a consistent basis. When her friends begin using make-up, she will use it more aggressively and consistently than they do. She will do this to cover up flaws in her face, that only she sees, as subconsciously, the neurons encoded with the First Fear Cycle exert a stronger influence on her, than those with the supportive male role model or father. It will be the same with perfume. She will be the first; she will use the most, covering up the odor that only she smells. Again, this is to offset the strong influence of the neurons encoded with the First Fear Cycle of Development that are dominating her subconscious. When she is the first to buy the newest clothes, it will be for the same reason. The entire purpose for her is to change the natural condition. This is because in her natural condition, she fears she has the death and decay inside of her. She will change her hair color often, never satisfied with the results. She will change her eye color, with contacts if possible. She may even change her name, having her friends call her a pet nickname. She will change everything, about herself; constantly running away from her natural identity and the death and decay, which consumes her subconscious. In general, she will be consumed with self-doubt and low self-esteem, yet she will have the appearance of quite the opposite.

As she gets older, the early lack of a supportive male role model or father will begin to show even more obvious signs. While most teenage girls will enjoy shopping, she will often become obsessed with it. After all, shopping is a stroll through aisles with new things, clothes and shoes. There are two major reasons she may become obsessed with shopping. The first is that because something is not alive, it has no nature in it. In other words, clothes that are new are not in a decaying state. Clothes in a decaying state, symbolize the decay of the intrauterine environment during the First Fear Cycle. And for her the influence of this cycle is stronger than for others, as many more neurons, encoded with the memory of this event, the First Fear Cycle of Development, remain in her subconscious. When shopping, she may not even have to buy anything, just to be surrounded, to look, feel and touch new things, not from Nature or altered from Nature, that have no death and decay, will make her feel better. Shopping will change her neural pattern to a positive association, thus, temporarily negating the negative First Fear Cycle influence. This desire or obsession to shop will be exaggerated during her monthly menstrual cycle, as Nature physically confronts her with her worst fears.

This increased desire for shopping, during her menstrual cycle, for the female with First Fear Not Relieved, can easily be contrasted to the female who does not suffer from this condition. The female, who had a supportive male role model or father during infancy and early childhood, will also have an increased desire during her menstrual cycle; often however, it will not be for shopping, however, for the opposite sex. It is important to realize that during the female's menstrual cycle, Nature's model that attracts the female to the male gender has reached its pinnacle. For, at this time, the female is physically confronted with her worst fears. For the female who had a supportive male role model or father, she will then seek disbelief of her subconscious fear, which she is now physically confronted with due to her menstrual cycle, by male companionship. Not only will her desire to be around him increase, however, her sexual desire will often increase as well. While this is true on one hand, on the other, she will be reluctant to expose the death and decay of her menstrual cycle to him. The initial desire, however, is what is important here.

This is in contrast to the female with First Fear Not Relieved. In her case, disbelief of the death and decay through shopping, replaces the disbelief she would receive from a male, in the same way that the doll, during infancy and early childhood, took the place as a symbol of no death and decay in the role that the father was supposed to fulfill.

Because she cannot control the death and decay she fears is inside of her, she will look out on the immediate environment outside of her and around her, to fight this battle. In addition to her appearance, being extremely clean and orderly, all that is around her should remain in this matter. Everything she does will be neat. Her room will often be the cleanest. Her reaction to a simple stain on her clothes or dress may be exaggerated. Even her handwriting will often be flawless. Everything will be organized to a science. Dirt will be her worst enemy. She will not want to associate herself with anything that in anyway mimics disorder or a state of decay. Even clutter will not be acceptable, as it, in itself, represents the decay of an organized state in which objects were once placed in.

Now, all this girl's self-doubt, low self esteem and masking of this perceived death and decay inside of her, will not keep the males from showing interest in her. In fact, quite the opposite will occur. Because she masks her perceived flaws in smell and appearance, males, especially during her late adolescence years, will be particularly interested in her. After all, perfume smells like the odors that were programmed during the Euphoric Cycle, she therefore smells like the Euphoric Cycle. The teenage boys, subconsciously, reason, that unlike other girls, she is obviously not the death and decay. They will often pursue her aggressively. Without a supportive male role model or father during childhood, this attention will be somewhat foreign to her. She will not know how to react and may make a series of bad decisions. These bad decisions in relation to Nature's model of reproduction are not bad at all, for she may engage in sexual intercourse earlier than her female counterparts.

Therefore, while lack of a supportive male role model or father may not affect whether or not she reproduces, it will have substantial implications on the method and manner in which she chooses male companionship. As the early substitution of object containing no death and decay, for the lack of male support during infancy and childhood, will exert a strong influence on the type of male, which will ultimately attract her attention. Indeed, her selection of a male will be focused on factors, which were based on this early environmental deficit and how she attempted to overcome the trauma involved in that deficit. While the male will be important to her, her quest is still to surround herself with objects that are new and therefore, contain no death and decay. Remember, this as a child was her only refuge, as there was no other aids to help her combat this very strong attack on her self-esteem and self-belief that is so integral to Nature's reproduction model. So now, when she looks for a male, or allows companionship of one of the many males who likely pursue her, she will make her decision based on his ability to obtain and control these new objects. For example, she will not be interested in a male who drives an old car, as this represents the death and decay. If she were to sit in this male's car she would, subconsciously, feel herself consumed externally by what she possesses internally. Therefore, the male who hopes to seek her attention and equations will posses new material goods. In contrast, when she sits in a new car, this negative association is absent. Indeed, her entire neural pattern shifts to a positive association and she feels better. Not only must his car be new, however, his clothes as well. He will be well groomed, not showing any sign of death and decay.

What is happened here is that due to a deficit of environmental factors for the female infant, child and young girl, a cascade of events begins to unfold. The implication of these events affects not only the female and male, but also, ultimately, the entire society of which they both define.

CHAPTER EIGHT

SLEEP AND DREAMS

Sleep

The primary purpose of sleep is to review the developmental aspects of the two cycles of intrauterine development and integrate that review into the individual's daily rhythm. To ensure this is properly accomplished, there are immune system implications, which will not be discussed here, if the individual's sleep requirements are not met.

So, what does this mean and why is sleep important? First, we will briefly overview the importance of sleep; then explain what the first part of the first sentence of this chapter means. In the previous chapter, you realized how the human species is motivated to reproduce by a method that was unlike the method used for any other species. This method, of course, was intrauterine development, and the motivation was established in the womb, long before birth. Now, for Nature to make this all work, a format was needed so that the individual could review this important intrauterine development and resultant motivation on a nightly basis. This format is sleep.

In other words, sleep is essential not only for survival, however, for reproduction and therefore proliferation of the species as well. It is so important that as you will see, Nature takes great care in many precautions to ensure that the individual returns to sleep each night.

Of course, like most aspects of Nature, sleep serves many other purposes, such as learning and, of course, survival. Here, we will focus on how sleep is essential in regards to reviewing the motivation for reproduction. While you have seen, how this works and the importance of it in the previous chapter, a more thorough explanation of the process involved in sleep will be given here. In general, you can look at sleep, as a nightly rehearsal for what Nature wants, in developmental terms, the individual to accomplish the next day.

Sleep as a Review of Development

Now, we will answer the first questions in this chapter. The question is, "What does the developmental review of the two aspects of development mean?" This simply means that every night when the individual falls asleep, they experience four major stages of sleep. For simplification, we will group them into two, slow wave or deep sleep and REM or light sleep. The purpose of REM or light sleep will be discussed in the next section. What we are interested in here is slow wave or deep sleep.

Slow wave or deep sleep is the stage of sleep where the cortical neurons encoded with the events of the First Fear and Euphoric Cycles of Development fire uninhibited. In other words, during this stage of sleep, the sleeper re-experiences all the events they realized as a fetus in the womb. So essentially, every night the sleeper returns to the fetal stage during slow wave or deep sleep. And this is exactly what happens, but it is not quite that simple, however. First of all, many of the neurons encoded with the First Fear and Euphoric Cycles of Development were eliminated during the first few years after birth. Therefore, the sleeper, after infancy, will not experience a true and completely accurate representation of the events they experienced as a fetus in the womb. In addition, of those neurons that remain through this period of infancy, many others that were not eliminated were reprogrammed. Therefore, other representations of the first few years of life will be included during this nightly review as well. With all that taken into account, however, it is important to realize that the neurons encoded with the two cycles of development fire uninhibited, or are completely reviewed during slow wave or deep sleep. Therefore, when the sleeper wakes up, during this stage of sleep, kicking, screaming, fighting for their lives, and thinking they are about to die, this is nothing more than the neurons encoded with the First Fear Cycle of Development firing uninhibited and thus, waking the sleeper. The process involved in this event, which is called sleep or night terror, will be explained later in this chapter.

Nature, however, does not want the sleeper to wake up screaming. From Nature's perspective, when this occurs nothing of value has been accomplished. Indeed, none of the important developmental aspects that were supposed to be reviewed will be realized. Besides, if everyone woke up reacting to those fetal apneas, screaming and fighting for their life, during slow wave or deep sleep, it is doubtful that anyone would want to go back to sleep the next night.

How REM Sleep Protects the Sleeper

Nature has, therefore, created a series of mechanisms, integrated into the human brain that prevents the situation that was just explained from happening. The first mechanism that Nature provides is light or REM sleep. The definition of REM sleep, Rapid Eye Movement, does this stage of sleep very little justice. Indeed, its purpose and content are much more involved than the title suggests. Over the next few pages, you will begin to realize, what the major purposes of REM sleep are.

A primary purpose of REM sleep is to protect the sleeper. Indeed, as with the example you have just seen, when the sleep or night terror occurs, REM sleep has failed his primary objective. A review of the First Fear Cycle of Development, while necessary during slow wave sleep, should not come so abruptly as to wake the sleeper up completely. Indeed, in most circumstances, before the individual ever woke up, kicking, screaming, and fighting for their life, REM sleep should have intervened and diverted this trauma into a lighter stage of sleep. This, of course, would have resulted in a horrific nightmare, as you will see later, but at least the individual would have remained asleep.

There is a very good reason that REM sleep accomplishes this. If too much of the First Fear Cycle of Development is reviewed and the review is too intense, the individual sleeping could actually die. As will be explained in a later chapter, this is actually what happens in the Sudden Infant Death Syndrome. Therefore, the primary way that Nature protects the sleeper from this trauma is the initiation of REM sleep. Before the trauma of the review of the First Fear Cycle of Development becomes too intense for the sleeper to survive, REM sleep kicks in, rescues the sleeper from this trauma.

How REM Sleep Suppresses Movement from Slow Wave Sleep

Now, this entire trauma that is reviewed has to go somewhere. Imagine if the sleeper actually acted out all the events they experienced as a fetus during the First Fear Cycle of Development, the kicking, punching and fighting for its mother's and therefore its own life. If this occurred, it would be an understatement to say that every member of the human species would sleep alone. If they did not, the sleeper would risk waking up black and blue every morning, bruised heavily from the nightly kickboxing match they had with their partner throughout the night. This obviously would not work. Nature had to come up with a way to suppress the entire trauma the sleeper experienced during slow wave sleep, while reviewing the First Fear Cycle of Development.

What Nature did, was to ingeniously suppress most of the sleeper's movement. This process can be explained in steps. The first step was to divert the trauma, reviewed during slow wave sleep, into REM sleep. This process of diversion will be explained in detail in the next section. The next step was to suppress most of the sleeper's movement during the REM sleep stage. Indeed, during REM sleep, the postural muscles of the body are at the most relaxed of any sleep stage. Therefore, during REM sleep the brain is handling this diverted trauma; however, the body is disconnected from the process.

The final step is funneling the remaining energy of the diverted trauma. Indeed, even for Nature it is not easy to stop a moving freight train. Therefore, the remainder of this movement that cannot be suppressed, which originated from the First Fear Cycle of Development, reviewed during slow wave sleep, then diverted into REM sleep, is further funneled into the movement of the eyes and fingertips. This is what gives REM sleep its name, Rapid Eye Movement, as the eyes are moving rapidly during this stage of sleep. It is quite a conversion process. What Nature has accomplished, is a model, which takes this vast amount of movement the fetus generated in the womb, then allows the sleeper to review it, diverts the energy, then suppresses movement, and finally funnels the movement that cannot be suppressed into the eyes and fingertips. Indeed, it is simply another testament to Nature's genius.

Of course, if the trauma is too intense even Nature's conversion can fail. If the sleeper realizes too intensive of a review of the First Fear Cycle or even of the Euphoric Cycle during slow wave sleep, the suppression of movement during REM sleep can fail completely or partially. In this case, instead of the energy being diverted to the fingertips or eyes, it overrides the suppression and is physically acted out by the sleeper. In this case, the sleeper would kick or punch. In most cases, however, this does not occur, however, a diluted movement instead. In other words, the suppression of movement partially fails and instead of kicking and punching the sleeper will simply shift sleep positions. This partial failure is most common during childhood, as the child is much closer to the actual events in the womb, and therefore the First Fear Cycle, than the adult. As most parents can witness, it is not uncommon to find a child in a completely different position in the morning than the position that they were in when they went to sleep, often at the opposite end of the bed.

How Dreams are Formed

Another major purpose, and the most obvious to most everyone, of REM sleep, is diversion and integration. Before the trauma from the First Fear Cycle review becomes too intense for the physical body to handle, the images from this review are diverted into REM sleep, this produces dreams, and in this case a nightmare. It is important to understand that this also occurs with neurons encoded with the Euphoric Cycle of Development, which would result in a good or pleasant dream. What happens in both these cases is that the uninhibited firing of neurons, encoded with the First Fear and Euphoric Cycles, occurs during slow wave sleep, produces images; these images are then diverted into REM sleep. During REM sleep these images of the two cycles mix or are integrated with images from the individual's daily life. An example will clearly illustrate the process of diversion that REM sleep accomplishes and how dreams are formed, which in the following case is a nightmare.

For this example, we will use a ten-year-old boy. During his deep or slow wave sleep the boy reviews the neurons encoded with the First Fear Cycle of Development. On this night, during this review, the most intense images are those of him as a fetus punching and kicking out at the intrauterine walls, trying to initiate a response from what it believes its dying mother. Again, this is nothing more than the review of the neurons encoded with the First Fear Cycle. Then, when this review becomes too intense for the boy's physical body to handle while he is asleep, REM sleep kicks in and diverts these images into other images of the boy's daily life. Now, earlier today this boy was riding his bicycle with his friend Tommy. They went for a two-hour bike ride in the city park. Therefore, during REM sleep the images of the First Fear Cycle and the images from the boy's daily life mix or integrate together, thus forming dreams. The nightmare the boy experiences will be as follows: the boy experiences a nightmare where his friend, Tommy, is attacking him. In this nightmare his friend Tommy is hitting him with a stick. The boy is trying to fight back, he punches at Tommy however, and his punches do not seem to have any effect. In fact, his punches seem to be thrown in slow motion and are powerless, for Tommy keeps attacking him.

The boy wakes up in a cold sweat, frightened for his life and calls for his mother. Now, what has just happened, of course, is that the boy realized a dream, in this case a nightmare of what we will define as a dream of "no effect." We will go through this dream step by step to see exactly what images were involved and how it was formed. First, we will look at the images of the First Fear Cycle. The images that were reviewed during slow wave sleep were those of the fetus kicking and punching out trying to save, what it believed to be, its dying mother. There is an important aspect of these images to be understood. While the fetus was punching and kicking with all of its energy, the effect realized by its mother, who, of course, was only sleeping, was very small. This was because, while the message to kick and punch, from the developing fetal brain was complete and strong, the neural and nerves system pathways between the fetal brain and the fetal arms and legs were not fully developed or myelinated. Therefore, while the fetus was kicking and punching with all its might, the pathways that delivered the information to the actual physical muscles, arms and legs, slowed the entire process down; this resulted in the fetus kicking and punching out in slow motion or at least a slower movement than was anticipated by the fetal brain. Now, because the actual punching and kicking was essentially in slow motion and powerless; its mother who was deep asleep did not respond to them by waking up. The fetus interpreted this event different, of course. How it perceived it was, that its mother who was dying would not respond to its attempts at saving her life. Because the fetus believed that not only was its mother, however, also itself, dying, the attempts to save its own life were futile after all. This was the review that the boy experienced during slow wave sleep, when the neurons encoded with this event fully fire or fire uninhibited. As the review of these images intensified, a neural switch or trigger was enacted, that signaled the boy was experiencing too high a level of trauma. In response to this, REM sleep was initiated. In REM sleep these images filter or mix with images of the boy's daily life, thus, producing this nightmarish dream. Once you understand this; the neurobiological aspects of the dream; interpreting the dream itself is quite simple.

In the nightmare, his friend Tommy represents the unknown attacker or monster, the fetus believed was attacking its mother and therefore itself. No matter how hard the fetus, which, of course, now is grown into the boy, tries to stop this attacker and save himself and his mother included, his attempts have little or no effect. This, of course, was the case, night after night, in the womb. Late at night, deep into the First Fear Cycle, its mother was in a sound, deep sleep. No matter what the fetus did to try to wake her up, she would not. Indeed, just like the fetus, the boy in the nightmare is throwing punches that have "no effect." It is just that, now, the punches are thrown at Tommy instead of the walls of the intrauterine environment.

After the boy wakes up from the dream, other important events occur that not only shed light on the purpose of REM sleep, however, also reveal aspects of its content as well. When the boy wakes up, from the dream he calls for his mother. This, of course, makes perfect sense. After all, it is she in the images reviewed during slow wave sleep that he was trying to save. Therefore, when he wakes up, he first wants to know, subconsciously, that she is all right. When its mother comes into the boy's room, he tells her about his nightmare. She listens and then reassures him that it is only a dream. She may even blame her son's hanging around with Tommy for the nightmare. She may also blame the scary movie the boy saw on television, or the pizza he ate that night. It does not matter, who the boy or in this case his mother blames, for this is a major purpose of REM sleep. No matter, after some reassurance from his mother, the boy will quickly return to sleep.

How REM Sleep Misleads the Sleeper

REM sleep and its resultant dreams are designed to forever mislead the sleeper, as to the actual reasons for the dream itself. This is extremely important; REM sleep has accomplished its job, tonight perfectly. For if the boy were to know that he experienced a horrific review like this every night, it would be doubtful he would want to return to sleep. Indeed, one of the major purposes of REM sleep is to divert or mask the true origins of the images reviewed during slow wave sleep.

If you are looking for important developmental aspects of this dream, you will be sadly disappointed, as there are none. There are no aspects in this nightmare that will help the boy with his eventual purpose of reproduction or even survival. This review was simply a remnant of development, a group of neurons encoded with First Fear Cycle that were not eliminated, during that important period, during the boy's infancy. Not every review, however, is this developmentally insignificant. It is just that Nature, or the human brain, cannot discriminate the neurons that fire during this review. In other words, all remaining aspects of the First Fear Cycle of Development are fully reviewed during slow wave sleep. This is because, during this stage of sleep the neurons fire fully or uninhibited, every image is conveyed, some are helpful for life outside the womb, some, as in this case, are simply remnants of earlier development. Later, we will look at another review of the First Fear Cycle of Development, during slow wave sleep and the resultant dream it creates, and in that case, the dream will have developmental relevance.

The Influence of the Memory Block on Dream Recall

Another tool, that Nature utilizes to ensure the individual returns to sleep the next night to face the same traumatic review, is encoded within the neurons themselves. Indeed, one of Nature's most effective tools to mask the content of this nightly traumatic review is the Memory Block encoded in the neurons themselves that are being reviewed. In earlier chapters you have realized, that encoded in every neuron, containing the events of the First Fear and Euphoric Cycles was the entire fetal experience itself. In other words, besides the kicking, punching and fighting to save its mother's life, also encoded is the Memory Block that caused the fetus to misinterpret the events in the womb, in the first place. Therefore, when the nightly review allows the neurons, encoded with the First Fear and Euphoric Cycles to fire fully or uninhibited, the Memory Block contained within them fires as well. This, of course, is why individuals have a difficulty remembering the exact contents of their dreams. Indeed, while sleepers dream every night, many people do not even know they have had a dream. This is because, laced into every nightly review of the two cycles of development, and therefore in every dream produced during REM sleep, is the Memory Block itself, causing the same block in short-term memory for the sleeper as it did for the fetus in the womb. Sometimes, of course, the trauma during the review is so intense that the Memory Block encoded fails to erase part of the review and resultant dream, thus producing the recall of a dream. In most cases, this occurs during nightmares.

While the Memory Block often fails when the individuals recalls a dream, it rarely fails if an individual is awoken during deep or slow wave sleep. For example, if there is a knock at the door, or if a book falls in the room where the individual is sleeping, even if the alarm clock goes off in the room and the sleeper is in the stage of slow wave sleep, it is unlikely they will remember this review. This, of course, is because during the review in slow wave sleep, the neurons encoded with the Memory Block are fully firing or firing uninhibited, then during REM sleep they fire less fully or inhibited. So essentially, during slow wave sleep the Memory Block is at its purest form; then during REM sleep a more diluted influence is realized, as the images from life in the womb mix with the images of the individual's daily life.

The experience upon awakening from a dream is, of course, as close as the child or adult sleeper will ever get to realize exactly how the Memory Block worked for the fetus in the womb. Often upon awakening, the individual will remember the content of a dream. This recall usually does not last too long. After a few minutes, the individual often struggles to remember specific details of the dream. Indeed, it takes deep concentration, often, to pinpoint the exact events. The reason that so much concentration is necessary and that often a complete specific recall cannot be achieved, is of course because the individual is fighting the Memory Block. For every detail they are trying to recall, the Memory Block is working equally hard to block that memory and the specific details of it. It is important to realize, however, that the Memory Block in the womb for the fetus was much stronger even than this. As you have already seen in previous chapters, the Memory Block was engrained into the neural pattern of the fetus. While the fetus experienced the events in each of the two cycles of intrauterine development, once in the next cycle, they quickly forgot about the existence of the other cycle. This, of course, is exactly what Nature wanted to occur. This ensured that the fetus would respond to not only the changes between cycles, however, also to the developmental aspects of each one. Understanding this, it becomes easier to realize just how simple it was for the fetus to misinterpret and misread the cues during the First Fear Cycle of Development, thus, believing that its mother, and therefore it itself, was in the process of dying.

Placement of Sleep Periods

The final mechanism that Nature utilizes to make sure the individual returns to sleep the next night is the arrangement of sleep periods. Typically, there are between four and six major sleep periods, the sleeper experiences every night. For simplicity, we will view these periods as two halves, one is the first period and the other is the second period. The first period occurs to the sleeper during the first half of the night, with the second period occurring during the second half of the night. A sleep period is a phase or cycle of sleep. In other words, it is a complete unit. This unit includes a phase of slow wave sleep and of REM sleep.

What Nature has accomplished here, in regards to ensuring the individual will return to sleep the next night is the arrangement of these periods. During the first half of the night or first period, the sleeper will review the most traumatic aspects of the First Fear Cycle of Development while in slow wave sleep. Then, during the second half or second period, the sleeper will review the less traumatic aspects of life in the womb including the Euphoric Cycle of Development while in slow wave sleep. Now, there are many variations of this, including the fact that during both periods of slow wave sleep, each intrauterine cycle of development is reviewed. However, the primary focus of the review during the first period is the First Fear Cycle and the primary focus of the review during the second period is the Euphoric Cycle.

By placing these two periods in this manner the individual realizes the longest amount of time between the traumatic review of the First Fear Cycle during slow wave sleep and going to sleep the next night. In other words, this traumatic review not only has a long time to filter into the subconscious, but also is followed by a more positive review of the Euphoric Cycle. This, theoretically, will lead the sleeper to a positive perception of sleep. This will encourage the individual to return to sleep the next night; completely oblivious to the trauma they will review during their first period of slow wave sleep.

This makes complete sense of course, as Nature painstakingly hides the trauma to be realized behind the more positive review of the Euphoric Cycle. What will then occur, again theoretically, is that during the first half or first period, the sleeper, during REM sleep, will experience nightmares. Then, during the second half or second period, the sleeper, during REM sleep, will experience good dreams. In most cases though, dreams in both periods of REM sleep will have somewhat mixed content, as the dreams recalled will have influence from both cycles of intrauterine development.

First Sleep Period must be Completed

It is important to realize that the first period review must be completed. What this means is, if for any reason the first period of sleep, which is heavily influenced by the First Fear Cycle of

Development, is interrupted, that the review will be continued before the second, more pleasurable, period of sleep can occur. This is very important; for Nature wants to make sure that the sleeper reviews the important developmental aspects of the First Fear Cycle, every night, even if this occurs at the expense of the second sleep period, which is heavily influenced by the Euphoric Cycle. For example, should the sleeper be awoken, by a noise or other event in their immediate environment during this important first sleep period, and then the sleeper returns to sleep, they will continue with the important First Fear Cycle review, before the second sleep period review begins.

This phenomenon can be easily understood by anybody who has awoken from a nightmare; then stayed awake for a few minutes, only to return to sleep and continue that same nightmare. What is happening here, of course, is that the First Fear Cycle of Development was being reviewed during slow wave sleep; then the neural mechanisms interpreted that the sleeper was reviewing too much trauma and was in danger. Next, to rescue the sleeper REM sleep kicked in and the mixing of the images from the First Fear Cycle and the images from the individual's daily life combined to create a nightmare. This nightmare was so traumatic that all mechanisms to keep the individual asleep failed, causing the sleeper to awaken. When the individual went back to sleep, they continued, essentially where they left off in the review of the First Fear Cycle. This shows, in a practical example, how no matter what interruption occurs, Nature wants the sleeper to completely finish this important review of the first sleep period heavily influenced by the First Fear Cycle of Development, even though this is a much more negative period of sleep. This is because, while the first sleep period is heavily influenced by the horrific events the fetus experienced in the womb during the First Fear Cycle, it is also heavily influenced with essential developmental aspects that are extremely important to be reviewed on a nightly basis.

For some individuals the inability to fully complete this vital first sleep period is a serious problem. As you will see in a later chapter, this is a common problem for individuals with the condition of First Fear Not Relieved. To these individuals sleep does little more than compound the influence they realize from the First Fear Cycle of Development. Because they have so many neurons remaining, encoded with the events of the First Fear Cycle of Development, too much trauma to be reviewed during slow wave sleep remains and REM sleep is continually pulling them out of this important review, before they can complete it. In their case, they simply spend the entire night trying to finish the vital first period of sleep. This leads to a negative association with sleep and often the condition of insomnia.

Why Nature Wants us to Return to Sleep

Throughout this chapter, you have seen some of the methods Nature utilizes to ensure that the individual has a pleasurable perception of sleep and that they return to this state on a nightly basis. You have realized that REM sleep diverts the trauma reviewed during slow wave sleep and mixes it into dreams that include the images of the sleeper's daily life, forever leaving the individual guessing and continually lost to the actual trauma they review on a nightly basis. You have seen, how the uninhibited review of the neurons, encoded with the First Fear and Euphoric Cycles of Development, are heavily influenced by the review of the Memory Block encoded in them as well, and how this makes specific recall of most dreams difficult. You have also seen how Nature arranges the sleep periods, having the most traumatic review first, then a review heavily influenced by the neurons encoded with the more pleasurable Euphoric Cycle during the second sleep period. This leaves the longest time possible between the negative aspects of sleep and the time that the individual will return to sleep. This, in addition to encapsulating the negative aspects of sleep behind a pleasurable period, in most cases, leaves the individual with a positive association of this vital function. With all these mechanisms in place, one thing becomes very obvious and that is, of course, that Nature wants the individual to sleep on a nightly basis.

Indeed, to Nature it is essential that every single night, the individual will get some sleep. It is the only way to make sure that we, as a species, stay, at least partially, focused on a primary purpose of our life, which is of course to reproduce. Besides survival, reproduction is our only obligation to Nature. And with six billion as the proof, it appears that the human species is fulfilling this obligation quite effectively. This all is a testament to the effectiveness of Nature's sleep model.

Here, we will look more closely at how the entire process of sleep in regards to reproduction works. We will first look at the male model and then at the more complex model of sleep for female reproduction. In the previous chapter, you looked at a summary of the male's sleep model in regards to reproduction. During the first period of sleep, the male reviews images of his intrauterine experience during slow wave sleep. This review is heavily influenced by images of the First Fear Cycle, these images include fighting for his mother's life and therefore his own. Indeed, the first period of sleep is heavily influenced by the theme and connection of the dying female, and therefore of himself. Later in the night, during the second sleep period, images of the Euphoric Cycle will be reviewed during slow wave sleep. All these images will be diverted to REM sleep for assimilation and mixing into images from the male sleeper's daily life. From this, dreams will form; however, most will not be remembered. Developing out of these dreams is a resolution from the images of the review of these two intrauterine developmental cycles. This resolution is experienced during the final REM sleep stage in some form of the male experiencing the Euphoric Cycle with the female, an image of his daily life, which is now a substitute for his mother. It is important to realize that the male's dream does not necessary have to be directly related to intercourse. Even an association with a female as a symbol of no death and decay will serve the same purpose. It is only essential that this resolution, and therefore this dream, develops images of a female, healthy and in some way mimicking the Euphoric Cycle. The female could simply be active or even showing some form of interest in the male. In the most obvious scenario, the male will be close to the female within the dream. Again, most of these dreams will not be remembered. When the male wakes up, often with an erection, the images of his dream will subordinate and further reinforce the influence of the neurons encoded with the intrauterine developmental events in his subconscious and form a motivation that will, upon seeing a female, rise to his conscious thoughts and generate behaviors with the ultimate goal of intercourse.

While this is how the model works, still some questions remain. For example, what would happen if the male missed this important second period of sleep? Would the sleep model still work, if the male only got three hours of sleep instead of his normal seven? What if he went to bed at 3 a.m. instead of his normal bedtime of 9 p.m.? The question of course is; would these variations in the model reduce the effectiveness of his motivation and desire to associate with the female and ultimately undertake intercourse? The answer is no.

Even if the male only gets three hours of sleep, no matter how late it is, the first sleep period will be at least partially reviewed. During this period of sleep, he will realize the important review of the First Fear Cycle of Development, even if he misses the more positive second period of sleep, it makes little difference. There are two major reasons for this.

The first reason is that even though the first sleep period is heavily influenced by the review of the First Fear Cycle of Development during slow wave sleep, aspects of the Euphoric Cycle of Development are also included. Therefore, this resolution and motivation, which develops during REM sleep, can essentially occur during any REM stage of any sleep period.

The second reason is much more important. As long as the male reviews the important negative aspects of the First Fear Cycle, that his mother and he himself are in the process of dying, then he will connect the health and survival of his mother and therefore the substitute female with the health of himself. This will, during his waking state, resolve itself within his subconscious. Indeed, while it is effective to mix images during REM sleep in the second sleep period, when the influence is heavily focused on the Euphoric Cycle and images of females from his daily life, what is even more effective is that he sees the female in person and makes this connection subconsciously. This is because the images in REM sleep from his daily life are only reproductions of the actual association with the female. In many ways, the second sleep period and REM sleep, for the purpose of reproduction, are not necessary at all. This is because, again, the resolution and motivation will be realized immediately, in his subconscious, when he associates with the female in his daily life. Indeed, the male who misses the second sleep period will even be more motivated to associate with the female and ultimately reproduce, than those who obtain the second sleep period.

To understand why the absence of the second sleep period will increase the male's motivation for association with the female and reproduction; it is first necessary to reexamine the neural patterns involved in sleep. The neural pattern involved in the first period of sleep is heavily influenced by the neurons encoded with the First Fear Cycle of Development. After this review is completed a second sleep period begins, which is heavily influenced by the neurons encoded with the Euphoric Cycle of Development. Now, if the individual were to skip, or were not be able to obtain the second sleep period, what happens is that this neural pattern, heavily influenced by the Euphoric Cycle, occurs anyways. In other words, if the sleeper misses the second period of sleep, the neurons encoded with the positive Euphoric Cycle will dominate his subconscious upon awakening. It continues, in many ways, just as if he was asleep, realizing his second sleep period. This is because, asleep or awake, the neural pattern of neurons encoded with the Euphoric Cycle will always follow the review of the neurons encoded with the First Fear Cycle. It is as if Nature, in this case does not differentiate between patterns of awake and asleep states. It matters little whether this neural pattern occurs during slow wave sleep when the neurons encoded with these events fire uninhibited or whether it occurs during the individuals awakened state and they fire inhibited within their subconscious.

This awake, subconscious review of neurons encoded with the Euphoric Cycle of Development can occur, because the signaling of the completion of the review of the neurons encoded with the First Fear Cycle of Development has been completed. While this signaling of completion usually occurs at night when the review of the neurons encoded with the First Fear Cycle of Development has been completed, the process of waking up and remaining awake for a variable period of time mimics the completion of the review of the neurons encoded with the First Fear Cycle of Development as well. This is important and has dramatic consequences for the individual, as you will see in later chapters. This is because, for individuals who cannot fully complete their first period of sleep, due to excess of neurons encoded with the First Fear Cycle of Development and therefore, too much trauma to be reviewed during slow wave sleep, they will actually realize on a continual basis, a positive association with awake states, primarily in the morning and a reinforcement of the negative association with sleep itself, thus, leading to the condition of insomnia. As you will see, in the case of the individual with depression, a reduction in the amount of sleep can often trigger a manic episode, which as you will learn, is nothing more than the strong influence of the neurons encoded with the Euphoric Cycle of Development firing in their subconscious. When we get to the section of manic depression, you will see just how much more effective Nature's reproduction model is when it is interrupted, as those realizing a manic episode are often impulsive and indiscriminant about sexual relations.

The Differences in the Female Sleep Model

In many ways, the female sleep model in regards to reproduction works essentially the same way as the male. The major difference is that she realizes a diluted version of the review of the First Fear Cycle of Development. This, of course, is because for the female her intrauterine experience was much less violent and intense than for the male.

With the female, Nature's major focus is on the review of the death and decay the female fetus realized during the First Fear Cycle of Development. Over and over again, night after night, during her first period of slow wave sleep, the female is confronted by the images of the death and decay, the olfactory development of foul and pungent odors and their negative association to the horrific events of the First Fear Cycle.

In the female's second period of sleep, the same review continues however, with more influence from the neurons encoded with the Euphoric Cycle of Development. This review includes the more pleasant smells, the more pleasant moving intrauterine environment that occurred during this cycle. Ultimately, in the REM sleep period, during her second period of sleep, resolutions will be developed.

When these images mix with images of the male from her daily life, she will be further motivated to associate with him in order to believe that she has no death and decay inside of her, however, instead only positive associations from the Euphoric Cycle.

It is important to realize that Nature's obligation to utilize the female's sleep model for reproduction is limited. There are many reasons for this. The first is; it can be limited. In other words, with the burden of initiating association and reproduction falling on the male, the sleep model in regards to reproduction must be more complete for him. The female, on the other hand, does not need an extensive resolution that will motivate her to seek out and be the aggressor in reproduction. This is the male's job. All that is necessary for Nature to accomplish within the female sleep model is that she realizes a review of the First Fear Cycle of Development that will yield a reduction in the female's self-belief and self-esteem that will, ultimately, lead her to the male.

Another reason that Nature cannot use the female sleep model too extensively for the purposes of motivation for reproduction is that an essential aspect is missing from the neurons encoded with both cycles of intrauterine development. This important aspect is the male. As you have already realized; with the female, Nature uses factors outside the womb to guide reproduction. The important role of the male, as reducing the young girl's fear that the death and decay is inside of her, is not encoded in these neurons reviewed during slow wave sleep. In fact, with the exceptions of these fetal neurons that were reprogrammed after birth, there is no male presence within the neurons encoded with the female intrauterine experience at all. Without this vital component, the overall effectiveness of sleep with regards to the generation of motivation for a female is severely limited. In other words, because the male came from the female it was easy to have him gain a resolution and therefore, motivation from the neurons encoded with intrauterine development. Because the female came from the female these neurons encoded with her intrauterine development lack the essential male component, and therefore, their usage is limited for the purpose of motivation that would lead to reproduction.

Due to the differences in the intrauterine environment between male and female, the nightly review of this experience for the female during slow wave sleep is not as traumatic as well. This affects many aspects of the female's relation to sleep. One way in which this sleep model between genders differs is the neural mechanisms, which conceal the purpose of sleep itself. With the male the trauma reviewed is much more severe; therefore, the neural mechanisms that define REM sleep fail quite frequently. This is especially true for the REM sleep periods that follow the review of slow wave sleep which focus on the First Fear Cycle of Development. This is not the case for the female. Therefore, the intensity of her dream recall, especially nightmare recall, will be less than for the male. In most cases, she will be more likely to successfully complete her review of her first period of sleep and begin her second sleep period uninterrupted on a nightly basis. This, theoretically, is how Nature intended the sleep model to work. In many cases, for reasons that will be discussed later, variations in these intentions occur. In general, the female will realize a more pleasurable sleep experience with a larger influence from the Euphoric Cycle than from the First Fear Cycle as the male experiences.

While in most cases the female sleeper realizes during her two sleep periods a larger influence of the Euphoric Cycle, there are exceptions to this. Just preceding her monthly menstrual cycle is one such exception. During this period, the amount of protective female hormones that not only diluted the intensity of the First Fear Cycle in the womb, however, also dilute the influence of these neurons in her subconscious, are substantially reduced. Another time when these protective hormones are diminished is during and after menopause. In both these cases, the reduction of these protective hormones intensify the review of the First Fear Cycle and reduce the influence of the review of the Euphoric Cycle during both sleep periods. This will lead to a breakdown of REM sleep mechanisms that prevent the recall of dreams. When this occurs, the positive association of sleep, the female once realized quickly diminishes and sleep quality is commonly affected.

Dream Recall during Pregnancy

As you have seen, both the male and female sleepers can recall a very low percentage of their dreams. Again, this is especially true for the female. The reasons for this include the diluted trauma experienced in the First Fear Cycle of Development that is encoded into the neurons the female reviews during her first period of slow wave sleep. This allows the neural process that masks the purpose of sleep to work exceptionally well for the female sleeper. Part of this process is to mask the content of most dreams, making dream recall difficult. Therefore, in most cases the female sleeper has very little idea of the developmental aspects she reviews during this important first period of slow wave sleep and the resultant dreams that are generated during this first REM sleep period. One of the exceptions to this is during pregnancy; it is especially true during the late stages.

In most cases, due to the reduced trauma reviewed during slow wave sleep the female is easily able to complete her first period of sleep, therefore, allowing the more pleasurable second sleep period to begin. Pregnancy often interrupts the full completion of the first period of sleep, especially, during late stages when fetal movement is more obvious. Earlier, you realized that the first period of sleep must be fully completed before the second sleep period can begin. In the late stages of pregnancy the completion of the first sleep period is often not obtained. This yields a nightly sleep experience for the pregnant female that has a stronger influence of the First Fear Cycle of Development. Because of the fetal micro movements the mother is unable to fully finish this review; therefore, she is constantly resuming the review of the neurons encoded with the First Fear Cycle of Development. When this occurs, the neural mechanisms that conceal the content of dreams, generated during the REM sleep stage, often fail and dream recall is realized.

A sample of this dream recall by the pregnant female can provide a "window" into the review she realizes during the first period of slow wave sleep on a nightly basis, however, in most cases she has no recall of the dreams, which are generated in the resultant REM sleep stage. As you have realized, the major theme during this sleep period that Nature wants the female to review during slow wave sleep is the death and decay, realized as a fetus, of the First Fear Cycle of Development. This, as you have already seen, is for the purpose of reduction of self-belief and self-esteem, which is intended to indirectly lead her to the male for confirmation. Therefore, when these images generated during slow wave sleep mix with images of her daily life, dreams are generated during REM sleep.

An example of a dream, or in this case a nightmare, that a pregnant female might recall, would be the mixing of the images from the review of neurons encoded with the First Fear Cycle and those images with her daily life, that by the late stages of pregnancy would most certainly be consumed with the anticipated arrival of her newborn infant. The mixing of images could generate nightmares during REM sleep with varied content. For example, the pregnant female may dream that she has her child and there is something wrong with it. She may dream that her child is an animal, maybe even an alien. What has happened here, is that the review of neurons encoded with the First Fear Cycle that reduce her self-belief translate into images; and therefore, dreams of not being able to properly give birth, or that something inside her is not normal. This, of course, is exactly what Nature wants her to believe, through the nightly review of the death and decay during slow wave sleep that the female believes this is inside of her. Nature does not necessarily want the female to believe that there is something wrong with the fetus, it is just that the soon to arrive infant is simply the image that the death and decay connected to, as this is what currently would be consuming the images of the pregnant female's daily life.

This enhanced dream recall serves another purpose as well. Because the pregnant female has temporarily lost her monthly menstrual cycle, the recall of dreams focusing on the death and decay Nature wants the female to believe is inside of her, will further reduce the female's self-esteem and lead her to the male.

Dreams

Now, we will enter into one of the most misinterpreted aspects of human behavior, the dream. As you will see, this misinterpretation is exactly what Nature wants to occur. The attempts, historically, to interpret dreams is nothing more than a testament to Nature's effectiveness at concealing the true purpose of sleep from her species.

While dreams are occurring all throughout the REM sleep stage, few are remembered upon awakening. As you have seen, when dream recall does not occur upon awakening, all the neural mechanisms to conceal the true purpose of sleep have worked effectively. On the other hand, when a dream upon awakening is remembered or in the case of a nightmare, the dream itself wakes the sleeper up, a failure within the neural mechanisms that conceal the purpose of sleep have failed. The primary reasons for these failures are that the review of neurons encoded with the First Fear Cycle of Development, during slow wave sleep, are too traumatic for the neural mechanisms, which contain them to handle. This failure is realized in many ways. One of which is the abrupt initiation of REM sleep. When this occurs a nightmare is generated during the REM sleep stage that often awakens the sleeper.

There are many reasons why the review of neurons encoded with the First Fear Cycle, during slow wave sleep, can be too traumatic for the neural mechanisms to contain them. The most obvious reason, which will be explained in detail in a later chapter, is for those individuals who realize the condition of First Fear Not Relieved. In their case, there are just too many neurons encoded with the First Fear Cycle of Development remaining and therefore, a complete review, on a nightly basis, during the first period of sleep, cannot be accomplished. Another reason that this review can be too traumatic is for reasons that you have already seen. For females this is, during and after menopause, during pregnancy, and just preceding the onset of their monthly menstrual cycle. Another reason that can lead to this is that an individual, who misses a night sleep on the previous night, may realize an intensified and traumatic review during the following night of sleep. This is because, a rebound effect occurs concerning the intensity of the review of the First Fear Cycle of Development, during slow wave sleep. In other words, if an individual misses a night of sleep; the intensity of the next night's review will be stronger and therefore, more traumatic.

Fever, the sleep experienced during this process can be too traumatic, and therefore cause the neural mechanisms that conceal the purpose of sleep to fail, allowing recall, upon awakening, of dreams or nightmares the sleeper experienced during REM sleep. How fever affects this process; will be explained in the appendix under "Neural Notes." For whatever reason these mechanisms fail, it is important to realize that when a dream and, in most cases, a nightmare are remembered, it is due to this failure.

Contents of Dreams

While the misinterpretation of dream content is a testament to the effectiveness of Nature's sleep model, there is still value in examining that content in respect to the two cycles of intrauterine development the fetus realizes. In many ways, this content when understood properly provides a clear perspective on the events the dreamer or the sleeper realized as a fetus in the womb. Therefore, we will look at a few dreams and their content in relation to the two cycles of intrauterine development. Most of these dreams will be in the form of nightmares, as they express effectively the First Fear Cycle of Development. Most of these nightmares will be recalled upon awakening during childhood and adolescence, as these time periods are closer to the actual events experienced in the womb. Much of this content will be recalled upon awakening from a fever-induced sleep. The term "fever dream" will apply too much of this recall. During a "fever dream" or more accurately a fever nightmare, the dream content is often very specific in regards to the First Fear Cycle of Development.

Before we begin to look at specific dream recall and its content it is important to remember how a dream is formed. During slow wave sleep the sleeper experiences a review of the neurons encoded with the two cycles of intrauterine development. The uninhibited firing of the neurons, encoded with the First Fear and Euphoric Cycles of Development, generates this review. During REM sleep the images of the two cycles of intrauterine development are mixed with images from the individual's daily life. From this mixing dreams and nightmares are created.

It is important here, to define the images of the individual's daily life. These images that are mixed with images of the two cycles of intrauterine development, during REM sleep to create dreams, are not exclusively from the individual's daily life. Indeed, they can be from any aspect or time frame throughout their life, with exception of life in the womb. In other words, these images can be all those the individual experienced throughout their life. In most cases, however, these images will be from the individual's recent memory. It is only important to define these images as not belonging to their subconscious, however, to their conscious realm of thought only. In some cases, the individual may have experienced these images during that previous day, or week, month or even years, before they enter into the REM sleep stage.

The following is a partial list of recalled dreams and their content in relation to the two cycles of intrauterine development. Again, the primary focus will be on the themes of this content and their relation to the First Fear Cycle of Development and the resultant nightmares generated.

Dreams of Falling

Dreams of falling can include falling; slipping, sliding, unable to gain a balance, fear of falling, weightlessness, tunnels, anything underground or underwater, and other variables and deviations from this theme. This of course, is nothing more than the neurons encoded with the First Fear Cycle of Development, specific through the process of birth itself. When the fetus, finally, decided it must leave the womb, the experience of labor itself through the birth canal was traumatic. As its mother's intrauterine water breaks, the fetus begins a process of sliding, if only for seconds, uncontrolled through the birth canal. This is important for the fetus, because for the first time it feels that the situation is truly out of its control

Dreams of "No Effect"

These dreams have been explained earlier in this chapter, in the nightmare example of a ten-year-old boy and his friend Tommy. Briefly, the images reviewed by the sleeper are of the fetus, during the

First Fear Cycle. The fetus tried to initiate a response from its dying mother are ineffective or have "no effect." These images reviewed during slow wave sleep, then, mix with images from the individual's daily life during REM sleep to create a nightmare where the individual is punching and kicking an opponent, however, there is no effect or little effect to attacking the opponent. Often the punches and kicks are in slow motion, during the process of the nightmare. This was due to the incomplete myelination between the fetal brain and the muscles involved in the punching and kicking.

Dreams of Being Pursued

Dreams of being pursued include dreams of being chased, attacked, followed, running for one's life, and other variations of this theme. Often, these nightmares are of homicidal intent. Usually, the sleeper is being chased by someone who is trying to kill them. In many cases, the sleeper cannot figure out what it did that caused this event to occur. While the attacker may have a face, more commonly they are faceless and ambiguous in identity. This is nothing more that the fetal experience, attempting to understand during the First Fear Cycle of Development, what is trying to kill its mother and therefore itself. The fetus cannot figure out what it did wrong to cause this attack. Of course, it is a question with no resolution. The fetus did nothing wrong, the intrauterine environment simply changed as its mother was lying down to go to sleep. It changed from the positive Euphoric Cycle to the horrific First Fear Cycle. Occasionally, the attacker in these dreams will begin as a helpful or friendly person, then, within seconds, the person may turn around, suddenly threaten to attack and begin chasing the individual. In this case, a representation of how quick the environment changed for the fetus in the womb can be realized. At one moment the womb was a pleasurable experience, as represented by the friendly person, then, the very next it was a place where the fetus must fight for its mother's and therefore its own life.

Dreams of the Death and Decay

These dreams include content related to unpleasant sensory experience. This unpleasant sensory experience can have a wide range of interpretation. It can be anything from slimy snakes to worms. It can include, for the female, giving birth to foreign objects. It can include, in the most extreme cases, the realization of poisonous gases. This dream content is all related to the fetal experience during the First Fear Cycle of Development. As you have already seen, Nature utilized this cycle to code the fetal olfactory neurons with pungent and foul odors. This connection was made between this sensory experience and the fetus fighting for its life. The slimy snakes and worms represent the fetal experience of feeling around the womb with its fingers and hands.

Sleep Disorders

You have seen how Nature's sleep model works in regards to the review of the two cycles of intrauterine development, and the resultant reproductive behavior it generates. In Chapter ten on "First Fear Not Relieved – The Disorders," you will realize what occurs to individuals, who cannot successfully complete Nature's sleep model.

CHAPTER NINE

FIRST FEAR NOT RELIEVED
– THE INDIVIDUAL

In the next two chapters, you will begin to realize what the repercussions are, when, for whatever reason, the minimum requirements established by Nature for development of the human species are not achieved. As you will see, these repercussions vary from subtle to extreme. In both degrees of severity, however, the consequences of the condition of First Fear Not Relieved are life long. In this chapter, we will focus on the individual with the condition of First Fear Not Relieved. In the next chapter, we will expand the scope to include the majority of the major behavioral disorders realized by the human species. As you will see in both chapters, the symptoms of the disorders for the individual originate from the same place.

Before we begin this look into the life of an individual who realizes the condition of First Fear Not Relieved, there are a few aspects that need clarification. The first is that it is not an exact line that separates the individual without First Fear Not Relieved from those who will realize this condition. In other words, an infant does not experience a certain given number of environmental factors that fail and then cross an invisible threshold only to realize a lifetime of repercussions from the condition of First Fear Not Relieved. Then, those infants who do not cross that threshold spend their life completely unaffected. This is not how it works after all. Just as there are varying degrees of environmental failures during infancy, there will be varying degrees of severity of this condition. While this is obvious, it is important to remember, nevertheless. For example; some individuals will realize one or more behaviors described in this chapter, yet will not technically suffer from the condition of First Fear Not Relieved. For simplicity, however, it is necessary to look at two contrasting conditions. The first is of individuals that express essentially normal behavior and do not have the condition of First Fear Not Relieved. The other is of individuals that express somewhat abnormal behaviors and have the condition of First Fear Not Relieved.

The second aspect, which is important to clarify, is that this is a textbook case. In other words, the individual and individuals explained in this chapter will have all the symptoms of First Fear Not Relieved. This is done, again, for simplicity. It is unlikely that a single individual, whether male or female, would express each and every symptom and behavior of this condition. Indeed, what we are looking at here, are a series of very extreme cases. What determines which specific behavior an individual with the condition of First Fear Not Relieved will express, depends on a number of variables. These variables include the specific intrauterine environment of the fetus, the genetic make up of the father, mother and therefore the fetus, the specific environmental factors that fail during infancy and other variables. What we are interested in here, are the behaviors and repercussions of the condition of First Fear Not Relieved and their expression from the intrauterine experience and their causation during infancy and childhood. Throughout most of this chapter, we will look at the male as an example. This is done for several reasons. The major reason is that when deviations from Nature's intended purpose for the human species occur, the male is most affected. This is because the First Fear Cycle of Development was stronger for the male than the female. Therefore, when deviations in environmental factors occur after birth, the male is more severely affected. Therefore, the behaviors demonstrated by the male will often be more obvious and easier to detect. This does not mean that these behaviors do not pertain to the female. In fact, most of them can be equally obvious when demonstrated by the female with First Fear Not Relieved as well. Specifically, in chapter seven on "Boys and Girls," we already have looked at a female who expressed the condition of First Fear Not Relieved. The environmental factor in that female's case- was that she lacked a father or supportive male role model. In that chapter, the focus was on the condition and how it related to her relations with the male gender.

Finally, it is a good idea to briefly restate the circumstances, environmental factors and ultimate expression of the condition First Fear Not Relieved that was covered in chapter five. First Fear Not Relieved is a condition realized by the individual when certain environmental factors during infancy and early childhood have not been met. The results of these environmental failures have substantial neurobiological and, ultimately, behavioral repercussions on the individual. Included in these neurobiological repercussions are implications on the individual's immune system. The ultimate result of this environmental failure is that the neurons encoded with the First Fear and Euphoric Cycles of Development do not realize a substantial reduction from elimination and reprogramming during infancy and early childhood. This results in a large amount of neurons encoded within these two cycles of intrauterine development becoming reinforced, and therefore, remaining in the regions of the brain that form the individual's subconscious. This, ultimately, results in a stronger influence from these intrauterine events on the individual's behavior throughout their life.

Infancy

While we have already briefly discussed the effects of First Fear Not Relieved during infancy in Chapter five, we will reexamine critical differences between the infant with this condition and the normal infant. The male infant with First Fear Not Relieved will have an especially difficult time during infancy. With too may neurons encoded with the First Fear Cycle of Development remaining the infant's immune system will be severely suppressed. As you remember, encoded in each neuron containing the First Fear Cycle of Development, is the resultant Memory Block that was an integral aspect of the fetal neural pattern during this intrauterine cycle. As you also remember, the Memory Block has a direct relationship to the individual's immune system; this relationship begins in infancy. This relationship is that, the more Memory Block remaining the more suppression the immune system will realize. Therefore, with a large amount of neurons encoded with the First Fear Cycle of Development remaining, the infant will realize an increased amount of suppression on its immune system. Again, for the male infant this suppression is especially severe.

Due to his suppressed immune system, the male infant with First Fear Not Relieved will be sick more often and for longer periods of time than its normal counterpart. The infections he realizes will be more severe, often resulting in a higher fever than the normal infant will realize. In advanced societies, where medical care is easily accessible, this will translate into more visits to the doctor's office, more antibiotics and more medical care required in general. The areas that will be especially affected will be those utilized most significantly during the First Fear Cycle of Development. These areas will include the ears, nose, throat, and lungs of the infant. It is important to remember that in underdeveloped regions where medical care is not readily available, he will likely not survive.

Over a period of time, or maybe immediately, the infant's immune system, to fight this suppression, will up-regulate itself and become hypersensitive. This will result in a myriad of allergies that the infant will suffer from. This may begin very early, such as an allergy to milk. The infant when he begins eating solid foods may become allergic to certain ingredients. His skin may become allergic to certain lotions or crèmes that the normal infant would tolerate without a response. Even the air he breathes contains dust mites and pollens that will affect little a normal infant; however, with his hypersensitive immune system they will generate a response.

The Memory Block itself will cause additional problems. Because its initial purpose was to block short-term memory for the fetus in the womb, it continues to serve that purpose during infancy. Because the male infant with First Fear Not Relieved has so many neurons encoded with the First Fear Cycle of Development remaining, he also has a larger amount of Memory Block remaining, which is encoded into each of those neurons. While the major effects of this will not be visible until childhood, early signs can already be seen during infancy. The focus of the effects of this increased Memory Block during infancy will be in his relation to his mother. Because he forgets quicker than the normal infant that he has just seen her and that she and therefore he himself is not in the process of dying, he will need to see her more often. This will result in a higher demand of his mother's time, and increased care for the infant will be necessary. This, of course, assumes that his mother is available and that her lack of presence is not the environmental factor that causes the condition of First Fear Not Relieved. The male infant with this condition will often be slow to reach milestones of development, such as organized speech, walking and bathroom training, as most of these activities require some form of short-term memory, the exact neural aspect that is blocked stronger for him.

While the male infant with First Fear Not Relieved will be more severely affected than the female with this condition, she will show early signs as well. Indeed, she will realize more illness, more medical attention required and a longer recuperation period than the normal female infant. While the female infant with the condition of First Fear Not Relieved will be slower to achieve developmental milestones than her normal female counterpart, compared to the normal male infant, it will hardly be noticeable. This is because, in all aspects of infant development, the female, because she did not experience as much trauma during her development in the womb, will always, in this early stage, reach these milestones quicker.

Childhood

Childhood is the turning point, the essential departure between those with First Fear Not Relieved and those without this condition. This is especially true for the male child. If there were slight noticeable differences between the male infant with First Fear Not Relieved and the normal male infant, now in childhood, the differences become obvious. Indeed, for the parents of this male child, they, for the first time, may be confronted with the fact that something with their son is unusual. While many of the behaviors due to the condition of First Fear Not Relieved could be masked or ignored or not recognized due to inexperienced parenting, in childhood, his behaviors and symptoms are often too obvious to ignore. This will, especially, be true when he begins the organized repertoire of school.

In school, the teacher will have a hard time dealing with the boy, who has the condition of First Fear Not Relieved, for many reasons. The first is that he cannot sit still. While, as you have seen, most boys will have a more difficult time sitting still than the girls will. You have seen that the reason for this is that the neurons encoded with the First Fear Cycle of Development are encoded with movement. During the late night hours, deep into the First Fear Cycle, the fetus was kicking and punching and moving in an attempt to save what it believed was its dying mother, who was only sleeping. For the boy, these neurons that are dominating his subconscious are sending continual messages to his brain that signal his body to move. While the young girl can easily suppress this movement, because the intensity of her First Fear Cycle, experienced as a fetus, was less than the young boy's was. For the boy with the condition of First Fear Not Relieved, this movement, this subconscious influence of activity that dominates every thought, is extreme. He simply cannot sit still. Indeed, the teacher cannot take her eye of him for a minute, before he is out of his chair and across the room. It is almost impossible for the teacher to instruct a class with this wide variation of activity levels between pupils. On one hand, the teacher has the young girl who sits still, and does not have the condition of First Fear Not Relieved. On the other hand of the spectrum, the teacher has the boy who realizes the condition of First Fear Not Relieved. In extreme contrast to the quiet, still young girl, he acts like he is powered by rocket fuel. So, what you have neurobiologically is; two distinct neural make-ups. For the normal young girl, you have a strong influence in her subconscious from the neurons encoded with the movement of the First Fear Cycle, although the neurons themselves are not encoded with as much movement as for the normal young boys. Then on the opposite end of the spectrum, you have the young boy with the condition First Fear Not Relieved. His remaining neurons are not only encoded with more movement, because he is a male, however, he also has many more neurons remaining than the normal young girl, because they were not eliminated or reprogrammed during the critical period of infancy and early childhood. To put the two together in the same classroom will simply not work.

The inability of the young boy with First Fear Not Relieved to sit still is just the beginning of his problems, however. For not only are those neurons of the First Fear Cycle of Development encoded with movement, however, with the Memory Block as well. The Memory Block was an integral part of the fetal neural pattern during both developmental cycles. Because the boy has so many of the neurons encoded with the First Fear Cycle of Development remaining, he also has a stronger influence from the Memory Block than the normal boy without this condition. As you remember, the primary purpose of the Memory Block is to block short-term memory. While it worked perfectly in the fetal environment, in the classroom environment it becomes a definite hindrance to the young boy. No matter what he is told, he forgets the information as quickly as he hears it. Concentration is almost impossible, as the Memory Block influences every thought and confuses his recall. The boy's teacher may think he is not paying attention or worse not trying. This is not the case at all. It is simply that the Memory Block is blocking his comprehension of any material the teacher presents. His attention span is very short and he is easily distracted. Now, if you add this to his inability to sit still, he becomes a problem in any classroom setting.

Unable to deal with this boy, the teacher may inform his parents that he needs professional help. Ultimately, he will be diagnosed with hyperactivity or Attention Deficit Disorder or whatever the current psychological terminology for this very old condition, which it is obvious that he has. This inability to function with the rest of the classroom is only the first step towards alienation from his peers that the boy with the condition of First Fear Not Relieved will realize.

Fortunately, in advanced societies medical help is available. Often, a child psychiatrist will prescribe medicine that can calm him down and get the boy back into the classroom setting. What is interesting about what the psychiatrist will prescribe is how it reveals the two cycles of intrauterine development. The psychiatrist will most likely prescribe an amphetamine for the boy to take. At first glance, this seems like exactly the opposite of what he needs. After all an amphetamine, in an adult, increases the activity level and this boy does not need any help increasing his activity level. When you look closer, at the chemical properties that amphetamine affect, you begin to realize why this drug will work perfectly for him. The net result of amphetamine is an increase in dopamine to the reward pathways of the young boy's brain. If you remember, the two cycles of intrauterine development and Nature's intention with each cycle, you can begin to realize why this works. During the Euphoric Cycle, it was Nature's intention to reduce or restrict the movement of the fetus so that its mother could move around, thus, reducing the amount of energy required by her in sustaining two lives in one body. To accomplish this Nature flooded the developing fetal brain with large amounts of dopamine. This reduced the desire for the fetus to move around. Now years later, as a boy with this problem and condition of First Fear Not Relieved, the doctor has essentially mimicked Nature and accomplished the same goal by administering the amphetamine to the boy. By increasing the dopamine flow to the boy's reward pathways, this signals the boy's neural pattern in his subconscious that he has, essentially, entered the Euphoric Cycle of Development and therefore, does not need to move around at the same rate he did when the First Fear Cycle of Development influenced his neural pattern.

The immune system of the boy with the condition of First Fear Not Relieved will also be affected. While it is doubtful that the suppression of his immune system from the overabundance of neurons encoded with the First Fear Cycle of Development will cause him mortal danger, as it could have during infancy, the suppression will begin to cause problems nonetheless. While he will still be sicker more often and for longer than his normal peers, allergies will often dominate his childhood. Asthma among other allergies will be very common, as his immune system up-regulates to battle this suppression from the large number of neurons encoded with the First Fear Cycle and the

Memory Block.

Overall, this young boy, or young girl will have a very difficult time in childhood. If most boys are slow to start out in life, this boy is crawling. Early signs of alienation and separation from his peers begin and foreshadow the fate that awaits him as he matures. All of this is due to failures in the environmental factors during infancy and early childhood. Of course, the young girl can realize very similar symptoms of the condition First Fear Not Relieved. In most cases, however, her symptoms will not be as severe and therefore, noticeable. This in itself has its own dangers. Indeed, the young girl with condition of First Fear Not Relieved may escape childhood, only to have her symptoms untreated and therefore, multiply by the time she reaches adolescence.

Adolescent Girls

In Chapter seven on "Boys and Girls" you have seen an example of a young girl with the condition of First Fear Not Relieved. In that case, the environmental factor that led to the condition was the absence of the father or supportive male role model. It is important to reinstate that this is not the only environmental factor for the female that can lead to this condition. In fact, any of the environmental factors listed in Chapter five on "First Fear Not Relieved" can generate similar behaviors as to those seen in the earlier example. While the example in Chapter seven focused specifically on the girl's relationship to the belief that the death and decay was inside of her, there are other behaviors that she will demonstrate not directly related to this fear.

Often, the adolescent girl with First Fear Not Relieved will have a difficult time remaining quiet. Indeed, she talks constantly. She talks in class, she talks to friends, she talks on the phone, and even talks in the middle of the sentences of others. She simply cannot stop talking.

While she may have a lot to say, this is not the primary purpose of her speech. If you remember in Chapter four on "Infancy," you realized why we, as a species, talk. You realized that in the womb, during the long hours of the night, sound was hope for the fetus. If it could hear a sound it could disbelieve, if even for a moment, that its mother and therefore itself was not in the process of dying. Through the long hours of the night, during the First Fear Cycle, the fetus would listen and listen. All this information was programmed into the neurons encoded with the First Fear Cycle of Development. A relationship was formed, sound meant life of its mother and therefore of itself; silence meant death of its mother and therefore of itself. After birth many of these neurons encoded with the First Fear Cycle are eliminated, others remain, however. These neurons form the individual's subconscious. The infant learns quickly to generate its own sound and offset the fear of its dying mother and the death of itself. Therefore, every time the individual makes sound they offset this fear that is influencing every thought they make. Talking is simply an extension of this process.

The young girl with First Fear Not Relieved has a larger amount of neurons encoded with the First Fear Cycle remaining. Therefore, to offset this stronger than normal fear she must create sounds more frequently than the normal young girl. This fear for her, that consumes her subconscious, is stronger than for her normal counterpart. Therefore, she must constantly talk to offset this fear. In her case, she is actually talking to hear herself talk, thus, reassuring her subconscious that she is not in the process of dying.

The young girl may also exhibit other behavior specific to the intrauterine developmental cycles. She may develop an oral fixation and chew gum constantly. Gum chewing is mimicry of eating. Eating is mimicry of dopamine-seeking behavior. It was Nature's intention that the fetus associated the sucking of its thumb to the obtainment of dopamine. The idea was that outside the womb, when the infant was in a situation that mimicked the First Fear Cycle in anyway that it would begin sucking to obtain dopamine, which would be released through its reward pathways. This sucking was intended for its mother's nipple. Therefore, an early association was made between obtaining dopamine and feeding or eating. Years later, with the strong influence of this development in her subconscious, the adolescent girl with First Fear Not Relieved is constantly seeking dopamine. For, even if the situations outside the womb do not mimic the First Fear Cycle, in her subconscious, the influence of this past event which influences every thought remains strong. The key area is her mouth. She may chew gum constantly. She may put a pencil in her mouth and suck or chew on the eraser during class at school. She may constantly apply lip-gloss, lipstick or lip-balm to her lips, as this all serves the same purpose, as it all mimics dopamine-seeking behavior. Of course, the lip-gloss and lipstick, serve a dual purpose, not only does it satisfy this oral fixation, however, it also alters Nature and covers up the death and decay that she, subconsciously, fears is inside of her.

For some girls, however, this dopamine-seeking behavior that was intended to encourage the infant to its mother's nipple, to seek milk and therefore, nourishment, can have no substitute. These adolescent girls will develop a problem with eating. For them, Nature's model of intrauterine development in regards to dopamine-seeking behavior that was explained in Chapter three on the "First Fear Cycle of Development" works too well. As you remember, in the womb during the First Fear Cycle, Nature essentially trained the fetus to obtain dopamine through the sucking of its thumb. After birth, this was translated into the infant sucking on its mother's nipple to gain dopamine, however, actually gained milk and therefore, nourishment instead. For the girl with the condition of First Fear Not Relieved, there are simply too many neurons remaining that are encoded with this developmental process. Therefore, when this adolescent girl is in pain she will seek dopamine the way she was taught by Nature and that is to ultimately seek nourishment through food. It is important to realize here that even if the girl with this condition is socially very outgoing, popular and well adjusted; she will still be in a tremendous amount of pain. The pain, in this case, is not caused by external factors; however, internal factors, as the neurons encoded with the First Fear Cycle are continually firing in her subconscious, influencing her every thought and motivation. In the womb as a fetus, she was taught when in pain to seek dopamine. This, later, translated into food. It is a pattern that will be with her during her entire life. When in pain, she will seek dopamine, and therefore, eat. And because, she has the condition of First Fear Not Relieved she will be, subconsciously, influenced by pain often. In many cases, the external pain from social criticism, either real or perceived of being overweight, may enhance her internal pain.

Adolescent Boys

In Chapter seven on "Boys and Girls," you learned the activities that boys become interested in, and why. Some of these activities included playing videogames, watching cartoons, playing in the dirt and their battle against Nature. For the boy with First Fear Not Relieved these activities will often become an obsession. For example, the normal boy may play videogames for an average of two hours a day. For the boy with First Fear Not Relieved, however, he must play seven hours or more a day, if possible, to get the same effect. It seems he can never get enough of watching the videogames characters die, and then reappear, which as you have seen is nothing more than the reenactment of, and the attempt to master his intrauterine experience. This intrauterine experience, of course, forms his subconscious. It is just that for him, in his brain, there are so many more neurons, encoded with the events he experienced as a fetus, remaining and therefore, exert a much stronger influence. So for him, these games are closer to the reality that is dominating his thoughts, than are the other activities the normal boy would participate in. Not only does an obsession with these games develop, but also a pattern that will dominate not only his adolescence but his life, as he matures as well.

Because the boy with First Fear Not Relieved has so many neurons encoded with the First Fear Cycle of Development remaining, he will always need more of everything to gain the same effect as the normal. This will be especially true when it comes to developmental aspects that originated in the womb. An example of this would be behavior related to reproduction. While most adolescent boys, as you have seen in Chapter seven, by this age will have interest in girls, the boy with First Fear Not Relieved will often be obsessed, not only with girls, but more specifically mimicking the Euphoric Cycle with them through the process of intercourse. In many ways, what motivates the normal adolescent boy will motivate him even further. There are exceptions to this, as you will learn in the next chapter on "The Disorders." For as you will see, this boy is a prime candidate for the early onset of mood disorders and other disorders of behavior.

While many adolescents will experiment with drugs and alcohol, for the boy with First Fear Not Relieved this experimentation will take on an added danger. To understand this, it is necessary to look at the neurochemical properties of the neurons encoded with the First Fear Cycle of Development. These neurons were programmed in the womb, in a time when high levels of dopamine were circulating around the fetal brain. Therefore, each one of these neurons has a very high demand for dopamine. Because this adolescent boy has a larger amount of neurons encoded with the First Fear Cycle of Development, his demand for dopamine is larger than for the normal boy. Therefore, throughout his life his demand for dopamine will always be higher than for the normal individual. The problem is that many recreational drugs and alcohol both, temporarily, increase the flow of dopamine to the reward pathways of the brain. So, when the boy with First Fear Not Relieved and his friends try drugs or alcohol, he will be the first to become addicted, as he will have the hardest time with the withdrawal symptoms from dopamine.

Indeed, for him, experimentations with drugs are the first of many attempts he will accomplish in order to self-medicate this imbalance. It is important to realize that not only do these neurons encoded with the First Fear Cycle of Development require a large usage of dopamine; however, they are also encoded with the physical pain the fetus realized during its development. In other words, inside each neuron encoded with the First Fear Cycle of Development is encoded the physical pain the fetus realized from living in the womb and growing at such a tremendous rate. There is muscle pain, the pain of the head and brain expanding rapidly, which results in a headache. There is the pain of being cramped in the womb. As you realized earlier, life in the womb would be intolerable, the pain level too high, without dopamine. After birth, the neurons that remain, after elimination and reprogramming, form the individual's subconscious. Now, for this boy, he has too many of these neurons remaining, therefore, the amount of nonspecific physical pain that he realizes is higher than for the normal boy. Of course, he does not know that he is in pain, because it has always been that ways and he has nothing to compare it to. However, when he takes drugs or alcohol that increases the dopamine flow, the contrast that he realizes from this increase of dopamine takes away temporarily; this nonspecific pain. Therefore, he is highly susceptible to addiction to these recreational drugs. All he is actually trying to do, however, is to realign a chemical imbalance that he has no control over whatsoever.

He also may begin smoking. While his friends might try smoking, for him addiction will become likely. This is because nicotine, like alcohol, cocaine and heroine, all, either directly or indirectly, increase the dopamine flow to the reward pathways of his brain. All of this, because Nature chose dopamine to neurochemically manipulate the behavior of the fetus and for whatever reason, during the boy's infancy and early childhood, the minimum environmental factors were not achieved in order to eliminate a large group of these developmental neurons.

Of course, drugs, alcohol and nicotine are not the only way to gain a net increase of dopamine to the boy's reward pathways. Physical exertion through sports can accomplish this task indirectly. During physical exertion large amounts of painkilling opiates are released to the same reward pathways of the brain. If the boy with First Fear Not Relieved has a positive influence, it is possible that his dopamine-seeking behavior will indirectly lead down this more positive path. Concerning his interest in sports the same rule will apply. Where the normal boy is interested in sports, he will likely be obsessed with it.

Regarding school, the boy's lagging development, due to the increased Memory Block, will begin to show more severe symptoms. By now, he has likely been diagnosed with a learning disability. Even if he has not, it is doubtful that he will have much interest in something that he does so poorly in, such as school. After all, school and book learning takes concentration and for him, with the increased Memory Block, concentration and memorization are difficult. Again, this was the initial purpose of the Memory Block, in the womb it worked perfectly, however, outside in the world, which he must face, it is a severe hindrance.

While school may hold little appeal to the boy with First Fear Not Relieved, activities that mimic the Euphoric Cycle likely will. While his friends might be into motorcycles, again, he will be obsessed with them. While his friends as they grow into late adolescence may have a fascination with cars, he will likely know everything about them. As you remember, the movement, vibration and speed of both, cars and motorcycles, directly mimic the fetal experience during the Euphoric Cycle. When its mother was walking around, the fetus was rocking, vibrating and moving in a dopamine-enriched environment. Riding a motorcycle or driving a car, especially very fast, creates a diluted effect of this cycle. When this occurs, a more positive association is realized, as the neural pattern changes and the influence of the Euphoric Cycle of Development dominates the individual's subconscious and they feel better. This, temporarily, shifts away from the negative association of the First Fear Cycle that normally dominates the subconscious of the individual with First Fear Not Relieved. With so many neurons encoded with the First Fear Cycle of Development remaining, this boy will be especially interested in shifting his neural pattern, in his subconscious, away from this cycle into the more positive Euphoric Cycle.

Pete and Irene — an Example

Because there are so many variations of individual's lives, who suffer from the condition of First Fear Not Relieved, an example is helpful to fully understand the lifelong impact this condition can exert. For during infancy, childhood and adolescence, many of the symptoms are somewhat homogeneous and standard. In other words, both infant and child with the condition will realize a suppressed immune system that will up-regulate it itself and become hypersensitive. Both infant and child will experience the effects of the increased amounts of Memoıy Block, making it difficult to concentrate and therefore learn. It is only as the individual with this condition ages and matures that the variations of the impact of First Fear Not Relieved can be realized. The choices these two individuals, in this example, will make throughout their entire life will be more focused on their intrauterine experience than the normal individual. As you will see, these two individuals, Pete and Irene, will spend their lives trying to obtain an imbalance that was created long before they can remember. They will spend their lives deeply affected by a failure in environmental factors they experienced during infancy and early childhood, failures that they had no control over whatsoever.

This example of Pete and Irene is a somewhat an extreme case. It is unlikely that every individual who realizes the condition of First Fear Not Relieved will suffer as many symptoms, behaviors and ultimate misfortunes as the two individuals used in this example. This, of course, has been done to give the most comprehensive range of effects possible from this condition.

Pete (Childhood History)

Pete was born after a long labor to a mother who was not in very good physical health. In fact, she was in such bad health that she died of cancer before Pete's second birthday. Pete was left, along with his two brothers and two sisters, to be raised by his father. Pete's father tried hard, however, was forced to work long hours to support his family and was rarely there. Most of Pete's early care was left to his eldest sister and brother. In school, Pete struggled. Concentration was difficult for him and he often seemed to be in trouble. While he was often sick as a child, he had no remarkable medical history.

In Pete's middle years of school, his grades improved. Under the guidance of a few good teachers Pete actually began to like attending class. While he had to work harder than most students, often reading the same text three or four times before comprehending it, he still did well. He was bothered by allergies to pollen and dust, however, so were many children at his school. Pete even enrolled in an after school basketball program, which he enjoyed thoroughly.

In high school, things started to change for Pete. He began hanging around the wrong crowd and rarely went to class. He was able to gain a part-time job after school; most of his money went to help his dad out. Pete began losing interest in high school and became more interested in his job. He tried drugs a few times in high school; however, had little interest in them. Alcohol, however, was a different story. He began drinking with his friends on the weekends; getting drunk quite often. The drinking helped him deal with the pain of his situation, which seemed to be deteriorating day by day. He finished high school, began working full-time and finally met Irene.

Irene (Childhood History)

Irene was born prematurely and raised by her mother. She never knew her father. He left before she was born. He moved out west to look for a better job, with the intention of sending for his family later, however, never did. As a child Irene loved dolls, she had no brothers or sisters, so she spent a lot of time alone. The dolls kept her company. For hours and hours, she could play with them. She was a very easy child, for her mother, to be raised. She was a quiet, pretty girl, who always had something nice to say. She was a healthy girl, not often sick. She loved to go shopping with her mother. While her mother had little time for her, because she was so busy working, when she did, she gave her daughter all the love she had.

In school, Irene did well. Her work was always organized and neat. In fact, everything about Irene was organized and neat. She paid attention to everything her teachers said. She also paid attention to everything the boys in her class did. She was a very alert, vibrant and hardworking young girl.

When her mom remarried, things began to change for Irene. She was about eight years old at the time. Irene did not like her new stepfather very well. He was not very nice to Irene. He never had anything good to say to her. In front of her mom, he put on a show, at first, that he liked Irene, later though; he did not even bother to do that. Irene began to spend more and more time away from home. She had a girlfriend from school, whose house was a better family environment, than hers was becoming.

In high school, Irene discovered boys. She actually had discovered them a long time ago, however, now their importance grew. While she liked being around her girlfriends, being around boys made her feel even better. She just could not seem to get enough attention from them. Irene began stealing her mom's make-up and putting it on in the bathroom at school. Irene was becoming very attractive. Older boys began asking her out on dates. Her mother said no, however, since her mother was often gone, busy working, Irene went out anyways. The older boys were nice, however, very pushy. They were always trying to get Irene into positions that she did not feel comfortable in. Most of the time, however, she escaped with only a good night kiss. Irene finished high school, got a job and met Pete.

Pete and Irene's Childhood in Relation to First Fear not Relieved

Now, you have seen a summary of Pete and Irene's childhood history. Both realize the condition of First Fear Not Relieved. The environmental factors for Pete that caused this condition were the sickness and ultimate death of his mother. The environmental factor for Irene that caused the condition of First Fear Not Relieved was the lack of a father or a supportive male role model. In Irene's case, this single factor was severe enough to trigger this condition. As you can see through both of their childhoods, while not obvious, subtle signs of the condition First Fear Not Relieved already began to materialize.

In Pete's case, his difficulty concentrating in school was the major symptom. This, of course, was due to the fact that during the critical period of neural elimination and reprogramming during his infancy and early childhood, when the neurons encoded with the First Fear and Euphoric Cycles of Development were supposed to be eliminated or reprogrammed, they were reinforced instead. Indeed, because Pete's mother was sick and actually in the process of dying, the fetal belief and therefore, the neurons that encoded that fetal belief that his mother and therefore himself was in the process of dying were reinforced. The end result of this was that compared to the normal boy, Pete had more neurons remaining that were encoded with the First Fear Cycle of Development. Now, because encoded into each neuron of the First Fear Cycle is the resultant Memory Block that was a part of the fetal neural pattern in the womb, Pete will realize a stronger influence from the Memory Block than will the normal boy without this condition. Therefore, when Pete is in school concentration is difficult. Concentration is difficult because the initial purpose of the Memory Block was to block the short-term memory of the fetus. In the womb it worked perfectly, in school it works against Pete. The Memory Block, as you remember, also suppresses the immune system. Because Pete has so much Memory Block, he realizes a stronger than normal suppression on his immune system. This is represented by Pete's sickness as a child and the up-regulation of his immune system in his early adolescent years, resulting in allergies. What is important to realize here, is that these symptoms of Pete's sickness are very subtle. In many cases, they could go undetected.

In Irene's case, the major symptom she displays of First Fear Not Relieved is her subconscious belief that the death and decay is inside of her. Because her environmental factor for First Fear Not Relieved was the lack of a father or supportive male role model, Nature's intention to have the young girl's association with her father help her disprove or disbelieve that the death and decay is inside of her failed. As you have seen, in the ideal situation the father would, through positive reinforcement of telling her that she was pretty and smelled nice, help her disbelieve that the death and decay was inside of her. The idea here is that she would then need the positive association of a father and this would, eventually, lead her to the male during her reproductive years. She would feel better in the presence of a male, thus, shifting her neural pattern, in her subconscious, away from the negative association of the First Fear Cycle to the more positive association of the Euphoric Cycle. In Irene's case, however, there was no father or supportive male role model to help her disbelieve or disprove that the death and decay was inside of her. Therefore, during late infancy and early childhood when Irene realized that her gender was the same as her mother's, her biggest fear was realized. This fear was that the death and decay was inside of her. With this belief, many of the neurons encoded with the First Fear Cycle of Development become reinforced, instead of eliminated or reprogrammed, as would occur to a young girl in a more ideal situation where the father can help her disbelief that the death and decay is inside of her, which would eliminate or at least reprogram the neurons encoded with the First Fear Cycle. This behavior for Irene can be demonstrated by her obsession with dolls, as dolls are symbol of a female with no death and decay. Also, the very organized and neat manner shows an early attempt at keeping the death and decay away from her immediate environment, as clutter, dirt and disorganization would symbolize the decay of something in his original state. This substitution of a doll as a symbol of no death and decay, for the father that she did not have, who was supposed to help disbelieve the death and decay was inside of her, is furthered as she matures and enjoys shopping. Shopping is important because by being around new material things, that contain no death and decay, she feels the positive association that Nature intended her to feel when she would be around the male.

Shopping however, will not be enough to help her disbelieve that the death and decay is inside her. This is because when she enters her adolescent years, Nature will provide her with a monthly reminder that the death and decay is indeed inside of her. When her monthly menstrual cycle begins, she will need further reassurance that the death and decay is not inside of her. Therefore, because the males do not have the death and decay inside of them, she will, if not become interested, at least allow their interest in her to develop.

Pete Meets Irene, and Their Early Adult Years

When Pete first saw Irene, he was riding his old motorcycle, just leaving work. Pete got a job as a welder in a factory. He was not dressed very fancily, wearing his blue work overalls. Irene worked as a secretary at the same factory. Pete was always looking at her, however, so, were most of his co-workers. She was dating a supervisor at the time. The supervisor was a neatly dressed, thin man. Pete was always trying to talk to her, when he would visit the front office; however, it seemed she looked down on his dress and position. Every time Pete would see Irene walking in the parking lot with her supervisor boyfriend, he would squeal the back tire of his motorcycle as he zoomed off, out of the parking lot. Irene would always notice this; however, her supervisor boyfriend would give her a short look when she did.

This went on for months and months. Finally, Irene's supervisor boyfriend broke up with her and Pete felt it was his big chance. He got up the nerve one day after work in the parking lot, to ask her out on a date. She just looked at him and laughed. This upset Pete, however, he was persistent, and he asked her why she would not go out with him. She told him that he did not want to know why. He assured her that he did. She said it was because of the way that he looked and dressed and that she would never date anyone who cared so little about his appearance. Even while she said this though, Pete could tell that she was interested in him. Every week he would ask her out. Every week she said no. Finally, as stubborn as Pete was, he decided to give in and buy some better clothes. He cut his hair neat and traded his old motorcycle in for a brand new pick-up truck. To Irene, Pete was a changed man. After a few more weeks of Pete's weekly rejection, she finally gave in and went out with Pete. He took her dancing, bought her a rose they fell in love and began dating. Eventually, after two years of dating Irene became pregnant and had a baby. By now, Irene was deeply in love with Pete and encouraging Pete to propose a marriage. Irene liked everything about the "new" Pete, except for one thing. It was Pete's drinking. It seemed every time when they went out to dinner or dancing, Pete could not stop at one or two drinks. In fact, often Pete would continue drinking until he was completely intoxicated. This was embarrassing to Irene, who felt Pete was a sloppy drunk and tried to discourage his drinking. When the baby was born they moved in together.

Early Adult Years in Relation to First Fear not Relieved

We will start at the beginning of this narrative of Pete and Irene's association, to see, even at the beginning of their acquaintance, how not only each individual's intrauterine experience shaped their motivations and actions, but how the condition of First Fear Not Relieved influences them both. From the moment Pete saw Irene, his riding the motorcycle, subconsciously, promised her that he could provide the Euphoric Cycle. The vibration and movement would mimic the fetal experience during this positive cycle of development. When Pete saw Irene, together with her supervisor boyfriend, he sped off very fast and squealed his back tire. Now consciously, this means very little, just a lot of noise. This action however, subconsciously, affects Irene deeply.

To understand why this, subconsciously, affects Irene deeply, it is helpful to look at the toys a young boy plays with and how he plays with them. As you realized in Chapter seven on "Boys and Girls," one of the first toys a young boy will choose is a car. To the young boy, the car symbolizes a fast escape from the death and decay in the womb. With that toy in hand the young boy will zoom the car across the floor as fast as it can go. This is to test it to see if it can escape the death and decay quickly enough. When a young girl, who knows that her gender is the same as her mother's, sees a young boy doing this, it is a confirmation to her that the boy knows that the death and decay is inside of her. Now, this is essentially a put down to the girl, to display this type of potential for escape. It reinforces the young girl's belief; and therefore, has fear that the death and decay is inside of her, and that the young boy is well aware. The same subconscious event occurs when a young woman sees a young man squealing or screeching the tires of his car or motorcycle very fast, from a given point, just like the young boy that raced his toy car across the floor. Now, to most women, this, while still a subconscious put down, will dismiss this type of behavior as childish. To Irene, however, or to a woman with the condition of First Fear Not Relieved, who has a stronger belief that she has the death and decay inside of her, this statement is a severe subconscious put down. Because Irene has so many neurons remaining, encoded with the First Fear Cycle of Development, this screeching of the tires, further reduces her self-belief and self-esteem. Now, Pete knows this. He could not tell you why he even does it, however, he knows it works. It not only empowers him, however, in some cases, such as Irene, it will get the girl's attention as well. While, consciously, Irene is rejecting Pete, subconsciously he knows she is interested. Even though Irene rejects Pete consciously, subconsciously Pete by squealing his tires is rejecting the death and decay that Irene fears is inside of her.

Irene's early forced substitution of a doll as a symbol of a female with no death and decay, in lieu of a father to reassure her that she has no death and decay inside of her, also dictates her choice in a boyfriend. As you have seen in Chapter seven on "Boy and Girls," the choice in boyfriends will reflect the attempt of the female with First Fear Not Relieved to control the death and decay of her immediate environment, this is because the influence, in her subconscious, of her fear that she has the death and decay inside of her, is so strong. Therefore, her choice in a boyfriend will be a male who looks neat and clean, a reflection of keeping her immediate environment free of the death and the decay. The supervisor, his superior dress and neat appearance represent this. While subconsciously, Irene may feel that she deserves to be with somebody like Pete, because his "old" appearance looks as if he is dirty and does not keep himself up well, therefore, representing the death and decay, Irene strives to change her environment, through positive association and be with someone who looks as though he obviously has no death and decay. This association, with a neat and clean individual, will make her feel better, changing her neural pattern in her subconscious from the negative influence of the First Fear Cycle to the positive influence of the Euphoric Cycle. Of course later, to get Irene's attention, Pete, will change his appearance to distance himself from any association with the death and decay, even though a dirty association to him means very little, as he knows he does not have the death and decay inside of him. Indeed, for Pete, he will as happy on his old motorcycle and in his dirty clothes, as he will in new clothes and a new truck, but he realizes however, at least subconsciously, that he will never get Irene's attention this way. The new truck Pete obtains represents to Irene a symbol of an object that has no death and decay, very much like the doll did for her as a child. When Irene was a little girl, subconsciously, she could visualize herself as a young adult woman with no death and decay inside of her, it is the same with new truck, she, subconsciously, visualizes herself in a new vehicle that contains no death and decay.

This is in contrast to being in an old car, truck or even motorcycle where, subconsciously, she fears the death and decay of her external environment could actually envelop her internally, thus, causing a continual negative association within her subconscious neural pattern.

Now remember, there is a lot at stake for individuals, especially those with the condition of First Fear Not Relieved, this is because encoded in those neurons of the First Fear Cycle, is nonspecific physical pain. This, of course, is the pain of one's own development as a fetus in the womb. Therefore, every time an individual, such as Irene, is around an association with the death and decay, this negative neural pattern dominates. On the other hand, if, in the subconscious, the neurons of the Euphoric Cycle are pulled up into a dominant pattern, then the individual, including Irene, will realize the influence of a neural pattern that was dominated by the reward of dopamine, which makes her feel good. This is important, when Irene makes her decision to surround herself with objects that represents no death and decay; she is doing so to avoid pain. She is not doing it, because she necessarily has lofty social ambitions. She, like most all other species, is simply avoiding pain and seeking pleasure.

When Pete and Irene go out on a date, Irene enjoys the dancing and companionship of Pete. The dancing, of course, makes total sense, because it is nothing more than a reenactment of the Euphoric Cycle, Irene realized as a fetus in the womb. This is a pleasurable experience and puts Irene in a good mood. However, after they have been dating a while, Pete begins to reveal his drinking problem to Irene, and becomes sloppy. In contrast to the dancing that brings up the positive association of the Euphoric Cycle, the sloppiness of a drunk brings up the negative association of the death and decay and the First Fear Cycle.

In Pete's case, after some time, his drinking problem begins to surface.

Because he has so many neurons, encoded with the First Fear Cycle of Development, remaining, and those neurons were programmed at a time of high dopamine usage in the womb, Pete's neural pattern has an increased need for dopamine. And the consumption of alcohol, temporarily, increases the dopamine flow to his reward pathways. So, Pete is essentially trying to regain a slight chemical imbalance that was created by circumstances beyond his control. It is a primitive attempt, however, an attempt nonetheless, to self-medicate.

Pete also has an obvious fear of commitment. Even though, Irene is pregnant, carrying his child, he still refuses to do the respectable thing and marry her. While this may seem to Irene cruel and heartless, there is actually a very good reason for this. To understand this, it is important to review the young boy's behavior during early childhood. Close to the memory of being entrapped by Nature in the female womb, young boys do not want to get too close to young girls. Indeed, many of the young boy's toys reflect his desire to liberate himself from the horrific events he experienced in the womb during the First Fear Cycle of Development. Now, for most young men, of Pete's age, this fear has long since diluted and subordinated, deep within their neural pattern. For Pete, or any male with the condition of First Fear Not Relieved, this influence, due to the increased amount of remaining neurons, encoded with the First Fear Cycle, remains strong. On one hand, these individuals, such as Pete, have an increased desire for finding a female and mimicking the Euphoric Cycle with her, through intercourse. This is because these neurons, which he has more of remaining than the normal male, contain developmental aspects concerning reproduction. On the other hand, these individuals, such as Pete, also have an increased desire to avoid ever being trapped again in the death and decay, such as the situation they realized as a fetus in the womb. This too, is because he has more neurons, encoded with the First Fear Cycle of Development, remaining than the normal male, which contain in addition to developmental aspects related to reproduction, aspects that the fetus experienced, such as being trapped in the death and decay of the womb. Now for Irene, Pete's behavior will be very confusing. In one way, he very much wants to be close to her, however, on the other, if he gets too close, he is afraid of becoming entrapped once again. To Irene, this means simply that he is afraid of commitment.

Pete and Irene's Middle Adult Years

Things began to settle down for Pete and Irene, once Irene had the baby. They had a baby daughter and named her Sandra. Pete appeared early on to be a good father. He spent many hours playing and dotting over their new baby daughter. He seemed to be getting his life together. He cut down on his drinking and even proposed marriage to Irene, who gladly accepted.

This period of relative domestic tranquility continued until their daughter, Sandra, reached the age of six. About this time, when Pete and Irene were in their early thirties, Pete lost his job. It was actually of no fault of his; the factory that he worked for simply had to cut back on their staff. To offset this financial setback, Irene began working overtime in her new job as an executive assistant at another factory. Pete told Irene that he would find another job easily and that she should not worry. This, however, failed to materialize. Instead, Pete began drinking again. He also began smoking cigarettes, about this time.

Pete became more and more depressed about not having a job. He entered a spiral of drinking to forget he was unemployed, then remaining unemployed because he was drinking. This went on for almost a year. Irene began to face the reality that she was married to an alcoholic. They then began to argue constantly. Less and less Irene had the desire to be around Pete. Finally, Irene said that she had had enough. She threatened to take Sandra and move into her mother's, who lived nearby, if Pete did not stop drinking. In an act of rage, during an argument, Pete began to act threatening towards Irene. First, he hit the walls with his fists. One night, he even hit Irene. This was enough for Irene and she left with Sandra.

Pete wanted Irene to come back. He sought counseling to solve his drinking problem; by now Pete realized that after fifteen years of off and on heavy drinking, he was an alcoholic. They remained separated for a year. During this time Irene began an affair with the owner of the factory, she worked for. The factory owner, who was married, promised to leave his wife and take care of Irene and Sandra. This, of course, never materialized as well. He would buy Irene expensive gifts, such as perfumes. The factory owner was very wealthy and kind to her. While Irene knew it was wrong to carry on with this married man, she really had no other hope in her life to speak of. Eventually, the factory owner's wife found out about the affair and persuaded him to stop seeing Irene. About this time, Pete was being very persistent about getting back with Irene. He had been sober for almost a year, and had found a better job at another factory. He told Irene he missed his daughter and her and would try to make up for the damage he had done. While skeptical at first, Irene gave in and moved back home with Pete. Now, the three were reunited together again as a family.

Middle Adult Years in Relation to First Fear not Relieved

Here we see that Pete's condition of First Fear Not Relieved has finally gotten the best of him. The event that triggered his drinking to become out of control was the loss of his job. Unable to grasp the loss of dignity and self-esteem that he previously had at his job, he began a downward spiral of dopamine-seeking behavior. What is important to realize, is that the loss of his job is only the trigger to his drinking.

Indeed, it could have been anything. It could have been the loss of a friend, a parent or even financial difficulties. If someone asked Pete why he started drinking again, it is likely that he would give one of these factors as the reason, as he is completely ignorant to the real cause and his condition. Before he lost his job, he was able to maintain this fragile neurochemical imbalance he has realized his entire life. The pain of losing his job, added to the pain he already realized from the condition of First Fear Not Relieved, finally, it was too much, the neurochemical imbalance of the dopamine needed to sustain a tolerable amount of pain was exceeded. Then, once this level was exceeded, Pete began the process of trying to self-medicate and to restore the dopamine or neurochemical balance. Of course, this did not work at all, like with any addiction, the more dopamine that his reward pathways were flooded with, the more the receptors that utilize that dopamine down-regulate and therefore require more dopamine, and in Pete's case more alcohol to obtain the same reduction in pain. This is the downward spiral of addiction, which in Pete's case was alcohol.

When Pete hits Irene, what has happened here is a severe deviation of Nature's intention concerning fetal development in the womb, and represents the grave physical danger that can occur from the condition of First Fear Not Relieved. What this means is, during the First Fear Cycle of Development the fetus was essentially conditioned by Nature to punch and kick out when it believed its mother was in the process of dying. This, as you have seen, had many important developmental purposes. One of these purposes was to strengthen the fetal heart and lungs and strengthen the fetal muscles that would be required during the process of labor. As you have seen, over time this conditioned response, violent as it was, worked effectively. Given the high consciousness of the fetal brain, its interpretation was this, in order to save its dying mother and therefore itself, it must kick and punch out.

Now years later, in the case of Pete, Irene has replaced the symbol of Pete's mother. Therefore, association with a healthy Irene assures, subconsciously, Pete that he will survive. Now, when Irene threatens to leave Pete he responds exactly how Nature conditioned him in the womb to respond to this threat. First, he punches the walls. This is exactly what he did as a fetus during the First Fear Cycle of Development. When Irene's threats to leave continued; the symbolism of the walls are not enough, however. At that time, he begins a process of dangerous behavior and actually strikes her. His subconscious intention, which is to save Irene and therefore himself, directly contradicts his physical action of striking and injuring her. Indeed, no longer do the neural and muscular connections between Pete's brain and his fist lack the myelination they did when he was a fetus and could do little damage to its mother. No, Pete is grown up and very capable of physically injuring Irene. The problem is these very old neurons, encoded with the First Fear Cycle, do not differentiate between Pete's fetal state and his adult, and physically stronger, state, they simply fire. Now, for most males, for those without the condition of First Fear Not Relieved, it is unlikely that they would ever strike a woman. This is because for them, the majority of the neurons, encoded with the First Fear Cycle of Development, have been eliminated or reprogrammed. Therefore, the influence of this aspect of development, that in Pete's case is deviated, is not that strong. For Pete, however, this is not the case.

In Pete's situation, because he has so many neurons encoded with the First Fear Cycle of Development remaining, the influence of this developmental aspect is very strong. He has now, essentially stepped over the line of his original intention. Pete's situation mimicked his intrauterine experience as well. Because he was drinking, he most likely realized a drop off or reduction in the amount of dopamine, as is common when drinking. When consuming alcohol the drinker will realize an initial rush of dopamine to their reward pathways, and then later, they will realize a drop off from that initial rush, unless they continue to consume greater amounts of alcohol. So, in Pete's case, if it was late into his daily or nightly cycle of drinking, it is possible that he was actually experiencing a temporary reduction in the amount of dopamine. This drop off in dopamine in the womb signaled the beginning of the First Fear Cycle of Development. This would change Pete's subconscious neural pattern to the negative association of the First Fear Cycle, thus, increasing the influence and the chances that he will reenact this deviated form of development, by striking the walls and then, ultimately, Irene. In the end, Pete has obtained the exact opposite situation that he originally wanted. Subconsciously, all he wanted to do was to save Irene's and therefore his own life, however, in reality, he has driven her away. All of these events occurred, because of an environmental factor during infancy and early childhood that he had no control over.

In Irene's case, when Pete's drinking became too severe and physical abuse began, she finally left. This was a very healthy and logical step for her to make, and not a typical step a woman with the condition of First Fear Not Relieved would normally accomplish. What is interesting about Irene's case is that when the association of Pete and his drinking, becoming a sloppy drunk, reminded her, subconsciously, of the death and decay she feared was inside of her, she once again attempted to change her immediate environment by a more positive association. She did this, not only by leaving, however, also by the acceptance of an affair with the owner of her factory. The owner of the factory represents the substitution of the doll for the lack of a father she experienced as a child. When she lost her husband, as she lost her father, she allowed herself to be pursued by symbols of no death and decay. This is represented by the material new gifts that she was given by the factory owner. The factory owner represents someone with the ability to provide this substitute symbol of no death and decay. It is important to realize that her interest in the factory owner, in this case, is not about some parental love that she never received. This is not true at all, for she has nothing to compare this to, as she never experienced it as a child. Irene's interest is, specifically, in the substitution value of the gifts he can provide, her association with these new material gifts help her to disbelieve that there is no death and decay inside of her, just as the doll did when she was a child.

Pete and Irene's Late Adult Years

It has been over thirty years since Pete first saw Irene, in the parking lot at his first job. Through all their difficulties, after all these years, they have been able to remain together. Their daughter, Sandra, has become a fine young woman. She is married and lives close to her parents. Irene spends every minute available with her daughter and new granddaughter.

Pete has long since stopped drinking. He still smokes extensively, however, the drinking was left behind years ago. Irene and he get along pretty good. His only complaint is that Irene is never home. Indeed, if she is not at their daughter's, she is at one of her girlfriends' house. Pete does not even mind that his wife spends so much money shopping. He must admit in the last five years she has cut down on how much she spends and how often she goes shopping. His only request is that she would be around him more often.

Both, Pete and Irene, suffer from health problems. Irene has arthritis in her fingers, which she blames on her years working as a secretary. It is very painful, especially in the morning. Since menopause, she has had trouble sleeping at night and bouts with depression. Pete has diabetes for five years now. He has a constant cough, however, has only missed work three times in the last two years.

Late Adult Years in Relation to First Fear not Relieved

As we prepare to leave Pete and Irene behind, we will look at one final segment of their life together and its relation to the condition of First Fear Not Relieved, of which they both suffer. For the female with First Fear Not Relieved the effects of menopause will be exaggerated.

To understand why menopause will affect the female with the First Fear Not Relieved more severely, than the normal female without this condition, it is first necessary to understand how menopause affects any female in relation to Nature's reproduction model and the female's intrauterine experience. Two major changes occur to the female during and after menopause in relation to the First Fear Cycle of Development and the female reproduction model.

The first major change is that the female loses her monthly menstrual cycle. This is important. After all, the monthly menstrual cycle was the pivotal aspect of Nature's reproductive model for the female, in many ways. It was the monthly reminder that reinforced the female's intrauterine development in relation to reproduction. In other words, because the female's subconscious fear that she contained the death and decay was a vital developmental aspect that was intended to lead her to the male, Nature reminded the female, consciously, on a monthly basis, that she had the death and decay inside of her. With this monthly reminder gone; the original danger of utilizing the intrauterine environment instead of the sole use of pheromones for attraction and reproduction surfaces again. In other words, because both male and female originated from the female and this origin is where all future attraction and the basis for reproduction begins, there is a danger that if the female does not believe that she has the death and decay inside of her that she will not be attracted to the male and that she will see other females as having no death and decay inside of them either. As you have seen, Nature's intention was that the female would seek companionship from the male, as through association with him she could believe that she has no death and decay inside of her. Now, when this monthly menstrual cycle ends, which occurs during menopause, the female will not be reminded of this death and decay that Nature wants her to believe is inside of her. The danger here, which occurs only in extreme cases, is that the female will then gain attraction and seek companionship from the female. In some cases, after menopause, this does indeed happen. In most cases, however, as it is with Irene, her desire to be around the male, or Pete will decrease and her desire to associate with a female, in a non-sexual matter, will increase. For Irene, being around her daughter and her girlfriends represents this association.

The second major change during and after menopause, in relation to the First Fear Cycle of Development, is the reduction of protective female hormones. It is important to remember, that it was these female hormones that diluted the intensity of the First Fear Cycle for the female fetus in the womb. It was also the protective female hormones that reduced the influence of the intrauterine experience within the female's subconscious. So, in many ways, what occurs to normal women during and after menopause is that, without these protective female hormones, they realize a condition very similar to First Fear Not Relieved. In other words, the influence of the remaining neurons encoded with the First Fear Cycle of Development, in the normal female increases. Now for Irene, this will be extremely difficult, because it will only enhance her condition of First Fear Not Relieved. So, on one hand, while she may not believe that she has the death and decay inside of her, on the other hand, she realizes many of the traumatic and somewhat violent development, within her subconscious, that the male fetus experienced. Indeed, some women during and after menopause will actually begin to gain an appearance that is more masculine in general, than they had previously looked before menopause. In Irene's case, this does not occur; what does occur is that she develops depression and cannot sleep. Both of these symptoms will be explained in detail in the next chapter on "The Disorders."

What you see beginning to happen with the male-female reproductive model, as this couple ages, is that both genders gain interest in the gender from which they originated. Indeed, if it were not for the protective female hormones and the subconscious belief of the female that all females, including her, have the death and decay inside of them, then this would always have been how the model worked. By providing these protective female hormones and the belief of the death and decay, Nature altered this attraction from the gender of origin for the female. As the female ages, however, Nature has no purpose to keep this altered model, as her intention for the female to reproduce at such a late age does not exist. Therefore, both male and female, as they age, will return to the gender of their origin. In Pete and Irene's case, the problem with this is that Irene will want to associate with her daughter; however, Pete will want to associate with Irene. Again, both genders in some ways, however subtle, will return to their gender of origin.

As you have seen, both Pete and Irene suffer from health problems, during their late adult years. Pete's coughing is a result from his years of dopamine-seeking behavior, which specifically in this case was the smoking of cigarettes. Over the years, every time Pete lit up a cigarette, he was providing testament, however altered, to Nature's original intrauterine model of dopamine-seeking behavior. As you have seen, in the womb the fetus, specifically during the First Fear Cycle, would be enabled an increase in dopamine by sucking its thumb or fingers. This, of course, was to be replaced after birth by its mother's nipple. This dopamine-seeking behavior was the primary method, Nature used to convince an infant, who had been force-fed for nine months in the womb, to learn to obtain food on its own. The cigarette, of course, is an alteration of this initial process. With the butt of the cigarette shaped very similar to a finger, the individual can suck on the filter and receive the nicotine that begins a chemical process, which increases the dopamine flow to the reward pathways within the brain. It is quite an ingenious innovation, unfortunately for Pete however; this innovation is resulting in health problems. With the condition of First Fear Not Relieved, it is doubtful that Pete will ever quit cigarette smoking. This is because the dopamine-seeking behavior, encoded in the neurons of the First Fear Cycle, is so plentiful for Pete that, subconsciously, he is constantly reminded of this behavior. In addition, Pete is still trying to make up for the neurochemical imbalance, due to the high dopamine usage of these neurons programmed in the womb, which he has an overabundance of remaining.

Both, Pete and Irene, suffer from other health problems as well. Unlike Pete's smoking, these other health problems are not from dopamine-seeking behavior. Both, Irene's arthritis and Pete's diabetes are a result of their condition of First Fear Not Relieved. If you remember the original model of development, you realize that programmed in all the neurons encoded with the First Fear and Euphoric Cycles of Development was the Memory Block, which was an essential part of the fetal neural pattern in the womb. You then, will also remember that the Memory Block had a direct relationship with the immune system. The relationship was, the more Memory Block remaining; the more the individual's immune system is suppressed. Therefore, the more neurons, encoded with the First Fear Cycle, remaining, the more the immune system is suppressed. And because both Irene and Pete have more neurons encoded with the First Fear Cycle remaining, than Nature had intended, both have realized a life of suppressed immune systems. However, because the immune system is not a static entity, it fights back and up-regulates. Years of this up-regulated immune system, causes it to fight back stronger and harder, attacking not only what is beneficial, but also the body's own cells.

This results in autoimmune disorders, such as rheumatoid arthritis and diabetes. It is interesting to note where this arthritis strikes Irene. In the womb, late at night, deep into the First Fear Cycle of Development, the fetus was too exhausted to kick and punch and could only use its fingers and hands in an attempt to initiate a response, from what it believed to be, its' dying mother. It could be any autoimmune disorder that the individual with the condition of First Fear Not Relieved suffers from. It could be colitis, lupus or problems with their thyroid. It will always be from the same cause, years of living with an up-regulated immune system that was suppressed by the Memory Block, which was contained in the neurons encoded with the First Fear and Euphoric Cycles that these individuals have too many remaining of. As you will see in Part Two of this book "The Organics," when there is an alteration in the initial intrauterine model that reduces the amount of Memory Block a fetus experiences, then this will result in reduced suppression of the immune system and, in that case, autoimmune disorders will be rare.

What you have just read is an example of two individuals, who both suffer from the condition of First Fear Not Relieved. While they have both managed to scratch a somewhat tolerable life, they did so, constantly, fighting an invisible enemy. The enemy was within themselves, throughout their entire life. If they are victims, they are not aware, yet they constantly were both fighting and struggling against the imbalance, caused by failures in their environment during infancy and early childhood.

Old Age and the Condition of First Fear not Relieved

Before we begin the next section in this chapter, it is important to clarify some aspects concerning the individual with the condition of First Fear Not Relieved. While we have not covered the disorders in this chapter, it is important to realize that by the time the individual with First Fear Not Relieved reaches their adult years, it is likely that they will suffer from one of the disorders listed in the next chapter. Because these disorders will be explained in detail in the next chapter, we have not covered them here. In general though, the individual with First Fear Not Relieved will very likely, during sometime in their adult years experience, depression, manic depression, anxiety disorders, panic attacks, sleep disorders, or other disorders. Again, the reasons for this become very obvious upon reading the next chapter.

For the individual with First Fear Not Relieved, old age is not a pleasant experience. While for most, it is the golden time of their life. It is the time to relax, to retire and to look back upon their past and figure out what they have experienced actually meant. The individual with First Fear Not Relieved in old age, however, is still fighting the same imbalance, the same invisible enemy, which has been consuming them their whole life. This, of course, is if they make it to old age at all. Indeed, they face a myriad of obstacles before they can even reach the golden years. There is likely the years of abuse on their body from their dopamine-seeking behavior, this could result in anything from lung cancer from smoking to cirrhosis of the liver from drinking. If the individual with First Fear Not Relieved needed a more direct source of dopamine, they may have turned to drugs and, ultimately, their abuse. They may have used cocaine, which will affect their heart. They may have used heroin, becoming infected with hepatitis from a needle they shared in the process. As you will see in the next chapter, there is a very good chance that they may commit suicide along the way. Then of course, there is that up-regulated immune system, suppressed by the Memory Block for many years. As you have seen, they must battle a host of autoimmune disorders.

Modern medicine is amazing, however. Indeed, it can work wonders. Over the years, improvements have been made, so that these unlucky individuals can survive. Survival, for those with First Fear Not

Relieved during old age, is not without its price. To understand the reason for this, and what this price is, it is first necessary to understand, at least some of Nature's intention, concerning the model of intrauterine development for the human species.

Mankind is Nature's favored species. Of this, there is little doubt. Throughout mankind's brief history, he has proved that there is little he cannot accomplish. Throughout this history though, there is one thing that Nature has made sure he cannot do. This, as you will see throughout this book, is to not meet the minimum requirements established by Nature for the successful reproduction of the human species. Some of these requirements were listed in Chapter five, titled "First Fear Not Relieved." When those environmental factors are not properly obtained, the infant begins the process of dying. This is always the case. It always has been and always will be. It is simply, for whatever reason Nature chooses, her way of pruning the human species. Mankind, however, has fought back. In advanced societies, he has lowered the infant mortality rate substantially. In advanced cultures, an infection, that could have killed an infant two hundred years ago, is now taken care of by a simple office visit and a prescription for the appropriate medicine.

What is important to realize, to gain from the previous paragraph, is that when environmental factors during infancy and early childhood are not met, Nature intended for this individual to perish. Indeed, in most cases, Nature never intended for the individual to successfully complete childhood. To accomplish this, Nature, again for whatever reason, made sure that if the environmental factors, listed in Chapter five, were not met, the infant's and young child's immune system would become and remain suppressed. This would not allow it to function properly. Again, however, mankind has fought back. These infants, now, in advanced societies, not only survive, but also flourish. Still, Nature never intended them to survive. So, while the suppression of their immune system is treatable and manageable, their entire neural make up is a different story. For those individuals with First Fear Not Relieved, who were never intended to survive, this neural make up is forever altered. By the time the individual with First Fear Not Relieved, if they survive, reaches old age, this altered neural make up, in some cases, shows its signs.

Indeed, the human brain was never designed to survive with such a strong influence and neural pattern from life in the womb, such as individuals with First Fear Not Relieved realize. It is important to remember, that these neurons encoded with the two cycles of development are fetal neurons. They were programmed at a time when the neural chemistry was unique to initial development. Many of these neurons, as you have seen, were supposed to be eliminated during infancy and others during early childhood. If they were not, an imbalance is created. The human brain, however, cannot indefinitely withstand this imbalance. It is simply too much stress on the mechanism.

A good example of the stress from this imbalance can be seen with the role of dopamine and the fetal neurons encoded with the First Fear and Euphoric Cycles of Development. As you have seen, individuals with First Fear Not Relieved have a greater demand within their neural chemistry for dopamine. This is because they have more neurons remaining, than the normal individual, that are encoded with the two cycles of intrauterine development. These neurons have a higher demand for dopamine than those reprogrammed or programmed outside the womb. In other words, they have more neurons that need higher amount of dopamine than the normal individual. As you have seen, they often spent their life, especially focused on dopamine-seeking behavior, trying to restore the imbalance. Now, this can go on for a while, this living with a neural imbalance. Maybe it can last five years, ten years, maybe even twenty or thirty. Eventually, however, the areas of the brain that produce dopamine cannot withstand the added demand and begin to fail. This makes sense, because for years they have been working overtime. In addition to being important during fetal development, dopamine in the child and the adult serves other purposes. One of them is that it suppresses the movement of muscles. Indeed, dopamine serves many purposes. Now, these fetal neurons, with their high demand for dopamine, are very old neurons. Because they are very old neurons, they take precedent over younger neurons. Indeed, they get fed first. Now, when the areas of the brain that produce dopamine begin to fail, due to all these years of overwork, and stop producing the same level of dopamine, these old fetal neurons, those encoded with the First Fear and Euphoric Cycles of Development, still get fed. They still take precedent; they still get the first share of dopamine. It is the other areas of the body, the other functions of dopamine that suffer from this reduced output.

Therefore, the individual with First Fear Not Relieved, who has overtaxed their dopamine reducing areas for years, is highly likely candidate to realize, in old age, although sometimes it occurs to younger individuals, a disease which was discovered by a doctor named Parkinson. The cause for Parkinson's disease has just been explained. A major symptom of Parkinson's disease is an involuntary tremulous motion. In other words, they realize a tremor. This, of course, is caused by the reduced amount of dopamine available, which itself is caused by the reduced functioning of the areas of the brain that produce dopamine, which itself is caused by years of overuse from these areas.

Another disease, even more serious, that awaits the individual with First Fear Not Relieved in old age, is Alzheimer's disease. Indeed, there is not a disease that more specifically pinpoints the neural mechanisms that are involved in the First Fear and Euphoric Cycles of Development. In the case of Alzheimer's disease, it is the neurons encoded with the First Fear and Euphoric Cycles themselves that become affected. This is what happens, when too many fetal neurons survive, avoid elimination and reprogramming, however, instead become reinforced. With too many of these old fetal neurons remaining, over time they simply stop functioning properly and either die or become a tangled mess. When this happens, certain parts of the neurons and certain groups survive and begin to express themselves, influencing the neural pattern even stronger than before. The part and group that survives, of course, are those areas encoded with the Memory Block. Therefore, with the remnants of the Memory Block expressing itself stronger, the individual realizes, even in old age, this old fetal pattern of a blocked short-term memory. They often have a hard time remembering even where they live, just as they did as a fetus remembering the existence of the previous cycle of intrauterine development. Again, here is the Memory Block, the same function that was so essential for intrauterine development. It is the same function that for individuals with First Fear Not Relieved made concentration difficult and was responsible for their learning disability as a child. It is the same Memory Block that caused them, in some cases, to be diagnosed with Attention Deficit Disorder. Of course, these terms were not around when they were children. Now, it is the same Memory Block, the survival neural mechanism within their decaying brain.

Of course, all areas that were utilized during the First Fear and Euphoric Cycles are usually affected. Even the olfactory system is subject to these neural tangles. The fetal olfactory neurons were, as you remember, the method in which the fetus interpreted the change in the cycles of intrauterine development. When the pungent and foul odors began, it was a signal of the conditioning for the fetus to begin punching and kicking, a signal that the First Fear Cycle had began, a signal that the fetus misinterpreted as the beginning of the process of its mother and therefore itself dying.

Death

While death is a normal process of existence, it can also be very revealing concerning the relationship between the Memory Block and the immune system. This is true for both, the individual with First Fear Not Relieved and for the normal individual. As you have seen in previous chapters, the Memory Block suppresses the individual's immune system. The more Memory Block, the more the immune system is suppressed.

You also realized that the immune system is not a static entity. To fight this suppression, it up-regulates itself and becomes hypersensitive. Another way in which the vitality and complexity of the immune system is demonstrated occurs upon death or upon a near death experience. If the individual's immune system is threatened to the point where death is imminent, the immune system, to reduce its suppression and save the individual's life, temporarily lifts the Memory Block. This then, allows the immune system, without this added suppression, to work more effectively.

What is interesting about this temporarily lifting of the Memory Block is that when this occurs the individual consciously reviews many of the events, which were encoded in the neurons that form their subconscious. This occurs in a backwards manner. This is why an individual will often say that their "life flashed before their eyes," which is common during a near death experience.

The last thing, of course, before death itself or during the process of dying, the individual will review; will be the first visual event they experienced upon initiating labor. They will see themselves going down the birth canal towards the bright light that awaited them outside. Unable to comprehend this experience, many individuals who have technically died, then come back to life, have remembered the exiting of a large dark tunnel into a bright light. Again, this is nothing more than the Memory Block lifting, temporarily, and the memory of their birth being consciously reviewed by them.

CHAPTER TEN

FIRST FEAR NOT RELIEVED
– THE DISORDERS

Every single disorder listed in this chapter is a condition of First Fear Not Relieved. We are about to embark upon an exciting chapter that will solve some of the oldest mysteries of human behavior known to mankind. Even with all of this, very little of what you are about to read, is new. Indeed, the perceptive reader can already see where the symptoms of these disorders originate.

As you will see, there is very little in these disorders that are original. In other words, all these symptoms expressed from every disorder listed, have all been experienced before. For, there are no creative symptoms to any of these disorders. The human brain does not work that way at all. For example, an individual who suffers the mood disorder of depression and expresses the symptom of not being able to sleep at night, however, is very tired and can sleep easily during the day, and is not doing so because of some neurochemical imbalance that generates this behavior or pattern. No, they are expressing this symptom because at one time and at one place this was exactly their sleep-wake pattern. Of course, there will be a neurochemical imbalance; however it is not the cause. Instead, like all aspects of those who suffer from First Fear Not Relieved, a neurochemical imbalance, as you have seen at the end of the last chapter, is a result of failures of environmental factors during infancy and early childhood.

Every single symptom of every single disorder while inconvenient to the individual, who suffers them, was once an essential aspect of that individual's intrauterine development. What occurs in every single disorder is that these essential aspects of intrauterine development were recorded into the fetal neurons. As you are already well aware of; these fetal neurons were encoded with the entire intrauterine experience: included in this intrauterine experience were the two cycles of fetal development, the First Fear and Euphoric Cycles. When an individual, who suffers from these disorders experiences symptoms, all that is occurring is that these fetal neurons are now firing in a collective pattern, so subtle that it is undetectable to any measurement, and, within their subconscious, are exerting a stronger than normal influence upon the individual's conscious thoughts. It is very much as if all the symptoms of these disorders are nothing more than the playing back of a very old tape. On that tape are the neurons encoded with the First Fear and Euphoric Cycles of Development. This tape was recorded by the individual as a fetus in the womb. This tape sits and waits, deep within the subconscious, for the day that it can replay. When that day comes, the play button is pushed and the tape rolls, unedited, once again, and the symptoms of these disorders are realized.

The question is then, with so many disorders and so many symptoms, what decides which individual, with the condition of First Fear Not Relieved, realizes which disorder? The answer that determines this is based on a number of variables. First, there are the genetic aspects that will not be discussed here. More importantly, however, than genetics is that most symptoms of most disorders are somewhat specific, just as everyone's experience was somewhat specific and similar, after birth the variables of the environmental factors and their complexity multiply. These complexities translate into different groups of neurons being eliminated, reprogrammed or, in this case, reinforced of the

First Fear and Euphoric Cycles for each individual. Just as every pregnancy is unique and every infancy and childhood is unique, so then are the specific disorders and symptoms that will be realized by the individual with First Fear Not Relieved. Still, there are some common experiences shared by every fetus, included in this common experience are the two cycles of intrauterine development. This makes it somewhat easy, as you will see, to understand what each major symptom of each major disorder listed, meant at one time in terms of fetal development and the resultant intrauterine experience.

Panic Attacks (Panic Disorder)

So, what is a panic attack? Well, to individuals who experience them, they are very real. They are embarrassing, debilitating and extremely frightening. Individuals who suffer a panic attack often end up, late at night, in the emergency room of a hospital. Here, they testify to the emergency doctor that they are having a heart attack or are in the process of dying. The victim of the panic attack describes their symptoms to the doctor. They feel dizzy and cannot breath. There is a severe pain in their chest and their heart is pounding. They may even tell the doctor that they think they are having a heart attack.

The emergency room doctor is sympathetic, yet reminds the individual that this is the third time this month that they have been in the emergency room with the same symptoms. The doctor reminds the individual that they have checked every aspect of their heart, of their lungs and of anything even related to their symptoms. On this response, the individual informs the doctor that something must have been missed. The individual informs the doctor that something must be wrong, because they have never felt this way before.

This, of course, is where this individual is mistaken. The last statement they made was definitely incorrect. When the individual with the panic attack stated that they had never felt this way before, this is where they were wrong. In fact, they have felt this way before, so has every individual that has ever been born. It is just that they do not remember where and why. For most individuals, they will never re-experience this event and therefore, will never realize a panic attack. The individual with First Fear Not Relieved, however, will likely suffer a panic attack and if they suffer enough of them, they will realize the condition of panic disorder. Yes, the individual with the panic attack has felt this way before, they just cannot remember where and when.

Most likely, by now, you know exactly where and when this individual first realized this experience. We will review a few of the symptoms of a panic attack, as we return to the fetus in the womb and realize their origin.

An individual, who experiences a panic attack, often realizes a sensation of shortness in breath and a feeling of choking. This is an accurate definition of the fetal response to one of the many apneas that occurred during the First Fear Cycle as the respiration from the mother to the fetus was cut off for short periods of time during this cycle. These apneas served an important purpose, as they not only strengthen the developing fetal lungs, but also served as a rehearsal for the long process of labor, when oxygen available to the fetus would be reduced severely. These apneas caused the fetal lungs to expand and contract, in response to the temporary cessation of air. It was a cruel and painful procedure the fetus had to endure, however, it was a necessary one. This choking sensation, the shortness of breath, was the exact sensation the fetus realized when these apneas began. This is also the exact sensation the individual, during a panic attack, experiences. A panic attack is nothing more than the replay of these fetal neurons encoded with the apneas from the First Fear Cycle of Development.

Another symptom of a panic attack is chest pain and discomfort. This, of course, originates from the same place, the fetal apnea. As the air supply was cut off, for seconds or minutes at a time, the fetal cardio-respiratory system failed, only to grow and expand from that failure. This was very uncomfortable for the fetus, as it felt like its entire chest was being pulled apart.

A fear of dying is another symptom that occurs to an individual during a panic attack. Once the apneas begin, the fetus realized its worst fears. While before, during the First Fear Cycle, the fetus believed that its mother was in the process of dying, once the apneas began, it was convinced. As you remember, the fetus directly connected the death of its mother to the death of itself.

During a panic attack, the individual may also experience nausea, or abdominal distress. There were two reasons the fetus realized this discomfort during the apneas. The first was a response to the intense pains of the apneas themselves. The second reason was the withdraw symptoms from the drop in dopamine that occurred when the fetus entered the First Fear Cycle from the Euphoric Cycle. The withdraw symptoms included sweating, chills and shaking as the fetus waited, with pounding heart, for what it believed to be its inevitable death, which was only another apnea.

The memory of this apnea, for the fetus would last anywhere between two and ten minutes, the apnea was so painful that it could even override the blocked short-term memory of the fetus for that short period of time. Of course, the typical panic attack will likely begin suddenly, as the fetal apnea did, and will reach their peak in intensity in about ten minutes, the same length of the blocked fetal short-term memory.

During a panic attack the individual may feel a sense of depersonalization. They may feel almost detached from themselves. This is very common, for the neurons that are firing, did indeed come from another time and place. It is just that they picked, this particular time to fire. The individual who is suffering the panic attack, however, has no idea where the sensation is coming from. The individual simply cannot understand what is going on. They go to the doctor and the doctor tells them there is nothing wrong with them. They reason, however, that they should know their own body and mind after all they have lived in it for many years. While professionals are telling them that nothing is wrong with them, it seems their brain and body are telling them something different. Once the individual, who suffers from panic disorder, realizes that there is nothing wrong with their body, they come to the conclusion that there must be something wrong with their brain.

Of course, there is nothing wrong with their brain. They are not going crazy. It is simply the neurons, encoded with the First Fear Cycle of Development, within their subconscious, that are generating a dominant, yet subtle neural pattern, are firing. It is just that, previous to the panic attacks, these neurons, while firing uninhibited remained within their subconscious and now, during a panic attack, this influence becomes so strong that they have burst through and into the individual's conscious thoughts.

As with all the other disorders listed, panic attacks and panic disorder all are a condition of First Fear Not Relieved. The individual, who suffers these attacks, has an overabundance of neurons, encoded with the First Fear and Euphoric Cycles of Development, remaining. Many of these neurons were intended to be eliminated or reprogrammed during infancy and early childhood, however, for these individuals, were reinforced instead. This was due to a failure in their environmental factors, explained in Chapter five on "First Fear Not Relieved."

Depression

Depression is one of the most common mental disorders within society; therefore, we will spend a large portion of this chapter looking at its symptoms and ultimate origin. In this section, we will look at a typical depressive episode or unipolar depression. In the next section, we will look at the more dramatic episode of depression, the manic episode or manic depression.

Depression can be a very subtle disorder. Unlike a panic attack that reaches up and grabs the individual's attention, depression can be very discreet. It can influence an individual's thoughts every day, little by little taking more of their life away.

To understand how depression affects an individual's life, how confusing the symptoms can be to them, and finally, to identify the origin itself, it is helpful to look at an example. For this example, we will use a female in her late twenties.

On the outside, looking in, Betty has the perfect life. She is well loved by her husband, and has two beautiful young children. Betty used to work, however, since the birth of her youngest daughter, and the family's improving financial situation, she has decided to stay home and devote her full attention to the important job of raising their children. She is a good mother, gives both of her children her undivided attention and rarely raises her voice at them. Every morning she wakes up, fixes breakfast for her husband and kisses him goodbye. After that, she wakes her children up, fixes them breakfast, drives them to school, kisses them goodbye, drives home and then it begins.

Inside their large, expensive home, all by herself, she falls apart. This has been going on for months. As soon as she takes her children to school and is back home, she pulls down the shades over the windows, sits on the couch and starts to cry. She has absolutely no energy; she is fatigued and exhausted, even though she has done very little. She cannot concentrate and barely moves off the couch. With all the energy she has left in her fingers, she turns on the television, however, turns it off almost as quickly. She gets up to walk over to the bathroom. It seems as if she is walking in slow motion, all of her muscles ache even though she has done very little. After she goes to the bathroom, she steps on the scale. She has lost another three pounds, she has not been eating lately at all, and she just has had no appetite to speak of. After the bathroom, it is back to the couch. After an hour on the couch, she falls asleep. She sleeps the rest of the morning into the early afternoon. She wakes up an hour before she has to pick up her children. She has not been able to sleep at night very well at all; it is only during the day that she can finally get to sleep for a few hours. At night, when it is time for bed she gets restless and ends up staying awake, reading until at least three o'clock in the morning.

After her long nap, Betty picks up the phone and calls her girlfriend. She tells her girlfriend about her problems. She tells her about not being able to sleep at night, about having no energy, and about the intense feelings of sadness she experiences. Betty's girlfriend listens as she usually does, carefully waiting until Betty is done. Then, the girlfriend asks Betty how she can be so unhappy? She tells Betty that she has everything that any woman would want. Her girlfriend continues, "You have a great husband, beautiful kids, the perfect house and more money you could ever want." Then, her friend tells her, "You should be happy!" After Betty hangs up the phone, she feels worse. She goes back to the couch, sits down and starts to cry. She feels guilty. She feels guilty about feeling this way. She feels guilty about her husband, about her children, and about what her friend told her. She even feels guilty about feeling guilty. She hates to feel this way. It seems she will always feel this way and things will never get better. She looks into the future and sees only the same. She looks at the clock and realizes that she is almost late to pick up her children. She looks for her keys, however, cannot find them. She searches for ten minutes, and then finally, realizes they were in her purse the whole time.

Betty is suffering from depression. No matter what her girlfriend tells her, about how she should feel, Betty feels miserable. Symptom by symptom, we will figure out exactly why Betty is feeling and acting this way.

By her sleeping pattern, it is obvious that Betty suffers from insomnia. Insomnia is a common symptom of depression. While there are other reasons for insomnia, which will be explained later in this chapter, here we will look at the most obvious. As the neurons encoded with the First Fear Cycle begin to fire, within Betty's subconscious, in a more dominant pattern, they begin to control her sleep-wake pattern. Because the neurons that are heavily influencing her thoughts are fetal neurons, encoded with the First Fear Cycle, they dictate her sleep-wake pattern as well. Encoded within those fetal neurons is the entire intrauterine experience the fetus realized in the womb. While the fetus slept during both cycles of development, in most cases it slept more during the day, when its mother was moving during the Euphoric Cycle, than at night, during the First Fear Cycle. Indeed, at night the fetus was awake and alert, busy trying to save its mother's and therefore its own life. Betty has no idea why she has difficulty sleeping at night, however, can sleep easily during the day. It is simply because, neurons encoded with events from another place and time, are dominating not only her thoughts, but her life style as well.

Betty also realizes a feeling of fatigue and loss of energy. This is another common symptom of depression. What is happening here, is that the neurons within Betty's subconscious, encoded with the First Fear Cycle of Development, are firing, exerting a stronger than normal influence on her thoughts. Encoded into these neurons is the fetal state and condition, it experienced during the First Fear Cycle of Development. After kicking and punching in an attempt to save its mother's and therefore its own life, the fetus was exhausted. It is important to remember, that physically, the fetus was not fully developed. The connections between its developing brain and its developing muscles were not fully developed or myelinated. The energy required to kick and punch and move about was enormous. The fetal lungs and heart were not fully developed either. The fetus tired very quickly, it was exhausted within minutes. It is also important to remember, how long the First Fear Cycle of Development lasted. In most cases, its mother would sleep for up to eight hours. The fetus had a very long exposure to the First Fear Cycle of Development, throughout the long hours of the night. As you have seen, these neurons encoded with this fetal exhaustion, are influencing Betty's conscious thoughts. While she has not done any hard physical work that makes her tired, these neurons, encoded with the First Fear Cycle, within her subconscious, are firing, thus telling her that she has just fought for her life for the last eight hours. This is the same reason that Betty's muscles ache when she got up to walk to the bathroom. After eight hours of attempting to save its mother's life, the punching and kicking and trying to initiate a response, the fetus has been through a tremendous workout. All of its muscles are sore and they ache. Again, this ache and fatigue is all encoded in the First Fear Cycle neurons, which are influencing Betty's conscious thoughts.

Also, when she walks to the bathroom Betty feels as if she is moving in slow motion. No matter how fast she tries to move, it seems that in a few minutes that she is back in the same slow pace. This is called psychomotor retardation and is a very common symptom of depression. To understand why Betty feels this way and moves this slowly, it is helpful to return to dreams or nightmares of "no effect," you have seen in Chapter eight on "Sleep and Dreams." While not everybody can recall these dreams or nightmares, everybody has them. If you remember, the major theme of these nightmares was the kicking and punching out at an enemy with all of the individual's strength, yet the punches and kicks had little or no effect. During these nightmares the individual, who is kicking and punching out at the attacker, seems to be doing so in slow motion. When a punch is thrown, it seems to be thrown at such a slow pace that the punch does little to stop the attacker. This nightmare, of course, is based on the fetal response to attempt to save, what it believed to be its dying mother during the First Fear Cycle of Development. No matter how many punches or kicks the fetus would deliver, its dying mother continued the process of dying. Its mother, of course, was only sleeping and would not likely wake up. The major reason its mother would not wake up, was because the fetal punches and kicks did very little to awaken her. This is because; while inside the fetal brain it was delivering a punch and kick with all of its energy an effort, however, because the connections between the brain and hand or foot were not fully developed or myelinated, the punch and kick was not thrown with very much force. This movement in slow motion that the fetus realized was not only limited to the punching and kicking. Indeed, while to its mother, the fetus appeared to be gently moving, the fetal brain was signaling its body, hands and legs, to move as fast as they could go. This was especially true during the First Fear Cycle of Development. Now, for Betty these are the same neurons, within her subconscious, that are dominating her conscious thoughts and actions. While Betty tries to move fast, and often can, for a short period of time when she stops concentrating on this quicker speed; her subconscious takes over, and once again, just like in her fetal state, she is moving in slow motion.

The reason for the weight loss Betty experienced is quite simple to understand. While eating is a dopamine-seeking behavior, it does not reach fruition until outside the womb. In other words, while the fetus was conditioned to suck its thumb or fingers in the womb to obtain dopamine, it was not until after birth that the infant would connect the sucking of its mother's nipple to the intake of food. Therefore, in Betty's case, because it is the fetal neurons that are dominating, through her subconscious, her conscious thoughts, her desire for food will often decrease. This is because the fetus in the womb was force-fed. As you have seen, it had no comprehension of obtaining its own food. In other words, those neurons, encoded with the First Fear Cycle of Development, are not neurons that have a complete comprehension of obtaining food. And it is these neurons, when experiencing an episode of depression that are dominating not only Betty's thoughts, but her actions as well. This lack of, or reduced, appetite should not be confused with anorexia or bulimia, as they are not related. The reasons for these disorders are very specific and will be explained later in this chapter.

When Betty loses her car keys, this is due to the blockage of her short-term memory from the Memory Block. Encoded in every neuron of the First Fear and Euphoric Cycles, is the Memory Block that was an integral aspect of the fetal neural pattern. In the womb, as you have seen, the Memory Block had a very important purpose. This purpose was to block the short-term memory of the fetus, thus, making its recall of the previous developmental cycle difficult. This allowed the fetus to conform effectively to the developmental cycle it was in at the time. These are the same neurons, those encoded with the First Fear and Euphoric Cycles of Development that are dominating Betty's conscious thoughts. Just as in the womb, this blocks Betty's short-term memory and causes her to misplace and forget things that she would normally remember. In the womb, the Memory Block played an important role, outside the womb, for those suffering an episode of depression; it is nothing more than a severe hindrance. The Memory Block blocks the short-term memory, makes concentration difficult, and for Betty it causes to lose her car keys.

The Development of Guilt as a Symptom of Depression

Guilt is another common symptom of depression. Sitting on her couch Betty feels guilty about her family, about her life and finally, feels guilty about guilt itself. Indeed, Betty is consumed in guilt. Guilt, as a symptom of depression, shows nothing more than the vast emotional maturity of the fetus towards the end of the pregnancy. As you have seen, the fetus believed that if its mother died it would die too. Over a period of months, this belief developed into the belief of a mutual dependence between the fetus and its mother. Not only did the fetus believe that its mother's life was connected to its own, but it also believed that it was keeping its mother alive. More than that even, it believed that its primary job was to keep its mother alive. The relationship between the fetus and its mother went very deep, emotionally, for the fetus. Night after night, week after week, during the First Fear Cycle of Development, the fetus believed that it had been saving its mother's life. It believed it was its job. It is important to realize here, just what the fetal perception of its mother was. The fetus never blamed or connected the horrific events of the First Fear Cycle of Development, the apneas, the increased pain, the reduction of dopamine, the nightly battles with death, with its mother. It never believed or perceived in any way that she was responsible for what was occurring. It simply believed that an outside force was attempting to kill them both. It also believed that it was its job to prevent this tragic condition. While the fetus did not blame its mother for any of these negative events in the First Fear Cycle of Development, it did credit her with the positive Euphoric Cycle of Development.

The reason that the fetus does not credit its mother with any of the negative aspects of the intrauterine experience, however, only the positive ones, is a very simple and logical reason. The reason is because during the Euphoric Cycle its mother is moving around and talking. Then, during the First Fear Cycle its mother has slowed or stopped her movement and is rarely talking. Therefore, the fetus interprets the high activity level of its mother during the Euphoric Cycle to be the responsibility of its mother. After all, this makes complete sense because the fetus not only hears its mother's voice, but also believes the movement that she is making, as she walks around, is that movement of her own. Now, when its mother is lying down or sleeping, the fetus believes that because its mother is not moving, that she is not responsible for her actions, nor is she in control of her actions. It is important to remember here, that the fetus has no comprehension about the process of its mother's sleeping pattern. It does not even understand what it is for her to sleep. Because of the Memory Block, the fetus does not remember or cannot recall that she goes to sleep every night and wakes up every morning. It simply cannot remember events, due to the Memory Block, for this long a period of time. The fetus then believes that while its mother is responsible for the Euphoric Cycle, she is obviously not responsible for the painful First Fear Cycle. It believes what affects itself affects its mother. So therefore, when the fetus is in pain during the First Fear Cycle of development it believes its mother is too and that it is responsible to save her and itself from this impending death.

Because the fetus credits its mother with only the positive aspects of intrauterine experience, it only sees her as someone who is positive and makes it feel better. This, of course, is because during the Euphoric Cycle high levels of dopamine are circulating to the reward pathways of the developing fetal brain. This, how the fetus perceives it, is what its mother is responsible for.

Because the fetus perceives its mother as only the cause of pleasure and that it believes itself responsible for saving both of their lives during the First Fear Cycle, a deep bond develops from the fetus for its mother. Now, as the intrauterine conditions deteriorate towards the end of the pregnancy, the fetus begins to think about leaving the womb. As you have seen, there are many reasons that initially prevent it from doing this. The first is that it is afraid that it may die. However, a more important reason is that it believes that if it leaves its mother certainly would die. As you have also seen, the fetus cannot believe that it is even considering deserting its mother. This is the origin of guilt. The fetus not only feels guilty about the possibility of leaving, however, also feels guilty about even thinking this thought.

Therefore, when Betty feels guilty about her husband, about her children and about feeling guilty itself, it becomes obvious that the guilt she feels is about nothing specific, however, essentially, a free floating guilt that is waiting to connect to something. She has done nothing wrong to her husband or children, yet feels guilty nonetheless. Finally, with no realistic reason to feel guilty, she feels guilty about feeling guilty. This is very much how the influence of the First Fear Cycle of Development works within the subconscious. The guilt that is encoded in the neurons of the First Fear Cycle is not a complete emotion. In other words, the guilt is not connected to anything. This, of course, is because the aspects of the fetal neurons encoded with that guilt, have been reprogrammed. Assuming its mother survives labor, these neurons are reprogrammed immediately, at least partially. While the guilt will remain, part of its belief that it left its mother to die, is immediately disproved, when the infant surprisingly realizes that its mother did not die, however, remained alive.

While this is true, it is important to realize that because the relationship between the fetus and its mother is the very origin of guilt, this relationship will almost always generate the strongest reaction of this emotion. This will be especially true for the female and especially true for the female with First Fear Not Relieved. The reason guilt towards her mother will, in most cases, be stronger than a male's guilt towards his mother, is because of the differences in the gender's intrauterine environment. As you remember, the First Fear Cycle of Development was for the male much stronger, more severe and more violent than it was for the female. Therefore, when the intrauterine environment began to deteriorate, as was a normal part of the end of the pregnancy, the male realized this deterioration much more dramatically. This deterioration for the male fetus was extremely painful, making the decision to leave the womb easier, than it was for the female fetus. Because conditions were better for the female fetus, it felt even worse, or guiltier about the prospect of leaving and deserting someone who had only caused it pleasure, at least until the time when it considered leaving.

A daughter may manifest this guilt towards her mother in many ways. She may feel that she has not been a good daughter. She may feel that she has not given her mother enough of her time. This will be especially true as her mother begins to enter old age. The daughter may, subconsciously, feel that she is somehow responsible for her mother's condition. When her mother actually does die, this will pull up, through association, many of those neurons encoded with the First Fear Cycle of Development, that were specific to the end of the fetal experience in the womb. Enclosed in the daughter's mourning for her mother is a certain amount of guilt. This is not to say that a son will not feel guilty concerning the attention he has given to his mother. Depending on how severe the final days in the womb were for him, his feelings of guilt may be close to comparable to the daughter's towards her mother.

Other Symptoms of Depression

There are other symptoms of depression that, while Betty does not demonstrate; are of equal importance. Suicide ideation, attempts and the act of suicide itself are other possibilities that the individual with depression will often experience. Suicide's relation to the fetal intrauterine experience is so obvious and important that it will be covered in its own section of this chapter. A feeling of hopelessness is a common symptom of depression, and will also be covered in this later section on suicide.

The feeling of worthlessness is a common emotion realized by an individual during an episode of depression as well. This emotion is easy to understand when you look, once again, at what the fetus believed to be its primary responsibility. This primary responsibility was to keep its mother alive. During the First Fear Cycle of Development, the fetus believed that it was failing this responsibility. No matter how much it kicked and punched, touched the intrauterine walls with its fingers, moved and jerked its body, it could not generate a response and therefore save its mother. It felt it was a failure and worthless. Concerning worthlessness, an individual may misinterpret environmental cues and its accomplishments, much as it did during its fetal state. For example, if a depressed individual loses their job, it would be a normal response to feel sad or upset. The depressed individual may misinterpret this event, by feeling that they are worthless and that nobody wants to work with them anyways. This, of course, is due to the strong influence of the First Fear Cycle of Development on the individual's subconscious, and therefore, perceptions, of not only their environment, but also of their own ability.

The expression of sadness on the face of an individual with depression, and the feeling of this sadness an individual experiences, are both common symptoms of this disorder. Sadness was an obvious emotion that the fetus experienced, which originated during the First Fear Cycle of Development. During the long hours of the night, deep into the First Fear Cycle of Development, after it was exhausted from the punching and kicking, the fetus essentially waited to die. It believed it was just a matter of time before death would completely consume its mother and therefore itself. The fetus believed that it was failing in its primary job, which was to keep its mother and therefore itself alive. The First Fear Cycle of Development was a painful experience; the reduced flow of the amount of dopamine enabled the fetus to feel the entire pain of its development. While it may not have given up the hope of survival completely, it certainly was close to doing so. All its attempts at saving, what it believed to be, its dying mother had failed. This feeling of sadness consumed the fetus for many hours. Indeed, the programming of the sadness from the First Fear Cycle was such a dominant aspect of this developmental cycle, that it consumed a large portion of each neuron encoded with this event. In other words, while the fetal apneas, which are encoded into the same neurons, were intense and devastating, they only represented a small part of the First Fear Cycle of Development. It was this emotional reaction of sadness that the fetus experienced in response to its situation that consumed a large portion of the First Fear Cycle of Development. Therefore, sadness, more than any other emotion or symptom, will be one of the most common signs that an individual is experiencing an episode of depression and ultimately suffers from the condition of First Fear Not Relieved.

Often times, individuals with depression will have a sad look on their face. When asked by others, what is wrong? They often reply nothing or they do not know. This is a very common response for an individual with depression. Indeed, they do not know what is wrong. What is occurring here is that, encoded in the neurons of the First

Fear Cycle, is not only the fetal emotion of sadness, however, the fetal facial response as well. This facial response, encoded within the neurons of the First Fear Cycle, which dominates the individual's subconscious, is not only influencing the individual's mood, but their facial muscles as well.

Manic Depression

Now, it is time to switch our thoughts from the negative aspects of depression, those influenced by the First Fear Cycle of Development, to the more positive influence of the Euphoric Cycle of Development. Yes, of course, just as there are two distinct cycles of intrauterine development, there are two distinct types of depression. Each type of depression mimics directly a single cycle of fetal intrauterine development. In the case of major or unipolar depression, the influence is the First Fear Cycle of Development. As you will see, with manic depression or a manic episode, the individual realizes the influence from the Euphoric Cycle of Development.

It must have been paradise. While its mother was moving around, busy with her daily tasks, the fetus must have been in paradise. After all, everything was working perfectly. Its mother was alive and active. The fetus was gently rocking, vibrating and moving to the rhythm of her steps. This rocking and vibration increased the flow of dopamine to the reward pathways of the developing fetal brain. It was the most pleasurable experience imaginable for the fetus. It felt little or no pain. The sound that represented life was plentiful. What Nature had taken away during the First Fear Cycle, she gave back during the Euphoric Cycle. And for a few brief hours the fetus was in paradise.

We will go through an episode of manic depression, a look at the symptoms of this disorder and how these symptoms directly mimic the Euphoric Cycle of Development the individual experienced as a fetus. Before we begin, it is important to realize that while the influence of a manic episode of depression is the positive cycle of fetal intrauterine development, the manic episode of depression is far from a positive experience. While the individual who suffers this episode is often happy, and elevated in mood, as you will see, this is a disorder and there are consequences.

An individual during a manic episode will often have an inflated sense of self-esteem and a feeling of grandiosity. This makes sense, as the fetus believed it was accomplishing its primary job perfectly; it was keeping its mother alive. This is the opposite emotion it experienced during the First Fear Cycle of Development. In that cycle, the fetus believed it was failing at its primary job of keeping its mother alive. This translated into a feeling of worthlessness for the fetus. Therefore, when the influence on the depressed individual from their subconscious originates from the Euphoric Cycle of Development, they will realize a similar misinterpretation, as the fetus did during the Euphoric Cycle. Just, as the fetus misinterpreted that it was keeping its mother alive, and therefore realized an inflated self-belief, so too, does the individual, during a manic episode, believes and therefore misinterpret that they are accomplishing or are capable of accomplishing some incredible task. After all, the fetal misinterpretation that it was keeping its mother alive, during her daily activities, is a severe misinterpretation. It actually believed that it was succeeding, that it somehow had something to do with all of these positive events. You will see this, as a common theme throughout the symptoms of an episode of manic depression.

During a manic episode of depression an individual will often talk incessantly, sometimes it will seem as if they will not stop talking at all. They will carry on conversations, often in depth conversations, with total strangers. This is nothing more than the reenactment of fetal perception of its mother during the Euphoric Cycle. To understand this, it is necessary to realize when the Euphoric Cycle happened. The very definition of the Euphoric Cycle was that it occurred during the time when its mother was active and moving around. During this time, usually during the day, its mother would not only be busy with her daily activities, however, during these activities would likely be talking to others as well. The people, who its mother would be talking to, would be to the fetus, total strangers. The fetus listened carefully to all these conversations, to the sound of its mother's voice and likely attempted to mimic these sounds. After all, to the fetus its mother was an advanced entity that could accomplish things that it could not, however, it was eager to attempt them. All this information was encoded into the neurons of the Euphoric Cycle of Development. These are the same neurons that are now firing, within the individual's subconscious, which is experiencing an episode of manic depression. This strong influence of the Euphoric Cycle, on the manic individual's behavior, results in them attempting to mimic every aspect of their mother's behavior that they realized, as a fetus in the womb. They will, like her, talk to what the fetus thought were total strangers. Because its mother was often talking during the Euphoric Cycle, they will talk, almost constantly, during an episode of manic depression.

Sometimes an individual during a manic episode of depression will have grandiose delusions. They may believe that they have a special relationship to God or somebody famous such as a celebrity. The key word here, of course, is special relationship. Indeed, there is no more of a special relationship with somebody than thinking that it is your job to keep them alive. This was exactly the fetal misinterpretation of its role with its mother. It believed that somehow it was responsible for somebody much larger than it was. This person was its mother. As you have already seen, the fetus believed that it was keeping its mother alive and therefore had an inflated belief in its own abilities. It had an inflated belief in its own importance. While the fetus felt its mother was responsible for the positive feeling it experienced during the Euphoric Cycle, due to the increase of dopamine, it also felt that she was very much dependent upon the fetus. It is important to understand the fetal perception of events that occurred during its intrauterine experience. In all situations, the fetus believed that it itself was responsible for everything that happened. When good things happened, it was because of something that it did. When bad things happened, while it did not always blame itself for those things, in the First Fear Cycle it very much believed that it was responsible for the failure to keep its mother alive. What you can begin to see, through both cycles of intrauterine development, is the fetus who essentially believed the world, its world at least, revolved around it. Therefore, as this perception influences the individual's thoughts during an episode of manic depression it is not difficult to understand how this fetal perception is projected on to the world outside. It is not difficult to understand why the manic individual believes that they have a special relationship with somebody that is bigger than them. This will be especially true, concerning a relationship with God. After all, to a fetus its mother was essentially a God, as one definition of this word must be the belief in someone who can do something more than oneself.

Individuals who suffer a manic episode depression are often very indiscriminate about their sexual relations. They may meet someone and quickly begin sexual relations with them. This would be in contrast to their normal or non-manic episode, where they would normally be more discriminate and cautious about such relations. This is a very important symptom of manic-depression, for as you have seen earlier, it shows the effectiveness of Nature's reproduction model within the individual's sleep-wake pattern. You have already seen that an individual with manic depression often sleeps only three hours. This, of course, is plenty of time to review the First Fear Cycle of Development, during slow wave sleep, in this first sleep period. Once this review is at least partially completed, the individual will be properly motivated to accomplish the essential task set forth for it by Nature. This task, of course, is reproduction, which will lead to the ultimate proliferation of the human species. How sleep works for the non-manic individual, and under normal circumstances, is that the first period of sleep is followed by a more positive sleep period, heavily influenced by the Euphoric Cycle of Development. Then, during the second sleep period, during REM sleep stage, the images of the Euphoric Cycle integrate with the images of the individual's daily life. This results in a dream of reproductive content.

Now, in the case of the manic individual, they simply act out consciously, the intention of the second sleep period, which is reproduction or the attempt there of. Again, this shows how effective Nature's sleep model is in regards to reproduction. It also shows the reduced importance of REM sleep for this purpose. By acting out, in a conscious state, the intention of the second sleep period their sexual drive is increased, this is because it has not been previously accomplished during their second period of sleep.

This brings us to understanding what causes a manic episode of depression in the first place. To this, there is a very simple answer. In fact, you have actually already seen the answer before in the chapter on "Sleep and Dreams." A manic episode of depression often follows an episode of major or unipolar depression. This pattern follows the placement of sleep periods perfectly. As you have seen earlier in Chapter eight on "Sleep and Dreams," Nature placed the most horrific sleep review during the first sleep period, which was that review heavily influenced by the First Fear Cycle of Development. Then, the second sleep period was intended to realize a heavy influence from the more positive Euphoric Cycle of Development.

Nature placed the more horrific review of the First Fear Cycle within the first sleep period for two reasons. The first is that it contains important developmental information concerning reproduction. The second is that by placing it in the first sleep period of the night, the time is the longest between the horrific review and the time the individual is to return to sleep the next night. This has all been explained in depth in Chapter eight. What is important to realize here is that the review of the Euphoric Cycle always follows the complete review of the First Fear Cycle. Now, this is true as you have also seen whether the individual is asleep or awake. Therefore, it is the same case with an episode of manic depression. This is because it is the same group of neurons that are involved. During an episode of major or unipolar depression, the neuronal influence is from the First Fear Cycle of Development. This is then followed, just as it is during sleep, by a neuronal influence of the Euphoric Cycle of Development, thus, the manic episode of depression.

However, an episode of manic depression does not always follow an episode of major or unipolar depression. There are many reasons for this, which are quite technical and will not be discussed here. What is important to realize is that there are other factors that can trigger an episode of manic depression. These factors can include the individual experiencing a traumatic situation or an emotionally painful one. What happens here is that, external events that occurred to the individual connect to the neurons of the First Fear Cycle of Development, within the individual's subconscious. In other words, external factors that cause the individual emotional pain mimic the pain experienced during the First Fear Cycle of Development; this then signals the completion of the review of the First Fear Cycle and is then followed by the review, within the individual's subconscious, of the Euphoric Cycle, which generates a manic episode of depression. We will look at a brief example, which will clarify how this complex process works.

John is a middle-aged man, who suffers depression. He has battled depression for the last twenty years of his life. His mother has been sick recently and now he has just received a phone call to inform him that his mother has passed away. Now, instead of mourning his mother's death, John is acting strangely upbeat and happy. At the funeral, he is even joking with other guests, who find his behavior strange.

What, of course, has happened to John is that the death of his mother has caused him great emotional pain. Now, this emotional pain, through association, connects, within his subconscious, to the neurons encoded with the First Fear Cycle of Development. This is understandable, because the central theme of the First Fear Cycle of Development was his attempting to save his mother's life and therefore his own. Once this connection to those neurons is made, this signals a complete review of the First Fear Cycle of Development, within his subconscious. Once this review is complete, it will be followed by a review, within his subconscious, of neurons encoded with the Euphoric Cycle of Development. Again, this is exactly what is supposed to occur on a nightly basis during the individual's sleep. What has happened here is that external events mimicked the First Fear Cycle, subconsciously, and then, consciously, John acts out the influence of the Euphoric Cycle, resulting in an episode of manic depression.

Misinterpretation as a Symptom of Depression

One thing that is very important to understand about depression; for both manic and major or unipolar depression is that it causes the individual to misinterpret their environment. While this is not an established symptom of depression, it is one of the most common dominating aspects of the disorder. First, we will look at why an individual with depression misinterprets their environment; then, we will look at ways in which this misinterpretation often affects their judgment and life. As you have seen, the entire intrauterine experience for the fetus was a series of misinterpretations. You have also seen that most of these misinterpretations were not only intentional, however, essential in the definition of the human species as well. You have also realized that most of these misinterpretations experienced by the fetus were due to the Memory Block. The end result of the Memory Block was that the fetus only knew part of what was actually occurring. For example, during the First Fear Cycle of Development, it believed that its mother was in the process of dying. This was due to its inability to remember that every night she went to sleep and every morning she would wake up. And this was due to its blocked short-term memory, which was made possible by this neural function of the developing fetal brain, called the Memory Block. When the fetus was in the Euphoric Cycle of Development, it believed that it was on top of the world that it was succeeding in its job to keep its mother alive. It also felt during this pleasurable cycle, under the influence of high levels of dopamine, that this Euphoric Cycle would last forever. If the fetus could remember the existence of the other developmental cycle, this horrific cycle, where it would be fighting for its life, was just around the corner, it would not be euphoric at all. Indeed, the fetus would be scared for its life, in both cycles. Because of the Memory Block, however, the fetus cannot remember the existence of the other cycle. Therefore, the fetus, during the Euphoric Cycle, can completely relax, oblivious to the existence of the horrific First Fear Cycle. When the fetus finally left the womb, it believed that it was leaving its mother behind to die; however, she did not die. This too was due to the Memory Block. If the fetus did not have its short-term memory blocked, it would have not believed that it was saving its mother's life every night, because it would not believe that she was even dying. Because of the Memory Block, however, it believed all of these things. And all of these things were misinterpretations. The fetus misinterpreted all of these events. The fetus only had part of the story, only knew part of the facts, and it only knew a part of what was going on. This all lead to misinterpretations. Indeed, as you have seen, life in the womb was one misinterpretation of the fetal environment built upon another.

For the individual with depression, both manic and major or unipolar depression, life is very much like this. Just as in their fetal state, the Memory Block, at least temporarily, heavily influences their neural pattern. This influence can cause a great deal of misinterpretation of the depressed individual's environment.

In manic depression, misinterpretation is a common occurrence. During a manic episode, an individual might spend money foolishly, not thinking about the consequences. This is a misinterpretation. Here, they misinterpret their financial situation. They believe because there is enough money or credit to pay for their spending spree, that there will always be enough money or credit to pay for their foolish spending behavior. This is because the Memory Block does not allow them to see the past clearly or the present clearly. It only allows them to believe that whatever condition they are in at the time, it will remain that way forever. In the womb, this was an important purpose of the Memory Block. In life, however, this type of misinterpretation is not helpful to the individual. The manic individual may also participate in sexual activity, not thinking about the risk of the consequences. They may be married to someone other than who they have sexual relations with. Consequences may arise out of this. The manic individual, however, misinterprets the situation and therefore, does not see the potential consequences. The manic individual may contact old friends that they have not spoken to in years. They may do this very late at night, even in the early morning hours, just to talk. Here, they misinterpret their friendship with the individual. They believe that this old friend will share the same intense desire to speak to them as they do to speak to the old friend. Indeed, the manic individual misinterprets other's feelings and emotions to be the same as their own, during this episode of manic depression.

The individual, with major or unipolar depression, also misinterprets their environment, although with more negative interpretations. For example, they may have a co-worker or friend, who they speak to on a daily basis. One day, this friend may be preoccupied, or not see them. The depressed individual may misinterpret this as proof that the friend does not like them anymore, or never really did. The depressed individual may also misinterpret their failures, as you have seen under the symptom of worthlessness. In that case, the individual thought that because they failed at a job that they were failures at life. This is not only a misinterpretation of the importance of one failure, but also likely a misinterpretation of the reason they lost their job in the first place.

Suicide

A threat to commit suicide or an unsuccessful suicide attempt is nothing more than a reenactment of the fetus initiating labor contractions. The act of committing suicide is nothing more than the reenactment of the fetus initiating birth.

To understand what this means, we will return to the final days in the womb for the fetus. As you realized, in the model of the First Fear Cycle in Chapter three, towards the end of the pregnancy, the intrauterine conditions deteriorate substantially for the fetus. Nature is signaling the fetus, in many ways that it is time to go. In addition, to signaling the fetus to leave, Nature is initiating changes to prepare the mother for the process of birth.

One of the most obvious signals that Nature utilizes to prompt the fetus to leave the womb is to allow it with a net reduction in dopamine. Dopamine, as you have seen, is the neurochemical that makes life in the womb for the fetus tolerable. Without dopamine or with severely reduced amounts of dopamine, the fetus will simply initiate labor and leave the womb. The actual dopamine flow available to the fetus does not necessarily decline, what occurs is that the developing fetal brain, as it matures towards the end of pregnancy, needs more dopamine than it previously did. As the fetal brain matures, it needs a larger amount of dopamine to realize the same effect that it once obtained with a lesser amount. In other words, the fetus needs more dopamine, towards the end of the pregnancy, to kill or numb the horrific pain that it is realizing. There is only so much dopamine available though, and the fetus is quickly outgrowing its supply.

Indeed, the fetus is growing in every way. Its head and body has grown so large that it can hardly move around inside the cramped womb. This makes its nightly battle with death, its attempt to save its mother's life on a nightly basis even more difficult. In fact, often in the last month its' kicking and punching may even decrease. This decrease in space and increase in pain, make life in the womb almost intolerable.

Not only is the fetus outgrowing its dopamine supply, however, it is outgrowing its nutrients supply as well. Nature is not only signaling the fetus to leave the womb by decreasing its dopamine level, however, its blood cholesterol level as well. The signal is clear; its mother simply cannot continue to support two lives in one body, especially since this second life has grown so large.

Yes, Nature is telling the fetus, in every way, possible that it is time to go. After all, it is all a part of the natural process. The fetus, however, knows nothing of the natural process. The fetus does not want to leave at all. If it could, it would stay forever encapsulated inside its mother.

The fetus has its own ideas about what is going on. While it wants to stay no matter what, conditions continue to deteriorate. The fetus decides that it must take action. No matter what it does, it seems that nothing is working. One night, during the First Fear Cycle of Development, it bluffs an attempt to leave. As you have seen, in Chapter three on "The First Fear Cycle of Development," the fetus bluffs leaving the womb, hoping that conditions will improve. As you have also seen in Chapter three, the conditions did not improve and the fetus realizing that there is no further hope in staying, that things are never going to improve, that it is faced with the insurmountable obstacles of the decaying intrauterine environment, finally, decides to leave the womb.

When an individual is suicidal, they are reliving the final days they experienced as a fetus in the womb. All that is occurring is the neurons encoded with the First Fear Cycle of Development, specific to the final days of pregnancy, are firing, within the suicidal individual's subconscious, exerting a stronger than normal influence. The brief description of the final days in the womb that you have just read, is exactly the perception of life outside the womb, the suicidal individual realizes.

The human species is the only species to initiate its own labor. The human species is also the only species to reenact that initiation through suicide. The decision to leave the womb is made completely by the fetus. The decision to leave the world, as we know it, is completely the decision of the suicidal individual. This is not to say that its mother has no effect on when the fetus will make this decision, if dopamine levels fall too dramatically for the fetus, it will leave. This is also not to say that the world has no effect on the suicidal individual, if conditions become too severe, they may leave the world.

The problem with suicide is that it has been confirmed. What this means is, when the fetus left the womb, it finally did so to escape a horrific situation. When the fetus evolved into infancy that horrific situation changed for the better. Therefore, when the suicidal individual reenacts these final days in the womb, encoded in those same neurons is not only the belief that things will be better once they commit this act, however, through reprogramming of those First Fear neurons outside the womb, proof that they are better. It is a sad deviation of Nature's intended purpose, when the individual reenacts their birth through suicide.

Then, there is the unsuccessful suicide attempt; the ideation and the completed act. Just as many fetal attempts to bluff leaving the womb ended up by the fetus going too far and actually initiating labor; so are many suicide attempts, which end up with the individual going too far and actually, successfully committing suicide.

Just like for the fetus during the last days in the womb, the suicidal individual will often have a low level of dopamine circulating within their blood. Just like the fetus during the last days in the womb, the suicidal individual will often have a low level of cholesterol circulating within their blood. And just like the fetus during the last days in womb, the suicidal individual will often realize an overwhelming sense of hopelessness.

Hopelessness is a very important emotion regarding suicide. The origin of hopelessness, of course, is the final days in the womb for the fetus. As you realized, in Chapter three on "The Fist Fear Cycle of Development" the fetus, during the long hours of the night, lived on hope. Indeed, it had little else. If it could initiate a response by touching its fingertips to the intrauterine walls, it had hope that it could save its dying mother, who was only sleeping. If it could only hear a sound, throughout the long hours of the night, deep into the First Fear Cycle of Development, then, the fetus would have hope that maybe its mother and therefore itself was not in the process of dying.

And finally, when it bluffed leaving the womb, its intention was hope. It hoped its mother, would somehow realize its importance and therefore, change the conditions for the better, in the deteriorating intrauterine environment. Hope was so much a part of fetal life. When it lost hope, it, finally, gave up and left the womb. Of all the symptoms a suicidal individual can exhibit; the most serious symptom in regards to their close proximity to reenacting birth through suicide would have to be hopelessness.

A motivation for suicide may include; a desire to give up in the face of perceived insurmountable obstacles. This is exactly what the fetus faced during the final days in the womb. No matter what it did, even threatening to leave the womb, conditions only deteriorated. A motivation for committing suicide is an intense wish to end an extremely painful emotional state. This is the exact state the fetus realized during the final days in the womb.

Anorexia Nervosa

"That's quite enough—

I hope I shan't grow anymore—as it is, I

can't get out at the door—I wish I hadn't

drunk quite so much!"

— Lewis Carroll

Alice's Adventures in Wonderland

These words were spoken in fear by Alice, as she had just drunk from a bottle that made her body grow larger. Growing larger was a tremendous fear of Alice's and as you will see, for some girls this fear is large enough to act upon. Of course, Alice's Adventures in Wonderland, where this excerpt originated from is filled with other references from life in the womb as well. There is the return to the womb, when she goes back down through the rabbit hole. There is all the crazy nonsense, things that made little sense, just like life in the womb, when looked back through the eyes of a child. Yet, we are only interested in one aspect of this classic tale, Alice growing too large.

This brings us to the world where everything is not upside down or backwards, however, tragic nonetheless. For the anorexic individual, there are often grave and dangerous repercussions to living life in the womb, years later.

To find out why the individuals, who suffer from this disorder, are primarily female, it is necessary to look back at the differences of the intrauterine environment between each gender. As you have seen, the conditions of the intrauterine environment, towards the end of the pregnancy deteriorate rapidly. This deterioration affected the male fetus even more severely. As you remember, the entire intrauterine environment, especially the First Fear Cycle of Development, was much more severe for the male than the female fetus. Therefore, as conditions worsened, the decision to leave, for the male, was much easier than for the female fetus.

The female fetus, truly, would have stayed forever. It would have endured the pain, in order to save, what it thought to be, its dying mother. The intrauterine conditions were never that bad for the female fetus, there was only one problem. The problem was that it just kept growing. Indeed, to the female fetus the walls were closing in, the womb was shrinking, as it continued to grow. The decision to finally leave was an extremely difficult one for the female fetus, and not one that was made without hesitation. It is important to realize that the female fetus absolutely did not want to leave the womb. It was consumed with guilt about leaving its mother behind to die that had given it so much more pleasure than the male fetus realized and so much less pain than the male fetus realized as well. This experience, of course, was encoded into the neurons of the First Fear and Euphoric Cycles of Development, specific to the final days in the womb.

For most female infants, many of these neurons are eliminated or reprogrammed. For the female with First Fear Not Relieved, due to environmental factors, these neurons are reinforced. As these females, with First Fear Not Relieved, mature, their neural pattern evolves, and these neurons, which form their subconscious, exert a strong influence on their conscious thoughts and motivations.

One of these motivations is eating. For the female with anorexia nervosa, her thoughts are dominated by the neurons encoded with these two cycles of intrauterine development, specific to the final days in the womb. Anorexia nervosa is a condition, where an individual, usually a female, refuses to maintain a minimal normal body weight, is intensely afraid of gaining weight, and exhibits a significant misinterpretation of the perception of their body size. This is all because, the neurons dominating her subconscious have pushed their influence into her conscious thoughts. Encoded in these neurons are the final days in the womb and the biggest fear of the female fetus. It is quite an ingenious distortion of Nature's intention. Subconsciously, the female believes if she stops eating, she will never have to leave her mother and therefore, neither she nor her mother will die.

This disorder has nothing to do with wanting to be thin, because of peer pressure. This disorder has nothing to do with living in a society that pressures a female to remain or to become thin. This disorder has everything to do with the condition of First Fear Not Relieved. This disorder has everything to do with the female, subconsciously, not wanting to leave her mother behind to die. Of course, this disorder, anorexia nervosa, is often associated with a stressful life event for a female, such as leaving home. In this case, the female's conscious leaving of home, triggers the neurons in her subconscious encoded with that very old fear of leaving her mother alone to die. The only way that she can make sure this does not happen is to stay very small. The only way to stay very small is to not eat. This disorder often begins a downwards spiral. The more weight the female loses, the more distorted her perception of her weight becomes, and therefore, the less she eats. A certain percentage of the females, who suffer from this disorder, will ultimately die, from starvation, electrolyte imbalance, or suicide. Suicide, of course, makes complete sense as an end result of this disorder. Because anorexia nervosa is a reenactment of the female fetal fears during the final days in the womb and the female fetus finally had to leave, it is appropriate, although tragic, that those with this condition often commit suicide, thereby reenacting this final option of birth, through suicide.

Sleeping Disorders

Could there be anything worse? To have your days filled with depression, panic attacks and other disorders is one thing, however, to have the one solace, the one retreat available to mankind which is sleep; could there be anything worse than to have this disrupted on a nightly basis? Indeed, the individual, with First Fear Not Relieved, in addition to the other disorders they will realize, will often suffer from disorders of sleep. It should not be surprising though, after all, if the neurons encoded with the First Fear Cycle are firing inhibited and generate disorders, such as depression and panic attacks, it is easy to imagine the impact these neurons will have when they fire uninhibited, exerting full force and influence, during slow wave sleep.

Yes, it is a series of many long nights for the individual, who experiences a disorder of sleep. As you have already seen, many of these disorders and behaviors listed from the condition of First Fear Not Relieved yield a disruption in the individual's sleep pattern. Here, we will look at exactly why this disruption occurs and a few of the major disorders of sleep. We will begin, in infancy, with an understanding to the origins and causes of what was once known as "crib death." While it is now termed "Sudden Infant Death Syndrome" or "SIDS," the cause remains the same. By the end of this section, we will look at some sleep related events and their ultimate cause.

Sudden Infant Death Syndrome (SIDS)

What occurs to the infant, who experiences Sudden Infant Death Syndrome, is a failure in the REM sleep mechanism. What you have seen earlier, in Chapter eight on "Sleep and Dreams", is that one of the primary purposes of REM sleep is to protect the sleeper. REM sleep essentially rescues the sleeper out of too traumatic a review of neurons encoded with the First Fear Cycle of Development, during slow wave sleep. You have also seen that due to too much trauma being reviewed, the REM sleep mechanism often fails this important purpose. In an adult sleeper, this failure may result in the realization of waking up during an apnea and the adult has a hard time catching their breath. For a child, this failure of REM sleep to accomplish its primary purpose of rescuing the sleeper from too traumatic a review can materialize into an episode of sleep terror, which will be explained later in this chapter. To an infant, however, a failure in REM sleep to accomplish its primary goal, which is protecting the sleeper from too traumatic a review of neurons encoded with the First Fear Cycle, during slow wave sleep, can be deadly.

To understand why an infant can die during sleep, which is exactly what occurs in SIDS, it is only necessary to review the neurobiological changes that occur during infancy that were explained in Chapter five on "First Fear Not Relieved." As you have seen, during infancy, Nature begins a process of eliminating and reprogramming many of the neurons encoded with the First Fear and Euphoric Cycles of Development. This period of neuronal elimination and reprogramming will either eliminate or reprogram millions of neurons encoded with the horrific events of the First Fear Cycle of Development. Because this intrauterine development occurred to the fetus, night after night, month after month, there is an overabundance of these neurons, than are necessary for the developmental aspects Nature utilizes them for outside the womb. This is an important event, as you have seen, it is the ultimate determination as to whether an individual will realize a lifetime of the condition of First Fear Not Relieved or will realize a normal life, in neurobiological terms, as those without this condition.

Imagine the developing infant's brain during the first year. Within their brain are the memories of the entire events, they experienced in the womb. Unlike, actually, experiencing the First Fear Cycle of Development, they have the memory, encoded in those neurons of many nights experiencing those events. Indeed, on any given night, if they were even allowed a partial review, uninterrupted, of those neurons, they would die immediately. It would simply be too much trauma for their physical body to withstand. In the womb, they were essentially supported by the life support of their mother and the intrauterine environment. Outside the womb, however, there is no life support. Their lungs, their heart, their entire cardio-respiratory system is not strong enough to return to the womb, to the nightly battle with death, even if it is only a review during slow wave sleep.

Nature, of course, realizes that the infant in no way can handle an uninterrupted review of the remaining neurons encoded with the First Fear Cycle of Development. The first reason, as you have seen, is that the infant cardio-respiratory system, at such a young age could not handle the trauma. The second reason is equally obvious. During infancy, there are simply too many of these neurons encoded with the

First Fear Cycle of Development, remaining in the infant's brain. At such a young age, there has not been time for Nature to effectively eliminate or reprogram these neurons encoded with this traumatic cycle of intrauterine development. As you have seen, while most of these neurons are eliminated, reprogrammed or reinforced, within the first two years, for some of these neurons, this process extends into early childhood. Certainly at one year of age, a period of extremely high risk for SIDS, not enough of these neurons have been eliminated, or at least reprogrammed. Simply not enough time has passed. To avoid an uninterrupted review of neurons encoded with the First Fear Cycle, during slow wave sleep, Nature heavily fortifies the infant's sleep with the protective neural mechanism of REM sleep. In fact, an infant, before the age of one year, spends almost half of its sleeping time, up to eight hours, in the protective stage of REM sleep. This compared to an adult sleeper, who will spend on the average, only one fourth of their total time asleep, two hours, in the REM sleep stage.

While it is obvious that Nature wants to protect the infant from death during its sleep, by the heavy fortification of the infant's sleep with the REM sleep stage, sometimes these protective mechanisms fail. When REM sleep fails to protect the infant from the traumatic review of the neurons encoded with the First Fear Cycle of Development, during slow wave sleep, the consequences are often grave. When this occurs, the infant during slow wave sleep simply is frightened to death. It may be the review of one of the many fetal apneas it realized, during the First Fear Cycle in the womb. It may be the review of it fighting to save its mother's and therefore its own life, during the First Fear Cycle. Whatever the specific event is within the First Fear Cycle that the infant reviews, when the REM sleep stage fails, the results are always the same. Whether the infant dies or is saved from death, in both cases, it has simply too much trauma.

The question then becomes, what criteria defines whether an infant will experience an episode of SIDS and what criteria defines those who will not? The answer to this, of course, is listed under the environmental factors in Chapter five on "First Fear Not Relieved." The infant who will die from SIDS was on their way to realizing the condition of First Fear Not Relieved. Something in the infant's environment, or in a very few cases within their intrauterine environment, has failed and the neurons encoded with the First Fear Cycle of Development, have been reinforced instead of eliminated or reprogrammed. When this occurs, even at this early age, REM sleep is unable to fulfill its primary objective to protect the infant sleeper.

Disorganization of Sleep Periods

Another disorder of sleep that is related directly to the protective aspects of REM sleep, which you have seen in the previous section on SIDS, is disorganization of sleep periods. What actually occurs in this situation is that the sleeper actually forfeits there positive second sleep period in order to attempt to fully complete their first sleep period.

To understand how this works it is helpful to remember the sleep model in Chapter eight on "Sleep and Dreams." In that chapter you realized that one of the ways in which Nature ensured that the individual would return to sleep the next night was the placement of sleep periods. In order to make sure the sleeper would not have a negative opinion or association of sleep, Nature placed the most horrific aspects of sleep within the first sleep period. During the first sleep period which occurs during the first half of the night, the individual experiences a review during slow wave sleep that is heavily influenced by the neurons encoded with the First Fear Cycle of Development. This horrific, however, necessary, review was followed by a REM stage of sleep, when the individual entered their second period of deep or slow wave sleep. The neurons the sleeper reviewed;

during slow wave sleep, in this second sleep period, were heavily influenced by the more positive Euphoric Cycle of Development. The intention of the placement of this positive cycle of development in the second sleep period is that the sleeper will wake up feeling refreshed and most importantly with a positive opinion of sleep in general. In many cases, however, the individual with First Fear Not Relieved does not realize this second more positive sleep period.

In many ways, it is as if they are actually cheated out of it. What makes matters worse for them, however, is that instead of the more positive review of the Euphoric Cycle, they get a second review that is heavily influenced by the First Fear Cycle of Development. This is because they are not able to fully complete this review during their first sleep period. Many times, they are not even able to finish it completely during their second sleep period.

To make this concept clear, it is helpful to use an analogy. Look at it as watching a movie. The normal individual watches two movies during the night. The first movie they watch is a horror movie. It is scary, frightening, and very horrific. The consolation is that, after they watched the horror movie, they get to watch a beautiful love story. The love story is wonderful, happy and joyful, and makes them feel euphoric. Of course, the first movie, the horror movie, is the review, during their first sleep period, of neurons encoded with the First Fear Cycle of Development, which occurs during slow wave sleep. The second movie, the love story, is the review, during their second sleep period, which is heavily influenced by neurons encoded with the Euphoric Cycle of Development, which also occurs during slow wave sleep.

Now, many individuals with the condition of First Fear Not Relieved are not as lucky as this. Instead of watching the horror movie and the love story, they only watch the horror movie. Not only that, however, they watch the horror movie twice. Even worse than this though is that they never get to completely watch the movie either time. This is because, right before the end of the movie, it shuts off. Therefore, they watch the same horror movie twice; never finishing it either time, and never get to see the more pleasant love story.

The reason the horror movie is interrupted for the individuals with First Fear Not Relieved is that the ending is too traumatic for them to withstand. The question is, then, who or what makes the decision that this movie is too traumatic, and who or what turns the movie off before its' ending. The answer here is the REM sleep mechanism itself. For at the end of the movie, it decides that the individual cannot handle the final scenes. Therefore, because they cannot fully complete the first sleep period, or fully finish the horror movie, they are not allowed to see the second, more positive love story. Instead, the human brain tries again. If it did not finish it the first time, maybe it will finish it the second. The horror movie rolls, this time during their second sleep period. Once again, however, right before the end of the movie, the projector is turned off and the sleeper is left in suspense to the final ending. Now, tomorrow night, when this individual lies down to go to sleep, the same thing will happen. Then again, it will happen on the night after that. It will happen, over and over again, as they will rarely finish watching the horror movie and will rarely get to see the love story.

The reason that the ending of the horror movie is too traumatic for them to watch is that there are simply too many neurons remaining, encoded with the First Fear Cycle of Development. The reason for this, as you have seen, is that during infancy and early childhood, when these neurons were supposed to be eliminated or reprogrammed, they were reinforced instead.

It is time to take a closer look at the method and the motivation behind REM sleep for turning this projector off before the end of the horror movie, and, basically, ruining the chances of this sleeper ever having a very good opinion of sleep. As you remember, from the previous section on SIDS, and the earlier chapter on "Sleep and Dreams," the primary purpose of REM sleep is to protect the sleeper. In SIDS, you realized that when the trauma of the review of the neurons encoded with the First Fear Cycle, during slow wave sleep, became too traumatic a neurobiological signal was sent within the brain to the areas responsible for REM sleep stage and this process was initiated. As you have seen, for an infant, the REM sleep stage was critical; it was a lifesaver. You have also seen that when REM sleep failed, the infant many times would die. REM sleep during infancy was that important. The problem is; it is unlikely that the adult, unlike the infant, would die if they were able to see the ending of the horror movie. They may wake up gasping for air, deep into the reenactment of a fetal apnea, however, in most cases, death would elude them.

The unfortunate part of the lifesaving aspect of REM sleep is that it cannot completely differentiate between the adult and the infant. In fact, in many ways, Nature cannot differentiate between the adult and the infant in regards to sleep. The thing about Nature is that she never intended this individual with First Fear Not Relieved to survive; more or less survive long enough to realize such a minor inconvenience as a sleep disorder. When Nature created the sleep model for the human species, included in this plan was that those who did not realize the minimal environmental factors during infancy and early childhood, would perish. As you have seen, this is no longer the case. Now, the REM sleep mechanisms operate on the principle of neuronal count. This neuronal count is defined by the amount of neurons remaining encoded with the events of the First Fear Cycle of Development. For example, if the REM sleep mechanism counts five million neurons (This is not an estimate, these are random numbers utilized for this example), encoded with the First Fear Cycle of Development, to be reviewed during slow wave sleep, an alarm goes off. The alarm states, "five million neurons, encoded with the First Fear Cycle of Development, have been detected, this is an infant." The reason this alarm goes off, of course, is that because the infant cannot withstand the trauma of reviewing more than five million neurons encoded with the First Fear Cycle of Development. Therefore, REM sleep kicks in and pulls the infant safely out of this review. For, as you have seen, Nature has invested a great deal of time into this infant and certainly does not want it to die in its sleep.

Just as REM sleep works off of an alarm system for the infant, the same is true for an adult. Now, the normal adult is supposed to have two million neurons remaining encoded with the First Fear Cycle of Development. (Again, this is not an estimate, these are random numbers utilized for this example). Now, when the REM sleep mechanisms detect that there are only two million neurons encoded with the First Fear Cycle of Development, the alarm will not go off. It will only go off for the normal individuals when the review of the First Fear Cycle of Development is complete. After the review is completed, REM sleep kicks in. This then, allows the sleeper, upon completion of this review, to enter the review heavily influenced by the Euphoric Cycle of Development, in the second sleep period. This is a much more pleasant sleep experience, where the sleeper reviews the more pleasurable aspects of life in the womb. In the movie example this was the love story. This, of course, is exactly how sleep is supposed to work.

When the individual with First Fear Not Relieved goes to sleep an alarm will also go off. During the review of the neurons encoded with the First Fear Cycle of Development, the REM sleep mechanisms will detect a certain number of neurons encoded with this intrauterine event. Instead of detecting two million neurons, however, this individual has five million neurons still remaining encoded with the

First Fear Cycle of Development. If you remember, instead of these neurons being reinforced, during infancy and early childhood, they were supposed to be eliminated or reprogrammed. So when, the REM sleep mechanisms detect this many neurons, five million in total, encoded with the First Fear Cycle of Development, the same alarm goes off, the one that went off during infancy. The alarm states, "five million neurons encoded with the First Fear Cycle of Development have been detected, this is an infant." Yes, the same alarm goes off, alerting REM sleep that this is an infant and it must be rescued from too traumatic a review and pushed into a lighter safer stage of sleep, even though, this is not an infant. In fact, this is an adult with the condition of First Fear Not Relieved, who, instead of having two million neurons remaining as the normal adult would have, has five million neurons encoded with the First Fear Cycle of Development remaining. Therefore, this individual will not be allowed to fully complete the review of the neurons encoded with the First Fear Cycle of Development, because the REM sleep mechanisms believe that because of this neuronal count that they are protecting an infant.

What has happened here is that the primary purpose of REM sleep, being to protect the individual and primarily the infant from too much trauma actually hinders the sleep of the individual with the condition of First Fear Not Relieved. Again, it is important to realize that the adult with this condition would not be likely to die in their sleep as the infant would. This is because their cardio-respiratory system, in many cases, is stronger than that of the infant, and the time that has elapsed between the actual events in the womb and infancy is much less than for the adult. In most cases, what would occur for an adult with First Fear Not Relieved, when REM sleep fails, is that they will wake up in the slow wave stage of sleep, either experiencing an event such as sleep terror, or deep into the reenactment of a fetal apnea.

The individual, who cannot successfully complete the entire review of the neurons encoded with the First Fear Cycle of Development, during slow wave sleep in their first sleep period, will then be forced to try again to complete this horrific review during their second sleep period. This gives this individual a very negative opinion of sleep. And who can blame them? After all, who wants to watch an incomplete horror movie twice, every night during their sleep? This, of course, explains why many individuals, with First Fear Not Relieved, will wake up after only sleeping four hours and feel better the next day than if they have slept an entire eight hours. In this case, they only had to watch the partial horror movie once, instead of twice, as they normally did. Technically, they only had to partially review the neurons encoded with the First Fear Cycle of Development, once instead of twice.

The normal individual, however, will not wake up feeling better after only four hours of sleep. They will feel better after completing their entire eight hours. This is because, if they only get four hours of sleep, they will get cheated out of the more positive second sleep period, which for them is heavily influenced by neurons encoded with the Euphoric Cycle of Development. In other words, if they only get fours hours of sleep, they do not get to watch the love story.

After understanding the difference between the normal individual's sleep experience and the sleep experience of the individual with First Fear Not Relieved, it is possible to explain how these different sleep experiences not only affect the individual's perception of sleep, however, how these different sleep experiences affect the world's perception of the individual as well. What we are talking about here is how sleep affects the individual's appearance, specifically the facial muscles. For the female, sleep was once called "beauty rest." This term was not coined by mistake. Indeed, when sleep works the way it should, both the female and the male sleeper should awake looking refreshed and in many cases better than they did when they went to sleep.

To understand how this works, it is only necessary to realize that sleep affects the individual sleeper's face. It does this for one reason. This reason is that, during both periods of slow wave sleep, the sleeper reviews neurons encoded with both cycles of intrauterine development. During this intrauterine development the fetal face changed by the influence of its emotional state at the time. For example, during the Euphoric Cycle, the fetal face was relaxed and smiling; this was due to its emotions that were dominated by happiness and pleasure. During the First Fear Cycle, the fetal face grimaced with pain. In contrast to the loosening of the facial muscles during the Euphoric Cycle, in the First Fear Cycle the fetal facial muscles were tense and contracted. The fetal nose, especially, was affected during the First Fear Cycle of Development. Because it was through the fetal olfactory system that the First Fear Cycle of Development was conveyed to the fetus, through pungent and foul smells, the fetal nose was formed in a reaction to these odors. As you have seen, this contrasting range of emotions, the fetus experienced between the two cycles of intrauterine development, gives the human species not only its emotional range, however, this range is programmed into the muscles of the human face. The primary purpose for these facial muscles was that they would be utilized during the head first delivery, experienced during labor. These facial muscles would be important during the process of labor, helping pull the fetus through the narrow birth canal.

Every night, during the two periods of slow wave sleep, these neurons, encoded with this facial development, are reviewed by the sleeper. For the normal individual, those without First Fear Not Relieved, this review affects their facial muscles in the following way. During the first sleep period, when the review during slow wave sleep is heavily influenced by the neurons encoded with the First Fear Cycle of Development, the individual's facial muscles tighten in response to the muscle memory encoded in the developmental neurons. In the second sleep period, in response to the review that is heavily influenced by the neurons of the Euphoric Cycle of Development, these facial muscles loosen. The combination of these two developmental cycles generates a toning effect on the individual's face. When they wake up, they look refreshed and often better than when they went to sleep.

Now, for the individual with the condition First Fear Not Relieved, who only gets two partial reviews of the neurons encoded with the horrific First Fear Cycle of Development, their facial muscles do not get the entire nightly workout. Instead, their facial muscles remain in a tense, tightened, un-relaxed position. Their nose responds to the fetal facial reaction, as it realized the pungent and foul odors and reacted to the pain of the First Fear Cycle of Development. Therefore, in the morning after eight hours of reviewing the First Fear Cycle of Development, including the memory of the fetal facial muscle response, their face often reflects the battle they have just reviewed.

Insomnia

From what you have read so far, it should be obvious why some individuals suffer from insomnia. After all, who would want to go to sleep? When you think about it, who would want to review a nightly battle of fighting for their life? It is not a pleasant experience to say the least. From what you have also read, you know that Nature definitely wants the individual to return to at least some sleep on a nightly basis. This you have seen demonstrated in many ways.

You have seen the ways in which Nature masks the trauma the sleeper experiences every night. You have seen how Nature places the most horrific sleep period first, this ensures the longest time period between the traumatic review and when the individual returns to sleep the next night. You have seen how REM sleep diverts the trauma reviewed, during slow wave sleep, into images of the individual's daily life, which forms dreams and nightmares and forever leaves the sleeper guessing as to their interpretation of what these dreams and nightmares are about. You have seen how encoded in every neuron reviewed, during slow wave sleep, is the Memory Block that makes the sleeper forget most of the events they reviewed during slow wave sleep, almost as quickly as they review them. You have seen, all of these methods that Nature utilizes to ensure the sleeper will return to sleep. Now you will see, what happens when these methods fail.

When these methods to ensure the sleeper to return to sleep fail, the individual realizes the condition of insomnia. There are two major reasons for insomnia. The first is when an individual with First Fear Not Relieved is unable to successfully complete the first sleep period. This, as you have seen earlier in this chapter, in the section on "Disorganization of The Sleep Periods," forces the individual to partially review the neurons encoded with the horrific First Fear Cycle of Development twice on a nightly basis. The result of this is insomnia. This is because, the sleeper will not want to return to sleep the next night, as fresh within their subconscious is the memory of the trauma they face on a nightly basis. This then, allows the individual with insomnia, to learn on a subconscious level, association with their nighttime routine that signals them to avoid sleep. This is the second reason. We will look at an example to see exactly what this means to an individual with insomnia.

Bob suffers from the condition of First Fear Not Relieved. He is a high functioning, successful adult male, who in the past has periodically suffered from bouts with depression. At the time, however, he has no symptoms of this disorder, with one exception. Bob still suffers from insomnia.

Indeed, for twenty years Bob has battled insomnia and tonight will be no different. It is eight o'clock Bob is exhausted. He almost falls asleep in his favorite chair, watching television. His wife tells him that he is tired and should try to go to bed. Bob gets up out of the chair, goes to the bathroom and brushes his teeth. He kisses his wife good night, lies down in bed and prepares to go to sleep.

Four hours later, when his wife comes to bed, Bob is still awake. He is frustrated that he cannot sleep. And this is why.

In addition to not being able to complete his review of the First Fear Cycle of Development, during his first period of sleep, on the previous night, which forced him to partially review this horrific cycle twice, Bob's subconscious is learning by association. What this means, is that through his nighttime routine, he is learning to avoid sleep. In other words, when Bob gets up out of his chair, goes to the bathroom, brushes his teeth, kisses his wife, and most importantly looks at his bed, events are occurring within his subconscious that are preventing him from sleeping. His subconscious has learned to connect the association of his nightly routine to the trauma that he will realize when he goes to sleep. For example, when Bob looks at that toothbrush, neurons fire and connect to other neurons encoded with his previous night's battle of the First Fear Cycle of Development he reviewed during slow wave sleep. This does not mean that by avoiding brushing his teeth, Bob will not suffer from insomnia. The worst association for Bob is his bed. Indeed, when Bob sees his bed, a string of subconscious events are initiated that warn him to avoid falling asleep. Bob, through his nightly routine and consistency, is his own worse enemy.

Now, if Bob were to left in his favorite chair, he would have likely fallen asleep easily. While he might have awoken with a backache, at least he would have been able to fall asleep. There is a very good reason for this as well. It is because Bob has no subconscious negative association between sleep and his favorite chair. His subconscious knows that before he can experience too much trauma, during the review of the neurons encoded with the First Fear Cycle, during slow wave sleep that his wife will wake him up and tell him to go to bed. In this case, his wife is his rescuer from the trauma he would normally realize during sleep. What is more important though, is that Bob has not experienced any sleep trauma in this chair.

This is the reason behind the restorative effect of a vacation. When Bob goes on vacation, he usually falls right asleep. This is at least true on the first night in a new bed, because with that bed there is no negative association within his subconscious at all. He has never slept in it; therefore he has not realized any trauma while in it. Of course, if Bob stays in this bed for a week the same pattern will return. Now, when Bob returns from his vacation, there is a good chance that he will fall asleep, for a few nights at least, very quickly in his old bed. This is because the association within his subconscious has been erased, at least temporarily. Within a few nights upon returning home, unfortunately for Bob, his same cycle of negative association with sleep and insomnia will begin again.

Now, if Bob would be creative and has the money to buy a large house with many bedrooms, he could place a bed in each bedroom and sleep in a different bedroom every night. This would help his insomnia, because this negative association, as you have seen, has very short life span. Or Bob could simply switch places with his wife from the side of the bed he normally sleeps on. Over a period of time, however, his subconscious would eventually figure out what he was consciously doing, and his sleep problems would return.

Another method Bob can utilize to battle his insomnia, would be to watch television or a movie, before he went to bed. This will be especially effective if it is a horror movie that he watches, as, the formula for horror movies is usually very consistent. The horror movies begin with a monster or attacker terrorizing an individual or a town. Then, through a series of close calls and near fatal encounters, the hero, almost always, slays the monster or attacker at the end of the movie. As ridiculous as this formula is, it is still utilized because it serves a therapeutic purpose. This is because, in a few hours, the sleeper or in this case Bob is going to go to sleep and review the same scenario. The ending however, that the sleeper will review will not have such a positive or definite ending to it. This, of course, is assuming that the sleeper will complete their first review.

By watching the horror movie with its ridiculously predictable ending, the individual can rehearse the horror that awaits them during slow wave sleep during the first sleep period. Not only can they rehearse it, but also they will realize a positive conclusion, this being that the monster or attacker will be slain. Once they rehearse this predictable ending, they are empowered, subconsciously, to face the fear, the First Fear, they will confront during their first period of slow wave sleep. This will then enable the individual or Bob to fall asleep.

Sleep Terror

It is important to realize that sleep terror occurs only during slow wave sleep. It occurs, usually, during the first few hours from when the individual falls asleep. The individual wakes up, often screaming or crying, occasionally punching and kicking, with a look of terror upon their face as if they had been fighting for their life. Sleep terror is not a nightmare, as those only occur during REM sleep. Sleep terror occurs during slow wave sleep and is more common in children than adults.

Sleep terror is a failure of REM sleep to rescue the sleeper out of slow wave sleep when the sleeper is reviewing too much trauma, which is occurring during the review of the neurons encoded with the First Fear Cycle of Development. This, of course, is why sleep terror usually occurs during the first few hours from when the individual falls asleep. This, as you have seen, is during the first sleep period when the sleeper reviews the neurons encoded with the First Fear Cycle of Development. Of course, sleep terror can occur in the second sleep period, if the individual were unable to complete their first review, during the first sleep period.

When the individual wakes up, during an episode of sleep terror, they are reacting to the review of the neurons encoded with their fetal experience during the First Fear Cycle of Development. They are reviewing the fighting for their life that took place every night within the womb. The individual will not likely remember the episode the next morning; this is because these neurons are heavily encoded with Memory Block.

CHAPTER ELEVEN

MAN VS. NATURE

In the womb, man's battle against Nature begins. As a fetus, it was Nature who controlled him. In the womb, it was Nature that tricked him into believing that his mother was dying, night after night. And it was Nature who made him kick and punch out, like a fool, trying to save his dying mother's life, who was only sleeping. In the womb, it was Nature who cut his air supply off, his life support and let him suffocate for seconds at the time. Finally, it was Nature, in the womb, who made him believe that he was leaving his mother alone to die, when he left the womb, only to find out that it was all a deception and that she was fine the entire time.

Of course, Nature did all of this with the best interest of the fetus. She did this for many reasons; a major reason was to ensure that the fetus survived the long difficult process of labor and evolved into infancy safely. At one time, for primitive man at least, it may have been necessary to ensure that mankind would have some vengeance against Nature. After all, it was a difficult world primitive man faced, full of variables that he could not control. Nature's ultimate goal, however, was that man would survive. It worked well. The initial seeds of rebellion, planted millions of years ago, still remain. The natural world, which was once full of variables, has come into order. Yet, the battle rages on.

Mankind, however, does not know this. From the womb his goal is to survive. Within his subconscious, encoded in his neurons is the memory of a nightly battle he fought for nine months in the womb. Once he defines the enemy, he will never forgive her. Even if he wanted to forgive, it would be difficult to do so, as the memory of the fight remains etched within his subconscious.

Yes, it was Nature who encapsulated man in the womb for nine months and he will spend the rest of his life attempting to control what controlled him once so severely. In most cases, as you will see, it is not a conscious attempt to control. While there may be a few exceptions, most individuals believe they have a good relationship with Nature. Yet, as you will see, their actions speak of a different relationship all together. It is a relationship where control is the key. It is a relationship so often, of such subtle control, that if you did not know exactly what to look for, you would be certain to miss it.

As you have seen, for the male, retaliation begins early. It may start off, by him stepping on a bee. It may be an ant, a snail or a wasp. He may put a bug in a jar and leave it to die. He may poke, with a stick, a spider in its web. He may break that snail's shell, watching it crawl for mercy. He may grab a puppy by its tail, laughing as it chases it. He may throw a stone at a cat. Then again, he may just throw a stone against a tree.

The key word is control. He may not even need to start the fight himself. His father may introduce him into the joy and discovery of battling Nature. It may be a BB-gun he gets for his birthday. With the BB-gun he can shoot at birds, dogs and cats. While he has been told not to shoot at animals, he will anyways. One thing you can be sure of, his first target will be Nature. It may be an ant farm he gets for Christmas. He may collect bugs, putting them neatly under glass.

He is a young boy, he is cute; however, his intentions are already deadly. As he grows older, his motivations will come more into focus. He will hunt; it is not an actual hunt, for mankind does not actually hunt anymore. No, this hunt, this sport, will be a careful reenactment; the odds will always be stacked in his favor. He will shoot with a bow, however, even that is not enough. He will shoot a gun, at a deer, at an elk. The animal has no chance. At one time, he felt he had no chance. After all, he was hunted on a nightly basis in the womb. This memory, these neurons influence every thought. It is a fascination, it is therapeutic, and it is empowering to finally be on the other side of that rifle. He will seek a trophy. He could careless about the body, but the head and especially the eyes he wants to see, again and again.

Taxidermy itself is a testament to man's battle against Nature. It is a bizarre proceeding; it is a bizarre science. It serves a purpose, however. It is not about a trophy, it is about a triumph. To hang the head of a deer or an elk, or a moose on the wall, projects a statement. The statement is "Nature is controlled here." No mountain tavern, no sportsman's bar is complete without an animal's head on the wall. It lets the traveler know, "Nature is controlled here." It lets the traveler know, lets their subconscious know, that the battle they once fought against Nature in the womb, so long ago, will not have to be fought here. By the animal's head on the wall, the traveler can see, man is in control here.

The problem with hunting is that it is such a violent hobby and Nature is so big, often times the hunter comes back empty handed. Fishing may be a better choice. After all, who could actually think that fishing would have anything to do with man's intrauterine experience? You fish for food; at least that is what it once was about. Now, it is about "catch and release." This sounds good. It sounds as if man cares about Nature. It is not the case at all. To understand this, it is only necessary to look at the actions of the average fly-fisherman. He is usually more educated, more cultured than the typical deer hunter. In fact, he will probably not even want his name linked with such a sport of carnage. Yet, through fly fishing and "catch and release," philosophy his need to control Nature is even more intense than for his less educated counterpart, who only wants to kill a deer with a couple of buddies.

In many ways fly-fishing is the ultimate control of Nature. It mimics what Nature did to man almost identically. In the womb, man was fooled by Nature. Man was forced to kick and punch, on a nightly basis to save his dying mother who was only sleeping. This man, who was once a fetus, was made a fool by Nature. Now, it is his turn. Now, he can make a fool of the fish, now he can make a fool of Nature. He will fool the fish with an artificial fly. Yes, it is Nature now who will be deceived. As he watches that stupid fish jump at a fake fly he tied with his own hands, he is reenacting how Nature made him feel as a fetus in the womb. The only difference is, this time he is not the fool.

Then there is the policy of "catch and release." To find any value in this aspect of fishing, you must look closely. For this is a sport without any understandable goal. Individuals will spend thousands of dollars; will fly thousands of miles to catch a fish. Once the fish is caught, they make sure they release it. Is there a more blatant statement of man's battle against Nature? This is especially true if the fisherman uses an artificial fly, an artificial worm or artificial lure to catch the fish. Now, not only has he fooled the stupid fish, thereby fooling Nature, but also he is rewarded by a moment of empowerment. He now controls the fish in his hands. He can keep it or he can release it. This is his choice. He is in control. In his hands he is holding Nature, what once controlled him, he now controls. He is at least somewhat educated, although misled as to why he fishes.

The closer man lives to Nature, the more obvious the battle becomes. After all, in the mountains and forests, Nature's presence is overwhelming. This affects the individual's subconscious. It makes him feel small which he is against her. Nature's overwhelming presence, within the individual's subconscious, reminds him of the battle in the womb. If man lives in such a natural environment, he must constantly fight back. To live in the shadow of a large mountain may be a city dweller's dream; however, to those who live under Nature's magnificent presence, it is anything but that. Where Nature is too powerful, man feels too small. By feeling small, it reminds his subconscious of another time when he was very small. In the womb, he was very small. In the womb, Nature controlled him. Living under the shadow of such a presence, man must fight back. He may write his name on a rock, spray paint it on a cliff. Even the early pioneers, faced with the magnificence of Nature, could not help but to write their name, to deface Nature in someway. It is an act of vengeance to deface Nature. Those who live in the country, where Nature is strong must always fight back. They will dump trash, at every chance they can get. They will pick the most beautiful spot, where Nature is at her strongest and dump upon her. They will dump their old refrigerators, old stoves and old cars, violating her at every chance imaginable.

A man who lives in a city will walk out of his way to throw his trash in a public trashcan. The same man, when visiting the mountains, when camping or hiking, will throw trash on the ground. While this is hard to believe, it happens all the time. This is because in the city Nature is controlled. Nature is weak; Nature is impotent. In the mountains, however, by a clear running stream, as beautiful as it is, it reminds the individual's subconscious of how powerful Nature is.

It is not a coincidence that those who want to save Nature the most, are those who see it the least. Those who live in the city will often want to save Nature. As you will see, this is only another form of control. For even in the city, amongst the high-rise and accomplishments of man, there is still a need to see Nature controlled. There is the city park. This is important, because nobody should be deprived of the right to see Nature under the control of man. There are the city gardens, the trees and shrubs under the control and order of man. And then there is the zoo.

What city is complete without a zoo? You would have to be a coldhearted adult to deprive a child a trip to the zoo, in order to see Nature up close. The sad thing here, all this really says, is that it is important for a child to go to the zoo, in order to see Nature controlled. A child can relate to the zoo more closely than the adult can. After all, they are closer to the events in the womb. Was it not they, just a few years ago, in a similar cage? Yes, it was, they were encaged by Nature in the womb. Now, however, it is Nature in the cage and man in control. It is Nature, not the child who is humiliated at the zoo. In the womb, it was the fetus that was made a fool and Nature was in control. At the zoo, it is the animals that are controlled, and it is man that makes them a fool. It is those wild animals, wild Nature under lock and key of man's control.

The problem with zoos, however, is that they do not humiliate the animals enough. It is not humiliating enough to see a polar bear sweltering under the summer sun. This is outdated, as man's need to see Nature as the fool, has grown. After all, the fetus was humiliated. It was led to believe that its mother and therefore it itself was in the process of dying. Many things misled the fetus. It kicked and punched out, when it did not really need to. Nature has violated man and man must violate her back. Again, the need to see Nature humiliated is more important for the child than the adult, as they are closer to the actual events in the womb, the very source of the original humiliation. So, it is off to the animal parks. Here, you can see a giant whale wearing sunglasses. If this is not humiliating enough, you can watch the animal trainer brush this giant mammal's teeth. See this beautiful creature, which once roamed the sea, now begging like a dog for a humble handout of frozen fish. This all serves a purpose; it affects the child's subconscious. It tells him or her that they have arrived; they have survived from the place in the womb where survival was in doubt. They arrived from the place where Nature was in control. A circus is an urban version of an animal park. Here, you can see the wild tigers tamed and giant elephants in silly hats. The list can go on and on.

It is not only the child that needs to see animals humiliated. This need often extends well into old age. The domesticated dog is a perfect example of this. It is man's best friend, so the saying goes, however, a dog may disagree. A dog is a perfect way to control Nature. Just to see the dog begging for food is a testament to man's domination of other species. To have a dog is a constant testament to man's control of Nature. The best thing about a dog is that it displays this dependence in so many different ways and on a daily basis. A dog will let its owner do just about anything to it, and still appear to love its owner. A dog will let its owner humiliate it. And there are many different ways to humiliate a dog. Some people will cut their dog's hair, giving them haircuts as if they were people. Some people will put a sweater on their dog, and dress them up as if they were cold. All is fair game, because Nature humiliated man first. The problem with a dog though, is that it is an animal and animals must be controlled. Nature must be controlled. To offset this problem are dog obedience classes. In these classes you can train your dog. You can teach your dog tricks. These are tricks that have nothing to do with being a wild animal, however, everything to do with humiliation and control of the animal.

Man's battle against Nature however, becomes much more serious than the control of a dog. Man will cut down forests, dam rivers, and poison ponds; all in the name of control. He will pollute the seas; divert the streams, and level the mountains, before the battle is over. He will leak oil into the oceans; start fires in the forests and dump chemicals in the ponds. While money is often cited as the purpose for this destruction, the motivation is deeper still. It is man's battle against Nature.

Then there is the management of Nature. There is forest management. There is wild life management. There is environmental management. There is the management of national parks. There is land management. There is water management. Somehow and in someway, mankind believes it is his job to manage Nature. For almost every aspect of Nature, there is likely an agency that manages it. If you look up the word manager in the dictionary, hidden down in the third definition you will find the true purpose for the management of nature; this definition states, "the person or persons controlling or directing an institution." Indeed, manager is just another term for control. The institution, these managers attempt to control, is Nature.

Mankind is Nature's favored species; of this there is little doubt. Yet, unlike any other species that has ever been in the existence, mankind has the power to completely destroy her. With the seeds of rebellion sown early in the womb, he blindly marches on to the battle. Little does he know its victory can only be gained upon retreat.

PART TWO

THE ORGANICS

CHAPTER TWELVE

AUTISM

All throughout Part One of this book, you have realized how important the Memory Block is in the development of the human fetus. You realized how this neural function of the developing fetal brain is responsible for many of the behaviors that define the human species. In the beginning of Part One you realized, how the Memory Block allowed the fetus to conform effectively to each intrauterine developmental cycle. You realized that during the Euphoric Cycle it enabled the fetus to rest comfortably, completely unaware of the horrific cycle that it would face in a few hours. You realized how the Memory Block was responsible for the initial fetal misinterpretation, this was that during the First Fear Cycle of Development, its mother was in the process of dying and therefore it was as well. You also realized how the Memory Block led to the second important fetal misinterpretation. This was the fetal belief, that it was responsible, that it alone was the one to save both of their lives. You realized how this prompted the fetus to kick and punch out, trying to generate a response from what it believed to be its dying mother, who was only sleeping. You also realized that this kicking and punching was essential for the physical development of the fetus. This was all due to either directly or indirectly to the Memory Block.

Yes, it is obvious that the Memory Block was essential for not only intrauterine development, but for development of the human species as well. However, what if it did not exist? What if the short-term memory of the fetus was not blocked? What if this important neural function of the developing fetal brain that is defined as the Memory Block, failed to form?

The most obvious answer to these questions is that without the short-term memory of the fetus blocked; the fetus would remember the existence of one cycle while in the other. More than that however, because the Memory Block prohibits learning, without the Memory Block the fetus theoretically could learn. This then, brings us to the most important question, which is, what if the fetus could actually learn in the womb? As a society, we tend to value the concept of learning. Learning in the womb however, as you can tell by the title of this chapter was not Nature's intention at all. While as a society we see learning as a positive aspect, in this case, as you will see, the outcome is not positive at all.

If the individual experienced life in the womb as a fetus, without the Memory Block, every aspect of their development would be forever altered. Instead of expressing behaviors that define typical human behavior, they would express a completely different type of behavior. They would express behavior that was specific to their intrauterine experience, which was one without Memory Block.

Welcome to the world of autism. While it is a sad world, there can be no denying of this, it is also one of the most fascinating journeys back into the origins of human development, which can be undertaken. We will begin this chapter, with looking at the reasons that the Memory Block fails to form for the autistic fetus. Then, we will look at the differences of the intrauterine experiences between the autistic fetus and the non-autistic or typical fetus. It is important to note here that throughout this chapter, the fetal experience that was explained in Part one will now be termed the non-autistic or typical fetus. This is in order to clarify the differences between the two intrauterine experiences. After we look at the differences between the autistic and non-autistic or typical fetal intrauterine experiences, we will look at the early symptoms and signs of the autistic infant. Then, we will look at the major neurobiological differences for the autistic individual in contrast to those of the non-autistic or typical individual. Finally, we will look at the classic or formal symptoms of autism and realize that they are nothing more than a reflection of their altered fetal development.

Reasons the Memory Block Fails to Form

To understand why the Memory Block fails to form for the autistic fetus; it is only necessary to look back at the model explained in Chapter three "The First Fear Cycle of Development." In that chapter, you realized that the fetal Memory Block suppressed its mother's immune system. You also realized, all throughout Part One, that Nature's primary concern was always with the mother. Therefore, should any situation during pregnancy arise, that would signal the mother's inability to maintain at least a minimum level of health; Nature will utilize whatever is necessary to protect the mother. In this case, in the case of the autistic fetus, its mother's immune system is unable to handle the suppression resultant from pregnancy. Nature, therefore, simply lifts or fails to develop the areas of the fetal brain that will suppress the mother's immune system, which, as you have seen, is the Memory Block. This event occurs very early in the pregnancy, during the first trimester.

In most cases, a failure of the Memory Block to form properly within the developing fetal brain is combined with other aspects of improper development and results in a miscarriage by the mother. In this case, the pregnancy simply fails to materialize. However, in certain cases, as you will see, the pregnancy will continue and the fetus will develop in the womb without this vital aspect of its evolving brain functioning correctly. This will lead to the condition of autism and is what the remainder of this chapter will explain.

Now, there are many neurobiological factors that signal the pregnant mother's immune system that it cannot tolerate the suppression inherent within a normal or typical pregnancy. These factors include, however, are not limited to; lack of proper nutrition, any illness early in the pregnancy, an early intrauterine insult, or even the preexistence of a suppressed immune system realized by the mother. Of course, there are genetic variables that determine these factors just listed, as well.

In all these cases, the end result will be the same. The result will be that the fetus will experience life in the womb, the two cycles of intrauterine development and finally birth, with the absence of the Memory Block.

Differences in Intrauterine Experience between the Autistic and the Non-Autistic or Typical Fetus

Think back a moment to Chapter three on "First Fear Cycle of Development." Think about all that the Memory Block led the typical fetus to believe. Think about the fetal misinterpretations, how the fetus was led to believe that its mother was in the process of dying. How the fetus misinterpreted that it was its role to not only save her life, but its own as well, through its kicking and punching. Remember, how its mother was only sleeping, the entire time. Think back about the emotions the fetus realized. Think about how the fetus felt in the Euphoric Cycle of Development, resting and relaxing, completely unaware that right around the corner, within minutes or hours, it would be fighting to save both its mother's and therefore its own life. Then think about the worthlessness the fetus felt, as it could not save her life. And the hopelessness of the situation, towards the end of the pregnancy, as the intrauterine conditions deteriorated. Then, think about the tremendous guilt the fetus felt at the decision to leave its mother behind, alone to die. Then, think about the surprise on the infant's face, immediately after birth, when it realized that its mother was not dead at all, however, alive and healthy instead. Yes, remember all of this. In the world of the autistic, however, you may as well forget it, because it all never happened.

As you will see, in the world of the fetus without Memory Block, which is the autistic fetus there was no Memory Block, therefore there was no fetal misinterpretation. There was also no deception, as there was nothing to block its short-term memory. The autistic fetus does not misinterpret its mother's lying down as her beginning the process of dying; it is not fooled by this at all. No, because the autistic fetus has nothing blocking its short-term memory, it remembers that this morning its mother woke up and tonight she will go to sleep. It also knows that tomorrow morning she will wake up. Yes, the autistic fetus can learn. And one of the first things it learns is its mother's schedule.

Without the Memory Block, the autistic fetus does not suffer the same misinterpretations as the typical fetus does. When the First Fear Cycle of Development begins, the autistic fetus does not have a First Fear. The First Fear is the belief that its mother and therefore itself is in the process of dying. The intrauterine environment changes for the autistic fetus in the same manner it does as for the typical fetus. No, the autistic fetus cannot escape this horrific cycle of development. Just like the typical fetus, when its mother slows down and goes to sleep, the autistic fetus realizes a reduction of dopamine and therefore, the pain of its own development.

Indeed, the autistic fetus realizes the same two cycles of intrauterine development, as does the typical fetus. The difference is how each fetus interprets the cycle which they are currently in. For example, the typical fetus during the First Fear Cycle of Development will constantly touch the intrauterine walls to try and gain a response from what it believed to be its dying mother, who, of course, is only sleeping. Every time the typical fetus touches these intrauterine walls, it realizes a burning or painful sensation upon its fingertips. It quickly withdraws its fingers, convinced never to try it again. However, due to the Memory Block, in three to five minutes it quickly forgets the last experience, including the painful sensation and therefore, reaches out and touches the walls again. The autistic fetus, during the same horrific cycle of intrauterine development, will not touch the intrauterine walls with its fingertips every five minutes in the same way the typical fetus does. It will not do this for two reasons. The first reason is that it does not believe that its mother is dying. Indeed, as you will see, its mother is just another variable in the complex equation to the autistic fetus. Because it does not believe that its mother is dying, it will not attempt or be misled into attempting to save her life. This, of course, is because the autistic fetus has no Memory Block. Again, it remembered that the same event happened last night and knows the same event will happen tomorrow night. It has learned this. It has also learned that trying to wake up its mother makes little or no difference whatsoever, as this horrific cycle will continue all throughout the night, and no matter what it does it has learned the least effective method of dealing with this horrific events is by trying to wake up its mother, who by now is sound asleep. The second reason the autistic fetus will not continually touch the intrauterine walls with its fingers is because it can learn. Not only can it learn, but also it remembers that every time it touches the intrauterine walls, it realizes a burning or painful sensation. Therefore, there is no reason for the fetus to continue doing something that is going to cause it pain. So, instead of touching the intrauterine walls fifty times throughout the First Fear Cycle like the typical fetus, the autistic fetus may only touch them three or four times.

Unlike the typical fetus, the autistic fetus will not spend much time listening to its mother's heartbeat. While for the typical fetus, its mother's heartbeat was the best indicator as to whether she was still alive, dying or coming back to life. Again, the autistic fetus never believes its mother is dying, so it has little interest in monitoring the speed of her heart rate. To the autistic fetus sound is not hope at all. It is only another variable to calculate.

Primary Focus of the Autistic Fetus

As you have seen, while the autistic fetus does not believe that its mother is in the process of dying, it is still forced to experience the changes within the intrauterine environment. Included in these changes are the two cycles of intrauterine development. It is important to realize that these developmental cycles were intended and designed for the typical fetus, with Memory Block. What happens to the autistic fetus, then, because it lacks the Memory Block, an entire different focus of development occurs altogether. Instead of the focus being on saving its mother's life and therefore its own like the typical fetus, the autistic fetus will focus on two aspects of these developmental cycles.

The primary focus of the autistic fetus is the painful fetal apneas. From morning until night the autistic fetus is consumed with the thought and anticipation of this horrific event occurring. The typical fetus, because of its Memory Block had no idea when the apneas were coming or even that they were coming. For the typical fetus, one moment it could be relaxing in the Euphoric Cycle of Development and than the next moment it could be in the painful First Fear Cycle of Development, gasping for its life as its oxygen supply is cut off momentarily. While this was sudden and startling to the typical fetus, there were some benefits to it. Indeed, when it was relaxing in the Euphoric Cycle, it could completely relax. The autistic fetus, however, cannot relax; it has no Memory Block and therefore can remember the existence of this battle with death, these painful apneas. The very fact that it knows the existence of the apneas changes its entire intrauterine experience.

Because the autistic fetus knows of the existence of these horrific fetal apneas, their entire intrauterine experience is defined by the attempting accomplishment of two primary goals. The first goal is to predict when these painful apneas are coming. The second goal is to somehow find a way to stop them from coming. To accomplish these goals the autistic fetus will utilize a form of primitive learning. This learning is happening in a place where learning was never supposed to occur. It is a sad set of circumstances the autistic fetus, due to its altered development, faces.

To predict when the apneas are coming, the autistic fetus has essentially unlimited resources. It is important to remember the autistic fetus has no Memory Block. Nothing is blocking its short-term memory whatsoever. If you think of a small computer or calculator, you will still not be close to the potential in memory that this autistic fetus commands. To predict when the apneas are coming, the autistic fetus memorizes everything. It memorizes everything, especially as it pertains to its mother. Unlike the typical fetus, which believed its mother is in the process of dying, the autistic fetus believes in nothing. The autistic fetus does not attach blame to anyone, or anything. To the autistic fetus, there is only the reality that these horrific apneas will come and that its mother is somehow part of the equation. Because its mother is part of the equation, it will memorize everything about her. It will memorize her schedule, her routine, how many times she stands up and how many times she sits down. It will memorize her trips to the bathroom; even how many words she speaks. It is memorizing all this, in an attempt to gain some form of order, in an essentially order less environment.

During both, the Euphoric Cycle and the First Fear Cycle of Development, the autistic fetus is assimilating every piece of information it can obtain. While the typical fetus was relaxing during the Euphoric Cycle, the autistic fetus is calculating. There is no variable it will overlook. One of the reasons it is so interested in finding out when the apneas are coming is that it needs to be able to rest. While the autistic fetus falls asleep from exhaustion, it never really rests. It is important to remember that one of the reasons Nature provided the Memory Block for the fetus was so that it could rest peacefully in the Euphoric Cycle, completely oblivious to the horror that would confront it within a few hours. The autistic fetus, however, lacks Memory Block and therefore, cannot rest during the Euphoric Cycle, as it is busy calculating and anticipating this horrific event that awaits it. While the apneas come during both cycles of development, as you have seen, they are more painful during the First Fear Cycle, as this is when the dopamine available to the fetus is reduced. The objective then, for the autistic fetus, is to predict just exactly when the apneas are coming, so that during the other times, it can relax and rest in the same way that was intended for the typical fetus.

The problem with these attempts to predict when the fetal apneas come is that they are essentially impossible to predict, as they are essentially random events. This does not stop the autistic fetus from trying, however. While it cannot predict exactly when the painful apneas will come, the autistic fetus has been able to pinpoint a few generalizations about them. The first generalization it realizes is that the most painful apneas, the ones that hurt the most, do not come during the Euphoric Cycle when its mother is moving and the fetus is rocking in the womb to her movement. This, of course, is because, while the autistic fetus realizes apneas in both cycles, because of the high level of dopamine in the Euphoric Cycle, they are not as painful, as during the First Fear Cycle. The second generalization that the autistic fetus makes concerning the most painful apneas is that they are temperature triggered. In other words, when the intrauterine environment cools down the most painful apneas occur. Therefore, when the womb is the warmest, the autistic fetus at least feels a little safer. This is because, during the night, when its mother is asleep, her body temperature drops. This, of course, is the same time when the First Fear Cycle of Development is occurring and also the reduction in dopamine available to the fetus. This is in contrast to during the day, during the Euphoric Cycle, when its mother is moving and her body temperature increases. During this time, even if the autistic fetus realizes an apnea, it will not be as painful; this is because the high levels of dopamine nullify much of that pain. Now, the autistic fetus calculates all of this as, when the temperature of the intrauterine environment drops, the most painful apneas occur and it should be prepared. The third generalization the autistic fetus makes in regards to the most painful apneas is through its sense of smell, or olfactory cortex.

To understand why the autistic fetus utilizes the smells of the intrauterine environment as a variable in calculating when the most painful apneas come, it is necessary to look back at the model for the typical fetus in Chapter three, "First Fear Cycle of Development." In that chapter, you realized that the First Fear Cycle of Development occurred during the same time that Nature was encoding the fetal olfactory cortex with the smell of pungent and foul odors. This, of course, was a matter of convenience for Nature, because as the mother slept, which was when the First Fear Cycle of Development was occurring, the bodily fluids and waste of the typical fetus were not flushed as rapidly from the intrauterine environment. To the autistic fetus, the changing of the smells in the intrauterine environment is just another variable to calculate when the most painful apneas occur. The autistic fetus memorizes every smell of its intrauterine environment. When it smells the pungent or foul odors it knows it is in the cycle where the most painful of the apneas will begin. It then knows at least, what to be prepared for. Therefore, it spends a large part of its time continually smelling for changes in the intrauterine environment.

Even with all these calculations of its mother's activities, these generalizations of the conditions of the intrauterine environment, the autistic fetus can still not accurately predict exactly when the horrific and painful apneas will begin. Again, this does not prevent it from trying. It has got to figure out a way to predict exactly when the apneas will come. The main reason that it needs to know exactly when they are coming is so it can attempt to try and stop them. For as you will see, all of these methods, the autistic fetus utilizes to try and stop these horrific apneas, will take a great deal of energy and the autistic fetus cannot do them all the time. Therefore, if the autistic fetus can pinpoint when the painful apneas come, then, it can begin its attempts to prevent them from coming.

One of the things the autistic fetus will do in the attempt to stop the most painful apneas from occurring is to attempt to recreate the Euphoric Cycle. It does this even during the First Fear Cycle of Development, while it cannot create the Euphoric Cycle directly, it can at least attempt to mimic its own movement that occurs during that cycle. As you have realized, during the Euphoric Cycle while its mother was walking and moving around, the fetus in the womb was experiencing a rocking motion. The autistic fetus remembers this and knows that when in this cycle, the most painful of the apneas do not occur. To try and recreate this cycle the autistic fetus begins rocking, believing that this will keep the painful apneas away. So, even if its mother is not moving and the Euphoric Cycle is not occurring, the autistic fetus will attempt to mimic its motion during that cycle by rocking. It will do this only during the times when it believes the painful apneas will come. Indeed, women who were sensitive to the fetal movement inside of them and have given birth to an autistic child have remarked that they actually felt their fetus creating its own rocking movement inside of them.

The problem with creating a rocking motion is that it takes too much energy for the autistic fetus to expend. After all, this is a very complex movement involving the entire body. No, the autistic fetus has to come up with something else to keep these painful apneas away. Because using its entire body takes up too much energy, the autistic fetus begins using its hands. Now this, while completely different than the typical fetus with Memory Block, does share some similarities. If you remember, for the typical fetus after quickly becoming exhausted from the kicking and punching that utilized its legs and arms, which were large muscle groups, turned instead to its fingers and hands in order to attempt to gain a response from what it believed to be its dying mother. The difference here, of course, is that the autistic fetus is not trying to gain a response from its dying mother, as it does not believe she is dying at all. No, the autistic fetus will use its hands for something completely different. The important thing to realize here is that when the fetus, whether autistic or typical, becomes exhausted from using its major muscle groups in order to accomplish a goal, they will turn to their smaller muscle groups, in an attempt to accomplish the same purpose or task.

Because it takes too much energy to use its entire body to recreate the rocking motion of the Euphoric Cycle to keep the painful apneas away, the autistic fetus begins to use its hands. Through trial and error, it plans movements using both of its hands in an attempt to keep the apneas from coming. It will try the left hand over the right, and then the right hand over the left. If this does not work, it will repeat the sequence backwards. The autistic fetus may try another combination, maybe this time it will be the left hand three times over the right, then touching its head or ear with the right hand. If that did not work and the painful apneas come anyways, it will then try another combination. Maybe this time it will be five spins of its right hand around its left and then the entire process backwards. The autistic fetus will keep trying different combinations of these hand movements until it can find one that will keep the painful apneas away. Of course, it never will actually work. There is no way to keep the apneas from coming. The apneas, however, are so painful that the fetus will never give up hope. It is deeply motivated, by pain alone to find someway to protect itself from what is only a natural, although altered in its case, aspect of intrauterine development. While no hand combination will work to keep the apneas away, eventually, it will settle for a particular hand combination that it finds, mathematically, works betters than others to either interrupt the apneas or prevent them. Again, for the autistic fetus this is flawed logic, as their hand movements have nothing to do with preventing or interrupting the apneas. What you are seeing here is primitive learning in the face of a cruel, horrific, but necessary, event.

All these planned movements the autistic fetus makes, will come with a price. This is because, Nature never intended on the fetus making any planned movements in the womb. It was never part of the plan. The autistic fetus was supposed to be kicking and punching in order to keep, what it should have believed to be its dying mother and therefore itself alive. Indeed, if it had Memory Block this is exactly what it would be doing. Because it has no Memory Block, however, it does not believe that kicking or punching has anything to do with keeping its mother alive, because it does not suffer the misinterpretation as the typical fetus does, it does not believe she is even dying. While it will kick and punch to some extent to obtain dopamine, it will not do so near as much as the typical fetus. Therefore, instead of using the parts of its developing brain that are responsible for a conditioned response, such as the kicking and punching, as the typical fetus does, it instead is using parts of its brain that are responsible for planned movements. Again, this is not what Nature intended, therefore, the autistic fetus will realize neural deficits from using this alternative neural pathway, at a time, when it was not intended to do so. This area is the cerebellum and will be discussed together with the neurobiological aspects of autism in the appendix under "Neural Notes."

By now, it should become apparent that no matter what the autistic fetus does to predict or try to prevent them, the painful apneas come anyways. The autistic fetus has found a way to even deal with this. As you have seen, in Chapter three on "First Fear Cycle of Development," the typical fetus will realize an increase in the dopamine flow to the reward pathways of its developing brain, when it sucks its fingers or thumb. This, as you have seen, was intended to train the fetus to eventually, as an infant, take its mother's nipple and therefore, receive her milk and ultimate nourishment. This same principle applies to the autistic fetus. The autistic fetus can realize an increase in the flow of dopamine to the reward pathways of its developing fetal brain, however altered, much in the same way as the typical fetus does. The autistic fetus, however, because it can learn, takes this dopamine-seeking behavior one step further. In fact, it takes it many steps further. Unlike the typical fetus that is limited to the accidental placement of its thumb or fingers into its mouth, thus, realizing an increase of dopamine, the autistic fetus has no blocked short-term memory and therefore, it can learn. One of the first things the autistic fetus learns is how to maximize this dopamine flow. Through trial and error, the autistic fetus realizes that if it receives a given amount of dopamine increase by sucking its thumb or fingers, it will receive even a larger amount of dopamine by putting as many fingers as it can into its mouth. Then it takes this one step further. The autistic fetus realizes it can maximize this dopamine flow by sucking and biting on its entire hand or wrist; this is because the dopamine is pressure-released by the developing fetal mouth. The stronger the autistic fetus sucks, the more pressure that is applied to the sucking, the greater the dopamine flow to its developing reward pathways will become. Therefore, a finger or thumb, because of its small circumference will not generate as much pressure within the mouth, as something with a larger circumference such as the back of the developing fetal hand.

Sucking on its hand is not the only way the autistic fetus realizes an increase in the dopamine flow in the womb. A much more violent way is also utilized. While the autistic fetus, like the typical fetus, can realize an increase of dopamine from kicking and punching, it finds more efficient ways to obtain this release. The autistic fetus will often pound its head against the intrauterine walls; this goes directly to the source and releases large amounts of dopamine within its developing brain. Again, because it can learn, through trial and error, it has found that this method is more effective than others.

Final Days in the Womb

Overall, you can begin to grasp a picture of what life is like for the autistic fetus in the womb. The best way, however, to understand what life is like for the autistic fetus is to realize what life is not like. As you have seen, because the autistic fetus lacks this one essential characteristic of development, this one neural function that is the Memory Block, almost every aspect of its intrauterine experience is forever altered. There is no fetal misinterpretation, not a single one. This is unless you would define the autistic fetus' attempt and belief that it is somehow stopping the apneas from coming by its repertoire of planned movements with its hands. No, the autistic fetus is very much in touch with the reality of its situation. It is a horrific situation and its entire intrauterine experience is devoted to reducing the amount of pain it realizes. This is an extreme departure from the typical fetus that experiences a wide range of emotions, as it experiences the full effects of the Euphoric and First Fear Cycles of Development. There is no range in emotions for the autistic fetus. There is no feeling of worthlessness, because it cannot save its mother's life. This is because, it does not believe that its mother is dying and therefore, it cannot be failing at the task of saving her life.

Because the autistic fetus realizes no Memory Block, there is no fetal misinterpretation concerning its mother. Because there is no fetal misinterpretation concerning its mother, there is no belief that she is in the process of dying. Because the autistic fetus does not believe its mother is dying, it does not believe that it is in anyway saving her life. In other words, because the autistic fetus lacks Memory Block, it can remember that its mother wakes up in the morning and goes to sleep at night. Indeed, it has her entire schedule memorized. What it does not believe is that she is dying at any time. Therefore, there is no connection between its mother's condition and the fetal condition for the autistic fetus. Because there is no connection to its own life with its mother's life, there is no reason for the autistic fetus to be interested in her condition. It is only interested in her condition as a variable in calculating when the horrific apneas are going to come. Even at this, she is not a reliable variable. This is because, the apneas occur all throughout the day and at night. It is just that the most painful ones occur during the First Fear Cycle, which is usually at night. Therefore, because its mother is not a reliable variable, it cannot even hold her responsible for the apneas. They simply occur at a random rate, at a random time, in random patterns, that it cannot find the formula to predict.

Because the autistic fetus does not connect its life to its mother's, no bond will develop from the autistic fetus towards her. While it will not hold her responsible for the horrific First Fear Cycle of Development, it will also not credit her with the pleasurable Euphoric Cycle of Development. After all, it never actually realized an extremely pleasurable Euphoric Cycle. As you remember, during the Euphoric Cycle of Development, the autistic fetus was busy planning, calculating and, worst of all, anticipating the horrific and most painful apneas that would consume it during the First Fear Cycle of Development, therefore, it could never really relax and feel the pleasure of this Euphoric Cycle.

For the autistic fetus, the womb is a horrific place that it wants to get out of very badly. As you will see, however, there is one very good reason that it does not leave immediately. Unlike the typical fetus however, this reason will have nothing to do with guilt. The autistic fetus feels no guilt towards leaving its mother. It cannot feel guilt, because when it finally does leave, it does not believe that it is leaving her to die. However, even if it were leaving her to die, it would not care because there would be no connection to it. There is simply no direct connection between its health and its mother's. This, of course, is exactly the opposite perception of what the typical fetus with Memory Block believed, as it always connected the condition of its mother to itself.

Indeed, for the autistic fetus the womb is a horrific place. The autistic fetus feels trapped and immediately wants to get out. There is a problem with this however, and this is where its lack of Memory Block works against it in its plans to leave. As you have seen, because the autistic fetus has no Memory Block, it can learn. You have seen this concerning its behavior with regards to the intrauterine walls of the womb. In this case, the autistic fetus, once it touches the walls will realize a burning response and painful sensation upon its developing fingertips. Unlike the typical fetus with Memory Block, who quickly forgets this painful response, the autistic fetus can remember and therefore, learn. Because it learns the intrauterine walls are hot to the undeveloped touch, it will avoid them whenever possible. This becomes a problem, when attempting to leave the womb. As you have seen, the areas it will need to cross to initiate labor are warm areas of its mother's body. To the undeveloped fetus however, this warmth is magnified and generates a hot or painful response. This hot or painful response, of course, decreases as the fetus matures. This is because the fetal dermatome matures as well. The problem for the autistic fetus however, is that it remembers touching those areas of the womb, long before its dermatome was mature enough to tolerate the warm sensation. Again, in this case, the autistic fetal memory is so good that it remembers the time when it was not fully developed and does not take into account that during the later months of the pregnancy, its dermatome has matured and developed, so that it could successfully initiate labor, without realizing the intense burning or painful sensation. In other words, the autistic fetus can remember back so long that its memory works against it when deciding to leave, as it fears a situation that is no longer pertinent. The situation, of course, was the undeveloped dermatome, which is now developed.

Finally, even with this extreme fear of burning up during labor, the autistic fetus can no longer withstand the deteriorating intrauterine environment and decides it must leave. For, just like the typical pregnancy, the pregnancy that carries the autistic fetus is subject to the same deterioration of conditions towards the end of pregnancy, as Nature is prompting the fetus to leave the womb.

The question then becomes, once the autistic fetus finally decides to leave the womb, how would it survive the process of labor? Theoretically, it should not survive at all. After all, its entire intrauterine environment was altered. For, as you have seen, one of the major purposes of the two developmental cycles was to ensure that the fetus survived the long process of labor successfully. And the autistic fetus was definitely not conforming to the two cycles of intrauterine development. How, for example, can you compare the kicking and punching that the typical fetus was undertaking to small hand movements that the autistic fetus was attempting. Again, theoretically, because the autistic fetus did not conform to this classical conditioning model in the womb that was established by Nature to ensure the fetus survived labor; it then should not survive the process. It simply makes no sense to believe that the autistic fetus could survive this difficult process without the proper intrauterine development. For was it not Nature that planned every single fetal movement, every single aspect of intrauterine development, every single apnea, kick, punch and touch that the fetus made, in order to assure that it evolved into infancy safely?

In addition to this, there is another important reason that the autistic fetus should not, theoretically, be able to survive the difficult process of labor. This reason has to do with the Memory Block itself. As you remember in Chapter three on "First Fear Cycle of Development" an important purpose of the Memory Block was to develop fetal reflexes and reactions. While in one cycle, due to the Memory Block, the typical fetus had no recollection nor could it anticipate the existence of the other cycle. The end result of this was the typical fetus could react quickly to changes within the intrauterine environment. For example, when the typical fetus was relaxing and resting in the Euphoric Cycle, then its mother lied down to go to sleep, the typical fetus immediately came to full attention, as it began fighting to save its mother's and therefore its own life. These quick changes the typical fetus experienced were essential in the development of fetal reflexes. These reflexes would be critical, as they were utilized during the difficult process of labor, as the fetus would have to react quickly to changes as it worked its way through the birth canal.

The autistic fetus, because it has no Memory Block does not experience the same benefits of reflex development as the typical fetus with Memory Block does. This is for the obvious reason that while in one cycle the autistic fetus is already anticipating the existence of the other. Therefore, when the intrauterine conditions change, as they do between developmental cycles, the autistic fetus is prepared for those changes. Indeed, it is anticipating them. When the intrauterine conditions change from the Euphoric Cycle, when its mother is moving around, to the First Fear Cycle, when its mother is lying down, the autistic fetus is not startled, it does not come to full attention and it is not likely awakened from a relaxed sleep to begin fighting for its life. No, it is completely prepared, either with its repertoire of protective hand movements or its advanced dopamine-seeking behavior. Because of this, it does not realize the full, effective reflex development as the typical fetus with Memory Block does. This is another important reason that, theoretically, the autistic fetus, partially lacking this important aspect of reflex development, should not be able to survive the difficult process of labor.

If you add the autistic fetus' lack of intrauterine development conformity to its limited reflex development, one question becomes clear. How could this fetus possibly survive the difficult journey that is labor?

There is an answer to this, as an autistic fetus can safely make the transition to infancy. Indeed, it happens almost every day. If you remember, earlier in this Chapter, you realized that the autistic fetus, unlike the typical fetus executed planned movements in the womb. These planned movements were a primitive form of fetal learning. The autistic fetus had its own particular repertoire that it accomplished with its hands, which it used in an attempt to keep the horrific apneas away. This was a planned movement. When, the autistic fetus experimented with its hands, to obtain a greater dopamine release from sucking, instead of merely sucking its thumb or fingers, like the typical fetus. This was a planned movement. When, the autistic fetus, intentionally, began rocking in the womb, to attempt to initiate the Euphoric Cycle. This too, was a planned movement. You may also remember that, by making these planned movements in the womb the autistic fetus was utilizing an alternative neural pathway; one, which included areas involved in executing planned movements. These areas included the cerebellum. It is important to realize that the typical fetus rarely executes planned movements. Indeed, most of the movements of the typical fetus are in response to the model of classical conditioning. For the autistic fetus however, the opposite is true. The autistic fetus executed very few classically conditioned response movements, however, executed many planned movements.

Therefore, when the autistic fetus initiates labor, in some ways, it has an advantage over the typical fetus. This is for the obvious reason that it has experience in executing planned movements. This experience may indeed save its life, when it utilizes the planned movements during the process of labor. Where as, the typical fetus, is reliant upon its experience of movement, within the context of the classically conditioned model. In other words, the typical fetus is somewhat forced to react to the changes in the intrauterine conditions during labor, while the autistic fetus can utilize planned movements to help it safely escape the womb. Now, this ability to execute planned movements during labor can work against the autistic fetus as well. For birth itself, is not an event experienced only by the fetus. The process of labor is a joint effort between the mother and the fetus as it evolves into infancy. Therefore, planned movement by the autistic fetus could, theoretically, contradict this joint effort, resulting in complications during labor. In most cases though, the autistic fetus will make this transition into infancy safely. After all, no matter how hard it tried to stop the fetal apneas; in the majority of cases it was certainly unsuccessful. Therefore, the lungs of the autistic fetus will not be that much weaker than those of the typical fetus and it should be able to withstand the periods of time without oxygen or with limited oxygen, during the long process of labor.

Early Signs and Symptoms

In some cases, the altered intrauterine development the autistic fetus realized in the womb can be immediately identifiable after birth. After all, the autistic infant, unlike the typical infant, is not surprised to see its mother alive. It never felt the guilt when it left the womb, because it never thought she would die when it left. To the autistic infant, while it does not hate its mother or hold her responsible for the horrific events it experienced, it does at least connect her to the womb itself. Therefore, it will have very little interest in being held by her, touched by her or even close to her. In some cases, the autistic infant will arch its back to avoid being held immediately after birth.

When the autistic infant arches its back to avoid being held by its mother, it is the culmination of an intrauterine experience that will forever distance the autistic from the rest of the world. As a child, the autistic will rarely watch its mother's eyes. This is in contrast to the typical infant, as you have seen in Part One, who will constantly watch its mother's eyes to make sure that they are still open. The typical infant will watch its mother's eyes to make sure that she is still alive. After all, the typical infant believed that its mother would die when it left the womb. The typical infant believed that it would die if something happened to its mother. For reasons you have already seen, the autistic infant never believed that its mother would die when it left the womb. The autistic infant never believed that there was any connection between its mother's health and its own. The autistic infant does not believe that if its mother dies, it will die, as the typical infant does. Therefore, there is no reason for the autistic infant to look at her eyes, as there is no connection between her health and its own. This is unlike the typical infant, who is always watching its mother's eyes to see if they are open and she is still alive. Again, the autistic infant will pay little or no attention to its mother at all, it will have little interest in her eyes, for it probably does not care whether they are open or shut, as neither condition represents anything more to the autistic infant than her being asleep or awake.

This more than anything else will symbolize the life of the autistic. Because there was no Memory Block, there was no misinterpretation or deception in the womb. Because there was no misinterpretation or deception, the autistic did not believe its mother was dying. It, therefore, never connected any link between its life and its mother's. This lack of its initial dependence, at least perceived, will determine every relationship it develops, which will, of course, be very few.

For the typical infant with Memory Block, it associates the condition of its mother with the condition of itself. This will later build into empathy for others, based on this initial dependence. The reasoning here being, "If she is alright, I will be alright." This then expands into, "If they are alright, I will be alright." This then build into an empathetic response to society in general, based on self-interest, which itself stems from its initial dependence. It is even more than that though, the typical infant, which had Memory Block in the womb, will need to see people alive and moving to feel better, to negate these First Fear Cycle neurons which form there subconscious. The reasoning here is that if its mother remains alive, the infant believes it will remain alive and will not die. Now later, to see other people alive will serve the same, although diluted, purpose, which is to offset the fear of death, which is, of course, the First Fear.

The autistic infant and later the autistic individual simply lack this. Their intrauterine development was different. Now, give the autistic individual something that pertains to their specific development and you will see a response that the typical individual will convey in regards to another person. For example, if you bring an autistic to a laundromat and it can watch a dryer spin around for hours and hours, this is something that relates directly to the development it experienced in the womb. Why? This is because, during the Euphoric Cycle, the autistic fetus was rocking in a semi-circular motion. During this cycle not only was its developing fetal brain flooded with dopamine, however, the few apneas that occurred were not as painful as the others. Therefore, during this cycle, the autistic fetus could at least relax a little bit. So, here is the autistic individual in the laundromat, in front of a dryer that is directly mimicking the fetal activity during the Euphoric Cycle. Therefore, the autistic is now safe from the painful apneas that occurred during that horrific First Fear Cycle. In short, the autistic has now found its idol, for here is a machine spinning not only halfway, but also all the way around. Here, they will always be safe as long as the dryer keeps spinning. Of course, when the dryer stops, the safety is then gone, as this represents, to some extent, the initiation of the First Fear Cycle. What is important to realize here is that it simply depends on the individual's intrauterine development as to what will be important later in life. For the autistic, because of a failure of the Memory Block to form, interpersonal relationships will never be very important.

While there are noticeable differences between the autistic and the typical infant, primarily involving eye contact, in many cases, the parents of an autistic child do not realize the symptoms until the third year of life. This does not mean however, that the autistic infant loses their autistic state during the first two years of its life. This is far from correct. It is just that the developmental signs, at this early of an age, are difficult to detect to the untrained eye, however, they are there, and they are always there.

One of the reasons it is difficult to detect autism in the earlier stages of infancy, is that the autistic infant shares some similarities with the typical infant. For example, both will cry when they need to be changed. For the typical infant the association of the death and decay of their own waste products signal the beginning of the First Fear Cycle of Development, within their subconscious. This signals the beginning of the death of their mother and therefore themselves. For the autistic infant, the situation is somewhat similar, as in the womb the autistic fetus constantly smelled the intrauterine environment for changes. And it was, during the First Fear Cycle, when the intrauterine environment was not flushed as frequently, and the autistic fetus was consumed in its own waste products that the most painful of the fetal apneas would occur. So, during infancy the autistic infant, just like the typical infant, will dislike the association of its own waste products. This association for the autistic infant will signal the beginning of the most painful of the apneas. Therefore, they will both dislike the association; it is just that they will dislike it for different variations and interpretations of the same event, this being due to their own specific intrauterine experience. Again, to the parents these differences are almost impossible to detect.

There will also be immune irregularities for the autistic infant. If you remember the model explained in Chapter five on "First Fear Not Relieved," there you realized that the Memory Block suppressed the infant's and later the individual's immune system. You realized that the more Memory Block the individual has remaining, the more suppression their immune system realized. For the autistic infant and later individual, the same model will apply. Only in their case, because they realized no Memory Block during their intrauterine experience, none will be remaining to suppress their immune system. Therefore, with nothing to suppress their immune system, they will often exhibit autoimmune type symptoms. What is important to realize from this is to show exactly how the model works. The immune system can appear hypersensitive or up-regulated for two reasons. In the first case, as you have seen in Part One, the individual or infant with the condition of First Fear Not Relieved, realizes such a large suppression on their immune system from the overabundance of Memory Block, that the immune system actually up-regulates itself to fight against the suppression. This is a deviation from Nature's intended purpose, as it was Nature's intention that many of these neurons of the First Fear Cycle of Development were to be eliminated. The second reason, as in the case of an autistic, is also a deviation of Nature's intended purpose. In this case, Nature expected a certain amount of Memory Block to exist. Because there was no Memory Block, there was nothing to naturally suppress the immune system. This imbalance, then, makes the immune system appear up-regulated or hypersensitive, as if it was fighting back against being suppressed. In both cases, there is an imbalance that will result in the appearance of a hypersensitive or up-regulated immune system; it is just that this imbalance is for a different reason in each case.

The lack of Memory Block, the autistic infant realizes, will have other implications as well, although in this case, as you will see, they are not so clearly definable. For example, for the non-autistic or typical individual, because of their intrauterine development was dominated by the neural function of the Memory Block; recall of events in infancy are almost impossible to remember. Again, this is because the Memory Block was still a dominating aspect to their neural pattern during this time. The inability for the typical or non-autistic individual to remember their infancy and early childhood is defined as childhood amnesia. For the autistic, however, because they had no Memory Block, they can essentially and theoretically remember these time periods. Therefore, they will not suffer this condition of childhood amnesia. In fact, in some rare cases, autistics can actually remember the process of birth itself.

Now, there are many problems to this recall. One of them is that it depends upon the functioning ability of the autistic as to whether they can verbalize or even reach these memories. The other problem is somewhat of a paradox. This is because, in many cases, the Memory Block that failed to form in the womb for the autistic fetus will partially form later. While this is not a full recovery, it is at least, in many ways, an improvement of their condition. When this occurs, some of these early memories are eclipsed behind the late developing Memory Block. The paradox is this, the more severe the disorder for the autistic, the higher chance they will have of grasping these early infant memories. At the same time, they will be the least likely to be able to communicate them, more or less articulate them. On the other hand, the partially recovered autistic, integral to the recovery, is the masking of these memories, due to the delayed, but eventual, development of the Memory Block.

Major Symptoms of Autism

Before we begin with the major symptoms of autism and their intrauterine origins, it is important to realize, how certain aspects of neural development, during infancy, for the autistic differ than from those of the typical infant. Due to the lack of Memory Block, as a fetus, the autistic will realize implications in their neurodevelopment during infancy. These implications will center on the development of their subconscious. While there is an explanation for this, it is very technical and will be covered in greater depth in the appendix under "Neural Notes." What is important to realize about the subconscious of the autistic individual, is that its influence is exerted much stronger than for the typical individual, who realized intrauterine development with the Memory Block intact. In other words, the events that happened to the autistic fetus in the womb; will dominate the thoughts of the autistic infant, child and in some cases the adult. For the autistic, the line between their subconscious and their conscious thoughts is very blurred. What you will see, throughout all of these symptoms, is that in many ways, the autistic, while living outside the womb is dominated by the same fears as it was inside the womb.

The autistic's neural pattern will reflect this, as many of the neurons encoded with their unique intrauterine experience will fire, during their awake and conscious state, in a much less inhibited pattern than the typical individual's neurons will. In other words, these neurons encoded with their intrauterine experience are firing many times during their awakened state in a similar pattern as that of the typical individual's neurons fire during slow wave sleep, when their intrauterine experience is reviewed. This, of course, means that many of the autistic's neurons encoded with their intrauterine experience are firing uninhibited or fully during their waking state. When, these intrauterine neurons fire in groups, uninhibited or fully; the autistic individual realizes an epileptic seizure. Seizures are very common for autistic individuals. The reason that seizures are mentioned here is to gain an understanding of just how weak the suppression of the autistic's subconscious is and therefore, how strong the influence of this subconscious is during their waking state. This will be important, as we look further into the major symptoms and behaviors of the autistic individual.

Social Isolation

One of the most common symptoms of autism is social isolation. While we have already covered this earlier in this chapter, we will add a little bit more here. What is interesting is to contrast the autistic to the typical child, than to the typical adult. If it was not for this one single function of our developing brain, the Memory Block, we realized in the womb, we would have no interest in people whatsoever. Try to think back to all the social contacts you have made in your life, from your first friend to the ones you have now. Think of how much time you have devoted to other people. All of this would never exist, if your intrauterine development lacked the Memory Block, the way the autistics did. Indeed, if it were not for this original misinterpretation or deception in the womb, we would not care much about anyone. It is amazing, how this one small aspect of our development, shapes our whole world. Small is the key word here, because the areas responsible for the Memory Block are very small aspects of the limbic system within the brain. They are too small to be seen clearly, so you must use a microscope, and to see the differences between the limbic systems of the brain with Memory Block in the womb and the autistic brain, you would have to know what you were looking for or you would never find it. It is that small, yet, responsible for the world we know.

Our entire development was based on a misinterpretation. This misinterpretation was made possible by that microscopic neural mechanism called the Memory Block. If it were not for the Memory Block, the development, the need for others, the interpersonal relationships would not exist. Because, the autistic lacks the Memory Block; the need for others and interpersonal relationship does not exist.

Stereotyped Behaviors

Autistics usually have a preferred repertoire of stereotyped behaviors, such as rocking back and forth, biting their hands, moving their hands in a specific motion or pattern. Many do these repetitious behaviors for long uninterrupted periods. While these behaviors seem strange to others, taken in context to the intrauterine experience of the autistic fetus, they make perfect sense. Each one is important, so we will treat them each separately here.

While you know that the autistic is rocking to mimic the Euphoric Cycle, to increase their dopamine release and be safe from the horrific apneas, it is helpful to look at the comparison between the typical child or individual and the autistic. Both the autistic and the non-autistic or typical individual, subconsciously, remember the Euphoric Cycle, when its mother was active, moving about and the fetus was rocking in a semi-circular motion, back and forth. Yes, both the autistic and the typical individual experience, to a certain degree, the pleasurable aspects of the Euphoric Cycle, including the high volumes of dopamine that flow through the developing fetal reward pathways. What is different, however, is to what degree the autistic and the typical individual remember this experience.

The typical individual, as you have seen in Part One, will spend a large part of their time reliving and recreating this cycle, either directly, such as being rocked by their mother as an infant, swinging on a swing or rocking on a rocking horse as a child, or indirectly through the vibration and movement of cars, motorcycles and even dancing. From the cradle of infancy to the rocking chair of old age; it all serves the same purpose, this being that it mimics the pleasurable Euphoric Cycle in the womb. The typical individual cannot help it, as the neurons of the Euphoric Cycle of Development form their subconscious, firing inhibited during their waking state and uninhibited during their deep or slow wave sleep. The reenactment of the Euphoric Cycle, when the typical individual, as a fetus, was moving and rocking and the dopamine was flowing freely, defines some of the most enjoyable aspects of the individual's life. It simply cannot be escaped, as it is nothing more than the reenactment of what every typical individual experienced before.

Now, the autistic will take this one step further. Instead of spending their life, influenced by the neurons of the Euphoric Cycle encoded within their subconscious, for them, these neurons are closer to the surface. Without the Memory Block, they recall the exact movement they were realizing and experiencing, which during the Euphoric

Cycle was rocking. So, when frightened or fearing the painful apneas will come, even outside the womb, they will return to this favored cycle and mimic their actions during it. Now, this is not so much different than the typical individual, which in the womb experienced development with the Memory Block intact. When things get bad or they feel down, they may get in their car and go for a drive to feel better. In both cases, the motivation of the behavior is similar, thus, being able to respond to an undesirable condition, either real or perceived, by mimicking, either driving or rocking, the Euphoric Cycle.

You will see this theme quite often throughout the next two chapters. You will see those with altered intrauterine development, undertaking behavior, although exaggerated or modified, very similar to those behaviors undertaken by the typical individual. Again, while many of these behaviors will be altered or unique to their intrauterine experience, some consistencies, such as seeking to reenact the more pleasurable Euphoric Cycle, are consistent for every individual regardless of the alteration in their intrauterine development.

The repetitious hand movements the autistic individual undertakes are nothing more then a reenactment of the primitive attempts, the autistic fetus executed in the womb, in order to keep the painful and horrific apneas away. If you remember earlier in this chapter; in the womb, the autistic fetus, as a primitive form of learning, was attempting to develop a method to keep the horrific and painful apneas away. It began moving its hands in certain combinations, in order to accomplish this task. While none of them worked; eventually, the autistic fetus settled on a combination of hand movements that it felt worked better than others. Therefore in the womb, every time they believed, based on their projections, the apneas would come, they would undertake this preferred repertoire of hand movements to prevent the apneas from coming. Outside the womb, when feeling threatened or in a new environment, the autistic individual begins again with their proven method of prevention. It is important to remember, these neurons encoded with the autistic's intrauterine experience are exerting a strong influence, even during their waking state.

The hand biting, the autistic individual undertakes, is another reenactment of their altered dopamine-seeking behavior that was accomplished in the womb. The problem here is that in the womb their teeth were not developed and outside the womb they are. For the autistic individual this often results in welts upon their hands, as testament to reenactment of a time and place when its teeth did not exist. The autistic bites its hand for the same reason the typical infant sucks on its pacifier or thumb. Both do this when frightened, just as they were trained in the womb to do, as this was how the fetus obtained dopamine. Of course, it was not Nature's intention that the typical infant sucked upon a pacifier or that the autistic infant bit its hand. In both cases, these are deviations of Nature's intended purpose, which was to ensure that the infant reaches for its mother's nipple, sucks upon it and therefore gain the nourishment of food. As, you have seen, the autistic, as a fetus and later outside the womb, takes intrauterine development one step further. Because the autistic fetus had no Memory Block, it could learn in the womb. One of the most essential things it learned was how to maximize the dopamine flow, it realized from sucking its fingers and thumb. Instead of sucking its fingers and thumb, it took this process one step further by sucking its hand. This released the maximum amount of dopamine to the developing fetal reward pathways, thus, making life in the womb more tolerable for the autistic fetus. After birth, as the autistic develops, it is doubtful that they continue to realize a dopamine increase from hand biting, just as it is doubtful that the typical infant realizes an increase in the dopamine flow from sucking its fingers and thumb, it matters little as its behavioral pattern, established in the womb, will be repeated after birth.

Resistance to Change in Routine

The autistic will usually have a resistance to changes in their routine. This is a very important symptom. Because the influence upon their intrauterine experience is so strong, the suppression of their subconscious so weak, an autistic individual will spend a great deal of its time focused on making sure the horrific events that occurred to it in the womb, never happen again. Everything for the autistic is focused on this. As soon as the autistic child can control their environment, they will want to make sure that nothing will signal the beginning of this event, of these horrible apneas and its fight for its life. It is an obsession, a devotion to ritual that rivals little else.

Just as the autistic lived in the womb, it will live outside the womb. The autistic is looking for patterns. Through trial and error, it will make sure that this horrible event never happens again. The autistic's reasoning is this; "If I walked to school this way yesterday and no horrific apneas occurred, then I can walk there tomorrow and here I am safe." This is now a safe-zone for the autistic. Tomorrow, it can walk to school in the same way and be safe. To the autistic this has been proven. It was proven today and will be further reinforced tomorrow. However, if tomorrow it sees a different car, a different person or a major change within the environment that defines this route, the safe-zone has been violated. In response, the autistic may panic a little bit. As now, the painful apneas could come at any time. The autistic may begin their preparation to prevent the apneas. They may begin rocking, repetitious hand movements and then the hand biting to increase the dopamine flow. Again, the apneas will not come, the hand biting will not likely increase the dopamine, however, the developmental pattern established in the womb, is destined to repeat.

This is due to the strong influence of the neurons encoded with the intrauterine events, the autistic experienced as a fetus.

Even if the autistic did suffer an apnea during this walking route, it is unlikely that it would be as painful as it once was. Their neural pattern is telling them something altogether different, however. For while they are not still in the womb, the neurons encoded with these events are firing with the same information that was important back there. The autistic's entire life is based on establishing and living around these safe-zones. It is a simply logic that they take to an extreme. This is how severe the fetal apneas once were, and how strong the influence, from those neurons containing that event, still are.

Resistance in Change of Environment

An autistic will also not like changes in their room, their house, their mother's clothes or the movement of furniture. They will dislike any changes within their immediate environment. Unlike their obsession for routine, the reason they do not like these changes are for something different altogether. To understand why the autistic does not like changes in its immediate environment, it is necessary to review the two cycles of intrauterine development for the typical fetus, with Memory Block. For the typical fetus, because of its Memory Block when it was in one cycle of intrauterine development, it had no idea that the other cycle existed. For example, when in the Euphoric Cycle, it had no idea that the First Fear Cycle existed. Therefore, it did not know that it was in the same place during both cycles. It would be relaxing in the Euphoric Cycle of Development then, when its mother would lie down, it would be thrown into the beginning of the First Fear Cycle of Development, never remembering the existence of the previous cycle. The purpose of this was to maximize fetal conformity to each cycle of intrauterine development. This also developed important reflexes for the fetus, as it quickly reacted without anticipation to the changes within the intrauterine environment. Indeed, these reasons have been discussed in detail in Part One. What is important to realize here is that the autistic fetus does not experience this.

The autistic fetus, because it has no Memory Block, can remember the existence of one cycle while in the other. They also experience the intrauterine environment changing around them. In other words, the typical fetus because they have no short-term memory does not remember the womb changing around it, however, the autistic fetus does. The autistic fetus felt the changes in the womb, smelled the changes in the womb, realized the temperature changes in the womb and in general was very sensitive to the subtle changes that occurred as one cycle transformed into another. The typical fetus with Memory Block, because its short-term memory was blocked was not as perceptive to these subtle changes. For the autistic, the womb essentially changed in front of them.

Now, outside the womb as an infant or as a child, the autistic is still heavily influenced by these neurons, as you have seen. If the furniture in a room of their house is arranged in a certain way, as you have seen, the autistic feels safe there. This represents the Euphoric Cycle where the painful apneas did not occur. Therefore, as long as the furniture stays the exact same, the autistic will continue living in the Euphoric Cycle where the painful apneas did not occur. However, should one little thing change, such as the color of a bedspread or the movement of a desk, this signals the change to the horrific First Fear Cycle, which contained the painful apneas. Just as the autistic fetus realized the intrauterine environment changing from good to bad, it has now witnessed the external environment changing from good to bad. Of course, no apneas will come if the autistic's mother changes the placement of her furniture; however, within the autistic's brain a different message altogether is being realized.

Sniffing and Smelling

This is also why the autistic child often smells things. If it gets something new or enters a new place, it will immediately start sniffing and smelling around. What it sniffs for is the same thing it once sniffed for, as a fetus in the womb. This was because, the changes in the intrauterine environment, from the Euphoric Cycle to the First Fear Cycle of Development, were related to the fetus through their olfactory senses. The change in smells signaled the coming of the horrific First Fear Cycle, where the autistic fetus remembered it would experience the most painful of the apneas. The autistic fetus smells for the death and decay of the intrauterine environment. Now, this is the same smell, of the death and decay that plagued the typical fetus with Memory Block, that occurred during the First Fear Cycle that signaled the death of its mother and therefore of itself. This is the same death and decay; that the typical young boy wants a toy car to escape, from. It is the same death and decay that the typical young girl, once she realizes her gender, fears is inside of her. This will be the same death and decay that will, ultimately, be directly responsible for the eventual relations bonding and reproduction of the human species between the male and female. Here, with the autistic we see, because of their altered intrauterine development, a different adaptation altogether. For the typical infant, smells that are associated with the First Fear Cycle of Development represent the death of their mother and therefore of themselves. To the autistic infant, however, these smells only represent the coming of the most painful apneas and their particular brush with death.

Abnormal Response to Sound

An autistic often shows an abnormal response to sound and noise. This will be especially true for anything of a sound in a bass range. To understand this, we must once again, look at the contrast between the typical fetus with Memory Block and the autistic fetus.

During the First Fear Cycle of Development, the typical fetus believed that its mother and therefore it itself was in the process of dying. As you have seen, after the typical fetus was exhausted from kicking and punching out, it listened, throughout the long hours of the night. What it listened for most was its mother's heartbeat. Hour after hour, it listened to her heartbeat. It would get encouraged when it increased, because this meant that she was coming back to life, and discouraged when it decreased as this represented she was dying. For the typical fetus, in the womb sound meant hope and the sound and speed of its mother's heartbeat was the best indicator the fetus had to determine whether she was alive or dying. Of course, she was only sleeping.

Now, the sound of its mother's heartbeat to the fetal auditory cortex represented a bass sound. Nature utilized the First Fear Cycle of Development for important aspects of auditory development, as the typical fetus differentiated the higher pitch sounds outside of the womb to the bass sound of its mother's heartbeat. All this information was coded into the fetal auditory cortex.

The autistic fetus however, did not have Memory Block and therefore, did not believe that its mother was dying. Because the autistic fetus could learn, it learned that she was only sleeping. In fact, the autistic fetus most likely knew how many hours on the average she slept. However, its mother's heartbeat was only another variable, that the validity of for prediction was disproved early within the pregnancy. Its mother's heartbeat was only another variable, the autistic, had to chose from when making its prediction as to when the most painful apneas would come. The autistic fetus would weight her heartbeat no higher than her trips to the bathroom. It meant very little to the autistic fetus. Unlike the typical fetus who was a captive listener to that heartbeat, the autistic fetus would listen to it not even one fourth of that amount of time. Therefore, the autistic fetus lacked this critical auditory development. As an infant or a child, when the autistic hears a bass sound, it will sound approximately four times as loud as for the typical infant or child. It may even sound like bullets, as it mimics the sound directing of its mother's heartbeat. For the autistic fetus, because of the lack of motivation to continually listen to its mother's heartbeat, this important neural programming of the bass sound did not occur within its auditory cortex. This, of course, is difficult for the autistic, because in the world in which it lives, that of the typical individual, the bass sound represents its mother's heartbeat and therefore life. The popularity of this sound can be witnessed in everything from the bass of a stereo to the explosion of fireworks.

Insensitivity to Pain

Autistic individuals often have insensitivity to pain. For example, when working around a hot stove, an autistic may burn its hands, then, leave them there, without realizing a painful response. Here, we see more incomplete intrauterine development. To understand this, we will once again return to the contrast of the typical fetus in the womb.

As, you have seen in Part One, because of the Memory Block, the typical fetus would repeatedly touch the intrauterine walls in an attempt to gain a response from what it believed was its dying mother. Every time the typical fetus touched these intrauterine walls, it realized a burning or painful response on its undeveloped hands and fingers. Because of the Memory Block however, the typical fetus would quickly forget this painful sensation and touch them again, within minutes. This, as you have seen, served an important developmental purpose, as each time the typical fetus touched these walls; this burning sensation encoded the pain receptors within the fetal sensory neurons.

The autistic fetus however, because it had no Memory Block, quickly learned that touching these intrauterine walls with its undeveloped fingers and hands would initiate a painful response. Therefore, it avoided them whenever possible. Because it avoided them, this essential coding of the pain receptors within the fetal sensory neurons did not take place. Therefore, the autistic can easily burn its flesh and feel little or no pain, due to this incomplete intrauterine development.

Failure to Communicate

Autistic children are often thought to be deaf, because they rarely respond to the voices of their parents and talk very little if at all. This is one of the most telling symptoms not only of autism, however, why we as a species talk. This is it. This is why we talk. The Memory Block, this function of the developing fetal brain is totally responsible for the human species' interest in creating sounds in an organized manner. Without the Memory Block, we, like the autistic, would feel the need to communicate very little.

Of course, the autistic does not talk or talks very little, because in the womb sound meant very little for them. Because they had no Memory Block, they did not believe its mother was in the process of dying. As you have seen, unlike the typical fetus, the autistic fetus did not listen intently upon the sounds its mother made.

For the typical fetus with Memory Block, sound in the womb meant everything. Sound was the only tool it had to negate its worst fear. This fear was during the First Fear Cycle of Development that its mother was in the process of dying and it would soon follow. During these long hours of the night, for the typical fetus sound was often the only thing that kept it from completely giving up hope. In the positive Euphoric Cycle, when the fetus was consumed with large volumes of dopamine, sound was everywhere, as its mother talked to others during her daily tasks and activities.

After birth, the typical infant learned to create its own hope, as it was consumed with the neurons encoded with the First Fear Cycle of Development, as they began the process of development of the subconscious. When the typical infant was afraid that its mother was in the process of dying and therefore itself, it created sound to offset this fear. It began with crying, and then graduated into making sounds, then words and finally, sentences. What is important to remember is that the primary motivation for all speech, for the production of all sounds, is to hear one's own self making noise, thus, offsetting the fear of death. The second reason the typical infant made sounds was to control its environment. Essentially, every word a typical individual says pays homage to the Memory Block and the First Fear Cycle of Development. In the womb, sound was hope; silence was death. It was the death of their mother and therefore one's self. Many of these neurons remained in the typical individual's brain, firing from the subconscious. Every time the typical individual speaks, talks, or makes a sound, they are offsetting the neurons encoded with the First Fear Cycle that form their subconscious. Every time the typical individual speaks, talks, or makes a sound, they are offsetting the First Fear, which is the death of their mother and therefore of themselves. Because of the Memory Block, this fear returns almost as quickly as it is offset. Therefore, the typical individual must keep talking, to continually offset the fear that keeps resurfacing. It is a continual process, based on a continual need. It is the need to believe that one is not in the process of dying. It is the need to offset the neurons, firing within their subconscious that tells them they are in the process of dying. More than this; the ability to speak, to form sentences and to communicate effectively, separates and elevates the human species above all others.

The autistic fetus had little to do with any part of this equation. There was no Memory Block, therefore there was no misinterpretation and no deception, as they learned their mother was not dying but sleeping instead. To the autistic fetus, there was no real connection between its mother's life and its own life. The autistic fetus never grouped its mother and itself together; she was a variable among many other variables it utilized in making its prediction as to when the horrific apneas would come.

Therefore, as a newborn infant, the autistic will cry, however, not for the same reason the typical infant does. For the autistic infant, there is no hope in sound. Sound was for those whose fears were based on its mother's death and therefore its own. The biggest fear of the typical infant is the death of its mother. The autistic infant, even if its mother were to die; would hardly notice. As, it would not believe death would consume it shortly thereafter. No, the autistic will focus its entire energy on avoiding the painful apneas. While, they will never come, the neurons encoded with their intrauterine development dominating their thoughts demand the autistic to act upon them. Yes, the autistic individual will spend as much time avoiding these horrific apneas, as the typical individual will spend communicating. There is no value in noise, in sound and therefore they see no purpose in communicating with their parents, with others, or with the world.

The Lie

Then, there is the lie. The autistic individual cannot understand the concept of the lie. They cannot understand the concept of deception. They cannot understand the concept of a joke, if it is based upon deception. Of course, by now, you likely know why this is. By now, this should no longer be an illusive.

The autistic cannot comprehend the lie and cannot comprehend deception for one simple reason. The reason is, as you have seen, the autistic fetus never experienced deception. It never misinterpreted that its mother was in the process of dying. It never believed, when it left the womb that it was leaving its mother alone to die, then, only to find out like the typical newborn, to its surprise that she was still alive. Not only will the autistic not understand the lie, but also they will have little interest in cartoons where the characters seemingly die and are born again. This is because in the womb, they never experienced their mother appearing to die every night, only to be born again the next morning. This will make little sense to them.

Without the Memory Block, the autistic fetus remembered everything. It remembered its mother would go to sleep and wake up the next morning. There was no magical veil of the Memory Block, to wash away the memory of the previous day, so that it would find itself, confused in another cycle. This never happened for the autistic fetus. The autistic therefore, will have little interest in magic, games of deception or the concept of untruths. Every single individual, ever born, would be the exact same way if it were not for the Memory Block. Because the autistic did not experience deception as a fetus, it cannot understand deception at all.

Of course, this lack of deception of misinterpretation the autistic fetus realized will have much more profound implications than not being able to understand a joke or a lie. As you have seen in Part One, Nature's entire reproduction model for the human species is based on this deception, on this misinterpretation of the intrauterine environment for the typical fetus. Because the autistic fetus never experienced this initial deception, this misinterpretation, it is also likely, even if they are fully recovered, they will never participate in this reproduction model.

Interest in Schedules

Autistics will often be interested in schedules, timetables and other facts. Of course, this makes perfect sense, as in the womb, to the autistic fetus, predicting when the painful and horrific apneas would come; it was an obsession. The pain level during these apneas for the fetus was almost unbearable. The autistic fetus knew its mother's schedule by heart. It had memorized her trips to the bathroom. It had memorized how many steps she had made. It memorized how many times she sat down, how many times she stood up. It knew her schedule, the timetable of her life, by heart. Outside the womb, for the partially recovered autistic this interest in schedules, timetables and facts will continue, reflecting their initial development. Besides maybe, just maybe, on one of these timetables, on one of these schedules is the exact figure they are subconsciously searching for. Maybe they can find, for once and for all, the equation that puzzled them in the womb, the final equation that accurately predicts when the painful apneas will come again.

Islands of Memory

The partially recovered autistic individual will often display abilities that are exceptional in regards to memory. Indeed, it is not uncommon for them to be able to memorize numbers that would almost rival an adding machine. In Part One of this book, you realized the primary purpose of the Memory Block. It was to block the fetal short-term memory. As you have seen in this chapter, the autistic had nothing to block this memory, for there was no Memory Block. Without the Memory Block, the human brain is capable of memory that is incomprehensible to most of us. Therefore, the autistic can memorize and recount a volume of information that is, for the lack of another word, unbelievable.

Of course, it has to be something they are interested in. An autistic will rarely memorize a face with the same effectiveness it will memorize a number, schedule or statistic. Again, the face holds little value to them, the statistic and fact is their hope. In the womb, for the typical fetus, sound was hope. The greatest musicians can memorize large quantities of sound. In the womb, for the autistic fetus, numbers and predictions were hope. For them however, there is nothing blocking their memory, therefore they can even memorize more. The theme for the autistic memory is predicting outcome based on past performance. This is what they did as a fetus in the womb, all through the day and all through the night. They memorized their mother's schedule, they memorized the changes in the womb, they memorized the temperature in the womb, and finally, they memorized when the last painful apnea came. From all this they based their prediction on when the next one would come. This was a prediction of outcome based on past performance of variables.

The Heater

Another unusual behavior the autistic child will display, concerns warmth and heat. When an autistic child enters a room with a heater in it, they will often huddle around it as if they were cold. This is true even if the room is very warm. The first aspect to understanding this is the fact that they have entered a room. This could signal a change in the environment. Therefore, to the autistic, the painful apneas could begin at any time. If you remember earlier, you realized that the most painful of the fetal apneas usually occurred during the First Fear Cycle of Development. This, in most cases, was at night when its mother was sleeping. At the same time its mother's body temperature was dropping. The autistic fetus put all these facts together into its unblocked memory and devised a prediction. The prediction was this, "When the womb is warmer, the most painful apneas will not come. When the womb becomes cooler, the most painful apneas will come." This was their prediction, and in most cases, it was very accurate. Therefore, when the autistic individual enters a room, or a new place, anything that signals a change in the environment their fear of the apneas consumes them again. The only place they can assure themselves that they are safe is by a heat source. Because as long as they are warm, as long as the room, which is symbolic of the womb, is warm, the apnea will not come.

Alienation of the Autistic

The unfortunate aspect of autism is that, until now, it has not been fully understood. Yet, without understanding the disorder and its origin, society has attempted to control and change the autistic. This is a shame, as these incredible people are so often forced to conform or attempt to conform to development that is completely foreign to them. This only further alienates the autistic. Imagine going to a school where you were forced to watch a spinning wheel go around in circles all day long. Imagine going to a school where you were forced to study train schedules all day long, while standing close to a heater. This is not only ridiculous, but also sad.

Of course, no typical individual would enjoy attending a school such as this. This, however, is symbolic of what so often happens to the autistic. It is only another example of mankind's battle against Nature. By wanting to fix and change, even those within his own species, it is another attempt to control Nature, as he is only reenacting a battle that was fought long ago.

CHAPTER THIRTEEN

SCHIZOPHRENIA

It would be easy if the Memory Block either formed, as in the case of the typical fetus, or failed to form, as in the case of the autistic fetus. Yes, it would be simple if there were only two degrees of Memory Block formation. Unfortunately however, this is not what occurs at all. Like so many aspects of Nature, the formation of the Memory Block realizes a range. In Part One, you realized the important aspects of the Memory Block. In the last chapter, you realized what occurred when the Memory Block failed to form for the autistic fetus. Here, you will realize what occurs when the Memory Block is weakened and the many ranges of its formation.

Indeed, there are many variations to the formation of the Memory Block. As there is a full nine months of pregnancy, there is a full variety of formations for this important neural function. This, more than anything else, becomes the major problem with schizophrenia. For example, during the beginning of the pregnancy, the Memory Block can fail to form, then, during the second trimester, if conditions improve for the mother, it will form in a delayed manner. Of course, in this case the Memory Block will always be weaker than if it had formed during the beginning of pregnancy, as was Nature's intention. Another example of the variation of the formation of the Memory Block would be that, during the beginning of the pregnancy it forms properly, then during the second trimester it breaks or lifts. The purpose here is the same as in the previous chapter on "Autism." The purpose is to protect the mother's immune health. The reason the Memory Block could lift or break during the second trimester of pregnancy may be due to something as simple as the mother contracting influenza. Then, there are all the months in between. For example, the Memory Block may form at the beginning of the pregnancy, then break, then reform, only to lift or break at the end. Again, this is the major problem with schizophrenia. As there are too many variations upon the formation and breakage or lifting of the Memory Block. Each one of these variations will result in development that is specific to that individual's altered intrauterine experience, as a fetus. Therefore, before the origins of schizophrenia can even begin to be fully understood; it is first necessary to realize that there are many variations to this disorder, just as there were many variations to the altered formation, breakage and lifting of the Memory Block.

In addition to this, because the Memory Block is weakened, due to an alteration in the intrauterine development, there are two major degrees or conditions of that weakness. The first occurs when the Memory Block is slightly weakened and the second is when the Memory Block is more severely weakened. When the Memory Block is severely weakened, the fetus will experience intrauterine development that is closer to that what the autistic fetus experienced. When the Memory Block is only slightly weakened, the fetus will realize intrauterine development that is closer to that which the typical fetus experienced. However, in both of these cases, the fetal intrauterine experience will be completely different. This only adds to the complexity and difficulty in understanding the variations of schizophrenia.

Yet, there is even more. Because in addition to these variations, there is the amount of time that the Memory Block remains in its weakened state or has broken for. The Memory Block may remain in a weakened state throughout most of the pregnancy. It may remain in a weakened state for only a month. This, again, adds to the variations of the intrauterine experience and therefore, the ultimate variation of symptoms that the schizophrenic will later exhibit.

So, what you have, even before we begin, is a wide variation of intrauterine experiences. You have the period within the pregnancy when the Memory Block weakens. You have the degree at to which it is weakened. And you have the length of time for it remains weakened.

An encouraging aspect however, is that schizophrenia can never be understood without first understanding the intrauterine experience realized by the typical fetus and the autistic fetus. As you will see, the understanding of schizophrenia is a multi-step process. And the first two steps you have already completed. Indeed, without understanding these two major variations of the fetal intrauterine experience, already discussed, you could look forever for the causes; you could look forever for an understanding to this complex disorder, however, you would never find it. This is because the origins of schizophrenia fall between the poles of the autistic intrauterine experience and the typical intrauterine experience.

Therefore, unlike the previous chapter on "Autism" however, it will not be possible to look at every major symptom and variety of symptoms for schizophrenia. Instead, we will focus on the two major types of fetal intrauterine experience in regards to the altered Memory Block. We will look at the Memory Block in its slightly weakened state and how this affects the fetal intrauterine experience and the symptoms of schizophrenia it will later generate. Then, we will look at the Memory Block in its more severely weakened state and how this affects the fetal intrauterine experience and the symptoms of schizophrenia it will later generate. Before we begin looking at these two unique intrauterine experiences, we will look at how this weakened Memory Block will ultimately affect the neurons encoded with their intrauterine experience, which form the subconscious of the schizophrenic and therefore, how it ultimately affects their neural pattern and their behavior.

The Subconscious of the Schizophrenic

As you have seen in the last chapter on "Autism," fetal development without this important neural mechanism of the Memory Block will have developmental implications long after birth. In the case of the autistic, because the Memory Block failed to form during the fetal stage of development, as Nature had intended, this ultimately affected the development of the autistic's subconscious. In other words, without this critical component of Memory Block, the autistic's subconscious always would exert a stronger influence than for the typical individual. This as you have seen in the last chapter, for the autistic causes the neurons, encoded with their intrauterine experience, which form their subconscious to continually dominate their conscious thoughts, as the suppression of their subconscious will always be weaker and the influence of their subconscious always stronger, than for the typical individual.

This is very similar to what occurs in schizophrenia, although there are some important differences. Because the Memory Block, realized as a fetus in the womb, was weakened, the individual with schizophrenia will always realize a stronger influence from the neurons encoded with their intrauterine development that form the subconscious, than typical individuals who experience fetal development with the Memory Block completely intact. For the individual with schizophrenia the influence of the subconscious will not be as strong as for the autistic. You can look at schizophrenia as a middle ground of the subconscious influence. The influence from their subconscious is not as strong as the autistic, however, much stronger than the typical individual's. The problem is, as you will see, the diversity of the intrauterine experience, which is encoded within the neurons that form the subconscious of the schizophrenic.

This is because, in almost all cases, the fetus, which will later develop schizophrenia, will realize, for at least some time period intrauterine development with their Memory Block intact. In other words, this fetus will experience some time in the womb as a typical fetus. Then, there will be other times when they will experience a time period in the womb with this altered and therefore weakened form of Memory Block.

In other words, the same fetus will realize two different types of intrauterine development, which results into two different intrauterine experiences altogether. For example, the schizophrenic fetus can realize the third and fourth months of pregnancy with Memory Block, and then, the fifth and sixth with a weakened Memory Block. The problem in this is, of course, the intrauterine events that occur during all four of these months are encoded in developing fetal neurons that will eventually form the subconscious. Therefore, in the case of schizophrenia, not only will their subconscious have a stronger influence than the typical individual's, but also completely different intrauterine experiences will define the same subconscious. In other words, a neuron encoded with the fetal experience of the weakened Memory Block will be located very close to a neuron encoded with the fetal experience of the Memory Block completely intact.

These two neurons or groups of neurons reflecting a completely different intrauterine experience will then, during the waking state of the schizophrenic, fire together and exert a strong influence upon their conscious thoughts and in many cases, their resultant actions.

This is unlike the autistic, which at least will have only one intrauterine experience, however altered, encoded within the neurons of their subconscious. This is also unlike the typical individual, who also has only one intrauterine experience encoded within the neurons of their subconscious. This you can quickly see becomes the major problem of schizophrenia. For, it is important to remember that the subconscious of the schizophrenic is strongly influencing every thought; and what is encoded in that subconscious is, at least, two completely different intrauterine experiences. This of course is why, at one time, schizophrenics were thought to have a "split" or "two" distinct personalities. Even though these terms are no longer utilized, you can now see where this perception originated.

While the individual with schizophrenia can express behaviors influenced by two distinct intrauterine experiences, it can also express behaviors influenced by at least three distinct intrauterine experiences. This is because when the Memory Block is at a weakened state, as is the case for the schizophrenic fetus, it tends to fluctuate within that weakened state. In other words, during some period of their fetal experience the Memory Block will be severely weakened and during other time periods, whether for months or only days, the fetal Memory Block will only be slightly weakened. Again, both of these fetal experiences, along with the fetal experience of the Memory Block intact, will be encoded into the developing fetal neurons that will eventually form the subconscious of the individual with schizophrenia. This is very commonly what occurs. Therefore, in this case, the individual with schizophrenia has three groups of neurons, each one encoded with a completely different intrauterine experience forming their subconscious. In some cases, all three of these neuronal groups are firing in a dominant pattern, at the same time, and thus, influencing the conscious thoughts of the individual with schizophrenia. Fortunately however, for these three groups to fire together is uncommon. What is more common is that two intrauterine experiences fire in a dominant pattern, at one time, within the subconscious of the individual with schizophrenia. And in most of these cases, one of the intrauterine experiences will reflect the time period when the fetal Memory Block was intact, similar to a typical fetus.

Disorganized Thinking

Because of the multiple influences of intrauterine experience, which is encoded within the neurons of the subconscious of the schizophrenic individual, thinking and communication can become a difficult task for them. This will represent the symptoms of schizophrenia that are disorganized. We will look at one disorganized symptom of schizophrenia. The symptom is "disorganized thinking." This disorganized thinking manifests itself in the schizophrenic individual's communication or speech. Often a schizophrenic with this symptom may reply to questions with answers that are not even related to the question asked. Also, when talking they may slip off track from one subject to another. While some of this is common to all individuals, with the schizophrenic individual it is so severe that it often disrupts the ability to communicate effectively. What happens to the schizophrenic here is that because there are more than one neuronal bases of intrauterine experience, within their subconscious, influencing every thought the schizophrenic individual realizes, a competition of influence occurs. This, essentially, divides the subconscious influence of every thought. Every time a typical individual speaks, the information they utilize to form that speech must go through the subconscious. For the individual with schizophrenia, the same is true. It is just that in their case, the information is influenced by at least two separate intrauterine experiences.

It is even more than that, however. This is because the neurons encoded with each of these intrauterine experiences have additional information built upon and around them, which reflects that particular perspective. A simplified example will clarify how these two intrauterine experiences, a schizophrenic realizes, can come into conflict.

For simplification, we will say that one of these intrauterine experiences influences the schizophrenic individual to like running. Then we will say the other intrauterine experience influences the schizophrenic individual to dislike running. Now, when the schizophrenic is engaged in a dialogue or conversation with someone about running, the information is channeled through the subconscious of the schizophrenic individual. Some of the influence reflects their desire to run, other influence reflects their dislike of running, both of these influences are competing, within the subconscious, to influence the conscious thoughts and resultant reply the schizophrenic individual will make. Now, this competition results in a conflicting neural dialogue and intertwines with each other to make very little sense to the schizophrenic who will express this through communication. The schizophrenic may say, "I like running, I hate running, I hate running, I like running."

Again, this is a very simplified example of running, which has little to do with the fetal intrauterine experience. What is important to understand about this however, is that the information processing for the schizophrenic individual is completely altered due to the existence of two distinct, and in the case of the example, often conflicting intrauterine experiences within the neurons that form their subconscious.

Thought Insertion and Thought Withdrawal

In certain cases, the schizophrenic individual will realize such a reduced suppression and such a strong influence from their subconscious that it will seem to them that their subconscious is not connected to their conscious thoughts at all. It will appear to the schizophrenic that the thoughts formed by the strong influence of the subconscious are actually foreign to them, or alien to what is contained in their subconscious. In this case, the schizophrenic will realize the symptom of thought insertion. With this symptom, the schizophrenic believes that someone is actually inserting thoughts into their own head. Of course, this is not what is occurring, it is just that the influence of their subconscious is so strong, the neurons from their intrauterine experience firing in a dominant pattern that they cannot control the force of the subconscious, as it pushes up into the conscious thoughts. Again, this is all due to the reduced amount of Memory Block experienced as a fetus in the womb, which therefore, led to altered neural development in relation to their subconscious. The same flaw in development materializes in the symptom of thought withdrawal. In thought withdrawal the schizophrenic individual believes that somebody or something is taking its thoughts away. Again, this is only their inability to control their subconscious and concentrate upon the thought they are attempting to form. In this case, the schizophrenic individual connects the failure of their subconscious to operate efficiently, with an utside force that is actually taking their thoughts away.

Symptoms that Reflect Periods of Typical Intrauterine Development

Not all of the symptoms the individual with schizophrenia will exhibit reflect their intrauterine experience that occurred with the weakened Memory Block. Some symptoms and behaviors will reflect their intrauterine experience when the Memory Block was intact. It is important to remember that almost every schizophrenic individual realized, at least some time period, as a fetus in the womb when the Memory Block was intact, very much like the typical fetus.

In fact, the schizophrenic individual can express behavior that is very similar to behaviors and disorders discussed in Part One. For example, schizophrenics can suffer from depression. Schizophrenics also realize a very high rate of suicide. Drug abuse, which is a dopamine-seeking behavior, is also very common for schizophrenics. And schizophrenics often smoke cigarettes heavily, which is, of course, another method of obtaining a dopamine release.

What is important to realize here, is that due to the strong influence and reduced suppression of the subconscious of the schizophrenic, in many ways, they will exhibit behaviors that will mimic the typical individual with the condition of First Fear Not Relieved. In other words, even in the best-case scenario for the schizophrenic, when their neural pattern is dominated by the intrauterine experience of a fetus with Memory Block intact, they will express symptoms of First Fear Not Relieved. They will display these symptoms for a completely different reason than the typical individual who suffers this condition.

As you remember from Part One, the typical individual with First Fear Not Relieved realized this condition, because there were too many neurons encoded with the two cycles of intrauterine development remaining in their subconscious. From time to time, these neurons would fire in a dominant pattern, which would result in behaviors and disorders that included drug abuse, suicide and depression.

Now, in the case of the schizophrenic, they will exhibit these behaviors for a completely different reason. It is not that the schizophrenic has too many neurons remaining encoded with the two cycles of intrauterine development, including the First Fear Cycle. This is not it at all. In fact, the opposite is true. This is because the schizophrenic individual's intrauterine experience as a fetus was divided into at least two time periods. One was when they realized intrauterine development with the Memory Block intact, much as the same way as the typical fetus. During this intrauterine experience with the Memory Block intact, this fetus would realize the full effect of the First Fear and Euphoric Cycles of Development. Then, in the other time period, this fetus would realize an altered intrauterine experience with the Memory Block weakened. The end result of this divided intrauterine development, of course, will be that the schizophrenic individual will actually have a reduced amount of unaltered neurons encoded with the two cycles of intrauterine development, including the First Fear Cycle. At first glance, it would appear that there is no way the schizophrenic individual, and then could display behaviors and disorders of those typical individuals with the condition of First Fear Not Relieved. If you look closer however, you will realize it is not that the schizophrenic has more of those neurons remaining, but instead, it is the influence of those remaining neurons that is so strong. This again is due to the strong influence and weak suppression of their subconscious, which is formed, at least partially, by the neurons encoded with the two cycles of development, experienced as a fetus with the Memory Block intact. In other words, in the case of the schizophrenic, it is not the amount of First Fear neurons remaining, however, the influence of those neurons, and because in schizophrenia, due to reduced suppression and strong influence of those neurons within their subconscious, symptoms that mirror First Fear Not Relieved can be realized.

To take this one step further, in the case of the schizophrenic, they could experience the ideal environmental factors during infancy and early childhood, as explained in Chapter five on "First Fear Not Relieved," and still express behaviors and certain disorders, such as depression, suicide and drug abuse that a typical individual with First Fear Not Relieved will express. It is important to realize that no matter how ideal infancy and early childhood environmental conditions were for the schizophrenic individual, they will always express symptoms, in at least some form, of the condition of First Fear Not Relieved. Not only will the schizophrenic express these symptoms, such as depression, drug abuse and a high risk for suicide, but also, they will be expressed in a more obvious manner. Therefore, they will appear as if they have a severe form of the condition of First Fear Not Relieved, this due to the strong influence and reduced suppression of the neurons encoded in their subconscious. For example, if the typical individual with First Fear Not Relieved occasionally uses recreational drugs, the schizophrenic individual will use them all the time. If the typical individual with First Fear Not Relieved smokes a pack of cigarette a day, the schizophrenic individual will smoke three packs a day. If the typical individual with First Fear Not Relieved occasionally thinks about committing suicide, the schizophrenic individual already has a plan.

Again, it is important to remember, for the schizophrenic it is not because of the amount of neurons remaining encoded with the First Fear Cycle of Development, but instead, the strong influence and reduced suppression of those remaining neurons within their subconscious.

Display of the Symptoms of Schizophrenia

The individual with schizophrenia does not always display obvious symptoms of this disorder. Often times, it will not be until the schizophrenic individual is in their late twenties or early thirties before they experience an active phase or outbreak of the disorder. In other cases, the schizophrenic individual will realize their first active phase or outbreak of the disorder, even earlier, possibly during their early twenties. Still in other cases, an individual with schizophrenia may not experience their first active phase or outbreak until they are in their forties. In almost every case it varies.

To understand why the age varies so immensely among schizophrenic individuals, it is only necessary to look to the last chapter on "Autism." In the case of the autistic individual, they begin showing signs of autism as early as their second or third year of life. This is because their intrauterine development was completely devoid of Memory Block. What occurs for the schizophrenic can be summed up in a general rule. The more severe the Memory Block was weakened in the womb, the earlier the schizophrenic individual will display symptoms and realize an active phase or outbreak of the disorder. The less severe the Memory Block was weakened in the womb, the later the schizophrenic individual will display symptoms and realize an active phase or outbreak of the disorder. For example, if a schizophrenic individual as a fetus realized intrauterine development with only a slightly weakened Memory Block, they may not begin showing symptoms and realize their first active phase or outbreak of the disorder until their early forties. Another schizophrenic individual, who realized intrauterine development with a more severely weakened Memory Block, will begin showing symptoms and realize their first active phase or outbreak of the disorder in their early twenties.

Then there is the amount of time the schizophrenic fetus realizes in the womb with the weakened Memory Block. This adds to the equation as well. The longer the amount of time the schizophrenic fetus realizes intrauterine development with the weakened Memory Block, the earlier the age of their first active phase or outbreak of the disorder. The shorter the amount of time the schizophrenic fetus realizes intrauterine development with the weakened Memory Block, the later the age of the first active phase or outbreak of the disorder.

Regardless of when the individual with schizophrenia realizes their first active phase or outbreak of this disorder, there will always be signs and subtle symptoms much earlier. Subtle is the key word here, as many times the symptoms are very difficult to detect. For example, much as in the same way as the autistic, a schizophrenic infant or child will not make the eye contact with their parents and especially their mother at an early age. This will be, especially, true for the schizophrenic infant or child who realized the longest and most severe weakened Memory Block during their intrauterine development. Again, this is a very subtle symptom and can easily be missed, however, this does not negate its importance. The reasons for this will be explained later in this chapter. Another early sign will be their exaggeration of certain symptoms of First Fear Not Relieved. For example, they may heavily undertake in dopamine-seeking behavior such as drug abuse and cigarette smoking. Again, in all cases, these particular symptoms of First Fear Not Relieved will be exaggerated due to the strong influence and reduced suppression of their subconscious and not from a large amount of neurons encoded with the First Fear Cycle of Development remaining.

Fetal Experience with Slightly Weakened Memory Block

Now we will begin to look at the fetal experience of the individual with schizophrenia. As, you will see in both cases, one with slightly weakened Memory Block and the other with more severely weakened Memory Block, their intrauterine development is a major departure from Nature's intended purpose. While it is a major departure, it is certainly not as severe as one as it is for the autistic fetus, which experienced no Memory Block whatsoever. No, the schizophrenic fetus realized some form of intrauterine development with the Memory Block almost completely intact, much in the same way as the typical fetus did. What you will begin to see is how the degrees of the strength of the Memory Block completely change the interpretation by the fetus of the events that are occurring within its intrauterine environment.

An example of this would be to look at the fetal interpretation of the First Fear Cycle of Development. For the typical fetus, with Memory

Block intact, as you have seen, it misinterprets this cycle of intrauterine development, to be the beginning of the death of its mother and therefore itself. It also misinterprets its role throughout the entire cycle, as it believes that it alone is responsible for saving both of their lives. In the case of the autistic fetus, with no Memory Block, it values the First Fear Cycle of Development, only as the developmental cycle where the most painful of the fetal apneas occur. It believes its role is to predict when these painful apneas occur and then take action to attempt to stop them. The schizophrenic fetus, with a slightly weakened Memory Block, interprets or misinterprets the First Fear Cycle of Development, as something completely different.

Because the schizophrenic fetus has Memory Block, however, its strength is slightly reduced, it can remember more than the typical fetus, however, not as much as the autistic fetus. This leads to a completely different interpretation of the First Fear Cycle. The schizophrenic fetus with slightly weakened Memory Block cannot remember long enough to realize that when its mother lies down at night to go to sleep that she will get up in the morning. Therefore, it will, like the typical fetus, connect her to the equation of the painful apneas. When the First Fear Cycle of Development comes, it will kick and punch and attempt to save its mother's and therefore its own life. It will do this, however, due to its weakened Memory Block; it also misinterprets this event in a different way. It will take this developmental cycle one step further. It not only believes that its mother is in the process of dying, but also that something is trying to kill its mother and therefore itself. It also misinterprets its role as that of being the one who is responsible to try and figure out what it is or who it is that is trying to kill them both.

This is simply a different interpretation of the same event realized by every single fetus. What defines a difference is the amount of Memory

Block, which, ultimately, results in how much recall that particular fetus has. As you will see in a later section, a general rule can apply. This rule is the more severely weakened the Memory Block is, the least likely the fetus will incorporate its mother in the equation. With the inclusion of the next section on the fetus with the more severely weakened Memory Block, you will begin to be able to see a pattern of degrees with regards to the fetal belief of its mother's involvement.

Because the schizophrenic fetus with slightly weakened Memory Block misinterpreted the First Fear Cycle of Development, as an attempt on its mother's life and therefore its own, its intrauterine experience was consumed by this thought. Therefore, this fetus was extremely sensitive to the environmental cues within their intrauterine environment. This was somewhat similar, however, not to the same degree as the autistic fetus was. For the autistic fetus, they utilized the intrauterine environment as an important part; however, only one part of the equation. For the schizophrenic fetus with slightly weakened Memory Block, it was a major part of the equation. This schizophrenic fetus paid attention to every aspect of the intrauterine environment, it noticed, like the autistic fetus did, the change in smells as the developmental cycles changed. This was one of its primary cues. Unlike the autistic fetus, which would focus on the memorization of the numbers and patterns of its mother's behavior, this schizophrenic fetus was focused on, due to its limitation of its partially blocked memory, the memorization of smells within the intrauterine environment. It attached an undue importance to the smells within the intrauterine environment, as it believed that these smells might be responsible in themselves, for this attempt on both its mother's and therefore its own life.

The schizophrenic fetus with slightly weakened Memory Block is not limited to the intrauterine environment in its attempt to find out who or what is trying to kill its mother, and therefore itself. This fetus also listens intently to its mother's speech and to the voices of others that she is conversing with. This occurs primarily during the Euphoric Cycle of Development. As, this was the time when its mother was active and moving, and therefore, usually around other people; and would be in a situation where conversation would likely occur. While the typical fetus would also listen to its mother's voice, there is a very large difference in the way these two fetuses listened. The typical fetus would listen to the sound of the voices; as they represented its mother in an alive state. This was all they represented, for as you have seen, in the womb, to the typical fetus sound was hope. The schizophrenic fetus with slightly weakened Memory Block would also listen to sounds of its mother's voice and those she was conversing with. Due to its increased memory capacity over the typical however, it was not only listening for sounds however, for words as well; and not only was it listening for words, but it was memorizing those words. More than words though, this fetus was listening to entire sentences, believing that somehow contained within those words and sentences was the answer it was seeking. Because the schizophrenic fetus with slightly weakened Memory Block believed that someone or something was trying to kill them, it spent a great deal of its time, during the Euphoric Cycle, listening to these voices and sentences.

It is important to realize, for this schizophrenic fetus with slightly weakened Memory Block, the intrauterine environment was still a very much disorganized place, as, there are major differences between this fetus and the autistic fetus. This is because this schizophrenic fetus' memory was still partially blocked. Unlike the autistic fetus it did not separate the painful apneas from its mother as a variable. This schizophrenic fetus interpreted the apneas as an attempt on both of their lives and spent a great deal of time attempting to figure out who or what it was that was attempting to do this. While we have looked at the two major areas of focus for this schizophrenic fetus, this was certainly not all it concentrated upon. Everything within the intrauterine environment was a possible source of what was trying to kill its mother and therefore itself. It would look for patterns and changes within the intrauterine environment to try and figure out what it was, however, the Memory Block even in its weakened state prevented it from doing so. This schizophrenic fetus was constantly frustrated at its inability to concentrate and therefore, ultimately, figure out what was actually occurring. Like the autistic fetus it would look for patterns, however, unlike the autistic fetus it could not remember and therefore, grasp these patterns. Again, this was due to the Memory Block, however slightly weakened.

There will be many developmental implications due to this slightly weakened Memory Block for the schizophrenic fetus. The first is that, because when in one cycle, it at least partially anticipates the next cycle. This slows down the transition between cycles for the fetus. Because of this its reflexes and response to startle, will be slower than that of the typical fetus. Also, it is not going to kick and punch as much as its typical counterpart. This is because, even with the limited Memory Block, it does not always believe that kicking and punching will save their lives. Both of these deviations of intrauterine development will affect the fetus when it attempts the process of labor. Unlike the autistic fetus, which utilizes planned movements throughout its intrauterine development, this schizophrenic fetus with slightly weakened Memory Block, in most cases, does not utilize this alternative neural pathway. As you have seen with the autistic fetus, because it can utilize planned movements, it is able to successfully complete labor. Because, in most cases, this schizophrenic fetus does not utilize planned movements and has not completely conformed to Nature's intended intrauterine development, it will often have difficulties in the labor process itself. As you will see in a later section of this chapter, when we look at the schizophrenic fetus with more severely weakened Memory Block, in that case, planned movements and posturing in the womb are more common.

The Symptoms of Schizophrenia Related to the Fetal Experience with Slightly Weakened Memory Block

In this section, we will look at the symptoms of schizophrenia that originate from fetal development with the slightly weakened Memory Block. We will first look at the symptoms themselves, then discuss their intrauterine origin.

Delusions

Delusions are a major symptom of schizophrenia. Delusion is a false belief that usually involves a misinterpretation of perceptions or experiences. There are many types of delusions a schizophrenic individual realizes, including persecutory, referential, control and somatic. All of these are important and will be discussed separately here.

Before we even begin to look at the origins of the various themes of delusions, it is helpful to look at the very definition of the word itself. Again, a delusion is a false belief that usually involves a misinterpretation of perceptions or experiences. This is exactly was the intrauterine experience was to the schizophrenic fetus. This is not only true for the schizophrenic fetus however, for as you have seen in Part One, Nature's entire intrauterine model of development was based on misinterpretation of perception. Indeed, as you have seen in the last chapter on "Autism," if the fetus does not experience a misinterpretation, which is due to the Memory Block, the human species would be very different altogether. So, it should not be surprising that the schizophrenic fetus would suffer symptoms that were an integral part of their intrauterine development. This is especially true, when you realize the intrauterine influence upon the conscious thoughts for the schizophrenic individual is so much stronger than for the typical individual. This, as you have seen, is due to their reduced suppression and strong influence of their subconscious, which, of course, is formed by the neurons encoded with this intrauterine development. It is just that, in the case of the schizophrenic individual, the misinterpretation that they realized was due to their altered intrauterine development and is therefore, not common to the typical individual.

Schizophrenic individuals often realize delusions of persecution. A schizophrenic with the delusion of persecution often believes that someone is out to get them, that they are being conspired against, obstructed from their long-term goals, or even worse, being poisoned or drugged. Indeed, persecution was a central theme of the intrauterine experience to the schizophrenic fetus with slightly weakened Memory Block. If you look in the dictionary, under the word persecute, you will see very quickly a brief representation of the fetal experience of the schizophrenic fetus with slightly weakened Memory Block. The first definition is, to pursue with harassing or oppressive treatment; harass persistently. This was exactly this schizophrenic fetus' interpretation of the First Fear Cycle of Development. This schizophrenic fetus believed that someone was out to kill its mother and therefore itself. Of course, all that was happening were the painful apneas during the painful First Fear Cycle of Development. The second definition is, to oppress with injury or punishment. Again, the punishment this schizophrenic fetus realized was the same punishment both the autistic and the typical fetus experienced, this being the horrific First Fear Cycle of Development and the painful apneas.

Another type of delusion of persecution this schizophrenic individual will express is a belief that they are being poisoned or drugged by someone. This, of course, is exactly the perception of the schizophrenic fetus with slightly weakened Memory Block of the two intrauterine cycles of development. If you remember in Part One, Nature neurochemically manipulated the fetus during the Euphoric Cycle of Development. She accomplished this neurochemically manipulation by increasing the release of large volumes of dopamine to the reward pathways of the developing fetal brain. This release was accomplished by its mother moving around and being active. The purpose of this was to keep the fetus still or reduced its movements while its mother was busy with her movements. To accomplish this, Nature essentially drugged the fetus with high levels of dopamine. As, you also remember from Part One, when the intrauterine environment changed from the Euphoric Cycle of Development into the First Fear Cycle of Development, the smells of the intrauterine environment changed as well. As during the long hours of the night, the intrauterine environment was not as flushed as during the Euphoric Cycle, therefore the fetus was left in its own waste products. Nature used this cycle for coding of the olfactory neurons with the smell of pungent and foul odors. Again, this is the death and decay that has been mentioned many times throughout the book. Later in life, the typical individual will associate the smells, programmed during this cycle, as negative, because when they were first experienced they, as a fetus, were in the process of fighting for their mother's life and therefore their own.

Now, the schizophrenic fetus with slightly weakened Memory Block interprets the changes between the two cycles of intrauterine environment in the following way. Earlier you realized how perceptive this schizophrenic fetus was to the intrauterine environment. You realized how this schizophrenic fetus constantly smells for these changes. It quickly realizes a pattern as to what occurs. It realizes that the most painful apneas, which it interprets as an attempt on its mother's and therefore its own life, come at the same time as these pungent or foul odors come. Therefore, it blames the odors themselves as the substance responsible for the attempt on both of their lives. These smells then become the poisonous gasses or substances that are attempting to kill its mother and therefore itself. The problem for this schizophrenic fetus however, is that it cannot find out who it is. This is because, during the Euphoric Cycle, when this schizophrenic fetus escapes the most painful apneas, or as it interprets them as escaping the attempts on its mother's and therefore its own life, it believes it is being drugged. And, of course, this is somewhat correct. This is exactly what is happening, for as you have seen, Nature through neurochemical manipulation is drugging the fetus to reduce its movement during the Euphoric Cycle. Of course, where this schizophrenic fetus was wrong is in its belief that this drugging or high level of dopamine was intended to keep it from finding out who was trying to kill it, as obviously nobody was.

Another type of delusion an individual with schizophrenia will express is a referential delusion. In this case the schizophrenic individual believes environmental cues are specifically directed at them. For example, two complete strangers may be carrying on a conversation in the close proximity of a male schizophrenic individual. This schizophrenic will then misinterpret this conversation as being about himself. Here the schizophrenic has once again misinterpreted his environment. This, of course, is very easy to understand, when you realize that every fetus believed the world evolved around itself. This was especially true for the schizophrenic fetus with slightly weakened Memory Block, who was not only overly perceptive of the intrauterine environment, but also attempted to be overly perceptive of what was going on outside of the womb, as it tried to figure out who or what was trying to kill its mother and therefore itself. For hours and hours, during the Euphoric Cycle it would listen to its mother conversing with others, as it tried to find a pattern in her conversation that would help it figure out who was trying to kill them both.

Another type of delusion the schizophrenic individual will often express, is a somatic delusion. In this delusion the central theme is the schizophrenic individual's body. They commonly believe that they emit a foul stench or odor from their skin, mouth, rectum or vagina. They may also believe that parts of their body; such as their large intestine is not working correctly. In some cases, they even believe, there is an infestation of insects either in or under their skin. The foul odor here that the schizophrenic individual believes they are emitting is, of course, nothing more than the death and decay, which occurred during the First Fear Cycle of Development. Here is an example of the over-sensitivity to the intrauterine environment the schizophrenic fetus with slightly weakened Memory Block realizes. As you have seen, this schizophrenic fetus paid very close attention to the changes in smells in the conditions within the womb. It paid such close attention that it realized, indeed, that the death and decay of the First Fear Cycle of Development, was coming from itself. This, as you have seen, is exactly what occurred, during the long hours of the night when its mother was sleeping, during the First Fear Cycle of Development, the fetus was left in its own bodily waste, as the intrauterine environment did not flush and circulate as thoroughly as when its mother was awake and active. This schizophrenic fetus however, misinterprets these smells as being responsible for the horrific apneas, which it interpreted as an attempt upon its mother and therefore on its own life. When all that was actually occurring was that Nature was utilizing this horrific cycle for the encoding of olfactory neurons with pungent and foul odors. This schizophrenic fetus connected these two events and misinterpreted them to mean that the odors themselves were responsible for the apneas and therefore, the attempt on both of their lives. To avoid this from occurring, this schizophrenic fetus attempted to stop its bodily waste. The reasoning here was, if it could stop its waste, then it could stop the horrific apneas, which it interpreted as an attempt on its mother's and therefore its own life. This of course, was only possible for so long. This schizophrenic fetus, then interprets its inability to suppress its bowel movement, inevitably, as a malfunction of its intestines.

The belief that bugs are crawling or insects are living under their skin is nothing more that the dopamine withdraws the schizophrenic fetus with slightly weakened Memory Block realized as the Euphoric Cycle ended and the First Fear Cycle of Development began. As you remember, one of the most important roles of dopamine within the intrauterine environment was to nullify or reduce the physical pain of fetal development. Sometimes this pain was as large as the head expanding and sometimes as minor as the dermatome forming on the developing fetal body, which without a high enough level of dopamine circulating throughout the reward pathways of the developing fetal brain, caused an intense itching sensation. This initial intrauterine sensation is, of course, re-experienced every time any individual reenacts this initial reduction of dopamine. As drug addicts, during withdraw from dopamine, commonly re-experience the itching of the skin. For those who withdraw from the dopamine realized by drug cocaine, this phenomenon is called "coke bugs."

Another common delusion for the schizophrenic individual to experience is the delusion of control. Here, the schizophrenic individual believes that their body or actions are acted on or manipulated by some outside force. Not much time needs to be spent on this symptom, as this, of course, accurately defines the schizophrenic fetus or any fetus within the womb. Indeed, every fetal body experienced this external control or outside force, which, of course, was its mother. In the case of the schizophrenic fetus with slightly weakened Memory Block, this is the definition of its perception of its mother. As its mother, or the outside force, was responsible for the fetal body and indirectly by her activity level, for the fetal actions in response to the First Fear and Euphoric Cycles of Development.

Hallucinations

Of all the hallucinations a schizophrenic realizes, auditory hallucinations are the most common. When an individual with schizophrenia experiences an auditory hallucination, they hear voices that are distinct from their own thoughts. To understand why the schizophrenic experiences auditory hallucinations, it is only necessary to look at the motivations of the schizophrenic fetus with slightly weakened Memory Block. As you have seen, their entire intrauterine focus is concentrated on an attempt to identify who or what is trying to kill its mother and therefore itself. As you have seen, this schizophrenic fetus pays very close attention to its intrauterine environment searching for the answer it is focused on finding. You have also seen that this fetus spends a great deal of time with its attention focused outside the womb. This was especially true during the Euphoric Cycle during the times its mother was most often engaged in conversation. This schizophrenic fetus listened not only for sounds, like the typical fetus did, however, due to its increased interest in identifying who was trying to kill it; it was listening for words and sentences as well. This worked out well because due to its slightly weakened Memory Block, this schizophrenic fetus could actually memorize not only words, but also entire sentences. All of these words and sentences were recorded and encoded into the developing fetal neurons, however, altered. These fetal neurons form the base of the schizophrenic individual's subconscious. Due to the strong influence and reduced suppression of the subconscious, these neurons fire, the voices recorded within them fire as well. Inside their head this schizophrenic individual hears these prerecorded voices and sentences. Often when a schizophrenic individual hears these voices, they begin to smile or laugh. This is because most of the neurons encoded with those voices were programmed during the Euphoric Cycle of Development. During the Euphoric Cycle, the fetus, both schizophrenic and typical, realized high levels of dopamine. This caused the fetus to smile or laugh. Therefore, when these neurons encoded with the Euphoric Cycle fire and the voices encoded in them are replayed, for the schizophrenic individual, other aspects of the Euphoric Cycle are replayed as well. This causes them to laugh or smile.

The problem with the schizophrenic fetus with slightly weakened Memory Block, remembering these entire sentences, is that, this was not Nature's intention at all. Like in so many other circumstances, when Nature's intentions are not met, there are consequences. One of the consequences of this advanced auditory development will be the processing of sounds even after birth. So, what occurs is that these sounds, this schizophrenic infant hears, during the period of neural elimination, reprogramming and reinforcement, will also be encoded within the neurons encoded with its intrauterine development. So, not only is this schizophrenic individual hearing words and sentences recorded in the womb, but those during their infancy and early childhood, as well. In addition, this intensified listening that the schizophrenic fetus undertakes in, will in some cases lead to slight malformations of the schizophrenic individual's ears.

Paranoia

The schizophrenic fetus with slightly weakened Memory Block will often, later in life, develop symptoms of paranoia. There should be no surprise to this symptom, as paranoia, in many ways, summed up the intrauterine experience for this schizophrenic fetus. This schizophrenic fetus believed that something was trying to kill its mother and therefore itself. Indeed, from the perspective of this fetus the painful apneas, which stopped its oxygen supply for periods of time, could easily have been interpreted as an attempt upon its life. The entire intrauterine experience for this schizophrenic fetus was unnerving to say the least. Because of its slightly weakened Memory Block, it got very little rest during the pleasurable Euphoric Cycle of Development. This weakened Memory Block allowed it to, at least partially, remember, the existence of the horrific First Fear Cycle and the painful apneas that awaited it, right around the corner, when its mother would lie down to go to sleep. Unlike the autistic fetus with no Memory Block who could concentrate fully and take some form of action, however primitive, this schizophrenic fetus had its memory partially blocked. Therefore, it could not concentrate long enough to find out what was causing these horrific events, more or less; devise a plan to stop them. This fetus was not wrong to be paranoid, as something painful was going to happen to it. Of this there was little doubt, it is just that because its memory was partially blocked, it could not figure out who or what it was; this therefore, led to a mental state of distrust and, of course, paranoia.

Later in life, the neurons encoded with this fetal experience, which form the subconscious of this schizophrenic individual, are exerting a very strong influence upon their conscious thoughts. This is for reasons that have already been explained. These intrauterine neurons await connection to events from the schizophrenic's conscious thoughts and the paranoid individual believes something is out to get them. Of course, while at one time, through their interpretation this was true, it no longer remains the case.

Fetal Experience with More Severely Weakened Memory Block

What you will see here, for the schizophrenic fetus with more severely weakened Memory Block, is an intrauterine experience that in many ways resembles the autistics. You will also see, for the first time in schizophrenia, a departure by the fetus, away from its mother. As this schizophrenic fetus will now only believe that something is trying to kill it, and its concern will not be focused on its connection to its mother. While it still has Memory Block, it is very limited. The schizophrenic fetus with severely weakened Memory Block can partially remember its mother waking up and going to sleep, therefore it will not connect her to the equation of the painful apneas and the horrific First Fear Cycle. Unlike the autistic fetus however, the schizophrenic fetus with severely weakened Memory Block is not organized enough to plan an attempt to anticipate when the painful apneas come, nor is this fetus organized enough to do much to attempt to prevent them. In most cases, the action it will take will be limited to posturing and bracing itself for the horrific apneas. This fetus definitely has a good idea about when they are coming. In many ways, this fetus has the worst intrauterine experience of all, as it has enough memory to realize what is going to occur, but not enough memory to plan and take serious actions or have the hope that taking action will do anything to stop its predicament. In a sense, this fetus experiences a condition similar to learned helplessness. For, no matter what it does, it realizes the horrific apneas will consume it. Its life during the Euphoric Cycle is nothing more than a period of waiting for this inevitable painful event. This is in contrast to the schizophrenic fetus with slightly weakened Memory Block, who at least occasionally, would forget the upcoming horror that awaited it, then at other times it had an idea that it was coming, however, was not sure when or what it exactly was. Therefore, the schizophrenic fetus with more severely weakened Memory Block will not realize the range of emotional experience as the schizophrenic fetus with slightly weakened Memory Block; and will certainly not experience the emotional range of the typical fetus. Again, this is because, when it was supposed to be resting, relaxing and happy in the Euphoric Cycle of Development, it was instead concerned about the oncoming horrific event of the First Fear Cycle of Development and the painful apneas that occurred during this cycle.

Concerning its mother the schizophrenic fetus with severely weakened Memory Block will pay her little attention. While it will listen to the sound of her heartbeat and to her voice, it will not listen like the schizophrenic fetus with slightly weakened Memory Block to her words and sentences, as it realizes no value in this. In general, this schizophrenic fetus does very little. It will rarely kick and punch in an attempt to save its mother's life, as like the autistic fetus it does not believe that she is in the process of dying.

There is a very fine line between the fetal development of the schizophrenic fetus with severely weakened Memory Block and the autistic fetus. The two intrauterine experiences are very close. The major difference is that, in the case of the autistic fetus, the Memory Block fails to form and, in the case of the schizophrenic fetus with severely weakened Memory Block, the Memory Block forms, but then is either damaged or forms in a very much weakened state. In many cases, the intrauterine experience each fetus realizes crosses the line over into the other. This is primarily true for the schizophrenic with severely weakened Memory Block.

There are many times, when the schizophrenic fetus with severely weakened Memory Block will undertake behaviors that are identical to the autistic fetus. As from time to time throughout the pregnancy, its Memory Block weakens even further. Occasionally, the schizophrenic fetus will begin rocking to try and bring back the Euphoric Cycle. Occasionally, it will sniff and smell the intrauterine environment for cues as to when the painful apneas will come. Occasionally, it will begin hand movements in an attempt to keep the horrific apneas away. This, however, is only temporary. This is because, once the Memory Block originally forms, as in the case of the schizophrenic fetus, it will gravitate in the direction of strengthening. Indeed, it may strengthen to the point where this fetus will emerge into the fetal experience of the schizophrenic with slightly weakened

Memory Block. And in most cases, it will, at least for some time period, resemble the intrauterine experience of the typical fetus. For the autistic fetus, this will never occur. As for the autistic fetus the Memory Block will fail to form through the entirety of the pregnancy.

The Symptoms of Schizophrenia Related to the Fetal Experience with Severely Weakened Memory Block

We will now look at a few of the symptoms of the schizophrenic individual with severely weakened Memory Block. As you have seen, a major departure occurs between the schizophrenic with slightly weakened Memory Block and the schizophrenic with severely weakened Memory Block. While they can both be understood under the same disorder of schizophrenia, they are miles apart. What separates both, so vastly is, of course, the fetal perception of its mother's role in the horrific events it experiences in the womb. This very slight degree of difference between the amounts of Memory Block for the fetal intrauterine experience will translate into a very large difference in not only symptoms and behaviors, but also in the possibility of the schizophrenic individual ever reproducing. For as you will see, the schizophrenic individual who experienced as a fetus, severely weakened Memory Block will value interpersonal relationships much in the same way, although to a lesser degree, as the autistic individual does. This is in contrast to the schizophrenic individual who experienced as a fetus, slightly weakened Memory Block. As this individual will likely value interpersonal relationships much higher, will function at a higher level and in some cases even reproduce.

Early Recognition of Symptoms

In contrast to the schizophrenic who realized only slightly weakened Memory Block as a fetus, the schizophrenic who realizes severely weakened Memory Block as a fetus will begin displaying symptoms of the disorder very early. Again, this is due to its perception of its mother's role throughout its intrauterine experience. Because as a fetus, this schizophrenic did not include its mother in the equation, because it did not believe she was in the process of dying, because it did not believe that it was its role to save her, as an infant, there will be very little attention paid to her. This schizophrenic infant will make very little eye contact with its mother, while it will make more than the autistic infant, it will make much less than the schizophrenic infant with slightly weakened Memory Block. Because it will make little connection between its mother's health and its own, it will also not transfer this perceived dependence onto others. This will result in the failure to develop early close relationship among their peers.

Affective Flattening

Affective flattening is nothing more than a reduced range of expression and lack of eye contact that this schizophrenic individual expresses. The schizophrenic with this symptom will also have the facial appearance of immobility and unresponsiveness.

 This symptom, of course, makes complete sense, when you realize the intrauterine experience of the schizophrenic fetus with severely weakened Memory Block. Yet to understand this, it is necessary to contrast their development to that of the typical fetus. As you remember from Part One, part of the purpose of the Memory Block was to ensure that the fetus conformed effectively to each developmental cycle. When in the First Fear Cycle of Development, the fetus did not know of the existence nor had any recall of the Euphoric Cycle of Development. Indeed, the typical fetus believed that when it was in one cycle that it would always remain there. This enabled not only complete conformity to each cycle, but also it intensified the emotional experience. For example, when the typical fetus was in the First Fear Cycle of Development, as you have seen, the emotions that consumed it were fear, worthlessness, a sense of hopelessness and an intense sadness, as it believed that its mother and therefore it itself were in the process of dying. On the other hand, during the Euphoric Cycle, the fetus realized emotions of happiness, joy, euphoria and the heightened sense of self-belief. Most of this, of course, was due to the high levels of dopamine that were circulating through the reward pathways of the developing fetal brain. While, as you have seen, conformity to both of these cycles of intrauterine development had many developmental consequences, they also established the emotional range of the fetus. This emotional range was all encoded into the neurons of the two cycles of development; these neurons would later form the individual's subconscious.

The schizophrenic fetus with the severely weakened Memory Block never experienced this range, however. This was because, its weakened Memory Block prevented complete conformity to each cycle of intrauterine development. For example, during the First Fear Cycle of Development, it did not realize the emotional experience of the typical fetus. It was not fighting to save its mother's and therefore its own life, so the emotions that were inherent to that process and belief never materialized. The same was true for the Euphoric Cycle. Unlike the typical fetus, the schizophrenic fetus with severely weakened Memory Block did not realize the emotions of happiness, joy, euphoria and the heightened sense of self-belief during this cycle. There were two reasons for this. The first was because this schizophrenic fetus did not believe that it was its job to save its mother's life, there was no heightened sense of self-belief when it was accomplishing this. The other reason was that this schizophrenic fetus was anticipating the horrific apneas that awaited it during the next cycle. It only knew about these, because its Memory Block was weakened, which therefore allowed partial memory to be restored.

When this occurred, this schizophrenic fetus could remember the previous cycle and therefore, anticipate the next one.

Because the schizophrenic fetus with severely weakened Memory Block did not experience the emotional range during both intrauterine cycles of development, this lack of emotional range along with the rest of its intrauterine experience was encoded into the developing fetal neurons. As you have seen, these neurons form this schizophrenic individual's subconscious. Therefore, when this schizophrenic individual reacts to an experience, this lack of emotional range within their subconscious is utilized and a response is formed. This response, of course, reflects their altered intrauterine development. This altered development affects not only their response, however, their facial features and body language as well. In addition, eye contact will be reduced; the reason for this has already been explained.

Lack of Goal Directed Activities

The schizophrenic individual, who realized severely weakened Memory Block as a fetus, will often lack motivation to persist in goal directed activities. They will simply sit for long periods of time and will have little interest in social activities. Again, this symptom demonstrates their altered intrauterine development. As a fetus they experienced something very similar to a condition of learned helplessness. They realized there was nothing they could do to stop the painful apneas from happening. Unlike the autistic fetus, which due to the complete lack of Memory Block believed that they could actually stop the painful apneas, this schizophrenic fetus due to the existence of the Memory Block, however weakened, was not able to concentrate enough to initiate a plan of action. This also is unlike the typical fetus with Memory Block, which believed its mother was in the process of dying and that it must do something to save both of their lives. The schizophrenic fetus with severely weakened Memory Block, with the exception of posturing, did very little throughout its intrauterine experience. This intrauterine experience, encoded in the neurons that form the schizophrenic's subconscious, will then influence future goal directed activities.

Catatonic Behavior

In certain cases, a schizophrenic individual will display catatonic behavior. In other words, they will sit, as if frozen, often for hours in the same bizarre posture. Even if the schizophrenic individual is asked to move, or told to move, or an attempt is made to gain a response out of them, in all of these instances they fail to respond. It is as if they are forever glued to a certain position. They will often do this for hours at a time.

While these behaviors seems bizarre to the typical individual, when taken in context to the altered intrauterine development of the schizophrenic fetus with severely weakened Memory Block, these behaviors make perfect sense. As you have seen, this schizophrenic fetus could do very little to stop the oncoming painful apneas. One of the few things they did was to position their body in a certain way to brace themselves for the oncoming apneas. At first, these positions were simply in defense. After a while, however, this schizophrenic fetus began to believe that these positions they were maintaining were actually preventing the horrific apneas from occurring. This then became a very similar technique, although less involved, to the autistic's hand movements. In both cases, an alternative neural pathway involved in planned movements was utilized.

The schizophrenic individual, who is expressing these catatonic behaviors, will then avoid or resist moving from these positions, as this would allow the horrific apneas to return. Each schizophrenic individual will have their own particular preferred position, just as each autistic individual has their own repertoire of stereotyped movements. In both cases, the goal is the same, which is to keep the painful apneas away. What is important to notice here is the progression in the involvement of planned movements. For this schizophrenic fetus, because of the existence of the Memory Block, however weakened, they are limited to a repertoire that is focused upon a pre-existing fetal position, which then develops into a planned position. Now, for the autistic fetus, with no Memory Block, the effectiveness of this pre-existing fetal position in keeping the apneas away has already been discounted. Therefore, they progress into more involved hand movements that focus on a new belief system to prevent the apneas.

Additional Effects on the Schizophrenic Individual Due to the Weakened Memory Block

In the final section of this chapter we will look at the additional effects from experiencing intrauterine development with the weakened Memory Block. We will look at both degrees of weakness for this important neural function. We will look at the immune implications and the effects on the schizophrenic's reflexes and reactions.

Immune Implications

Due to the decreased amount of Memory Block realized during its fetal state of development, the schizophrenic individual will realize immune implications. As you remember in Part One, the Memory Block maintained a direct relationship with the individual's immune system. This relationship was, the more of the Memory Block that remains encoded within the neurons of the two cycles of intrauterine development, the more the individual's immune system was suppressed. For the typical individual, in every neuron, encoded with the First Fear and Euphoric Cycles of Development, the Memory Block was encoded as well. Therefore, the more First Fear and Euphoric Cycles neurons that were remaining within their subconscious, then, the more their immune system would be suppressed. In the case of the typical individual with First Fear Not Relieved, because an overabundance of these intrauterine development neurons remained and were not eliminated or reprogrammed, they realized an increase in the suppression upon their immune system. Their immune system, to fight this suppression, up-regulated itself thus, becoming hypersensitive. This then made the typical individual with First Fear Not Relieved very susceptible to autoimmune disorders and physical ailments that were resultant of this up-regulated and therefore, hypersensitive immune system.

In the last chapter on "Autism," you realized that without the Memory Block during their intrauterine development, the direct relationship between the Memory Block and the immune system, for the autistic would become imbalanced. Without anything to suppress the autistic's immune system, it would react in a very similar way as if it was fighting suppression and therefore, would appear up-regulated. This also could leave the autistic individual susceptible to autoimmune disorders, although for a completely different reason.

The schizophrenic individual is in the middle of these two extremes, between the autistic and the typical individual with First Fear Not Relieved. Because the schizophrenic realized during fetal development more Memory Block than the autistic, the immune system will not be susceptible to the same degree of hypersensitivity and autoimmune disorders, as the autistic will. In contrast, because the schizophrenic fetus realized less Memory Block than the typical fetus, it will also not be susceptible to the same degree of hypersensitivity and autoimmune disorders, as the typical individual with First Fear Not Relieved will be. So, on one hand, you have the autistic's immune system, which has nothing suppressing it, and therefore is so overactive that it fights against itself. Then, on the other hand, you have the immune system of the typical individual with First Fear Not Relieved, with too much suppression upon it; in defense it up-regulates self and begins fighting against it itself. Now, in the middle of both of these, you have the immune system of the schizophrenic individual, which in some ways has the ideal immune system. The reason the schizophrenic's immune system is ideal, is that it will never up-regulate its self. This is because, as a fetus, it did not realize the full Memory Block. It will also never fight against itself, because it had at least some Memory Block. As an end result of this, a schizophrenic individual will rarely suffer from autoimmune disorders, such as rheumatoid arthritis.

Now, there is a major exception to this. It occurs during infancy and early childhood. During this time period, Nature expects the immune system of the typical infant and young child to be disproportionately suppressed. This is for the obvious reason that the period of neural elimination, reprogramming and reinforcement is not completed. Therefore, the infant and young child will have more neurons encoded with the two cycles of intrauterine development than the adult will. Because the infant and young child will have more of these neurons remaining, they will also realize more suppression on their immune system.

This anticipated period of suppression affects the schizophrenic infant and child differently than it does the typical infant and child. Because there is already very little suppression on the immune system of the schizophrenic infant and child in the first place, the effect of this anticipated suppression is exaggerated. Therefore, the immune system of schizophrenic infant and child acts as if very little or nothing at all is suppressing it; this, results in it fighting against itself and it will, temporarily, remain in a state of hypersensitivity. Temporary, is the key word here, because once this period of infancy and childhood has passed and Nature no longer anticipates this suppression to occur, the effects will no longer be exaggerated, which will result in the schizophrenic's immune system no longer remaining hypersensitive.

Reflexes and Reactions

Because the schizophrenic fetus realized a weakened Memory Block, it did not fully conform to both cycles of intrauterine development. As you have seen, one of the purposes of the Memory Block was to develop quick fetal reflexes and reactions. These reflexes and reactions would then be essential during the process of labor, as the fetus would have to quickly respond to changes in the conditions. These fetal reflexes and reactions were developed during the quick changes between the two cycles of intrauterine development. For example, in the Euphoric Cycle the fetus was in a completely relaxed state, then, within seconds, as its mother lied down and the First Fear Cycle began; the fetus immediately came to attention and began fighting for its life. Again, this all happened very quickly. Every time this occurred the fetal reflexes and reactions were developed. This was the case for the typical fetus. This, however, is not what occurred for the schizophrenic fetus.

Because the schizophrenic fetus had a weakened Memory Block, it could anticipate the existence of one cycle while in the other. This is exactly what Nature did not want to occur, as that was one of the reasons the Memory Block was there to begin with. Because the schizophrenic fetus could anticipate these changes, it was expecting them and therefore, did not react as quickly. Indeed, Nature wanted the fetus to be taken completely by surprise, the schizophrenic fetus was not surprised at all, and instead, it was expecting the changes and therefore, failed to obtain these vital reflexes and reactions. Not only will this make the process of labor more difficult for the schizophrenic fetus, often resulting in complications, but also it will leave the schizophrenic individual, in general, with slower reflexes and reaction times.

CHAPTER FOURTEEN

OBSESSIVE-COMPULSIVE

In this final chapter, we will combine elements of Part One and Part Two of The Theorem. We will look at obsessive-compulsive behaviors and their intrauterine origins. Obsessive-compulsive behaviors have been placed in Part Two of this book, because they represent an organic aspect of intrauterine development. Unlike autism and schizophrenia however, they are not resultant from a break, weakening or a failure in the formation of the Memory Block. Obsessive-compulsive behaviors reflect the natural process of the Memory Block slightly lifting towards the end of the pregnancy. This is a common aspect of almost every pregnancy and therefore, a common aspect of intrauterine development.

The reason this chapter will incorporate aspects of Part One, is that while most every fetus, towards the end of the pregnancy, realizes the slight lifting of the Memory Block, in most cases, these neurons after birth will be eliminated or reprogrammed. In order to realize the disorder or behaviors of obsessive-compulsive, an individual must first realize the condition of First Fear Not Relieved.

What you have here then, is a combination. There is the organic lifting of the Memory Block towards the end of the pregnancy. Then, there are the environmental factors during infancy and early childhood that determine whether behaviors related to this organic lifting will ever be realized. These environmental factors during infancy and early childhood have already been discussed in detail in Chapter five on "First Fear Not Relieved" and will not be reviewed here.

The major reason Nature lifts the fetal Memory Block towards the end of the pregnancy is to protect the mother. As you have seen in Part One, Nature's concern and priority is always with the mother over the fetus or infant. You have also seen in Part One, that the fetal Memory Block suppresses its mother's immune system. With the long process of labor, right around the corner, the mother's suppressed immune system is a concern of Nature. It is important to remember, historically, in most cases, if the mother after childbirth were to become sick or die, the infant would likely die as well. This has been discussed in detail in Chapter five on "First Fear Not Relieved." Therefore, Nature wants to make sure that this does not occur. It is important that the mother has her immune system strong for the process of labor. After all, it is a difficult process at best, one from which the mother may realize some damage.

The Slight Lifting of the Memory Block Towards the End of Pregnancy

It is important to realize, concerning this natural process, to what degree the fetal Memory Block will slightly lift. For the typical fetus, the Memory Block will not weaken to the extent of the schizophrenic fetus. And the fetal experience towards the end of pregnancy for the typical fetus will in no way mimic the fetal experience for the autistic. No, this is a very slight reduction or lifting of this important neural mechanism. Towards the end of the pregnancy, the typical fetus will in no way be able to completely remember the existence of one cycle while in the other. Towards the end of the pregnancy, the typical fetus will in no way be able to remember that when its mother goes to sleep at night that she is not in the process of dying and will wake up in the morning. The slight lifting of the Memory Block for the typical fetus is not that severe.

There also is no danger for the typical fetus, towards the end of pregnancy, to begin to disbelieve the connection between its mother's life and its own. The major reason for this is that the developmental aspect connecting the fetal perception of the dependence upon its mother's activity level to the continued survival of the fetus has already been accomplished. In other words, the typical fetus, towards the end of the pregnancy, still very much believes that if its mother dies, it will die as well. The typical fetus, towards the end of pregnancy, will still kick and punch during the First Fear Cycle of Development in an attempt to save its mother's life and therefore its own. As you have seen, however, the intrauterine environment becomes so cramped towards the end of pregnancy, fetal movement will become somewhat reduced.

This is not to say that the slight lifting of the Memory Block, towards the end of the pregnancy, does not affect the typical fetus at all. This would be untrue, because it affects the fetus in subtle ways. With this newly realized increase of memory capacity, the typical fetus begins to notice very subtle patterns. Again, these patterns, in no way resemble the sophistication of the patterns the schizophrenic fetus connects concerning the oncoming horrific apneas. No, the patterns the typical fetus begins to notice are very subtle and vague. One pattern it begins to notice is that this horrible event that is occurring, the First Fear Cycle and these painful apneas that it interprets as its mother's and therefore its own nightly bout with death, seem to occur at the same time the pungent smells and foul odors consume the intrauterine environment. Even as the typical fetus, towards the end of pregnancy, begins to notice this subtle pattern, it cannot concentrate long enough to consistently predict the arrival of this horrific event of the First Fear Cycle and the painful apneas. Again, the Memory Block is still too strong. All that it can do is connect the smells of the death and decay, which are a normal part of olfactory development, to the arrival of this horrific event that it cannot quite comprehend.

It is important to reemphasize how strong the Memory Block still is for the typical fetus, towards the end of the pregnancy. It is constantly forgetting, constantly unable to concentrate, yet, at the same time, it has realized this pattern. The pattern is when the death and decay consume the intrauterine environment; something bad is going to happen. There is nothing the fetus can do to stop it; however, it will be alert and conscious of it anyways. Unlike the autistic fetus, which has figured out the entire puzzle months before, the typical fetus, towards the end of pregnancy, has only found a few pieces. The typical fetus is, basically, chasing shadows. It is chasing them in a very disorganized manner. The few pieces of the puzzle it has found are the connection between the death and decay during the First Fear Cycle and a horrific event that will occur.

Another reason the typical fetus, towards the end of pregnancy, is not able to comprehend a more sophisticated pattern of predicting the First Fear Cycle and its painful apneas are the intrauterine conditions themselves. As you have seen, the intrauterine conditions, towards the end of the pregnancy, deteriorate substantially. This alone, is the major focus of the typical fetus during this time. Not only has the womb, become a cramped place for the developing, growing fetus, but also the amount of dopamine available is no longer enough to reduce the physical pain of its own development. Then, there are its plans for leaving. As the conditions worsen, the typical fetus, after it has failed in its attempt to change things, for the first time contemplates leaving the womb. There is the guilt that consumes it. For the typical female fetus, as its intrauterine conditions are not as bad as for the male, the guilt of possibly leaving its mother behind to die, consumes every thought. For the typical female fetus, its major problem in staying is that it is growing too large. Therefore, throughout all of this emotional experience, it is difficult for the typical fetus to pay too much attention to the patterns of the intrauterine environment.

The Disorder

During infancy and early childhood many of the neurons encoded with the First Fear and Euphoric Cycles of Development will be eliminated, others will be reprogrammed and even others reinforced. This has been explained in Part One. Included in the neurons encoded with the First Fear and Euphoric Cycles of Development, are those that were specifically programmed towards the end of the pregnancy. In most cases, those neurons were eliminated or reprogrammed during infancy and early childhood. In other cases, due to environmental factors, those neurons were reinforced instead. If, for whatever reason, those neurons encoded with these two cycles of intrauterine development, specific towards the end of the pregnancy, become reinforced and therefore remain, the individual, later in life, will realize the disorder obsessive-compulsive.

The Symptoms

Obsessions are persistent ideas, thoughts, impulses or images that are experienced as intrusive and inappropriate by the individual. For the individual with the obsessive-compulsive disorder, this means is that the neurons encoded with the First Fear and Euphoric Cycles of Development are firing within their subconscious in a dominant pattern, which forces their influence up into their conscious thoughts. These, of course, are the First Fear and Euphoric Cycles of Development neurons, specifically programmed towards the end of the fetal experience in the womb.

The most common obsession is repeated thoughts about contamination. The individual with this disorder simply cannot seem to get things clean enough. To them, there are too many germs, which need to be cleaned.

The germs are everywhere. They are on people's hands, in public restrooms, around the kitchen's sink, indeed, they are everywhere.

It is likely that by now, you have already figured out that this is nothing more than the death and decay, which consumed the fetus in the womb during the First Fear Cycle of Development. Then, you also know, that encoded in the same neurons, specific to those programmed towards the end of the pregnancy, is the belief that whatever is trying to kill both its mother and itself, is right around the corner.

So, what does this individual with this obsession of contamination do? They wash their hands. They wash their hands to defeat the germs. They scrub their sink to defeat the germs. They wash things twice to defeat the germs and contamination they fear is around them. These are the compulsions. Now, while it makes sense to wash your hands, from time to time, these individuals with this disorder, wash them over and over again. It is almost as if, they forgot that they just washed them. It seems as if, they just cannot get them clean enough. They feel compelled to wash them. This makes them feel better.

Now, if they do not give in, to this compulsion, if they do not wash their hands, they are afraid that something bad is going to happen to them. Of course, they do not know what exactly is going to happen, if they fail to give in, to this compulsion. Nor do they know exactly in what context bad means. It is bad enough however, to keep them washing their hands over and over again. By now, you know exactly what context bad is, however. You know that this individual is washing their hands over and over again to keep the horrific First Fear Cycle of Development and the painful apneas, which they as a fetus interpreted as the death of their mother and therefore of themselves, away. Indeed, losing your complete oxygen supply, which is exactly what occurred to the fetus during an apnea, is enough motivation to get most individuals to wash their hands.

To the typical fetus, the contamination, which was the death and decay, towards the end of the pregnancy, signaled one thing, "Something bad is going to happen and you better do something about it." Of course, for the typical fetus, even with the partially lifting of the Memory Block, it still could not concentrate long enough to figure out what exactly it was it should do. Therefore, it did very little or nothing.

The obsessive-compulsive individual, however, can do something about it. Indeed, they can change the very state of their environment. Where it was once the womb, it is now their home. They can empower themselves, not to fight the fear, but instead to attack the very source of the fear, which to them is the contamination itself. Again, this is simply another word for the death and decay.

The big question then becomes, why do they continually repeat these behaviors? In other words, why do they wash their hands, then two minutes later have to rewash them? The most obvious answer, why they must keep repeating them, is that these neurons that are compelling them to act out or stop these obsessions, are part of the permanent formation of their subconscious. In other words, they are not going anywhere. For these neurons encoded with the First Fear and Euphoric Cycles of Development form their subconscious and the period of neural elimination has long since expired, therefore, these neurons will continue to fire inhibited, influencing the individual's conscious thoughts and forcing or compelling the individual to react upon them.

The second reason is not so obvious. The answer again is in the very neurons that contain the fears of this death and decay or in the case of obsessive-compulsive individual the contamination. When this individual washes their hands, it is almost as if they forgot that they just washed them, therefore, they are compelled to repeat the process.

The key words here are "is almost as if they forgot." This is because encoded in every one of these neurons that compel the individual to wash their hands, is the Memory Block as well. Therefore, when the individual with the obsessive-compulsive disorder washes their hands, subconsciously, they immediately are forgetting that they accomplished this task. While, consciously, they know they are washing their hands over and over again, subconsciously, however, it is the neurons encoded with the Memory Block, which forget that the contamination has been taken care of. In other words, encoded within the same neurons that tell them to wash their hands, is the Memory Block that makes them forget that they have just completed this process.

This is the same process that occurs when an individual is compelled to continually check the locks of their doors. Here, they are attempting to symbolically keep the horrific First Fear Cycle away, which has manifested itself into a criminal or burglar who may come into their house. Checking their locks once is not enough, however. Instead, they must check them over and over again. This is because encoded within the same neurons that tell them to check their locks, is the Memory Block that makes them forget that they have just completed this process.

Final Days in the Womb

You would think that because obsessive-compulsive behaviors reflect the neurons encoded during the final days in the womb, there then, would be other behaviors or disorders that would reflect the final days in the womb as well, which would co-exist with obsessive-compulsive disorder. In other words, because the same neurons programmed during the final days in the womb, reflect obsessive-compulsive behaviors, they also should express other behaviors that reflect the fetal experience at that time. This, of course, is exactly what commonly occurs.

For the typical female fetus, as you remember, one of its major concerns during the final days in the womb was that she was growing too large. As you have seen, these concerns can later translate into the disorder of anorexia nervosa. As you would expect, it is then not uncommon for the individual with anorexia nervosa to experience obsessive-compulsive behaviors as well. Again, this is because the entire intrauterine experience, during the final days of life in the womb, is all encoded within the same neuronal base. Therefore, it is not uncommon, when these neurons fire in a dominant pattern within the subconscious, for the complete experience of those final days in the womb to influence the individual's conscious thoughts.

The same is true for guilt. As you remember, the most dominant emotion experienced by the typical fetus, during the final days in the womb, was guilt. This was because the typical fetus felt guilt towards its mother at the thought of leaving the womb, and therefore leaving her behind to die. The individual with obsessive-compulsive disorder, along with their behaviors will often experience a strong sense of guilt, as well.

While not a symptom or behavior commonly associated with this disorder, a common perception has its origins during the fetus' final days in the womb. This perception is, when things are going very good or "too good," something bad is going to happen or something bad is right around the corner.

This is exactly what the fetus, when the Memory Block slightly lifted, during the final days of the pregnancy, realized what was occurring. While, in the Euphoric Cycle, when things were going good; the fetus had an idea of the existence of another cycle that was right around the corner, where things would be very bad. This, of course, was the First Fear Cycle. What is important about this belief or perception is that it accurately characterizes the fetal perceptions during the final days in the womb. The fetus could not completely anticipate or predict when the First Fear Cycle and the painful apneas were going to occur; yet, it had a definite idea of the existence of both cycles. This is demonstrated in the opposite of the saying as well, this being, when things are bad, they can only get better.

AUTHOR'S AFTERWORD

Page by page, you have witnessed the answers that man has been seeking since his beginning unfold in front of you. You have seen all the beauty, grace, and genius that are in Nature open up for mankind, her greatest species. You feel "The Theorem" to be right. You are sure that this makes sense. If you are a careful reader, you may have even noticed such behavior in others, or in yourself. And, if you are a perceptive reader, a true observer of life; you may be already making connections of these behaviors with their early origins. Yes, you are on your way to acceptance. You are well on your way to seeing, believing, and feeling the world in a way that you could only experience by knowing this. Still, you may have doubts; and if you do not have doubts, assure yourself that you may very well seek out those around you who do have doubts. While this is a natural element in the process of acceptance, these doubts are valid and deserve to be answered. After all, mankind has been looking for these answers for a very long time, for so many years: why have they been found now? To think that the model in The Theorem contains the answer to a single disorder is one thing; however, to accept that this model yields all the answers to all of these disorders and behaviors may be simply too much. Again, the question arises: why has not anyone seen this before?

The answer to this is partially contained in The Theorem body itself. The answer rests with the small fetus who is responsible for so much that we now know. To forward the idea or even the possibility of a conscious fetus, would have been a difficult position anytime throughout our history, and would have likely been met with resistance. There are reasons for this, as well. For, mankind is the greatest of Nature's species; and while he has inherited a great many things upon this throne, one of them is arrogance. This arrogance is authentic only to our species; inherent only to this mammal that is above all the others. To know what is right or wrong in his judgment, decisions, or actions towards the world around him would still make him the king. Well, this is the glory of man. We know this story too well, as this is a part of us all. If another species cannot talk to us, then it must not be able to communicate. Also, because it cannot communicate, it must not be important — simply a pawn to move out of the way, if it ever should be so bold as to put itself there in the beginning. This is the arrogance of man. This arrogance is as archaic as our civilization itself and has not only been confined to our perception of other species.

So strong was his arrogance that once it colored his perception of the entire earth: and a colorful episode it was. Rich in its deception and telling in its extent. Yes, at one time man was convinced his world was flat, truly believing that if one sailed far enough they would fall off the face of it. After all, the earth, like man's vision, must have a definitive end. So, man, in all of his arrogance, assumed that the earth must be flat. It is comical now to look back and think that men, against strong evidence to the contrary, were arguing and convincing brave explorers how they would fall off its face. Sad, how misled they were! How their own arrogance blinded them to what was right! Yes, it is comical now; however, at the time it was not comical at all. For, these were men of science, educated to see the answers, yet, they could not see past themselves. It would have been much the same way with the case of the conscious fetus. To think that a fetus could experience and be capable of experiencing these things without us being able to see them, without the fetus being able to tell us these things, well, this violates man's arrogance, and in the history of human thought, this has simply not been acceptable. Even though all the evidence would have pointed towards it, even if it felt right to those who understood it, and even though it was logical and correct, the fetus could not talk to us and tell us the answers; so, they would not be accepted as correct. In his search for the truth, it is man himself, in all his arrogance that stands in his own way on his journey towards the answers. It has always been this way. Yet, there is more to it than this.

Yes, there is more. After all, there have been so many wrong answers. There have been so many twisting, turning roads, leading optimistically into nowhere that it sometimes seems as if the answers are intentionally hidden. It is almost as if we were never supposed to know the answers in the first place. Because we did not know the answers, a mystical wall was built around the discovery of them. It was almost as if the answers were somehow hidden in a mythical kingdom and this kingdom was surrounded by a giant wall. Yes, this must be it. And at the base of this wall, men stood steadfast, and strong; however, they could not scale it. These were men of science, of medicine, and of psychology. These were not ordinary men: for, only the best earned the right to stand at the base of this wall. These were dedicated individuals who had devoted their lives in an attempt to scale this great wall. As you would imagine, most of their days were spent attempting to figure out ways to get up over the top and into this mythical palace that embraced the answers. Of course, everyone had a different opinion on which method was the best, and about which technique and which route one should take to get over the top. Most of the time, a spirit of cooperation dominated at the base of the wall, as these men would share their knowledge on the best approach. Other times, these men, as all men do, would disagree. Sometimes, these disagreements would become heated, and in a mad race to the top of the wall, these men would even stand upon each other's backs in an attempt to scale it.

There were other men at the base of this wall as well. These men, while not men of science, attempted to climb it, nonetheless. These were the artists and philosophers; and while they took a different approach, their goal was the same, this being to scale this great mystical wall and obtain the answers from this kingdom enshrouded. Like the others, these men also fell short. What was remarkable, however, about these men and their attempts, was the style and grace of how they scaled the wall. And, even though they failed, they inspired the other men at the base of the wall. They were so inspiring that their stories consumed the talk at the bottom of it for days, weeks, and, even, years.

These philosophers' and artists' stories inspired me, as well. Yes, like those who stood at the base of the wall, I felt that they carried my spirit with them as they made each and every one of those attempts. Unlike the others, however, I was not at the base of the wall. No, I was nowhere near this caliber of an individual. So, I admired these great artists and philosophers from a far distance. This mattered little as I admired them nonetheless. It was more than admiration: for, I was a student of their stories, their philosophies, and, of course, their interpretations of the human condition. I read them all — at least, as many as one could fit into the short lifetime I had experienced. More than just a reader, in my mind I elevated these great thinkers, writers, and philosophers to a category to which very few positions are reserved. I not only read and assimilated their works, but like many a young man does, I also looked hard to read between their lines, in order to find direction in what was, otherwise, a confusing world. While I never found answers, I was certainly inspired by the style and grace of their writings.

Obviously, after I made the initial discovery for the model of The Theorem, I had little time to continue to read these great works. I was busy with other things, such as asking myself why in the world it was

I who stumbled onto this. As you would imagine, these types of questions do take a large part of one's day. Still, I had to look at those men at the wall and wonder why they had not seen then what I now realized so clearly. I knew that it certainly was not due to lack of intelligence, as many of these men were brilliant. It was also not due to their lack of motivation, as most of them were very driven in their quest to understand the human condition. Year after year, through the long course of history, man had attempted to get up over the top of this wall and into this mythical palace that contained the answers. I simply could not understand why nobody had seen this before, as it was right there all the time. Of course, I now had the courage to confront these great men, these famous philosophers, artists, and writers not as a distant observer but as a peer; as, I was prepared to hold my discovery up to and at least equal to theirs. While I was giving away these great books, I wondered again, asking them, challenging their ghosts as to why they did not see what I had seen so clearly in the night sky. Still, I received no reply. Ten years came and went, and I still received no answer.

It was only recently that the answer to this question hit. And I must say that as a man, this answer cut quite deeply into me. Yes, it hit me very hard when I saw it. All this occurred as I was reading through The Theorem and working on the revisions for the book you just finished. I was assessing the work and I suddenly realized that if there was a hero in this book, it certainly was not a man. Yes, this was it; man was not the star of my little book that contained the answers mankind had been looking for since his beginnings. In fact, unfortunately, it was women who had secretly stolen the light of this show. Yes, while I had initially written the book for men like myself who had struggled and fought to understand life, it was women who looked for such things, which I had accidentally elevated in this book — in these answers. Of course, I had no such intention, as it was not I, after all, that had elevated them — it was Nature herself. It was only that I was so focused on the answers that I was blinded as to what gender possessed them. It was only after I had finished re-reading this work that I realized it was too late to change the way it was written.

This, of course, to a man was a large blow. I was very disillusioned in my brothers and in myself. I hoped to be wrong in my judgment and borrowed back these great books I had given away. Page by page, I scanned over them, only to be disappointed in the end. While I wanted to be wrong, I was, unfortunately, right. All these great books were written by men and were about men. All the heroes, every Faust, the philosophies, and their protagonists were all men. In fact all of man's stories including his theology was about, who else but, other men. Even in his own creation (stories) there must be a man involved playing the central role. There was no objectivity in this. Again, it was not only ridiculous but disappointingly inaccurate. For, it is one thing to not know the answers, but it is another altogether, to spend and devote your life in a self absorbed frenzy searching for the answers and not allow yourself for one moment to accept that you are not the star of the show. Yes, and that maybe — just maybe in all our greatness, we may have been horribly misled. And, maybe, all our immortality we sought to obtain, all of our great works we were to leave behind, the great books we had to write, the buildings we had to build that would last long after we were gone, and all our myths we had to create were somehow a consolation prize for not being the chosen one by Nature to accomplish her primary task. Certainly, few women, when compared to men, have devoted their lives to leaving something immortal, such as great paintings, literature, or philosophies behind when they left. This was only for one reason, as they had immortality running through them. Once they had experienced this, once they bore witness to creation itself inside of them, little else would compare. There was no need to look any further than the child at her side. While a few would continue looking, such as those who could not comprehend what they had already completed, in most cases, there was no need to look any further than the babe she was nurturing at her breast. Yes, this child could grow up to replenish successive generations, which itself would then further replenish. Compared to this, all buildings, bridges, paintings or works of art, literature, and science meant little. Indeed, they all paled in comparison. An elder once told me, many years ago, something that I have never forgotten. He said, "Nothing man can ever or will ever create can begin to equal the process of birth itself." While I never knew what he meant by this or why he felt the need to tell me, it now, in a very mystical way, made complete sense. This, of course, was it. The answers were obvious all the time — they were written on the wall itself. Yet, man was unable to see past himself and find them. Perhaps, the pain was too much to accept and perhaps the greatest insult against man from Nature came after birth itself. Knowing this, I felt small. It did not just make me feel small — the discovery itself, the very discovery that man had been looking for since his beginning, seemed to shrink in my hands from what I had learned.

Yes, I had learned so much from this discovery. I had found out so many things, some I really did not want to know. I learned that all the greatness of man, this myth I had been spoon-fed as a child, from the very books I sat on to boost me up to the table in order to eat, were not great at all. The mystery was unveiled and far from the heroic character as I once viewed him, man now seemed almost comical in his delusion of himself. Yet, I learned even more, as all of this recorded history of human thoughts, these incredible accounts of countless journeys into the mind, human beings were nothing more than a result of the neurobiological process itself. They were nothing more than man's subconscious interpretation of events he had experienced during his intrauterine development. Also that this was nothing more than a memory occluded, then, built upon by the countless folds of development, thus influencing every single thought and perception. About these men who had written great accounts of this journey, I learned that this was nothing more than the most damaged of individuals because it had to be this way. As it was only from the early damage that these memories and perceptions would reinforce and grow, when they went to write these random thoughts down, they were not random at all, but very specific accounts of the journey taken, the journey of our own development. And, when any reader would see this, while they might not agree with it all, they at least would recognize in his words remnants of their own journey. The damage that caused this wellspring of genius also sprouted a great deal of pain. This is what his undamaged neighbor could never understand, as to why this great artist would destroy his own life. It simply had to be this way, as the very pain and raw perceptions that deemed them great, stemmed from the same pool, the same experience that would be his downfall. It had always been this way and it always would be. The greater the pain, the greater the potential for genius; while, for most, the pain was too much and they would end up locked away in a cell or asylum somewhere, occasionally, one of these damaged individuals would take a few minutes out of their self-destruction to jot down their thoughts. When this happens, greatness was always the result; however, then, uncomfortable in a surrounding he was never meant to be, and deafened by the intense pain ringing in his ears, he would continue his slow suicide to the disbelief of those around him. Indeed, the greatest writings were never written, the best paintings were never painted and the greatest speeches were never spoken, muffled by the very pain from which they began.

Yes, it would always be this way. All of man's philosophy, psychology, doctrines, treaties, and theology were nothing more than the result of this conscious but obstructed interpretation of his own development and of these two cycles. In one cycle, almost heaven like, everything was provided for him; then, within minutes, the fallout of this beautiful garden and into a hellish cycle, a cycle of pain where he must now work hard for the precious neurochemicals he received, the ones given to him freely just seconds before. Man would fight, kill, and ultimately die to protect his interpretation of this journey. He would fight because others interpret this journey differently. Both, of course, were likely accurate as Nature's intrauterine environment would likely, in the spirit of true genius and ingenuity that was there, change ever so slightly for climatic differences. While both interpretations, because they were subjective, were no more flawed than the next, both were flawed, nonetheless. Also, all of the time, the answers were right there in front of him, standing next to his side and laying next to him on the bed he built for her with his own hands.

Yet, man still looked to himself for answers. He would create stories to fulfill some psychological need that it was not he that was the chosen one. Yes, in these stories, he would reverse the truth and claim that he was responsible, in some ridiculous way, for her and his creation. He would even take himself seriously in the study of this deception, convincing himself that he was somehow compelled to devote his entire life studying of fallacies. All the time, he was only compelled to not face the truth, and the resultant pain that accompanied it because Nature and all her evidence did not agree with these twisted tales; man turned against her, as well. Nature and human nature; this that was borne by women, was something wild, untamed and if went unchecked by the shackles of man's distorted doctrines, could be dangerous. Still, he looked up to the sky and in all sincerity, actually had the boldness to ask for answers, and the naivety to believe that he would receive anything of value, in return. Indeed, he could look for a million years in the mirror for the answers and he would be no closer than he was yesterday. Yes, the truth was piercing in its pain for this was a play, these answers, for which he was not cast as the central character. There was mercy in Nature however for she would keep the answers hidden from him, stored in the deepest regions of his subconscious his entire life. Only at his death would the truth be revealed to him, as he again slid down the twisting, turning tunnel and into the white light that was once life and was now death, in a last desperate act by the body human to lift the suppression on his immune system these memories had demanded.

The answers had always been there all right; you simply had to know where to look to find them. You, and I as well, were not immune from this charade. I had struggled hard to bring this work forward; it was a heroic struggle against almost insurmountable odds. In bringing this work to publication, for every man I met who knew the world was round; I met a thousand who could not see past themselves and the flat earth they stood on. Yet, I did not quit, I could not quit. After all, I had found what so many men before had looked for. Still there was no golden cup; there was no eternal fountain for me to drink from. There was only the distant murmur of a child's voice. While I too had looked for the answers I must be guilty of trying to obtain immortality through the written word, there could be no other reason one would work this hard. And this immortality in all its greatest glory was still inferior to the single cry of a newborn infant. So I decided then, as I tell you now that I will bow down to Nature not out of respect, although I do respect her immensely, but so that I shall not waste another living breath in trying to defeat her in a battle that was lost long ago for me and for all men.

Yet, this is only one view of our history. And it is certainly not a view that I want to see in mankind's future. A theorist and philosopher may be guilty of many things: this is true. One of these however is always an undisputable love for mankind, as even in his callous conscious exists — the true genuine desire to seek and sprout the seeds that can lead mankind into a better tomorrow. So, it is with this spirit that we must go forward. While it may be a bold statement to make, by looking at our past, I think we can do better. I must admit that I will gladly contribute the words on these pages if they will further the cause of advancement. My only hope is that it is not for the sake of advancement itself, but rather to lead us into a more enlightened tomorrow. Enclosed on these pages are answers to human behavior, use them wisely.

Douglas M. Arone
December 2004

APPENDIX
THE NEURAL NOTES

INTRODUCTION

When you do not understand something, it takes on a presence all of its own. It becomes bigger and larger than it has to become. To understand "The Theorem", is to understand the human brain. To understand the human brain, you must first have realistic expectations of what it can and more importantly cannot do. While it is an amazing function, there are limits. This book deals more than anything, with the limits of what the human brain can accomplish.

While, upon first sight of this work, its title, and the answers it provides, one would expect a radical approach. In all actuality, however, this work is very conservative in its estimation and is an accurate representation of what the human brain can do. In fact, as you have just read, The Theorem essentially de-mystifies what the human brain can accomplish. For the purpose of this work, it is necessary to think in terms of these limitations. In this context, the brain can record perceptions. It can record those perceptions, organize them, and play them back in a network, with a sophistication that is only now beginning to be understood.

Therefore, when you see an individual that is expressing symptoms of depression, schizophrenia or autism, you must first and foremost realize that they are expressing a large portion of previously recorded or encoded stimuli. There is simply no exception to this. Now the brain, through its vast network can twist and distort this original information, but again there is the necessity of initial source. So, these individuals are displaying behaviors that are very unoriginal to the present moment, however, that were always relevant to the moment they were recorded. The brain simply doesn't pick original material out of the sky and insert it into our thoughts, unless, we, of course, are looking into the sky.

Once, you understand this, then, you are very well on your way to a deeper understanding of human behavior and its resultant disorders, set out before you here. For, there is no magic region of the brain, yet to be discovered. No, its anatomy is well mapped. And, once you understand this, you quickly realize that the answers are right in front of you, and it is only your limitation of interpretation of those answers that has prevented you from this.

A major limitation of our interpretation is of course paradoxical in nature. To understand our own development is to learn the process of subtraction. While we were all taught the process of subtraction in school at a very young age; when, you are dealing with the human brain, the equation becomes much more complex. Of this I am certain you are aware. And from the vantage point where you and I sit now, with our subconscious influencing every single thought and action, it is difficult, if not impossible to project this onto the human fetus. Yet, it is not necessary, in fact it would not even be accurate, for while the human fetus has a remarkable complexity, the very origin of us all; it too has limits. The human fetus is limited by its source material. While, there are other important factors such as genetics, essentially the human fetus is limited by the very experience, sensory and other, and then, limited again by the developed mechanisms to record that experience it is exposed too.

The human fetus brings with it to this theatre, a very limited group of neural mechanisms, to record the sensory experience realized in a simple fear conditioned model. This is nothing very original here, for even the most primitive of mammals can be conditioned in this format. It is one of the simplest functions of animal learning; a tried and true tool, and one among many of the tools close at Natures side. One could even argue, from an evolutionary perspective that allowing the fetus a limited conscious presence during its own development is not so remarkable. When you speak in terms, however, of utilizing this same fear conditioned model for the purpose of reproductive motivation, and further, to gamble the entire survival of the species on this model, well, then you quickly begin to realize the genius you are dealing with here. Indeed nothing ever invented or discovered can match the beauty, economy and utter brilliance of her performance in this respect. So, while it is not so much that Nature generates new and unusual neural anatomy to produce these behaviors; it is more of how she utilizes what has already existed in such a unique application that begs of nothing less than aspiration of respect.

This is indeed a major breakthrough, a major discovery. Some will embrace this as such, for others it will be simply too much. It matters little, as everyone has a part to play. And, by choosing not to participate, you are participating, nonetheless. For the history of human thought holds a special place, a sentimental sanctuary for those who could not accept what was correct, because it did not arrange tightly into their acquired perception. Yes, this is a place that has always a vacancy, a solid shelter to hide from the shinning brilliance of progress and discovery. This discovery was a gift to me; and this is the same spirit with which I present it to you here today. I want nothing for it in return. I have no hidden agenda in presenting it to you. To believe so, is tragic. My only agenda is to the process of discovery itself. I have tried to bring this discovery to as many possible, so that, they and you too can continue where this one ends; which, from where I stand can only be defined as infinity.

While Nature is a genius, I certainly am not. This will become even more apparent as you read the neural notes enclosed. Please keep in mind as a writer and by fate a theorist, neurobiology is not my native language, nor do I want it to be; therefore, certainly some aspects were misinterpreted during translation. Please also keep in mind that to present such a vast work, such a complex structure that defines us all a great many generalizations and simplifications were essential. I am sure that you are aware that if I were to give this work this space it deserves, the space we all deserve, this work would be 10,000 pages and still not yet complete. However in condensing the majority of this, I have attempted to maintain the integrity of the original discovery. I am speaking of the general model here of course. One should be cautious of over interpretation of the specifics of the overall model for the reason just stated.

With that said, however, even with these limitations there is substantive value. While many aspects of the model were either omitted or did not fully materialize into these neural notes — this, while it is less than 2% of the research utilized in preparation for The Theorem, it is an important 2% nonetheless. Therefore, it is with all of my idealistic, yet, tempered enthusiasm that these notes will be enough, along with the primary model, to guide those to make major strides in solving two of the largest mysteries in the spectrum of human disorders, schizophrenia and autism.

First Fear, Memory Block and Autism

An important aspect of The Theorem is the identification of the two cycles of intrauterine development. While in no way is this intended to dismiss the value of independent testimony and opinion of the millions of women who have given birth and will tell you, "Yes, at night or whenever I lay down this fetus inside of me begins to kick and move, and that, yes, something likely very important is going on inside there." No, here it will begin to define from a scientific vantage a more specific description of the First Fear Cycle. Even though, it has been shown that pregnant women successfully define and identify their fetal movements correctly 87% of the time (1); to properly define this cycle, it is first necessary to define fetal movements in relation to independent fetal breathing, leg movements, trunk movements, jaw movements and a combination of all. Due to a lack of research focus on human fetal states in regards to psychologically significant behavior states, most data reviewed is mixed, and pertains to different aspects of independent fetal behavior. Therefore, it is difficult to produce two specific behavioral states and their relevance to The Theorem model. This is not to say that the definition of two specific fetal states has not been defined. Generally, human fetal behavioral patterns have been divided into two specific states: these states by late gestation have been defined as quiet sleep (1a), and active sleep (1b).

Of course, even the most skeptical observer would have to agree that it is naive to think that the human fetus only sleeps throughout its entire tenure in the womb. They would have to then believe that the fetus essentially sleepwalks through birth or magically awakes seconds before, and then through some grand genetic influence can initiate, and even if it seems impossible, successfully accomplish the process of birth itself. Now, as you will see, there is clear evidence that the fetus at least from mid-gestation realized not only organized behavioral state but also that these states are clearly linked to factors of mother-fetal relationship not yet determined. The definition of these behavioral states will be explained in general throughout, as it is likely that active sleep is misinterpreted, through EEG recordings as the fetal neural pattern with this function intact.

It is unlikely that the fetus is only sleeping as it moves on an average just over 50 times an hour (2). Fetal movements can be witnessed by ultrasound at 7 weeks gestation; this is much earlier than most mothers' notice or report movement, which usually occurs about 18 weeks (2a). During this 7th week the fetus realizes general reflex movements (1c). As gestational age progresses these early nociceptive reflexes graduate to the level seen in a newborn by the 14th or 15th week (1d). Development of these reflexes will not only be critical for the process of birth itself, but for our purpose, will be useful in our attempt to date the approximate onset of the First Fear Cycle of Development. By the ninth week, convulsive type fetal movements can be observed. These occur without fetal dislocation and occur with movements of the developing arms (1e). With increasing gestational age also comes an increase in the complexity of fetal movements. In addition to these complex movements, a definite rhythm as to their frequency also develops. These more involved movements include swinging of its arms vigorously and kicking the walls of its intrauterine environment (1e). This, as you have seen in the model included, is the very specific of the fetal reaction to changing intrauterine conditions during the First Fear Cycle of Development. In addition to these movements the fetus also actively moves in its intrauterine space and of course returns to its original position (1f). A number of fetal position exchanges increase from 10 weeks onward and reaches its peak between the 13th and the 15th week, then, shows a decrease after the 17th week of gestation (3).

There have been other reports of even earlier organized movements. One study conducted fetal monitoring from 6 to 17 weeks gestational age and found very early movement patterns. These included, startle, general movements, sucking, swallowing, rotation and ante flexion of the head, jaw movements and hand to face contacts. Early independent breathing movements and hiccups were also noticed in this study (3a). Other evidence suggests that by nine weeks while still considered an embryo, it can bend its body, hiccup and react to loud sounds (2b). By the end of the first trimester the embryo or fetus can yawn, suck, smell and more importantly, feel. This early organization of behavior suggests that the first Fear Cycle of Development could begin as early as the beginning of the first trimester. Further support comes from a study indicating that by the end of first trimester the embryo or fetus has already established regular patterns of exercise which include rolling, turning, leg kicks, flexing and waving of arms (4). Pattern is the key word here. And, again, these movements are a very accurate definition of the fetal behavior in the First Fear Cycle of Development.

Fetal heart rate is also an important modifier of the First Fear Cycle of Development. For over 70 years a direct relationship and association between fetal heart rate and fetal movements has been established (5). By the third trimester virtually all fetal movements are coupled with increases in fetal heart-rate. Instead of merely a result of increase body movements, a significant amount of research now suggests that these accelerations are almost simultaneous to the movements themselves (4a). This suggests that the fetus is responding to a change of conditions either within its intrauterine environment or internally. Whatever generates these changes is then substantial enough to motivate the fetus to kick and thrash out violently, and in some cases this activity is preceded by accelerations in the fetal heart rate. The question then, becomes, of course, what is generating this increase in fetal heart rate? The answer to this comes from studies of the fetus during amniocentesis. If a fetus is stuck with needle during the process, the fetal heart rate accelerated rapidly. If not stuck, the fetus shows no major change in fetal heart rate (5). It is then obvious that pain, in this case at least, is the generator of the acceleration and changes in fetal heart rate. This is of course what is going to increase the fetal rate every time; and it is also what is going to motivate the fetus in what should be an otherwise self contained complacent environment. While this seems cruel to utilize pain to prompt the fetus into action, it is only with this intent of Nature that the fetus is capable of surviving the long process of labor. Further support for pain relation to fetal heart rate in correlation to the First Fear Cycle of Development, comes from studies showing a decrease in fetal heart rate when the mother is reading a story to her unborn child (2c).

With the understanding of how the fetal heart rate increases in response to pain, you can begin to understand how the primitive model of classic conditioning or fear conditioning works during the First Fear Cycle of Development. Strong evidence for this model comes from fetal heart rate and fetal movement coupling. In this context, coupling defines a direct association between movements and heart rate of the developing fetus. While this sounds as a logical connection, if the fetus moves, then, their heart rate should increase (6). This, however, is not what occurs, at least during many movements. In fact, what is often the case is heart rate acceleration actually precedes the movement, showing that the acceleration of heart rate is not a response from the increased movement the fetus experiences. This of is what occurs in the model of classical conditioning or more specifically classical fear conditioning (7). The fetus realizes painful or noxious stimuli as witnessed by the accelerating heart rate and begins to move their body in response. The motivation likely for this organized movement is to bring some relief of the painful or noxious stimuli, which as you see comes likely as a direct result from the neurochemicals generated by this movement itself. Thus begins the start of this classical fear-conditioning model with the fetus responding in attempt to reduce the pain associated. Dopamine and L-dopa are an attractive possibility for the neurochemical motivation for this model. Dopamine is not only a significant, but also a plentiful catecholamine for the fetus. It has been concluded that L-dopa and dopamine are important during fetal development, and between 15 and 20 weeks gestation L-Dopa constitutes 80% of total circulating fetal catecholamines. These fetal levels were 2 to 3 times higher than in maternal plasma (8). And dopamine reward and release has been shown to be a result of a new behavioral strategy acquisition (9).

In addition to changes in movement by the mother, it is likely that other variables are involved in the changes of intrauterine environment and resultant behaviors the fetus experiences. Researchers have identified hormonal changes with maternal circadian rhythms. In the pregnant mother there are daily rhythms of prolactin, cortisol, melatonin and TSH (10). Rhythms of HCG in the placenta have also been found (10a). This has been substantiated by the fact that triamcinolone administration to the mother, which eliminates the maternal corticosteroid rhythm, also eliminates the diurnal variation in fetal activity (11). If dopamine in all its abundance is the pain relief and motivator for reward seeking activity for the fetus then prolactin may play an important role in changes of the intrauterine environment during the First Fear Cycle of Development. Prolactin increases during the time when the pregnant mother is sleeping and spikes at the end of pregnancy (12). Prolactin has been shown to inhibit the release of dopamine (13, 14). This reduction in dopamine would lead substantial discomfort as described in the model. This increase in prolactin and resultant decrease in dopamine could then explain fetal movement patterns and maternal sleep during the third trimester; an established and direct relationship exists between the movements of the fetus and awakenings of the mother during her sleep (15). Here the fetus is fighting for its life trying to wake the dying mother who is only sleeping.

This reduction of fetal dopamine availability throughout the night could also increase the pain level associated with the initiation of independent fetal breathing. Alterations and increases in maternal glucose levels are thought to be responsible for initiation of independent fetal breathing (16, 17). Fetal breathing movements increase during the second and third hours after breakfast, however, then reaches a minimum before lunch and dinner (17a). However, the same study also showed a significant increase of independent fetal breathing at 4am. This initiation was independent of maternal glucose level. Clearly another factor is involved in addition to glucose that triggers this independent breathing (17b). While this is not only likely to bring more discomfort to the fetus that is experiencing this painful initiation of independent breathing, but it also portrays the careful timing of Nature. This independent fetal breathing at 4am directly parallels the exact hour when most births occur worldwide, this is 4am (18). Yes, there is little doubt here that to Nature it is important that not only the fetus rehearse with its new lungs, however, that it does so at the exact hour it will need them the most during the long process of labor and birth itself.

Before, we can begin to identify the neurochemicals and or neuroanatomical regions associated with the Memory Block it is first necessary to pinpoint the neural regions related to the First Fear Cycle of Development, specifically the neural regions involved in the classical fear conditioning model the fetus experiences. Overwhelming evidence pinpoints the developing fetal amygdala brain for this role. The amygdala has been implicated in involvement of the classical fear-conditioning model in both animals and humans (19, 20, 21, and 22). Also, the amygdala and its extended regions have been shown to be involved in the processing of fear (23). And, the nucleus accumbence within the extended amygdala has been demonstrated to be involved in defensive and fear related behaviors (24). In addition, seratonin is also known to alter fear processing by modulating amygdala activity (19a). The amygdala also has been shown to generate appropriate emotional behaviors in response to, emotionally salient, fearful stimuli (25). Finally, the amygdala and interior insula have been shown to have an important role in conditioned taste aversion, unpleasant taste, pain perception, anxiety and nausea (26). The amygdala has also been established to have a general role in modulating learning and memory under stress (22a), learning about rewards (22b), associating stimuli with positive or negative reinforcement (21a), and AMPA receptors on the central nuclei of the amygdala play a key role in both acquisition and expression of fear potentiated startle (28). AMPA receptors on the central nuclei also exert a strong stimulatory action on dopamine neurotransmission especially in the prefrontal cortex (28a). In animal studies lesions of the basolateral amygdala suppress second order responding for conditioned reinforcers associated with sexual reinforcement (29). Indeed much of what you have read in the model that the First Fear Cycle is responsible for could be authentically represented and encoded within these neurons of the amygdala and its closely related structures.

There is more however, as drugs of addiction, through their dopamine release exert a strong influence on the amygdala. The basolateral amygdala has been implicated in the reinstatement of drug seeking behavior (30), and is also responsible for a variety of stimulus-reward associations (30a). In animal studies lesions of the basolateral amygdala severely impair acquisition of cocaine under second order schedule of reinforcement (30b). And the amygdala shows strong activity and becomes highly activated upon exposure to drug paired cues in human cocaine users (30c). Dopamine neuronal terminals are densely localized in the basolateral amygdala and dopamine is important in cue-induced cocaine seeking behavior (30d). Dopamine receptor activation in the basolateral amygdala, upon activation by dopamine, acts as a filter by inhibiting projection neurons and exciting interneurons by the stimulation of D1 receptors, thus reducing input from the medial prefrontal cortex (30e). It is clear that the drug taking individual through the exertion of dopamine is selectively reducing the influence from the firing of the neurons encoded with the First Fear Cycle of development and thus reducing the pain of their own development that is encoded in these neurons. With this neuronal firing selectively blocked the baseline level of pain they are accustomed to, a level that most are not even aware of, is temporarily eliminated and they feel euphoric once again, just as it occurred during the Euphoric Cycle of Development.

The amygdala has been linked to memory formation that is linked to emotion (20a). In a classic fear-conditioning paradigm, patients with amygdala damage, fail to show a normal physiological response to fear (20b). The amygdala can influence hippocampal dependent episodic memory (20c) and amygdala, through MRI studies, shows an enhanced response to fearful faces (20d). One theory forwards the idea that the amygdala receives information very early about the emotional significance of a stimulus in stimulus processing and through feedback connections enhances later perception, depending on the value of the stimulus. This influence then alters the encoding of hippocampal dependent episodic memories and then prioritizes those that have emotional relevance (30,20e). This of course is likely what occurs. When a man meets a women or sees a picture or object, then the stimulus presented, is first run through the amygdala to code it for either low priority if it does not have relevance to the First Fear Cycle of Development or to high priority if it does; and then, if, it does have significance it is pushed over and prioritizes to the hippocampus to develop a memory of this event. And this memory formation will take precedent over the memory of say a rock or stick. You could imagine how if you did not understand this model of First Fear Development the fetus experiences; how this research in relation to the amygdala could be quite confusing. After all, what in the world is the connection, between a man seeing a women jogging, fearful faces, and a classic fear conditioned model all doing in the amygdala? Indeed it would make little sense. When, however, you understand the model it all comes into view. This is because during the First Fear Cycle of Development the fetus was kicking and punching out in pain in response to this classical fear-conditioning model established by Nature. And, as you have seen, as fetal neural development progressed and a limited consciousness was allowed; the fetus began to make associations that its mother was in the process of dying and that the fetus was somehow by its activity preventing this. Therefore, during its fetal stage and well after birth the infant made the obvious association that the health of its mother and the health of itself; thus, as long as its mother was active and alive, then, it would not realize the pain of the First Fear Cycle of Development, its initial fetal perception of death. Now, years later he sees a woman jogging and looks at her, but what is actually happening is that these same neurons encoded with the First Fear Cycle of Development in the amygdala are firing and to some extent being disproved either by excitory action or inhibition depending on which group. For example, by seeing her jogging he has identified two things; one that she is moving and two that she is healthy. Both of these will thus inhibit the firing of those neurons encoded with the First Fear Cycle of Development, but more importantly the fact that she is moving will light up those neurons associated with the euphoric and more pleasant cycle the fetus experienced during that cycle. In response to this he may see her and smile at her, it is not that he is thinking of sex or even wants to have sex with her. No, not all, it is something much simpler than that. She is simply shifting his neural pattern from an unpleasant baseline level and nullifying those fears of a dying female and therefore a dying self, to a positive and Euphoric Cycle or neural pattern. He feels better just seeing her there and knowing that by this association he will be alright until those fears creep up into his subconscious once again, this of course later after these neurochemicals are depleted and the inhibitory neurons or excitatory neurons reduce their firing. Again, he may smile at her to acknowledge and reinforce her behavior. Now, if, for example this girl running reminds him of someone he used to know, maybe a previous girlfriend then this stimulus and reaction will very liked be pushed over to the hippocampus for consolidation, cueing and possibly storage. In this case, he may remember her over and over again or maybe this other girl that he used to know. And, this subtle transaction takes place billions of times a day all around the world, without either party truly understanding the neural mechanisms involved in the process, because it is primarily occurring on a subconscious level. And the amygdala, which is encoded with the First Fear neurons of development, is largely responsible for this. Now, for the female it is quite different, while the First Fear Cycle of Development is still encoded in the amygdala a different part or nucleus area will generate more activity, when she sees an attractive and well-dressed man. Now, it is not the dying mother, but the death and decay associated with that negative First Fear Cycle that will gain more activity. By looking at this man and hopefully him looking back at her, she is essentially offsetting those neurons encoded with the death and decay. Some neurons encoded with this event will be inhibited while others will be excited, because she is essentially disproving the fears that are consuming her subconscious. Because, he looks at her and he obviously has no death and decay inside of him and she begins to believe that through him or some other male he represents desiring her and wanting her then she can disprove these subconscious fears, Nature has encoded her with, and that she is reminded of on a monthly basis. Again all of this occurs in the amygdala and surrounding regions within seconds of the stimulus; which is the nicely dressed man, and all of it happens on a subconscious level so that she is not even aware of it. She just knows that it makes her feel better and if he made a strong impact on her, if he was extremely well dressed, fit her tastes or reminded her of someone else she knows then again this stimulus might be coded and pushed over to the hippocampus for consolidation into memory. Brain imaging studies have found similar results to these, this gender specific response to stimuli in different regions of the amygdala. In these studies the left amygdala is associated with later memory to emotional stimuli in females and the right amygdala is associated with memory of emotional stimuli for males (20f, 31, 32). It is important to not read too much into this example as the purpose of presenting it is only to show that because the First Fear Developmental Cycle is encoded for both male and female in the same general region of the amygdala, yet both genders motivation in this regard, stems from different areas of this development cycle and therefore will be reflected as such in imaging studies. It is also important to realize that this is a very simplified outlook and many other regions of the limbic structures and neurotransmitter systems are involved in the encoding of the First Fear Cycle of Development. The amygdala is very specific to this event however and therefore lends itself easily to this brief examination of its relevance. Along the same theme, the amygdala has been shown to be responsive to happy and or positive expression of faces (33, 34). The amygdala also has other important outputs and inputs worth mentioning here. The cortical amygdala receives profuse inputs from the olfactory bulb and olfactory cortex. Yet, the amygdala is not essential for olfactory discrimination (35). In mammals this connection is utilized for pheromone exposure in order to motivate mating behaviors (36). This occurs in almost all mammals except one; that is in humans. Some will argue that this is just some left over connection that evolution will eliminate. This however is not likely because, as you have seen in reading The Theorem model, Nature is extremely efficient and economical when it comes to our species and would not waste such an essential connection to the limbic region. And, indirectly through the death and decay it is utilized for mating behavior, but not exclusively on a pheromone level. No, as you have seen these connections are essential for the fetus to react to changes in the intrauterine environment. The results of this are widespread throughout human behavior, as will be seen in the sniffing behavior from the autistic; olfactory hallucinations by the schizophrenic, unusual odors from the epileptic during seizures and finally tangles in the olfactory region for the Alzheimer's patients. All of these originate from the same experience, the fetus reacting to changes in the intrauterine environment in response the First Fear Cycle of Development, this fear conditioned model that was essential for our development and ultimate survival.

It is the amygdala and its extended regions that are most obvious areas encoded with the day-to-day, cycle-to-cycle, fetal reaction in the classically conditioned or fear conditioned model that is The First Fear Cycle of Development. As you would expect, because of the failure of the Memory Block the autistic fetus did not fully conform to this classically conditioned model. Because this fetus could anticipate and plan and essentially prepare for these changes there should be some reflection and deviation of the typical neuroanatomic structures of this region. This is exactly what has been found in the brain of those with autism, the regions involved in the classical fear conditioning model, pathologic abnormalities of the forebrain, including the amygdala (27). These abnormalities which are generally consistent between cases include reduced neuronal cell size and increased cell packing densities and increased number of neurons per unit volume bilaterally (27a). Autism is a helpful assessment in identifying neural structures, primarily limbic, encoded with the fetal reactions to the dynamic development event that was The First Fear Cycle. This is because the autistic fetus due to its lack of Memory Block did not experience the development of this cycle as the typical fetus did. Therefore, we can go further to look at abnormalities of the limbic region of the autistic, and to a lesser extent the schizophrenic brain in order to determine the regions directly involved in The First Fear Cycle of Development and more specifically the Memory Block. Other regions of considerable abnormalities in the forebrain of the autistic individual include the hippocampus, mamillary body, entorhinal cortex, anterior cingulate cortex and the septum (27b). Like the amygdala these areas showed reduced neuronal cell size and increased cell-packing density along with increased number of neurons per unit volume bilaterally (27c). While these areas could be candidates for the encoding of the First Fear Cycle of Development, they are likely involved in the Memory Block the developing fetus experienced. And in the case of the autistic fetus this accelerated or enhanced memory will begin our investigation into the Memory Block.

The question then is which one of these areas; the hippocampus, mamillary body; entorhinal cortex, anterior cingulate gyrus and septum are responsible for the Memory Block. The answer in all its simplicity is, all of them. They are all directly involved in the Memory Block. Indeed all of these regions that are of considerable abnormality in the brain of the autistic individual were intended to keep the fetus in conformity of the two cycles of intrauterine development. More than this however, as we explore each of these areas, you will begin to get a very clear picture, possibly more lucid than in the model itself about Nature's intentions during the First Fear Cycle of Development. Most of the research that enables us in understanding of what these areas accomplish; derive from lesion studies on animals. By knowing the purpose of each area and understanding the accelerated development of the memory functions in the autistic fetus, we realize that, unlike the typical fetus, these regions were developed for the autistic fetus. Therefore the typical fetus, much like lesioned animals in these studies, during intrauterine life does not have these yet functioning, as they are blocked. Again in the autistic fetus these areas are functioning and are therefore not blocked. And this more than anything else is cause of the disorders of behavior that define autism.

Spatial navigation and place reference memory are disrupted in animals with lesions of the medial septum area (37, 38). Here we see that Nature did not want the fetus, much like the lesioned animal, in one cycle to remember the existence of the other. Therefore, when the intrauterine environment changed from the positive Euphoric Cycle to the intolerable First Fear Cycle the fetus could react to changes in the environment effectively. For the typical fetus, even though it was in the same place in both cycles, because it lacked spatial navigation and place reference memory, it was as if it was in another place altogether during the First Fear Cycle. This is why people when they are stuck in a situation that is undesirable will often want to get out. They might take a drive; take a vacation or even a walk outside of their house. Much like during their development they believe in the distinction that changes in latitude and or location can change their situation. This would be just as it once had; only they never actually went anywhere, as it was just that their reference memory or spatial navigation skills that were blocked, so they, as a fetus believed they were in a different place. Now, for the individual with autism it is much different, because they had these skills in place there was no deception, and they were not fooled that they were in a different place. No, they realized that the same place and what was to them somewhat euphoric only minutes before became intolerable and life threatening seconds later. This was because they had intact memory of the reference and space they were in. This is why the autistic child or individual will often become upset when furniture is moved around or changed in the house. For here we have the same place, but suddenly everything is changing. This represents an association to this experience.

The subiculum is responsible for reward directed navigation, memory retrieval and delay activity associated with working memory (39, 40, 41, 42). Here, we have a combination of not only memory retrieval but also reward directed navigation. So, we understand that for the typical fetus these were not in tact. And there was a very good reason for this, primarily in reward directed motivation. Remember that Nature wanted the fetus to kick and punch out to get its dopamine (reward). Or else, she wanted the fetal thumb to inadvertently end up in its mouth, as it always does due to fetal positioning, in order to begin the association of dopamine with sucking so that it will take to its mother's breast. Nature does not want the fetus figuring out that there is much more effective and easier ways to obtain dopamine. Thereby, Nature blocks the fetal ability of reward directed navigation. Now, for the autistic fetus because it does not have this ability of reward directed motivation blocked, it can quickly figure out that there are other and much more effective ways to gain dopamine. They figure out that if a finger produces a little bit of dopamine and therefore pain relief, they will experiment with an entire hand. And of course the larger object allows more pressure and suction from its undeveloped roof of its mouth. And here we go; now this fetus doesn't have to kick out so much, because it can get the dopamine by an easier method. When it comes time for labor however, well then it will pay the price from all those missed work out and conditioning sessions Nature had intended for it, as it will likely realize complications during the process of birth itself (43, 44, 45). Concerning memory retrieval and delay activity associated with working memory, these are both classic definitions of the Memory Block. Again the autistic fetus had these functions intact and could anticipate and plan accordingly, but the typical fetus like the lesioned animal could not recall or remember.

The mamillary body has been associated with spatial processing (46) and spatial working memory (47) Animals with lesions of the mamillary body do not know where things are around them. In addition they also cannot remember the location of things around them. This is especially true of allocentric spatial processing, which is judging the location or distance one object is from another (46a). This of course is exactly what nature wanted to occur for the fetus. It was important that the fetus forget that the walls in front of it were hot to the touch so that it would touch them over and over again. This would develop the sensory perception of its fingertips. These skills would not only safely navigate the fetus down the birth canal, but later in life, save it from burning its fingers, hands and body. The autistic fetus however has the ability of spatial processing and it can remember exactly where those warm places on the intrauterine walls are and more importantly what it means when it touches them. Therefore, the autistic fetus will avoid them whenever possible. Not only will this hinder the fetus during delivery as it will not go the correct route with its hands and cause all kind of complications, but also later in life, it may not realize that something is hot and accidentally burn its fingers and maybe its entire arm. For this reason the individual with autism will be insensitive to thermal pain as these senses were never encoded with these initial burning sensations (48, 49). In the case of the autistic individual these thermal sensory regions are essentially empty, as they have not been coded properly. The opposite of intact spatial memory can be observed in a child that as a fetus experienced typical development. They may be under a table and grab a ball. In the process they may stand up and slightly bump their head. If it doesn't hurt too much they will go on looking for the ball. Then you can almost be assured that minutes or even seconds later they will do the same thing again, thus bumping their head at the same spot. And it is this development, this lack of spatial working memory, which is encoded into each of these neurons that is responsible for this, causing them to forget their surroundings and orientation almost as quickly as they are aware of them.

The anterior cingulate cortex has been established with involvement of processing remote fear memories (50) and is thought to play an integrative role in the cognitive control process (51, 52). For the typical fetus this is about as much memory and intellect as they receive. I will explain what this means momentarily. Yes, we are going to see the anterior cingulate cortex involvement with schizophrenia (53, 54), obsessive-compulsive disorder (55, 56) and anorexia nervosa (57, 58). And while I haven't seen any research to document this, I would imagine that studies will come out and show a connection to pathological gambling, as with OCD and anorexia; all three are related to the fetal experience at the end of the pregnancy. If you remember at the beginning of The Theorem in the first chapter I spoke of the lie. I said the autistic never experiences it, the schizophrenic sees through it and everyone else essentially cannot escape its impact. Well it is this region that is essentially responsible for most of this. When the fetus finally begins to figure out at the end of the pregnancy, as the memory block lifts, it will be in this region that they will make this distinction. Yes, for the typical fetus at the end of the pregnancy the maturation that is a result of the memory block lifting allows them a slow realization. They begin to realize that all this kicking and punching they accomplished to try and keep the mother alive is not working and that no, they are not in two separate places and yes, something is coming right around the corner about to get them and instead of enjoying this Euphoric Cycle they better get prepared and try and do something about it. And this something that they do maybe nothing more than doing the same things that they are doing right at that minute, and that is to try and figure out what to do.

The anterior cortex is essentially an integration system of all information related to the First Fear. Without this functioning properly or blocked in the case of the typical fetus it cannot figure out what is going on, it only assimilates bits and pieces and attempts to make connections, but all the information is just a confusing blur.

Without this functioning properly the typical fetus makes incorrect assumptions based on the variables around it. The main variable of course that Nature wants the fetus to misread is the mother is in the process of dying and that the fetus should kick and punch in order to keep her alive. How important is the cingulate cortex in fetal development? Let us put it this way, if it was fully functioning during intrauterine development and not blocked for every fetus, then our species would certainly have faced extinction long ago. Because, there would be no misinterpretation, there would be no association between the mother's life and our own. And for the male this lack of connection would sever Natures reproductive model and he would simply have no interest in the female. This would translate into no reproduction and therefore no species.

As you have seen for the autistic fetus, the anterior cingulate cortex is already functioning at a time and in a place that it was not supposed to be functioning. Therefore, this fetus has the ability to not only process those remote fear memories that define the First Fear Cycle of Development, but it can also anticipate and plan about the coming cycle. And, as you would imagine, these will lead the autistic fetus developing behaviors and planned movements that the fetus was not intended to accomplish at this early stage of development. It is important to realize here that at no time during its development did the autistic fetus realize development in the same way as the typical fetus experienced it. Therefore, the autistic fetus could process remote fear memories, and because of this, it quickly began to take steps to prevent the impending doom when the intrauterine environment changed. This fetus began making connections, and one of the connections was that when the intrauterine environment slowed, the conditions deteriorated. Therefore, the autistic fetus began a series of planned movements, even to become as extreme as to mimic the rocking of the womb. Of course this took a considerable amount of energy and had little effect. Later in gestation, as you have seen in the model the autistic fetus became more efficient in its methods to prevent the First Fear from consuming it and the horrific episodes of independent fetal breathing. Therefore, it developed planned movements. It developed a specific group of hand movements to keep this cycle away. Of course, later in life, two common behaviors the autistic child displays are rocking motions, and unusual and repetitive hand movements (59,60,61). Because both of these were planned movements and Nature had no intention of planned movements at least to this extent and at this early of gestation in the womb, the autistic fetus will realize abnormalities of the areas involved with planned movements and that is the cerebellum and related structures. And, indeed, one of the major and most consistent findings in autism, in addition to limbic pathology, is abnormality in the cerebellum (62, 63, 64, 65). Areas of abnormality have been limited to the cerebellum and related inferior olive (65a). The absence of glial hyperplasia suggests that these lesions of cerebellum were acquired early in development (65b) and likely before thirty weeks of development (65c). In this study, researchers go onto to build the hypothesis that these lesions are due to the functioning of a primitive circuit utilizing the cerebellum before it was mature (65d). This of course is exactly what occurs, the autistic fetus is not supposed to be using this cerebellar circuit at this time and for this purpose, this being to generate these planned movements. So, what we can begin to identify here is a cascade of developmental abnormalities. Due to the accelerated development of the limbic region, in particular the anterior cingulate cortex, a secondary deficit occurs in the cerebellum. In other words because the autistic fetus can identify the two cycles of intrauterine development (anterior cingulate cortex) especially the First Fear Cycle, it begins to take steps to prevent it by utilizing planned movements (cerebellum). We will see this pattern again for the schizophrenic fetus but not nearly as consistent in terms of detectable abnormalities, as during development their enhanced memory was much more transitory in nature. What is exciting here is that from the model we begin to look at patterns of the individual neurons or groups of nuclei and how they respond to accelerated development from this enhanced or accelerated memory. In other words, when neurons are utilized before their intended purpose, such as you have seen in the model, they appear to exhibit specific changes as the individual matures. For example, in these same cerebellar related neurons just noted a distinct pattern can be detected. The neurons in the brains of young autistics seem to be large and then later atrophy and either eliminate or shrink in size with the older autistic brains (65e). And this observation is not only confined to the cerebellar regions. In the limbic region, the neurons that define the septal region that was mentioned above, the diagonal band of Broca also show a similar pattern. In the brains of younger individuals with autism (9–12 years of age) these neurons are unusually large and present in adequate numbers, however in brains of older individuals with autism (22–29 years of age) the neurons of the exact same nucleus are small and in size and significantly reduced in number (65e). Relevant here as well are the findings that show enlarged head circumference size, which is a good indicator of brain size (66) up to two years of age in children that are either diagnosed with autism or will be in the future (66a). If you add these to the model presented you begin to get a clear picture on behavior on the neurobiological and individual level for the child with autism. Due to an intrauterine insult early in gestation, the limbic structures realize an accelerated development, thus forfeiture of the typical fetal neural chronology i.e. the Memory Block. This then results in an accelerated memory function, thus resulting in atypical intrauterine development. As a secondary result of this atypical development the autistic fetus generates planned movements that cause further abnormal development in the cerebellum and related cerebellar structures. In the macrocosm this accelerated neurodevelopment results in increased head size at an early age then atrophy later. In the microcosm this accelerated neurodevelopment results in increased cell size at a young age then atrophy later, in some areas. In the majority limbic structures this accelerated neurodevelopment follows logical order and shows increased cell packing density and smaller cell size. And finally on a behavioral level, the individual with autism portrays the behaviors highlighted in the model you have just read, which define the current symptomology of the disorder.

We will revisit the importance of the anterior cingulate cortex one more time. As you have seen above the anterior cingulate cortex works as an integrator of information, combining all the other information from these other limbic regions. For the typical fetus not only is the integrator of that information not functioning, but the information, which it is supposed to be integrating, is itself blocked or not functioning. So, far from the autistic fetus that has all these limbic regions fully functioning very early in development, the typical fetus only knows that something is occurring. This fetus, while in one cycle, doesn't know what is coming, as these other limbic regions are not relaying information of any value, it just begins to realize that something is going to happen to it. Because of its' newly realized intellectual abilities it can begin to make simple connections. One of these connections is that when the foul odors come the First Fear will come. This behavior that defines the end of the pregnancy will later surface for the individual with First Fear Not Relieved, as behaviors in an aggregate that are termed as obsessive compulsive disorder. Again, this slow lifting of the Memory Block, component by component, is a diluted version of what occurs for the schizophrenic fetus that likely has had two or three of these regions functioning earlier in the pregnancy and even this, is nothing compared to the autistic fetus that has had them all essentially functional since very early in the pregnancy. Still, it is enough to shut things down for the fetus and cause it to reduce its conformity to this First Fear Cycle of Development. This is likely what Nature wants to occur anyway as the fetus is so large now and myelination is advancing; the fetus could likely do some extensive damage to the mother if it were still kicking and punching on a nightly basis with the same intensity it once did. Then of course there is the fact that the intrauterine environment is becoming so crowded. There is evidence to support that the First Fear Cycle of Development decreases in intensity at this time. As coupled movements between fetal heart rate and fetal movements decrease (5b) Ironically, some studies have even suggested that this is when organized or purposeful movements begin, after all the major development work has been accomplished. While certain aspects of the First Fear Cycle such as independent fetal breathing will actually increase, as Nature fine tunes the developing fetal lungs, for the important process of labor, most of the important work for the typical fetus will now be neurobiological. And, again one of these major steps is the gradual lifting of the Memory Block and allowing the consolidation of information in the anterior cingulate cortex. This essentially is the fetal awakening, the moment when it realizes a sense of what has occurred. It has been kicking and punching in order to keep the mother alive on a nightly basis and now it realizes slowly that it is not working and that maybe it has been mislead. It has believed in something for a long period of time and that something is not accurate. Indeed this fetus misinterpreted events around it, and someone or something is responsible. Again, because most its memory is still blocked it cannot be sure. It is the origin of deception, the origin of the lie. This has such a powerful impact on it that for the rest of its life when in a position or situation of fear, similar to the fear it realizes now it will almost instinctively mimic Nature. It then should be of no surprise to realize that in brain imaging studies when an individual lies or deceives it is this area, this anterior cingulate cortex and superior frontal gyrus that will show the most activity (67, 68). Of course, it is important to realize that the autistic fetus never experiences this misinterpretation as it has these memory functions intact much earlier than the typical fetus, due the acceleration of the development of these limbic regions. And, as you would expect the individual with autism, has difficulty understanding deception and lies (69, 70, 71).

Of all the areas we will explore as aspects of the Memory Block, we will spend the least amount on the hippocampus. This is not to downplay its importance; as the exact opposite is true. It is for only one reason and that is the hippocampus has been so well established as a region involved function of memory (71, 72, 73, 74, 75, 76, 77, 78) that its involvement in the Memory Block should be obvious. Instead of exploring the multiple functions of the hippocampus and its individual regions we will focus on how it relates directly to The First Fear Cycle of Development. However, a very good case could be made that it is in the day-to-day, cycle-to-cycle repetition of these two cycles of intrauterine development and the subsequent blocking of the developing fetal memory that lead to some of the plasticity by this limbic structure that leads to the extraordinary ability of this species, but this would be out of context here. Instead, we will focus on the hippocampus as it relates to the Memory Block.

While, all the CA regions of the hippocampus are affected in the brains of individuals with autism, a very consistent abnormality occurs in the CA1 region. In hippocampal CA1 depletion studies, animals realized deficits in spatial and relational memory (79-84). Here, we see again this is very similar to the typical fetus with the Memory Block intact. Relational memory here refers to the making of associations and this is very much a stepping-stone to learning. As you have seen the fetus is not supposed to make associations that are too accurately connected. Instead, the fetus is intended to misinterpret associations, which is what occurs. The autistic fetus without its memory blocked can make associations that are accurate and purposeful. The autistic fetus makes the association that when the intrauterine environment is moving, the First Fear Cycle of Development does not occur. This is why at one time, usually early in pregnancy, the autistic fetus begins rocking itself in the womb even when it is not moving. This, as you have seen, takes a substantial amount of energy and therefore only occurs until the autistic fetus can figure out a way to reduce its energy expenditure, which will usually involve their hands. However, there have been reports of the mother feeling the autistic fetus generating their own independent rocking movements later in gestational age (85). There is ample evidence to support this change of movement patterns for even the typical fetus as the gestational age increases. With the fetus making large quick progressive head flexion movement that was repeated resulting in a somersault within the intrauterine cavity, thus allowing the fetus to change positions (86). Then, in later periods of pregnancy, the hands became more important and the fetus directs them not only to the intrauterine wall but other areas including their own developing body itself (86a). In all cases the movements appeared purposeful and with variations in intensity and in most cases directed toward the intrauterine wall (87). These movements suggested primary and secondary circular reactions as if the movements had a functional importance to the fetus (87a). As you have seen for the autistic fetus because it could make associations it did not make these same repeated movements over and over again directed at the intrauterine wall. Once or twice in a day was likely enough for them to remember that they were hot and should not be touched. Yet, there are much more advanced associations the autistic fetus made, ones that took much less physical energy and more mental energy to accomplish. And, because these CA1 regions of its hippocampus were not blocked and were therefore functioning; it could make advanced associations enabling a primitive form of learning. As you have seen in the model the autistic fetus made associations between everything its mother did, with the hope that it could at least predict and hopefully prevent the upcoming cycle of intolerable pain. And, certainly, the hippocampus has been well established in the process of learning and memory (86, 87, 88). The autistic fetus with its memory functioning is making many associations; and while these will do it little good: the First Fear Cycle of Development is regulated by variables unknown to it, such as hormones and glucose levels; it has made some general associations about the mother's schedule. This fetus knows exactly when the mother usually goes to the bathroom, when, she usually lays down and when she usually gets up. This fetus is counting her steps and anticipating her movements. This, of course, is why later in life the child or adult with autism is fascinated with associations. They will watch a dryer spin for hours; watch a top spinning; as this mimics the movement of what was to be the Euphoric Cycle. They will also be interested in other things such as train schedules, bus schedules, and anything that predicts or anticipates when something will occur; this of course for those higher functioning individuals (89,90,91). It is a rigid belief-system based on what was effective in keeping the First Fear Cycle away. All of this effort to find variables in an uncontrollable environment will also later in life yield a reduced startled response for the individual with autism (92). This is because all of its associations and predictions at least kept it on close watch for the changes in the intrauterine environment, and therefore it was not as surprised as the typical fetus was, when the First Fear came.

The entorhinal cortex in the brain of the autistic individual has been continually reported to show many abnormalities consistent with those described above. The cortex has important connections with the hippocampus and it has been suggested that there is no other regions more closely connected than the entorhinal/hippocampal region (94).

While, the entorhinal region has been implicated in many functions related to this model, we will focus only on one of them and this as its function receiving important sensory information (94a). The cortical field of the olfactory complex impinges directly on the rostral entorhinal field (94b). The entorhinal region is thought to play an important role in relaying sensory information to the hippocampus and then relaying its significance back to other regions once it has passed through the hippocampus (94c). You can see clearly why Nature wanted this sensory information blocked for the typical fetus, as it did not want the fetus to be able to anticipate the coming cycle of the First Fear. While some associations and connections would be made as inevitable, as some conditioning was essential for the developmental process associated with the "death and decay," the typical fetus with this function blocked would not be able to anticipate the coming cycle through olfactory identification. This would then maximize reflex and startle development. The autistic fetus with the entorhinal region functioning could however anticipate the coming cycle by not only sniffing for the changes in the intrauterine environment but by tasting them as well. For the fetus this essentially is the "eyes and ears" in the womb. And, again, it would use these senses, as it found in them a reliable indicator of the changes in the intrauterine environment and could therefore anticipate the First Fear Developmental Cycle by this. As you would expect outside the womb the child with autism continues to use these senses in the same way. It will lick and sniff at toys and objects (95,96), continuing to use these senses as a primary input to make sure their environment is not going to change into the horrific cycle.

Of course, in the context of fetal development, the purpose of blocking the entorhinal cortex for the typical fetus may have been for a different reason altogether. In animal studies, lesions specific to entorhinal cortex caused an animal to have difficulty with flexible manipulation of memory between familiar items (97). This would have had important implications for the First Fear Developmental Cycle. If this is correct, then it would be likely the amygdala, which would process this olfactory information, as it as well has an important role in the process of olfactory identification and memory (98).

While understanding the origins of autism and defining the developmental model responsible for its behaviors is certainly a breakthrough, this still does not answer the question of what neuronal properties are completely responsible for the Memory Block, and in the case of autism, this accelerated neural development. While an in-depth investigation of each possibility would exceed the limitations for this appendix, one can essentially take two positions on this development. One is that the Memory Block is a consequence of typical fetal development, this being that these limbic functions are not yet mature during intrauterine development; and, therefore, the sensory information encoded into these neurons that contain The First Fear is this immature pattern of undeveloped memory, and that, this is what causes the difficulty in concentration and memory associated with disorders such as depression, ADHD, learning disabilities and during-dream-recall; when these neurons fire, and synaptic connections are made for the individual in this aggregate condition or upon awakening. In this case, then, the autistic fetus would realize accelerated intrauterine development of these memory functions, thus representing the limbic pattern of small densely packed neurons. Certainly, this perspective would follow a more conservative, although historical perspective viewpoint on our development. From, this perspective, there is evidence to at least suggest that an unfavorable intrauterine environment accelerates neuronal maturity (99). In the case of autism, however, this environment would have to be very unfavorable and at a very early stage to cause such a dramatic acceleration. This would leave one to believe that somehow in a final grasp to maintain the functioning pregnancy this acceleration is the final phase before the pregnancy terminates itself.

The other and more extreme perspective is that there is a functioning, although, primitive memory circuit is in place very early in gestation, and is intentionally blocked by a neurochemical or group of neurochemicals, in order to ensure that the fetus conform strictly to these two important developmental cycles. Dopamine, GABA and Seratonin could all play parts in this role. Serotonins importance during embryogenesis has been well established (100), where it works as a hormone, growth factor and neurotransmitter, and displays complex pharmacological properties (101). Further support for the existence of an early functional, although primitive memory function, early during development, comes from identification of a functional circuit very early in development that could at least partially support this model of classical fear conditioning. Robust reciprocal connections between the entorhinal cortex, hippocampus and the subiculum were continuously present at 19 weeks gestation (102). And, this was the earliest date examined. These projections to the hippocampus and subiculum originated from neurons in layers 2 and 3 in the entorhinal cortex (102a). These, early reciprocal projections to the entorhinal cortex originated from pyramidal neurons in the CA1 region of the hippocampus and the subiculum (102b).

There is of course another possibility, and if correct, would have some interesting implications. In the complex search to find some component of fetal development that would enable enhanced fetal memory capacity which defines the autistic intrauterine experience; it could be that the most obvious has been overlooked. It very well indeed may be the cholinergic system in autism that realizes or is responsible for this accelerated memory capacity.

Evidence to support this, comes from a diverse range of research. There is substantial evidence of abnormalities of the cholinergic system in autism (A1, A2, A3, A4). Much of this evidence derives from the low levels of muscarinic and nicotinic receptors in the in cortex of autistic brains (A4a). In addition, and complimentary to this cholinergic dysfunction, are findings of high levels of brain derived neurotrophic factors in autism (A4b, A5). In the rat hippocampus, brain derived neurotrophic factor is up-regulated by hippocampal activity (A6), suggesting that in the autistic brain, high levels of brain derived neurotrophic factor results from high levels of hippocampal activity. More importantly are the findings that these high levels of brain derived neurotrophic factor are present at birth. In 62 of 64 newborn babies that would later be diagnosed with autism, brain derived neurotrophic factor was elevated in blood levels (A7). This further suggests that cholinergic activity and in particular hippocampal activity was increased during fetal development for the autistic individual.

To understand the importance of this finding in relation to the model; it is important to take a detailed look at effects of accelerated cholinergic development in animal studies. Most of these studies focus on the effects of choline or folic acid supplementation during fetal development Folate and choline are interrelated metabolically (A10). Choline is necessary to establish a pool of acetylcholine during fetal development (A8). Acetylcholine is the neurotransmitter of cholinergic neurons. Plasma or serum choline concentrations are seven times higher for the fetus and for the neonate than they are for the adult (A9).

Here, in regards to autism, things become very interesting. It is well established that during fetal development progenitors of neurons divide with unnecessary cells dying by apoptosis while other cells migrate and reach their final brain regions (A10) Apoptosis is an important and well-studied aspect of human development. Approximately 50% of cells generated during development of the central nervous system are ultimately eliminated (A11, A12). There are many theories as to the purpose of this massive cell die off, most theories however agree on one aspect and that is apoptosis serves an important neurobiological function. One thing is certain and it is that maternal choline or folic acid supplementation interrupts or at the very least alters this process of naturally occurring apoptosis. For example, an inverse relationship has been identified between maternal choline supplementation and apoptosis in the fetal hippocampus (A13). In other words the more choline given to the pregnant rat, the less the hippocampus of its fetus will experience its natural cell die off. This would then lead one to believe that it would lead to a greater or possibly earlier maturation of the circuits surrounding the hippocampus. There is also evidence that maternal choline supplementation leads to a more efficient utilization of acetylcholine in the basal forebrain and hippocampus in particular (A14), with glutamate receptor stimulated phospholipase activity in the hippocampus doubled over control rats (A14a). In addition, maternal choline supplementation led to increase in the somata of cells of the medial septum and diagonal band to be 15% larger than non-supplemented controls (A15). This, now, becomes very important, because we have seen this in autism. If you remember, in the diagonal band of the young autistic brain (ages 9–12) the neurons were unusually large and plentiful, but then later in the older autistic individuals (ages 22–29) the neurons of the same nucleus are small in size and reduced in number (A16). Further support to this similarity comes from the same study that found this increased cell size of the septal region and diagonal band resulted in enhanced spatial memory function.

This finding is again very significant, because, we have a very direct correlation between increased cell size of specific nuclei in both autism and the choline-supplemented rat. This possibly could be the strongest evidence on what neurobiologically occurs in autism to date. In addition to this, we also see an increase in spatial memory. This, not only strengthens the model substantially, as it shows an increased memory capacity that is consistent with the altered intrauterine development the autistic fetus experiences, but also foreshadows a potential catalyst generating the disorder. This would of course be the involvement of the cholinergic system at a very early gestational date.

There is even more evidence. In a radial arm maze performance test these choline-supplemented rats made fewer working and memory errors than control littermates (A15a). It is also interesting that in this study memory enhancing effects were greater in males than in females (A15b). This is also another consistent finding in autism, as a much greater number of males when compared to females are diagnosed with this disorder. This could demonstrate how this increased utilization of acetylcholine and its potential enhanced early fetal memory is distributed between genders. Other animal studies have found prenatal supplementation or availability of maternal choline alters embryonic development of the hippocampus and septum (A17), advances hippocampal development (A18) and alters postnatal hippocampal structure and function (A19). Again these are all patterns consistent with the neurobiological findings in autism.

What is even more convincing for the role of acetylcholine in altered fetal development; which we witness in the model of autism, is the memory enhancing performances of choline supplementation. Here, maternal choline supplementation reduces proactive interferences in spatial memory (A20) produces long-term facilitation in spatial memory (A21) enhances temporal processing (A22) and increases spatial and configural learning in rats (A23). Even more than morphological irregularities and similarities to the disorder, these enhanced memory capacities are likely very relevant to the autistic model of fetal behavior. As you remember Nature went to great lengths to force conformity to these intrauterine cycles of development, indeed the very reproduction and ultimately survivability of the species depends on it. An important step in this conformity was to block the fetal memory so that the fetus would misinterpret cues. The autistic fetus because it realized enhanced memory capacity did not conform to these cycles and therefore realized and generated a unique intrauterine experience, which ultimately leads to the plethora of symptomology in autism. If memory for the fetus is intentionally blocked by continual apoptosis or a reduced amount of acetylcholine availability, it is likely for an intended purpose. And for the human fetus we have seen the reason for this intentional blocking.

Indeed, here we may have come to the limitations of animal models. For, we are likely at the very junction where the mankind continues to accelerate even with similar neuroanatomy, while development of other species stabilizes. There are a great many differences between the rat and human brain; and with the intrauterine environment of both species. It may very well be that what is beneficial to one species in terms of neural development is not beneficial or is even harmful to another species. While supplementing rat development with choline may be beneficial to long-term memory, in humans these effects may have quite the opposite effect, thus interfering with conformity to the very intrauterine development that is responsible for our superiority — in terms of neurobiology and intellect, over other species. The reason I bring this up here is that it is interesting to take this model one step further. While, it is understood that autism has strong genetic factors and even though there are other neurotransmitters involved, the evidence for the role of acetylcholine, as you have seen in context to the model is substantial and convincing. It is possible that through a genetic tendency or intrauterine insult the autistic fetus processed this acetylcholine at an increased efficiency, and was therefore, enabled the advanced memory capacity which then was the catalyst for this altered intrauterine development. The next step would be then be to see if this model could explain the current increase in rates or rise in cases of autism reported.

While, it is not likely the reason for an increase in autism rates, there are interesting parallels between the increases in the rise of autism rates and the supplementation of additional folic acid during pregnancy. While folic acid has substantially reduced the rates of neural tube defects, it could have a secondary effect that is somewhat unanticipated. This of course happens quite often when man attempts to intervene with Nature and if a direct relationship is eventually discovered it should not come as a great surprise to many. Because this is somewhat out of the scope of this work however, we will just examine a few aspects of this relationship. For example, in 1992 the United States Public Health service recommended that women of childbearing age take 400 milligrams of folic acid. By 1998 the Food and Drug Administration instituted the Folic Acid Fortification Program (A23). This program required the manufacturers of breads, flours and cornmeal, rice, noodles, macaroni and other grain products to add supplemental folic acid to their products (A24) Between 1998 when this policy was adopted until 2003, when children born in 1999 would be three years old, the autism rate in California had increased by 97% (A24). And from 1987 to 1998 a 237% increase in cases were reported (A24). In addition, both embryonic and fetal cells are entirely dependent on maternal folate to support their precisely timed proliferative bursts during gestation, as folate receptors mediate transport into cells and are central to transplacental maternal to fetal folate transport (A28). Again, this is very much out of the scope of this work, and it was only presented to show a possible relationship between the choline supplementation of research animals that realized accelerated or enhanced neural development and the autistic fetus that realized enhanced or accelerated neural development.

A more probable candidate to examine would be an in-depth microanalysis of the first five weeks of pregnancy. As it will likely be the factors related to the initiation and maintenance of pregnancy that will generate large advances of the molecular understanding of the locus of autism. It would be of interest to apply the hypothesis of an enhanced utilization of acetylcholine in context to measurements of female or pregnancy related hormones such as estrogen or progesterone. This would be especially appropriate in the time frame previous to the primary production of these by the placenta. For example, estrogen, which facilitates cholinergic transmission in the septohippocampal pathway, as it can increase activity and mRNA of choline acetyltransferase, high affinity choline uptake and acetylcholine release (A29) may play an important role in the early generation of the pregnancy that will generate autism. Estrogen also has been shown to increase synaptic proteins by 20–30% in the CA1 region of the hippocampus, increase excitatory synapses, and induce changes in the synaptic markers in the hilus of the dentate gyrus and CA3 region (A35). And In animal model estrogen injected directly into uterine arteries increases blood flow in the uterus (A30) and maternal first trimester bleeding during pregnancy has been reported as a risk factor for autism (A31). In addition high estrogen levels or low progesterone or estrogen dominance can increase copper levels in blood and this has been found in autism (A32). While, it is extremely unlikely that estrogen levels alone during pregnancy increase the risk for autism, rather what may be important is the interrelationship between estrogen, progesterone and acetylcholine and genetics, very early in pregnancy, before most women are even sure that they are pregnant. This then may explain the difficulty in determining potentially elevated levels, as they may later normalize when the placenta takes over primary production of these and other pregnancy related hormones.

It is unlikely either hypothesis is particularly correct, as I have not investigated them fully because again, they are out of the scope of this work. However, this should demonstrate the benefit of isolating a potential variable such as acetylcholine that may very likely be involved and partially responsible for this enhanced or accelerated neural development. Once this isolation is accomplished, the researcher has a solid criterion to apply to other potential models, such as we have done here. These models can then can be compared and contrasted to risk factors associated with the disorder, to evaluate their validity. In the case of acetylcholine, many factors during pregnancy likely have the potential to increase not only its quantity, but more importantly its utilization. We are interested here in essentially any property that through genetics or maternal environment could enhance and or accelerate fetal neural development of these important limbic regions and yield the likelihood of the developmental model you have seen here.

In addition, there is the availability of growth factors to consider, as we have not even examined the relationship of brain derived neurotrophic factor and its affect on acetylcholine, which is well established. Brain derived neurotrophic factor; stimulates choline acetyltransference activity in the septohippocampal pathway of ethylcholine mustard aziridinium treated rats (A25), prevents degeneration of medial septal cholinergic neurons (A26) and modulates synaptic transmission in the developing hippocampus (A27). Therefore the findings in the brain of autistic newborns of elevated brain derived neurotrophic factor may be itself the primary catalyst for these developmental abnormalities that are responsible for this enhanced or accelerated neural development that define autism.

What you have just read is an in-depth behavioral, neurobiological and neurodevelopmental model of autism. There are however certain important aspects of the model vacant such as genetic and immune considerations. In addition, no model can completely explain autism without explanation of excitory and inhibitory properties resultant of this altered fetal development; GABA in particular, and its early importance of neural development in autism has not been discussed here. Indeed, there are important aspects left out, due to spatial limitations. Still, I am confident that the skilled researcher, when taken in context to the model presented can apply these aspects. At the very least this model represents a bold and progressive step toward understanding the disorder, where synchronicity coexists between the correct behavior and the precise mechanisms of neurobiology. At its best, this may very well be true, the previous is the final pieces of the autism puzzle and when inserted properly into existing research provide a complete understanding of the disorder, defined as autism. The later judgment however is not for me to make. In either case, and from either the perspective of neural science or psychology, what you have just read can only be described as a major breakthrough.

Infant Development and Aggregate Disorders of First Fear Not Relieved.

In this section we will overview the neurobiological changes that occur after birth in respect to reinforcement and elimination of the neurons encoded with the First Fear Cycle of Development and their resultant synaptic connections. Then we make the connection between some of the catalytic events involved in this condition, examine the connection between disorders and behaviors and briefly look at the immune implications involved with the model, First Fear Not Relieved and the resultant disorders and behaviors.

It is generally understood that from late gestation and well into infancy and second decade of life there is a period of dendrite and axonal outgrowth, synaptic production and neuronal and synaptic pruning. In addition, changes occur to the sensitivity of neurotransmitters. We will take a brief look at how these events relate to the neurons encoded with The First Fear Cycle of Development. In the model presented in the main text you saw the aggregate term "neurons" utilized, as stated this was for simplicity. What we are really interested in here is the synaptic connections these "neurons" make to other developing neurons in the human cortex and how after birth, these neurons and their synapses compete against other for newly acquired sensory stimuli in the developing infant's brain. Also, how these neurons compete for the available trophic factors and most importantly how the environment either reinforces or eliminates these neurons.

Consistent with this model, is current opinion concerning neural events that precede birth, thus the establishment of very transitory or labile synaptic contacts between select groups of neurons (103). These liable contacts are then, during infancy, susceptible to environmental influences on the cellular level. As you have seen the dynamic locus of these initial contacts is development itself that accompanies the major migratory and proliferative events of the fetal brain. This has been defined as the two cycles of the intrauterine life, the Euphoric and First Fear Cycles of Development. These neurons encoded with these events have already begun, by late gestation, not only establishing these initial labile synaptic contacts, but also have already undergone synaptic pruning themselves. This occurs before the fetus even leaves the womb (103a). In other words the neurons encoded with these two cycles of intrauterine development, including the events of the First Fear Cycle of Development, have already made established contacts with other neurons related to these events, and these neuronal connections have already been refined. So, by the time of infancy there are very specific perimeters, which will drive the competition to establish and maintain functional synaptic connections among these developing sensory neurons. And, as you will see these perimeters narrowly define the majority of the fetal experience during its development.

The principle behind this competition is quite simple. To generate the dominant or functional synaptic contact on these newly developed neurons, such as those neurons encoded with The First Fear Cycle of Development, they need one thing and that is reinforcement. Sensory information in the environment during infancy must connect to sensory information encoded in these neurons or the synaptic contact will be lost to other synapses receiving other sensory information. The neurons encoded with the First Fear Cycle of Development must be reinforced with sensory input that connects to information encoded within them or they will not be able to obtain the limited amount of growth factors in the developing infant's brain.

We know what the criteria is for this reinforcement and that is any sensory experience that directly mimics the fetal perceptions, or more accurately misperceptions experienced during The First Fear Cycle of Development.

In the model enclosed in the main text you realized an overview of the fetal experience during the two cycles of intrauterine development. It is these experiences that are encoded into the developing neurons and their liable or transitory established contacts. You also realized in the model, some of the environmental conditions that would reinforce this fetal experience encoded in these neurons and strengthen their synaptic contacts. We will now look at a scenario of how the environment for the infant can reinforce these neurons. We will look at a situation where a husband or boyfriend is physically abusing the infant's mother. During infancy the neuronal base of brain is expanding, new neurons are being formed all the time. These new neurons are establishing synaptic contacts driven by many factors. A major factor is current sensory stimuli. If, for example, the infant watches its mother being physically abused by this man, then, at each episode of this and likely thereafter the cumulative group of neurons encoded with the fetal perception of its mother dying will make synaptic connections to these newly developed neurons. If the infant watches this enough times these synaptic contacts will strengthen, thus winning the competition over other sensory inputs that tell the infant its mother is not dying. The reinforcement of the established fetal fear has occurred. It is important to remember that encoded in many of these same neurons is the aggregate experience of the intrauterine experience. These experiences are thus defined as the symptomology of the majority of affective disorders established. This has been well documented in the main body of the text. So it is not the exclusive fetal fear that is being reinforced, but also the symptomology of depression, panic disorder and others, as this is all a cumulative aspect of the fetal experience. Now, these neuronal properties have not only been reinforced, but also have established and strengthened new synaptic connections. When this occurs over an extended period of exposure, the synaptic contact is made and or strengthened. If this occurs often enough the labile synaptic contact becomes well established and dominates, thus becoming the functional contact of these new neurons. And, if, this occurs over a long period of time and to enough neurons, the infant will realize the aggregate condition of First Fear Not Relieved.

As the brain matures and myelination proceeds, these neurons and their synaptic connections generate a dominant pattern of neuronal activity and the experiences encoded within them will fire in a dominant pattern. When this occurs the individual will realize the symptoms of the individual disorder or group of disorders they experience at that time. All of this symptomology is nothing more than the aggregate of specific fetal experiences realized during these two developmental cycles, as they are encoded in these individual neurons that have by now, made well established synaptic contacts.

What is even more accurate is that these neurons continue to make synaptic contacts through an individual's lifetime. And, it likely mimics the same process, however, on a much more transient level. For example, if an individual's parent dies, synapses form from these neurons encoded with The First Fear Cycle of Development. Especially, if, it is their mother that dies; these neurons reach out beyond their normal range and consume the individual with the cumulative experience encoded in these neurons. As you have seen in the model one of these emotions was guilt, in fact, it is the primary emotion the fetus realizes as it believes that it is leaving its mother alone to die, when it leaves the womb. Because the individual cannot understand or reach the dynamics of this previous encoding as it left the womb, they will likely come up with another reason for their guilt, "Oh I never called her enough," or something of this theme. The synaptic connection has been made because it is reinforced over and over again. There may be tears shed at the funeral home, when sorting through her stuff or during any of the routine associated with this loss, as all these events are sensory input that is strengthening this connection. However, after the mourning process is over these synapses because they are weak and not as plastic as the ones generated very early in infancy will die off or be pushed off by competing synapses.

Now, if the individual has too many of these synaptic connections from these neurons encoded with The First Fear Cycle of Development reinforced during infancy they will obviously experience this death differently. For them, the emotions are stronger and closer to the surface. In fact, for them, they may and usually do not need a death to experience the feelings encoded in these neurons encoded during intrauterine life. This individual with First Fear Not Relieved may just talk to their mother on the phone and feel guilty that they do not call more often. Maybe, it is a coworker calling their mother. It will be enough to generate this guilt. For this individual, these connections are constantly made because there are so many neurons encoded with these events remaining.

All of this of course begins during infancy when the brain realizes an immense amount of plasticity. We will now observe how a few studies of these environmental influences during infancy result in the increased likelihood of developing disorders, behaviors and immune irregularities described in the model. All of these risk factors lead to the aggregate condition of First Fear Not Relieved.

In animal studies, young animals separated from their mother for several hours a day for the first two weeks of life realized decreased dopamine transporter expression and a significantly increased dopamine response to stress (104). In other animal studies, repeated brief separation of young animals from their parents over a prolonged time period and exposure to a new environment caused an up-regulation of D1 and 5ht1a receptor density in the CA1 region of the hippocampus and the acoustic presence of the mother during this separation nullified some of these changes (105). And, animals that realized periodic maternal separation, suffered not only emotional implications but those of the immune systems as well (106). In men, childhood loss of a parent has shown a connection to later deregulation of the HPA axis and increased levels of cortisol (107). Disturbed regulation of the HPA axis is also increased in women who were abused during childhood (108). Past childhood trauma in both men and women is associated with increased risk of diabetes, lung disease, heart disease, peptic ulcers, autoimmune disorders (109) and rheumatoid arthritis (110). The HPA axis is disregulated in abused children (111), sexually abused girls (112), adult women sexually abused as children (113); and a relationship between women were physically abused as children and HPA disregulation exists (114).

Children have a disregulated HPA axis after early trauma (115) as do women who endured long lasting childhood abuse (116). And adverse experience in childhood is a risk factor for altered immune status in adult years (117).

In addition, to immune implications, adverse childhood events also has long lasting implications on future disorders and behaviors, as these adverse events through environmental influence reinforce these neurons encoded with the First Fear Cycle of Development and promotes their synaptic connections. Adults who were abused as children have an increased risk of attempted suicide throughout their lifetime (118), and shattered childhood, is a key issue in suicidal behavior among drug addicts (119). Major depression and manic episodes have been directly linked to childhood physical and sexual abuse (120); and panic disorder has a direct relationship to early traumatic life events (121). Women who reported sexual abuse histories had higher lifetime rate of suicide ideation and suicide attempts (122). Negative childhood experience is involved directly with alcoholism and psychiatric disorders (123) and women who experienced sexual abuse as children had deficits in verbal and declarative memory (124).

Parental loss or separation from parents will achieve the same neurobiological phenomena; this being the neurons encoded with the First Fear will become reinforced. Early loss of mother or father predicts depression in college students and old age (125,126). Unhappy childhood experiences and early parental loss increase the chances of hostility and depression (127). And early maternal loss is more common among individuals with depression than controls (128). Early parental loss and or separation increase the chance for alcoholism in men and women (129,130). And early parental separation increases the chances of both manic and unipolar depression (131). We could go on and on here, but the connection should be clear, Parental loss, abuse by or separation from, increases the chances of almost every major affective disorder, substance abuse and suicide risk.

To show this is not a large group of disorders with any relation to each other, we will look at comorbidity between them. Indeed, all of these disorders display the same origin of symptomology, as many the same neuronal regions and all the disorders, when in acute phases, are expressing the fetal experience as explained in the Theorem model. Individuals with panic disorder have and increased risk for depression (132). A strong connection exists between substance abuse, depression, panic disorder and pathological gambling (133). Individuals who were diagnosed with ADHD had an increase risk for completed suicide (134). Cocaine dependence is strongly linked to depression (135). Eating disorders are strongly linked to obsessive-compulsive behaviors (136,137)) as is drug use (138). When panic disorder and major depression occur together they increase the risk of suicide (139). Depression increases the intensity of anorexia nervosa (140) and panic disorder is also increased with anorexia nervosa (141). Depressed individuals realize sleep disturbances, including insomnia and shortened REM latency (142,143), as do individuals with panic disorders (144). And panic disorder is strongly linked to obsessive-compulsive disorder (145).

As shown in the model, individuals with First Fear Not Relieved also commonly have immune irregularities. The pattern of early suppression to later up-regulation and hypersensitivity can be seen here. Panic disorder is associated with a high frequency of asthma and allergies (146). Immune irregularities are seen in children that suffer obsessive-compulsive disorders (147). Circulating lymphocyte subsets were elevated in individuals with obsessive-compulsive disorder (148) and decreased levels of tumor necrosis factor (149). Immune irregularities and autoimmune disorders are common of adults (150) and children with depression (151), and in individuals with panic disorder (152). And, immune irregularities are reported in women with anorexia nervosa and those who have recovered from the disorder (153-156). Also infants that died from sudden infant death syndrome commonly have immune irregularities (157-160).

The pattern of immune irregularities is consistently disregulated. Again, what is occurring is that after birth many of these neurons that are encoded with the fetal pattern of immune function are intended to be substantially reduced or eliminated. When these neurons and their resultant synapses are reinforced instead, the individual with First Fear Not Relieved immune system up-regulates with the result being autoimmunities or hypersensitivities, preparing itself for an attack that never comes.

Individuals with First Fear Not Relieved will also often have receptor irregularities as well, as the proper synaptic pruning did not occur for them. Increased 5-HT receptor densities (2A) have been found in suicide victims (161) and in individuals with depression (162), and decreased binding in patients with anorexia (163). Of course, some of the most obvious evidence that these disorders have a single locus and a closely related neuronal basis is that one class of drug, the antidepressant, treats so many disorders. Antidepressants are used to combat eating disorders, suicidal behavior, panic disorder, ADHD, insomnia and of course depression (164-169). While the pharmacology behind them is complex, the concept is not at all so. As again, the aggregate fetal experience, thus encompassing all these disorders; even though expressed by different receptors, are located within similar groups of neurons or individual neurons; all encoded with an incomplete fetal memory (Memory Block) and more importantly the two cycles of intrauterine development (First Fear and Euphoric Cycles of Development). These antidepressants simply suppress their firing and expression.

We will take a brief look at the effects of First Fear Not Relieved on particular aspect of behavior, and how early adverse events can have a profound affect on the individuals life, in this example, we will look at how the sleep model is realizing a lifetime of impairment by early adverse advents. We will not take an entire look at the model; instead, will focus on how these early adverse events influence REM sleep and slow wave sleep. Keeping in mind that the purpose here is not intentional accuracy, which may not be accomplished, but, rather, as the building of a general model to explain complex properties.

Individuals with Depression and panic disorder, which falls under the aggregate condition Of First Fear Not Relieved, realize reduced amounts of slow wave sleep, reduced REM latency and increased REM density (A33, A34).

During infancy, this individual with First Fear Not Relieved experienced adverse events. These events generated a reinforcement of cholinergic neurons encoded with First Fear Not Relieved in their basal forebrain; an area with a large amount of neurons encoded these events. Indeed, there are areas of the basal forebrain, where the neurons, only fire during SWS (A35). During infancy, however, these neurons were reinforced by environmental stimuli. Because these neurons were reinforced at a time when more acetylcholine was available — infancy over fetal development; they utilized and contain a greater amount of this neurotransmitter. In addition, because of the early competition for synaptic dominance during the development of the mature pattern, these cholinergic made profuse synaptic connections to areas involved in the generation of REM sleep. One of these areas is the Pontine Reticular Formation (A35a). In addition, the receptors on these neurons become very sensitive to acetylcholine, essentially supersensitive. This is very much the same it occurs for the dopamine neurons on the maternal separation model previously mentioned. Only, now we are talking about muscarinic and nicotinic receptors.

It is 20 years later now, and this individual lies down to go to sleep at night. As the night progresses they fall deeper into sleep, slow waves begin to dominate as these neurons encoded with the First Fear begin to fully fire and exert their full imagery. The problem for this individual is that these neurons because they were reinforced are essentially full of acetylcholine. And, as neurons fire large amounts of this acetylcholine are released, in addition, these profuse projections and synapses on the pontine reticular formation receive a strong signal and begin REM sleep, thus, desynchronizing these neurons and others from firing. This occurs through partial or full inhibition. The REM response because it is initiated by the acetylcholine from the cholinergic neurons in the basal forebrain is not only premature but intensely strong. This is for the simple reason that these neurons are full of twice the amount of acetylcholine than they are intended to contain, and their connections are twice as profuse. All the information encoded in them has not only been experienced once, but also reinforced during infancy. This large amount of acetylcholine generates a premature REM response or short REM latency and a very intense response or increased REM density. In fact there is so much acetylcholine that even after this "dumping" of the neurotransmitter a large amount remains. Therefore, in the next sleep cycle this process will begin again, for the cycle is incomplete for this individual and they are therefore destined to repeat it.

On a behavioral level this individual realized a horrific nightmare during this intense REM episode. They were punching and kicking a friend who was in the dream, an enemy, but the punches had no effect. This dream then shows the lack of myelination the fetus realized, as it kicked and punched out to try and save the mothers life, thus, all the kicks and punches went slow and the mother did not wake up. The friend as an enemy was then experiencing of the two cycles as one. One was positive and euphoric and the other was horrific and negative; all assimilated into the lunch this individual had with their friend yesterday. It is unlikely they will even remember this dream, because they are quick into one after another. Tomorrow night when they lay down to go to sleep, they will have a hard time sleeping. It is no wonder it is so.

Schizophrenia

Initially, I was convinced that the model relevant to schizophrenia in relation to The Theorem was as follows: The positive symptoms of schizophrenia reflect the fetal experience in the Euphoric Cycle of Development. The negative symptoms of schizophrenia reflect the fetal experience in The First Fear Cycle of Development. This was an attractive hypothesis for many reasons. The most obvious reason for this hypothesis was the very existence of the two cycles. After all, Nature had neatly divided the intrauterine environment into two cycles, one essentially positive and the other essentially negative. The expression of these two cycles is very clearly displayed in manic or bipolar depression. One group of symptomology, unipolar depression expresses the First Fear Cycle very accurately; the other symptomology manic states express the Euphoric Cycle. It made sense, then, that researchers and clinicians had done a very good job of categorizing the symptomology into the two distinct cycles that every fetus, including both schizophrenic and typical fetus, experienced.

There were even other more obvious reasons. In the Euphoric Cycle the schizophrenic fetus would be subject to more noise and sounds, as this was when the mother was talking, moving and going about her daily routine. This fetus would of course be listening. Unlike, the typical fetus that was just listening to the sounds and noises, the fetus that would later develop schizophrenia would be listening carefully for voices of not only the mother but of those she was talking to. This fetus would do this for two reasons. One, it had enhanced memory so it could not only listen but would have enough length of attention or span necessary to handle complete, although short, sentences. More importantly, this fetus had motivation to do so. After all, in a few minutes or hours, the horrific First Fear Cycle was coming, and it was convinced that someone was responsible for this; therefore, it was trying to identify who it was, so that when it came the fetus would be prepared. Now, I will explain why this fetus identified a "someone" and not a "something" later in the text. Because this fetus was utilizing its auditory system and memory at a time and place where it was not intended for this purpose there would be later implications in functioning and abnormalities in neural development in these areas. Indeed, in schizophrenia the superior temporal gyrus, of which the primary auditory and auditory association cortex is located, is consistently found to have reduced volume, which included pyramidal cells size reduction (170,171,172). In addition, this fetus would later realize auditory hallucinations, as Nature had not intended this extensive auditory recording at this early stage of development. And, auditory hallucinations are a core feature of positive symptoms (173,174,175).

Delusions would also likely originate from this cycle and they are a core positive symptom (176,177). This was the motivation for the listening in so much detail. This fetus was convinced that someone outside the womb was responsible for this horrific event. These would later manifest as delusions of persecution or paranoid states, even though paranoia was not a core positive symptom. A "delusion of control" could easily generate from this cycle as well, as someone else was definitely controlling the fetus, this being its mother. Olfactory hallucinations, while less common, would generate from this cycle. The fetus, not unlike the autistic, would be sniffing for changes in the intrauterine environment. For the individual with schizophrenia, this recorded olfactory information would arise later in an acute phase of the illness where they would realize a burnt smell or the smell of "poisonous gases." Olfactory hallucinations also occur as a positive symptom (178,179). At the same time if the schizophrenic fetus were to prepare for the upcoming horrific cycle, it may place its body in a particular position hoping that by remaining in that position it could prevent the First Fear Cycle from coming and remain thus in the Euphoric Cycle. It would follow that movement was typically reduced during the First Fear Cycle; therefore this fetus with its advanced memory could make this simple connection. It would be very similar to the autistic fetus rocking the womb itself, in order to stay in the Euphoric Cycle or to generate a new one. Later in life this fetus will display catatonic motor behavior, a positive symptom (180). This schizophrenic individual with catatonia will sit for hours in a rigid position and oblivious to the world around them, becoming agitated, when they are moved. This, of course is, because, very much like the child with autism in a new environment, they both fear the same thing, the horrific First Fear Cycle; it is just that their techniques are different in preventing it.

Another strong indicator that positive symptomology derived from the Euphoric Cycle is treatment itself, as positive symptoms are reduced by narcoleptics, which have a high affinity for dopamine receptors (181,182183,184). This made sense because I had stated in the model, that increased levels of circulating dopamine levels, generated the Euphoric Cycle. Again, dopamine is not the only neurotransmitter or catecholamine, for that matter, responsible for this cycle. Therefore, it would follow logical order that these dopamine neurons would record the sensory information the fetus experienced during this cycle, as they would at the least indicate expression from this readily available catecholamine. And amphetamines and other dopamine agonist generate a euphoric feeling. This becomes quite paradoxical. Is it the property itself that generates the euphoria or stimulation, by dopamine agonists, of the neurons encoded with the original fetal sensory experience of the

Euphoric Cycle, which is encoded in dopamine neurons? If this were the case, then, possibly other neurochemicals would have to be involved or responsible for the original fetal state of euphoria that was then, mimicked or revisited by stimulation of these dopamine neurons encoded with this original experience. These neurochemicals could include endorphins. Another possibility would be that the fetus reacted to dopamine in a different manner than in the mature nervous system. Again, it becomes quite paradoxical and likely would be difficult to test. Concerning positive symptoms, however, if you were, through neuroleptics block these dopamine receptors then the sensory information encoded in these neurons would not fire and the influence on the schizophrenic's thoughts of this fetal experience would be blocked as well.

It is important to remember that the fetal sensory experience encoded in these neurons differs greatly from that encoded in the typical individuals, as the fetal experience for the schizophrenic reflects altered development due to its enhanced memory. This fetal experience is explained effectively by positive symptomology. Therefore, the dopamine neurons for the schizophrenic individuals should be altered or at least, the receptors should function unique to the typical individuals. There is ample evidence to support this. Altered levels of dopamine receptor-interacting proteins in the cortex of schizophrenic patients have been reported (185). There is some evidence that dopamine transporter activity is altered in some individuals with schizophrenia (186), alterations in D2 receptor gene (187), suggestions that inadequate D1 signaling cause cognitive deficits (188) and at least two dopamine receptor interacting proteins are upregulated in schizophrenia (189). The interest in regards to The Theorem is this as secondary effects of altered dopamine neuronal encoding during the Euphoric Cycle, as dopamine transporter or receptor abnormalities may arise from a cascade of other although related etiologies. For, as you will realize later in the text, many abnormalities that are considered primary in schizophrenia are secondary, resultant of the enhanced memory function this fetus experiences during gestation.

It would also follow logical order that negative symptoms arise from the encoding of the fetal experience during The First Fear Cycle. And, it would make sense that schizophrenic individuals with predominately negative symptoms would have a poor long-term prognosis (190,191) and earlier onset (192) when compared to those with primarily positive symptoms. Those with predominate negative symptoms were less likely to be married. Whereas, individuals with predominately positive symptoms were more likely, to have been married (193). This is strong evidence to suggest that the negative symptoms are derived from the First Fear Cycle for a few reasons. A primary purpose of this fear-conditioned model defined as The First Fear is, besides delivering the fetus safely out of the womb, produce reproducing-motivation. Therefore, if there were non-conformity to the cycle, it should surface, when, through neural maturity and myelination: at a time this cycle would promote its greatest influence. This would then be the prime reproductive years, presumably for the male in his early twenties. Whereas, the influence of the neurons encoded with the Euphoric Cycle would follow and occur later in life, as it would not be the primary push for reproduction. The fact that those with negative symptoms, would not marry, as often, is important. Here however convincing research is inconsistent. The obvious reason is that those who did not completely conform to The First Fear Cycle, such as the fetus that will later develop negative symptoms, motivation would be lacking, as again this was a primary purpose. Not unlike the autistic fetus in this respect, the fetus that would later generate negative symptomology that does not include the mother in the equation. This individual may share positive symptomology, as often episodes are mixed, but if the predominate symptoms are negative; as a fetus, it realized that the kicking and punching are not keeping the mother alive. Because of this partial functioning memory, this fetus remembers that no matter what it does throughout the night, it will make little difference, or at least it suspects this. While this fetus does not have enough functioning memory, in most cases, to attempt to stop the First Fear, it does not experience the misinterpretation of the typical fetus. This schizophrenic fetus that will later develop negative symptoms will then fail to make the connection of its mother's health to its own. In addition, because this fetus fails to conform to this initial goal directed behavior of saving the mothers life and therefore its own; it will display this behavior during an active phase of its illness as a child or an adult with schizophrenia. Avolition is a core condition of negative symptoms (194,195). Avolition is the inability to initiate and or continue in goal directed activity. The poor eye contact of affective flattening, another negative symptom (194a) derives from the fetal lack of connection and conformity to The First Fear Cycle. The eye contact as you have seen in the model of autism is only to make sure that the mother and therefore it is still alive. Both the individual with autism and the schizophrenic with negative symptoms do not see the mother as a major variable of this horrific cycle due to their increased memory capacity.

While the fetus that will generate negative symptoms does not include its mother in the equation, the fetus that will generate primarily positive symptoms certainly does. Now, in the Euphoric Cycle this fetus that will develop positive symptoms, with its memory functioning at a more advanced level than the typical fetus, can connect and group together its previous sensory experience, which is the kicking and punching in order to save the mothers life. Therefore, the connection between its mother's life and its own is established.

When, it attempts to decipher events there is always a "someone" in the equation. Remember each fetus with whatever memory capacity it has available is limited to utilizing that memory for current sensory information or sensory information that was previously experienced. This fetus knows it is not its mother that is responsible for trying to kill it because of its current vantage point, this being it is in the Euphoric Cycle and this cycle is very pleasurable. It simply lacks the mental development to think that what is nurturing it is responsible for this horrific cycle, because of its memory, while, advanced, is still partially blocked. It is from this perspective; this fetus attempts to find out who is responsible for this cycle. It accomplishes this; primarily from listening. This is very important observation as to why auditory hallucinations are much more common than olfactory hallucinations. The "someone" this fetus believes is responsible is outside of the womb. This then is where the focus is, outside the womb, not inside. This, of course, is for the fetus that will later generate positive symptoms.

The neurobiological evidence also supports that negative symptoms are derived from The First Fear Cycle of Development. Before we go into the neurobiological abnormalities of the negative symptoms in relation to the model, it is important to point out however that there always must be some limbic pathology in both positive and negative symptoms. Often times however this pathology is very subtle, sometimes it is missed due to difficulties with control groups or technical considerations. The problem with detection of abnormalities that is specific to schizophrenia will be covered later in this section. In general, there always must be some involvement in limbic regions, because as you have seen this is the region that is directly responsible for the accelerated or enhanced memory the fetus realizes. Every other abnormality is then secondary to this etiology and is part of the cascade of neurodevelopmental abnormalities the fetus generates from its response to an altered intrauterine experience, due to this increased memory that is demonstrated by this limbic pathology.

The areas of abnormalities that are consistently mentioned in relation to negative symptoms are areas of the prefrontal cortex, limbic region and the basal ganglia (194,195). These abnormalities would strongly support a direct relationship to The First Fear Cycle of Development. Of primary regions would be the limbic structures and basal ganglia, with advanced development of the prefrontal cortex being directly influenced by the deficits in these limbic regions. As you have seen in the section on memory block and autism, the amygdala in particular is involved in recording the events of The First Fear Cycle of Development. Reduced volume has been consistently found in cross sectional areas of the hippocampus, amygdala and parahippocampal gyrus (196,197,198,199). Activation of the amygdala occurs during facial emotional processing (200), facial and vocal representations of fear or disgust (201), and in a cognitive representation of fear (202). Individuals with schizophrenia, however, have an altered amygdala response to representations including sadness (203) threatening facial expressions (204) and negative stimuli (205). In all studies listed the amygdala in individuals either showed reduced activation or no activation at all. In one study, individuals with paranoid schizophrenia showed more amygdala activation than the non-paranoid subgroup (204a). This is important and gives further strength to the model because the paranoid group experienced the First Fear Cycle with its memory blocked similar to the typical fetus. They would then, like the individual with positive symptoms, realize enhanced memory during the Euphoric Cycle and thus anticipate the arrival of this cycle coming again, thus paranoia. The non-paranoid has already identified the First Fear Cycle and realizes that there is little it can do about it; certainly, it will not participate in it. More importantly this fetus does not connect the mother to the equation and therefore will not pay particular attention to the mother's face later or any face for that matter because there is connection to the health of its mother and therefore the health of others with its own.

The basal ganglion is of interest here as well. The first step is to define what this region accomplishes. The basal ganglion is essentially inhibitory where the cerebellum is excitatory. It is generally believed that the basal ganglia works as brakes that fine tunes and inhibits movements. The question is then what movement and where does it originate these abilities? Possibly, the answer is that this ability is programmed during the movement of the First Fear Cycle. As there are a large amount of dopamine neurons in the basal ganglia region, it could be that by kicking and punching the fetus realizes an increased level of dopamine to its developing brain which thus reduced the pain of this fear conditioned cycle. In other words this was the reward in the conditioning cycle. Therefore, much of the movement associated with the First Fear Cycle of Development may be either stored in this region or it regulates its storage in the cerebellum. Evidence for this would then come from Parkinson's disease. Loss of dopamine neurons in the basal ganglia, especially the substantia nigra pars compacta, is responsible for Parkinson's disease. What we are interested in here, however, is that the movement essentially released when these dopamine neurons dissipate. At rest they experience tremors, hinting towards dopamine's role, as a suppressor of movement, and this movement was very encoded during The First Fear, this classical fear conditioned model. Indeed irregularities of the basal ganglia are consistently reported in schizophrenia (206,207,208,209). If indeed this is where the movement is encoded or transferred through of the First Fear Cycle, there would be irregularities because this fetus did not participate in this cycle as was intended. Abnormalities in the basal ganglia are very difficult to assess however because it is often the region affected by neuroleptics. It should be also noted that many of these abnormalities have been shown for individuals with primarily positive symptoms. The general perception remains however that they are predominately related to negative symptoms. Other strong evidence that would connect The First Fear Cycle to negative symptoms is obstetric complications. It would make sense that if negative symptoms are generated from this cycle and a primary purpose of it is to safely deliver the fetus out of the womb then there should be a connection to more obstetric complications. Indeed, studies do connect obstetric complications to a predominance of negative symptoms of schizophrenia and earlier onset of the disorder, which as you have seen typically leads to more negative symptoms (210, 211, 212, 213, 214,).

It is appropriate at this section of the basal ganglia and the cerebellum, to clarify the role of the cerebellum and its related abnormalities to schizophrenia, and in autism for that matter. As you have seen in the text and throughout, the fetus experiences a classical fear conditioned model, which has been defined as the First Fear Cycle of Development. This cycle of development is very physically active for the fetus involved. There is kicking of the legs, thrashing of the arms and hands, rolling of the body and pushing and punching at the intrauterine walls. As you have seen, this fetus is fighting, for, its life support system has been shut off temporarily, as it realizes the initiation of independent fetal breathing. Again, this is a very horrific situation, and the fetus responds violently. All physical aspects are utilized in a full force fight to survive. All of this activity is essential for the preparation of birth itself and life outside the womb. Birth is a dangerous journey for this fetus and Nature is preparing it well.

Every physical aspect of this cycle involves the cerebellum; it is essential for this purpose. Therefore, it should not be surprising that if the fetus deviates from this important physical developmental cycle at all there will be consequences in these regions. The missed kicks, punches and swings of the arm will all reflect in a deviation or volume or neuronal structure in these regions. Also, any additional movement that were not part of the regime intended, anything outside of the spectrum of this classically fear conditioned model will also have consequences. An example would be the stereotyped movement the autistic fetus made or the rigid posture the schizophrenic fetus accomplished. These were planned movements and Nature obviously had very little intention of encouraging the fetus to make these. This is evidenced by the fact that the fetal memory in most cases was blocked. To initiate planned movement some has to assume at least a minor amount of memory existed. By understanding the model, it should also come as no surprise that these regions are likely to be involved in conditioned learned, are implicated occasionally in panicked states and most importantly in anticipatory planning. All of these are either a direct reflection of this developmental cycle or the neural mechanisms for it are established for future utilization here. The reason I mention this all here again, is that the study of the cerebellum in relation to these two disorders can be quite confusing. It is essential to understand that they are at best secondary to the limbic abnormalities associated with this fetal experience. Without this enhanced memory there would be little purpose or ability for the fetus to deviate from this established fear conditioned intrauterine model. In other words, if the fetus realized a disruption of development in the cerebellum they may indeed realize a great deal of abnormality, but without at least mild limbic pathology they would not develop autism or schizophrenia.

As I stated earlier, I, at one time did and still do particularly like this aspect of the model, this being that negative symptoms derive from The First Fear Cycle of Development. The positive symptoms would then generate from the Euphoric Cycle. And it is likely this model is exactly what occurs. One would wonder why I presented the other model. There are several important reasons for this. One of the reasons is the problem with the model. The major problem is the flat effect. While I am aware that flat effect is a negative symptom, in the context of the model, it should not exist without at least one positive symptom at some time through the schizophrenic individual lifetime. I doubt that it does, but I could not find research as none, likely exists to support this particularity. To understand the origin of flat effect you have to realize that what generates the range of emotions and expressions for the typical fetus is exposure to the Euphoric Cycle that generates the happiness and smiles. The horrific First Fear Cycle generates the sadness, negative emotions, frowns and of course expressions of fear. More than just encoding the neurons with the sensory experience of these cycles, the actual muscles in the face are formed and strengthened. These two cycles generate the range of not only emotion, but expression as well. In the case of the autistic fetus, they do not experience a great range of emotion. This is because when they are in the Euphoric Cycle they are preparing for the other. There is typically not the euphoric range in either emotions or their face. Much of the same can be said for the schizophrenia with flat effect. To gain this limited range they have to be in the Euphoric Cycle and be aware that the horrific cycle is impeding on them. Therefore, they have to be aware in the Euphoric Cycle of the next cycle. This should then generate positive symptoms.

This is the major reason I included the other model. With that said there are still very strong arguments, including those you have seen for the validity and strength of this model. A possible explanation is the co-occurrence or prevalence of both positive and negative symptoms. This happens quite frequently. For example, in long term observations of patients in a psychiatric hospitals over a twenty five year time period, showed few patients with more than one episode of exclusively positive symptoms (18%) and even fewer with only negative symptoms (6%) (215). It would therefore to unlikely that an individual with schizophrenia over an entire lifetime would have all negative symptoms and not a single positive one, especially with flat effect. This, while being the primary reason was not the only reason. I did not include this model in the main body. I will of course let the general readership decide which is more accurate. There is evidence that both could be correct however. If it is dopamine that blocks fetal memory function during these cycles, then the schizophrenic fetus might have realized a reduced memory function of memory in the euphoric cycle and an increased memory in The First Fear Cycle. This would be correct even though in both cycles the schizophrenic fetus has realized an increased memory over the typical fetus. Indirect support for this comes from the fact that when a fetus at 32 weeks gestation realized a high level of b-endorphin, it failed to habituate at the same rate as it did previous to exposure. This study also referenced a role of the opiod system in hippocampal function (216). As it generally understood that opiates decrease movement and generate euphoria, perhaps, Nature uses these b-endorphins or other natural opiods reduce movement while the mother is active. This would then decrease the memory capacity during the Euphoric Cycle, even for this fetus with accelerated or enhanced memory. Both models are dynamic and in either case will lead to a clear understanding of the origins of schizophrenia.

A major consideration in interpreting these models is to understand first and foremost that no matter the level of enhanced memory the schizophrenic fetus realizes it still experiences a large aspect of its gestation with its functioning memory essentially blocked. In other words the schizophrenic fetus realizes the part of their development in the exact same way as the typical fetus does. This of course is why they do not spend their entire life with active symptoms of schizophrenia

No, there always must be some typical development and that is reflected in their behavior before the onset of the disorder and during times when not in an acute phase of symptomology.

Because, this was such an important time for neural development, the timing of the insult the fetus and or intrauterine environment realizes will ultimately determine the severity of the symptomology and the duration and onset of the illness. The importance of the timing of the insult is so critical that it should likely be measured in days rather than weeks and months. There is an overabundance of evidence for the role of coincidental influenza epidemics during the second trimester leading to a higher risk of schizophrenia (217,218,219,220). Another study pointed to the first trimester influenza exposure to be a seven-fold risk for developing schizophrenia (221). It has been suggested that this influenza exposure results in an immune response, which includes a cytokine response (222). And, that cytokines can be neurotoxic to serotonergic, dopaminergic and hippocampal neurons (222a).

This is only one of the many, but a very likely scenario as both dopamine and seratonin likely play a role in the formulation of blocking fetal memory. The temporary reduction of these neurochemicals may lift block on the fetal memory and the schizophrenic fetus realizes an enhanced memory.

This then, begins the cascade of secondary neurobiological abnormalities, as this fetus realizes, and alters intrauterine experience as described in the models. What we are really interested here however is not the time period the schizophrenic fetus experiences altered development with enhanced memory, but instead the amount of time it spends experiencing typical development with its memory blocked just like the typical fetus. All this time this fetus is conforming to the First Fear Cycle of Development and Euphoric Cycle. This is very important especially when you consider not only how dynamic the second trimester is, but also how long it is, in terms of developmental differences. There is a large difference from a fetus at 14 weeks and a fetus of 27 weeks in terms of development. Each week is so dynamic with such a large amount of neurobiological changes that a single day will make a large difference for the future disability of this individual.

Interpreting this, it is easy to see how difficult it is to determine consistent limbic abnormalities or secondary abnormalities with schizophrenia samples. For example, if the Memory Block fails temporarily during the beginning of the second trimester a great many more abnormalities will likely be identifiable than at the later stages. Especially, when you consider that during the later stages of gestation many of these limbic regions are already at an advanced level of maturity. This consideration further renders subtle abnormalities difficult and depending on the controls, often impossible to detect.

Because the schizophrenic individual experiences at least some of their intrauterine development as a typical fetus they will likely realize the aggregate condition of First Fear Not Relieved. This is essentially independent of childhood and infancy variables that determine these factors for the typical individual. While, you have seen in Chapter 13 that this is due directly to the lack of Memory Block, it experienced during development. This will be explained in the final section of these notes

An important aspect of applying current research in schizophrenia to the model is an understanding the method of application. Every study, every abstract and every observation the clinician make is important as the model explained here is somewhat general and it will be through these other variables that the picture of the disorder continues to come into tight focus. Indeed, with every article, study, and observation applied to this model a clear and more precise picture will emerge as to exactly what this fetus experiences and how this later translates into the unique symptomology that defines this disorder. Again, it is helpful to realize that all the information and research necessary to completely understand this disorder is available already and has been for quite sometime, yet it has always only been our inability to interpret it correctly. Once, you understand this, it quickly becomes apparent, what an exciting time is ahead for the field of human behavior, this can be. The first step in this dynamic process is to understand that most of the current research in regards to this disorder has been substantially misinterpreted. It is from this vantage point that we will begin. A general rule is this. If the schizophrenic individual has a deficit or abnormality in some area it is because this function matured before it was time and therefore will dysfunction. This is extremely helpful. This also gives you a clear view into what capacity this fetus had.

In other words, if, the schizophrenic individual has deficits in olfactory identification (223,224), it is because as a fetus it realizes enhanced ability of olfactory identification. Then, due to the level of this advanced utilization of this region there will be deficits. This is because it is utilized in a time and place where this advanced utilization and application was not intended. In addition there will commonly be abnormalities in the neural regions responsible, for these functions, such as for olfactory identification. Schizophrenics have been shown to have reduced cortical volumes in brain regions that receive afferents directly from the olfactory bulb (225). As you have in the case of olfactory, this early recording of sensory experience results in later hallucinations of that recorded sensory experience. The rule is also accurate for auditory deficits and regions for auditory discrimination in the brain of individuals with schizophrenia. In an MRI study, activation of the left inferior frontal and right middle temporal gyri was evidenced between 6 and 9 seconds previous to an auditory hallucination by an individual with schizophrenia (226).

This is helpful for the model because now we know the precise neural region where this early fetal auditory sensory information is encoded and stored. We also know what we are looking for in the form of neural abnormalities in this region. Remember the pattern, if a sensory neuron or region of sensory neurons is utilized before their intended maturity there should be a deficit in this region. And indeed in another study we find decreased gray matter volume in the middle temporal gyri (227). In the same study there was a direct connection between the severity of hallucinations and the volume reduction in this region (227a). So, here you can see further support for this pattern, the more intensive the utilization at this early stage results in more intense hallucinations, as there was more auditory (sensory) information encoded. Of course, this, like the pattern in autism, has implications far beyond schizophrenia. To identify neural patterns of early utilization and their long-term affect on the nuclei, this will be essential in the identification of similar neuronal patterns in a variety of disorders. However, the skilled researcher should already be looking ahead here in respect to understanding of another consistent finding in regards to schizophrenia and that is the brain weight of these individuals. More specifically, brain weight, brain and intracranial size have all been found to be reduced in schizophrenia (228,229,230). This makes sense; as you begin to understand premature utilization of these regions by the fetus ultimately result in reduced groups of nuclei and therefore in the aggregate reduced brain volumes. This of course has potential for application as an additional diagnostic tool, not only in estimating the time of onset but also understanding the level of premature utilization this schizophrenic individual experienced as a fetus. This however, is only but a small aspect of this puzzle, the model solves.

A very important aspect of understanding schizophrenia is to understand these global implications that arise from non-conformity to this fear conditioned model. While this is especially true for the fetus that has enhanced memory intact during the First Fear Cycle of Development, both will realize effects. As you have seen in the model of the main text, one of the most important aspects of these two cycles of intrauterine development is to prepare the fetus for the difficult process of birth. To accomplish this, Nature establishes an intrauterine developmental regime aptly titled The First Fear Cycle of Development. To maximize conformity and therefore development, Nature blocks the developing fetal memory, a very primitive limbic circuit. Therefore, when the fetus is in one cycle it cannot remember the existence of or anticipate the arrival of the other. The fetus believes essentially that the state it is in will last forever. This as you have seen is very important, for the fetus is limited to its intrauterine environmental influences. And these changes take place very quickly. For example, when the mother is walking around, the fetus is in the Euphoric Cycle completely naive to the existence of anything else. When, the mother lies down on her bed to go to sleep, the complete intrauterine environment changes. The fetus begins to kick and punch out fighting for its life. What occurs here, however, is that the global changes occur for the fetus. Just seconds ago is was completely relaxed, now it is not only tense but all of its muscles are in flexion. The fetal reflexes are being not only developed, but also fine tuned. It is an amazingly effective development scenario.

The schizophrenic fetus, however, has enhanced memory and therefore is not so easily fooled. While in the Euphoric Cycle, it knows, because it can remember, that the situation is likely to change at any second. Therefore it is prepared. As you could imagine missing out on the simple fear conditioned model will have dire consequences for this fetus. For, this is the origin of reflex and neurological development and this fetus is missing it. These consequences will include a difficulty with the process of birth itself. If the fetus does accomplish this task, as many schizophrenics likely never survive birth, evidence of this altered development is obvious. Even in childhood from a simple neurological examination, the signs will be obvious. These signs or "soft signs" reflect this altered fetal experience and are easily observed by any pediatrician. Indeed, these are first signs to the outside world that this individual is at risk for schizophrenia (240,241,242).

REFERENCES

1. Vecchietti G & Borruto F, Echotomographic evaluation of embryo-fetal movements, Ann Ostet Ginecol Med Perinat, 102(6): 398-400, 1981.

2. Hopson JL, Fetal psychology, Psychology Today, 31(5): 44, 1998.

3. De Vries JP & Prechtl HFR, The emergence of fetal behavior, Eraly Human Dev, 7: 301-322, 1982.

4. Van Dongen LGR & Goudie EG, Fetal movements in the first trimester of Pregnncy, British J of Obstet and Gynec, 87: 191-193, 1980.

5. DiPietro JA, Hodgson DM, Costigan KA, Hilton SC & Johnson TR, Development of fetal movement — fetal heart rate coupling from 20 weeks through term, Early Hum Dev, 44(2): 139-51, 1996.

6. DiPietro JA, Hodgson DM, Costigan KA, Hilton SC & Johnson TRB, Development of fetal movement and fetal heart rate coupling from 20 weeks through term, Early Hum Dev, 44: 139-151, 1996.

7. ArmonyJL, Cohen JD, Servan-Schreiber D & LeDoux JE, An anatomically constrained neural network model of fear conditioning, Behav Neurosci, 109(2): 246-257, 1995.

8. Peleg D, Munsick RA, Diker D, Goldman JA & Ben-Jonathan N, Distribution of catecholamines between fetal and maternal compartments during human pregnancy with emphasis on L-dopa and dopamine, J Clin Endocrinology & Metabolism, 62: 911-914, 1986.

9. Stark H, Rothe T, Wagner T & Scheich H, Learning a new behavioral strategy in the shuttle-box increases prefrontal dopamine, Neurosci, 126: 21-29, 2004.

10. Seron-Ferre M, Ducsay CA, Valenzuela GJ, Circadian rhythms during pregnancy, Endocrine Reviews 14(5): 594-609, 1993.

11. de Vries JP, Visser GHA & Prechtl HFR, The emergence of fetal behavior: individual differences and consistencies, EH Develop, 16(1) 95-102, 1988.

12. Health Guide, Prolactin, //www.WebMDHealth.com, 2004.

13. Hernandez ML, Fernandez-Ruiz JJ, Navarro M, De Miguel R, Cebeira M, Vaticon L & Ramos JA, Modifications of mesolimbic and nigrostriatal dopaminergic activities after intracerebroventricular administration of prolactin, J Neural Transm, 96: 63-79, 1994.

14. Brown RE, An introduction to neuroendocrinology, Cambridge University Press, 1994.

15. Worth J, Onyeije CI, Ferber A, Pondo JS & Divon MY, The association between fetal and maternal sleep patterns in third-trimester pregnancies, Am J Obstet Gynecol, 186(5): 924-925, 2002.

16. Bocking A, Adamson L, Cousin A, Campbell K, Carmichael L, Natale R & Patrick J, Effects of intravenous glucose injections on human fetal breathing movements and gross fetal body movements at 38 to 40 weeks' gestational age, Am J Obstet Gynecol, 142(6 Pt 1): 606-611, 1982.

17. Patrick J, Campbell K, Carmichael L, Natale R & Richardson B, Patterns of human fetal breathing during the last 10 weeks of pregnancy, Obstet Gynecol, 56(1): 24-30, 1980.

18. Power M, How the body renews itself hour by hour, Pretoria News, August 11, 2004.

19. Burghardt NS, Sullivan GM, McEwen BS, Gorman JM & LeDoux JB, The selective serotonin reuptake inhibitor citalopram increases fear after acute treatment but reduces fear with chronic treatment: a comparison with tianeptine, Biol Psychiatry, 55: 1171-1178, 2004.

20. Phelps EA, Human emotion and memory: interactions of the amygdale and hippocampal complex, Current Opinion in Neurobiology, 14: 198-202, 2004.

21. McDonald AJ & Mascagni F, Cortico-cortical and cortico-amygdaloid projections of the rat occipital cortex: a phaseolus vulgaris leucoagglutinin study, Neurosci, 71(1): 37-54, 1996.

22. Carter RN, Pinnock B & Herbert J, Does the amygdale modulate adaptation to repeated stress? Neurosci, 126: 9-19, 2004.

23. Paradiso S, Johnson DL, Andreasen NC, O'Leary DS, Watkins GL & Ponto LL, Cerebral blood flow changes associated with attribution of emotional valence to pleasant, unpleasant, and neutral visual stimuli in a PET study of normal subjects, Am J Psychiatry, 156: 1618-1629, 1999.

24. Beck CH & Fibiger HC, Conditioned fear-induced changes in behavior and in the expression of the immediate earle gene c-fos; with and without diazepam pretreatment, J Neurosci, 15: 709-720, 1995.

25. Calder AJ, Lawrence AD & Young AW, Neuropsychology of fear and loathing, Nature Reviews Neuroscience, 2: 352-363, 2001.

26. Yamamoto T, Azuma S & Kawamura Y, Functional relations between the cortical gustatory area and the amygdala: electrophysiological and behavioral studies in rats, Exp Brain Res, 56(1): 23-31, 1984.

27. Edited by Bauman ML & Kemper TL, The neurobiology of autism, John Hopkins University Press, 1994.

28. Stalnaker TA & Berridge CW, AMPA receptor stimulation within the central nucleus of the amygdale elicits a differential activation of central dopaminergic systems, Neuropsychopharmacology, 28: 1923-1934, 2003.

29. Everitt BJ, Cador M & Robbins TW, Interactions between the amygdale and ventral striatum in stimulus-reward associations: studies using a second-order schedule of sexual reinforcement, Neurosci, 30: 63-75, 1989.

30. Davis M & Whalen PJ, The amygdala: vigilance and emotion, Mol Psychiatry, 6: 13-34, 2001.

31. Cahill I, Haier RJ, White NS, Fallon J, Kilpatrick L, Lawrence C, Potkin SG & Alkire MT, Sex-related difference in amygadala activity during emotionally influenced memory storage, Neurobiol Learn Mem, 75: 1-9, 2001.

32. Canli T, Desmond JE, Zhao Z & Gabrieli JD, Sex differences in the neural basis of emotional memories, Proc Natl Acad Sci, USA, 99: 10789-10794, 2002.

33. Breiter HC, Etcoff NL, Whalen PJ, Kennedy WA, Rauch SL & Buckner RL, Response and habituation of the human amygdale during visual processing of facial expression, Neuron, 17: 987-887, 1996.

34. Canli T, Sivers H, Whitfield SL, Gotlib IH & Gabrieli JD, Amygdala response to happy faces as a function of extraversion, Science, 296: 2191, 2002.

35. Edited by Kandel ER, Schwartz JH & Jessell TM, Principles of Neural Science, third edition, Appleton & Lange, 1991.

36. Fewell GD & Meredith M, Experience facilitates vomeronasal and olfactory influence on Fos. expression in medial preoptic area during pheromone exposure or mating in male hamsters, Brain Res, 941(1-2): 91-106, 2002.

37. Hagan JJ, Salamone JD, Simpson J, Iversen SD & Morris RGM, Place navigation in rats is impaired by lesions of medial septum and diagonal band but not nucleus basalis magnocellularis, Behav Brain Res, 27: 9-20, 1988.

38. Noonan M, Penque M & Axelrod S, Septal lesions impair rats' morris-test performance but facilitate left-right response differentiation, Physiology &Behav, 60: 895-900, 1996.

39. Zeineh MM, Engel SA, Thompson PM & Bookheimer SY, Dynamics of the hippocampus during encoding and retrieval of face-name pairs, Science, 299: 577-580, 2003.

40. Martin PD, Locomotion towards a goal alters the synchronous firing of neurons recorded simultaneously in the subiculum and nucleus accumbens of rats, Behav Brain Res, 124: 19-28, 2001.

41. Hampson RE, Hedberg T & Deadwyler SA, Differential information processing by hippocampal and subicular neurons, Ann NY Acad Sci, 911: 151-165, 2000.

42. Cooper DC, Moore SJ, Staff NP & Spruston N, Psychostimulant-induced plasticity of intrinsic neuronal excitability in ventral subiculum, J Neuroscience, 23(30): 9937-9946, 2003.

43. Glasson EJ, Bower C, Petterson B, de Klerk N, Chaney G & Hallmayer JF, Perinatal factors and the development of autism, Arch Gen Psychiatry, 61(6): 618-627, 2004.

44. Zwaigenbaum L, Szatmari P, Jones MB, Bryson SE, MacLean JE, Mahoney WJ, Bartolucci G & Tuff L, Pregnancy and birth complications in autism and libility to the broader autism phenotype, J Am Acad Child Adolesc Psychiatry, 41(5): 572-9, 2002.

45. Glasson EJ, Bower C, Petterson B, de Klerk N, Chaney G & Hallmayer JF, Perinatal factors and the development of autism, Arch Gen Psychiatry, 61(6): 618-627, 2004.

46. Neave N, Nagle S & Aggleton JP, Evidence for the involvement of the mammillary bodies and cingulum bundle in allocentric spatial processing by rats, Eur J Neurosci, 9(5): 941-55, 1997.

47. Conejo NM, Gonzalez-Pardo H, Vallejo G & Arias JL, Involvement of the mammillary bodies in spatial working memory revealed by cytochrome oxidase activity, Brain Res, 1011(1): 107-14, 2004.

48. Autism Society of America, Autism Characteristics, //www.autisminfo.com, 2004.

49. Edelson SM, Lack of attention to physical problems in autism, Center for the Study of Autism, 2004.

50. Frankland PW, Bontempi B, Talton LE, Kaczmarek L & SilvAJ, The involvement of the anterior cingulated cortex in remote contextual fear memory, Science, 304: 881-883, 2004.

51. Carter CS, Botvinick MM & Cohen JD, Rev Neurosci, 10: 49, 1999.

52. Robbins TW, Prog Brain Res, 126: 469, 2000.

53. Suhara T, Okubo Y, Yasuno F, Sudo Y, Inoue M, Ichimiya T, Nakashima Y, Nakayama K, Tanada S, Suzuki K, Halldin C & Farde I, Decreased dopamine D2 receptor binding in the anterior cingulate cortex in schizophrenia, Arch Gen

Psychiatry, 59: 25-30, 2002.

54. Laurens KR, Ngan ETC, Bates AT, Kiehl KA & Liddle PF, Rostral anterior cingulate cortex dysfunction during error processing in schizophrenia, Brain, A Journal of Neurology, 126(3): 610-622, 2003.

55. Rosenberg DR, Mirza Y, Russell A, Tang J, Smith JM, Banerjee SP, Bhandari R, Rose M, Ivey J, Boyd C & Moore GJ, Reduced anterior cingulate glutamatergic concentrations in childhood OCD and major depression versus healthy controls, J Am Acad Child Adolesc Psychiatry, 43(9): 1146-1153, 2004.

56. Dept of Psychiatry, Understanding obsessive-compulsive and related disorders, Stanford School of Medicine, 2004.

57. Uher R, Murphy T, Brammer MJ, Dalgleish T, Phillips ML, Ng VW, Andrew CM, Williams SC, Campbell CT & Reasure J, Medial prefrontal cortex activity associated with symptom provocation in eating disorders, Am J Psychiatry, 161: 1238-1246, 2004.

58. Fillon M, ENDO: Testosterone may help treat anorexia nervosa, Doctor's Guide Publishing Ltd., 2004.

59. Sullivan RC, Definition of Autism, Autism Society of Pittsburgh, 1997.

60. Crescent Life, Autism. //www.crescentlife.com/disorders/ autism.htm, 2004.

61. American Psychiatric Association: Diagnostic and Statictical Manual of Mental Disorders, fourth Edition. Washington, DC, American Psychiatric Association, 1994.

62. Lee M, Martin-Ruiz C, Graham A, Court J, Jajors E, Perry R, Iversen P, Bauman M & Perry E, Nicotine receptor abnormalities in the cerebellar cortex in autism, Brain, 125(7): 1483-1495, 2002.

63. Hashimoto T, Tayama M, Murakawa K, Yoshimoto T, Miyazaki M, Harada M & Kuroda Y, Development of the brainstem and cerebellum in autistic patients, J Autism Dev Disord, 25(1): 1-17, 1995.

64. Piven J, Nehme E, Simon J, Barta P, Pearlson G & Polstein SE, Magnetic resonance imaging in autism: measurement of the cerebellum, pons, and fourth ventricle, Biol Psychiatry, 31: 491-504, 1992.

65. Edited by Bauman ML & Kemper TL, The neurobiology of autism, John Hopkins University Press, 1994.

66. Courchesne E, Redcay E & Kennedy DP, The autistic brain: birth through adulthood, Curr Opin Neurology, 17: 489-496, 2004.

67. Langleben DD, Schroeder L, Maldjian JA, Gur RC, McDondals S, Ragland JD, O'Brien CP & Childress AR, Brain activity during stimulation deception: an

event-related functional magnetic resonance study, NeuroImage, 15: 727-732, 2002.

68. Kozel FA, Padgett TM & George MS, A Replication study of the neural correlates of deception, Behav Neurosci, 118(4): 852-856, 2004.

69. Leekam SR & Prior M, Can autistic children distinguish lies from jokes? A second look at second-order belief attribution, J Child Psychol Psychiatry, 35(5): 901-15, 1994.

70. Reinecke DR, Newman B, Kurtz AL, Ryan CS & Hemmes NS, Teaching deception skills in a game-play context to three adolescents with autism, J Autism Dev Disord, 27(2): 127-37, 1997.

71. Grant CM, Grayson A & Boucher J, Using tests of false belief with children with autism: how valid and reliable are they? Autism, 5(2): 135-145, 2001.

72. Grossberg S & Merrill JW, A neural network model of adaptively timed reinforcement learning and hippocampal dynamics, Brain Res Cogn Brain Res, 1(1): 3–38, 1992.

73. Eichenbaum H, Hippocampus: cognitive processes and neural representations that underlie declarative memory, Neuron, 44(1): 109–20, 2004.

74. Aggleton JP, Kyd RJ & Bilkey DK, When is the perirhinal cortex necessary for the performance of spatial memory tasks? Neurosci Biobehav Rev, 28(6): 611–624, 2004.

75. Buckley CT & Caldwell KK, Fear conditioning is associated with altered integration of PLC and ERK2 signaling in the hippocampus, Pharmacol Biochem Behav, 79(4): 633–40, 2004.

76. Burwell RD, Bucci DJ, Sanborn MR & Jutras MJ, Perirhinal and postrhinal contributions to remote memory for context, J Neurosci, 24(49): 11023–11028, 2004.

77. Kirwan CB, Gilbert PE & Kesner RP, The role of the hippocampus in the retrieval of a spatial location. Neurobiol Learn Mem, 83(1): 65–71, 2005.

78. Kier EL, Kim JH, Fulbright RK & Bronen RA, Embryology of the human fetal hippocampus: MR imaging, anatomy, and histology, Am J Neuroradiology, 18(3): 525–532, 1997.

79. Tsien JZ, Huerta PT & Tonegawa S, The essential role of hippocampal CA1 NMDA receptor-dependent synaptic plasticity in spatial memory, Cell, 87: 1327–1338, 1996.

80. McHugh TJ, Blum KI, Tsien JZ, Tonegawa S & Wilson MA, Impaired hippocampal representation of space in CA1-specific NMDAR1 knockout mouse, Cell, 87: 1339–1349, 1996.

81. Rondi-Reig L, Libbey M, Eichenbaum H & Tonegawa S, CA1-specific N-methyl-D-aspartate receptor knockout mice are deficient in solving a nonspatial transverse patterning tasl, PNAS USA, 98: 3543–3548, 2001.

82. Fukaya M, Kato A, Lovett C, Tonegawa T & Watanabe M, Retention of NMDA receptor NR2 subunits in the lumen of endoplasmic reticulum in targeted NR1 knockout mice, PNAS USA, 100: 4855–4860, 2003.

83. Shimizu E, Tang, Rampon C & Tsien JZ, NMDA receptor-dependent synaptic reinforcement as a crucial process for memory consolidation, Science, 290: 1170–1174, 2000.

84. Cui Z, Wang H, Tan Y, Zaia KA, Zhang S & Tsien JZ, Inducible and reversible NR1 knockout reveals crucial role of the NMDA receptor in preserving remote memories in the brain, Neuron, 41: 781–793, 2004.

85. Cesaroni L & Garber M, Exploring the experience of autism through firsthand accounts, J Autism Dev Disord, 21(3): 303–313, 1991.

86. Sparling JW & Wilhelm IJ, Quantative measurement of fetal movement: fetal-posture and movement assessment (F-PAM), Physical and Occupational Therapy in Pediatrics, 12(2/3): 97–114, 1993.

87. Sparling JW, Van Tol J & Chescheir NC, Fetal and neonatal hand movement, Phys Ther, 79(1): 24–39, 1999.

88. Cao J, Chen N, Xu T & Xu L, Stress-facilitated LTD induces output plasticity through synchronized-spikes and spontaneous unitary discharges in the CA1 region of the hippocampus, Neurosci Res, 49:229–239, 2004.

89. Williams E, Costall A & Reddy V, Children with autism experience problems with both objects and people, J Autism Dev Disord, 29(5): 367–379, 1999.

90. American Psychiatric Association: Diagnostic and Statictical Manual of Mental Disorders, fourth Edition. Washington, DC, American Psychiatric Association , 1994.

91. Edited by Bauman ML & Kemper TL, The neurobiology of autism, John Hopkins University Press, 1994.

92. Ornitz, Lane, Sugiyama & Traversay, Startle response in autism, J Autism Dev Disord, 23(4), 1993.

93. Edited by Bauman ML & Kemper TL, The neurobiology of autism, John Hopkins University Press, 1994.

94. Jakob H & Beckman H, Circumscribed malformation and nerve cell alterations in the entorhinal cortex of schizophrenics, J Neural Transm, 98: 83–106, 1994

95. Wood D, Autism, pervasive development disorder, //www.aurorahealthcare.com, 2004.

96. Kaufman Children's Center, Sign and Symptoms, //kidspeech.com, 2004.

97. Buckmaster CA, Eichenbaum H, Amaral DG, Suzuki WA & Rapp PR, Entorhinal cortex lesions disrupt the relational organization of memory monkeys, J Neurosci, 24(44): 9811–9825, 2004.

98. Buchanan TW, Tranel D, Adolphs R, A specific role for the human amygdale in olfactory memory, Learning & Memory, 10: 319–325, 2003.

99. Gould JB, Gluck L & Kulovich MV, The relationship between accelerated pulmonary maturity and accelerat neurological maturity in certain chronically stressed pregnancies, Am J Obstet Gynecol, 127(2): 181-186, 1977.

100. Vitalis T & Parnavelas JG, The role of serotonin in early cortical development, Dev Neurosci, 25: 245–256, 2003.

101. Wu C, Dias P, Kumar S, Lauder JM & Singh S, Differential expression of serotonin 5-HT2 receptors during rat embryogenesis, Dev Neurosci, 21(1): 22–28, 1999.

102. Hevner RF & Kinney HC, Reciprocal entorhinal-hippocampal connections established early in human fetal gestation, J Comp Neural, 372: 384–394, 1996.

103. Webb SJ, Monk CS & Nelson CA,. Mechanisms of postnatal neurobiological development: implications for human development, Dev Neuropsychology, 19(2): 147–171, 2001.

104. Brake WG, Zhang TY, Diorio J, Meaney MJ & Gratton A, Influence of early postnatal rearing conditions on mesocorticolimbic dopamine and behavioral responses to psychostimulants and stressors in adult rats, Eur J Neurosci, 19(7): 1863–1874, 2004.

105. Ziabreva I, Poeggel G, Schnabel R & Braun K, Separation-induced receptor changes in the hippocampus and amygdale of octodon degus: influence of maternal vocalizations, J NeuroSci, 23(12): 5329–5336, 2003.

106. Wigger A & Neumann ID, Periodic maternal deprivation induces gender-dependent alterations in behavioral and neuroendocrine responses to emotional stress in adult rats, Physiol Behav, 66(2): 293–302, 1999.

106a. Matthews K, Dalley JW, Matthews C, Tsai TH & Robbins TW, Periodic maternal separation of neonatal rats produces region- and gender-specific effects on biogenic amine content in postmortem adult brain, Wiley InterScience, 40(1): 1–10, 2001.

107. Nicolson NA, Childhood parental loss and cortisol levels in adult men, Psychoneuroendocrinology, 29(8): 1012-1018, 2004.

108. Altemus M, Cloitre M & Dhabhar FS, Enhanced cellular immune response in women with PTSD related to childhood abuse, Am J Psychiatry, 160: 1705–1707, 2003.

109. Goodwin RD & Stein MB, Association between childhood trauma and physical disorders among adults in the United States, Psychol Med, 34(3): 509–520, 2004.

110. Carette S, Surtees PG, Wainwright NW, Khaw KT, Symmons DP & Silman AJ, The role of life events and childhood experiences in the development of rheumatoid arthritis, J Rheumatol, 27(9): 2123–2130, 2000.

111. Kaufman J, Birmaher B, Perel J, Dahl RE, Moreci P, Nelson B, Wells W & Ryan ND, The corticotrophin-releasing hormone challenge in depressed abused, depressed nonabused, and normal control children. Biol Psychiatry, 42(8): 669–679, 1997.

112. De Bellis MD, Chrousos GP, Dorn LD, Burke L, Helmers K, Kling MA, Trickett PK & Putnam FW, Hypothalamic-pituitary-adrenal axis dysregulation in sexually abused girls, J Clin Endocrinol Metab, 78(2): 249–255, 1994.

113. Stein MB, Yehuda R, Koverola C & Hanna C, Enhanced dexamethasone suppression of plasma cortisol in adult women traumatized by childhood sexual abuse, Biol Psychiatry, 42(8): 680–686, 1997.

114. Heim C, Ehlert U, Hanker JP & Hellhammer DH, Abuse-related posttraumatic stress disorder and alterations of the hypothalamic-pituitary-adrenal axis in women with chronic pelvic pain, Psychosom Med, 60(3): 309–318, 1998.

115. King JA, Mandansky D, King S, Fletcher KE & Brewer J, Early sexual abuse and low cortisol, Psychiatry Clin Neurosci, 55(1): 71–74, 2001.

116. Rinne T, de Kloet ER, Wouters L, Goedkoop JG, DeRijk RH & van den Brink W, Hyperresponsiveness of hypothalamic-pituitary-adrenal axis to combine dexamethasone/corticotrophin-releasing hormone challenge in female borderline personality disorder subjects with a history of sustained childhood abuse, Biol Psychiatry, 52(11): 1102–1012, 2002.

117. Surtees P, Wainwright N, Day N, Brayne C, Luben R & Khaw KT, Adverse experience in childhood as a developmental risk factor for alter immune status in adulthood, Int J Behav Med, 10(3): 251–268, 2003.

118. Dube SR, Anda RF, Felitti VJ, Chapman DP, Williamson DF & Giles WH, Childhood abuse, household dysfunction, and the risk of attempted suicide throughout the life span: findings from the Adverse Childhood Experiences Study, JAMA, 286(24): 3089–3096, 2001.

119. Rossow I & Lauritzen G, Shattered childhood: a key issue in suicidal behavior

among drug addicts, Addiction, 96(2): 227–240, 2001.

120. Levitan RD, Parikh SV, Lesage AD, Hegadoren KM, Adams M, Kennedy SH & Goering PN, Major depression in individuals with a history of childhood physical or sexual abuse: relationship in neurovegetative features, mania, and gender, Am J Psychiatry, 155(12): 1746–1752, 2001.

121. Bandelow B, Spath C, Tichauer GA, Broocks A, Hajak G & Ruther E, Early traumatic life events, parental attitudes, family history, and birth risk factors in patients with panic disorder, Compr Psychiatry, 43(4): 269–278, 2002.

122. Talbot NL, Duberstein PR, Cox C, Denning D, Conwell Y, Preliminary report on childhood sexual abuse, suicidal ideation, and suicide attempts among middle-aged and older depressed women, Am J Psychiatry, 12(5): 536–538, 2004.

123. Saleptsi E, Bichescu D, Rockstroh B, Neuner F, Schauer M, Studer K, Hoffmann K & Elbert T, Negative and positive childhood experiences across developmental periods in psychiatric patients with different diagnoses — an explorative study, BMC Psychiatry, 4(1): 40, 2004.

124. Bremner JD, Vermetten E, Afzal N & Vythilingam M, Deficits in verbal declarative memory function in women with childhood sexual abuse-related posttraumatic stress disorder, J Nerv Ment Dis, 192(10): 643–649, 2004.

125. Mireault GC & Bond LA, Parental death in childhood: perceived vulnerability, and adult depression and anxiety, Am J Orthopsychiatry, 62(4): 517–524, 1992.

126. Kivela SL, Luukinen H, Koski K, Viramo P & Pahkala K, Early loss of mother or father predicts depression in old age, Int J Geriatr Psychiatry, 13(8): 527–530, 1998.

127. Luecken LJ, Attachment and loss experiences during childhood are associated with adult hostility, depression, and social support, J Psychosom Res, 49(1): 85–91, 2000.

128. Kanugi H, Sugawara N, Aoki H, Nanko S, Hirose T & Kazamatsuri H, Early parental loss and depressive disorder in Japan, Eur Arch Psychitary Clin Neurosci, 245(2): 109–113, 1995.

129. Furukawa T, Harai H, Hirai T, Fujihara S, Kitamura T & Takahashi K, Childhood parental loss and alcohol dependence among Japanese men: a case-control study. Group for Longitudinal Affective Disorders Study (GLADS), Acta Psychiatr Scand, 97(6): 403–407, 1998.

130. Kendler KS, Neale MC, Prescott CA, Kessler RC, Heath AC, Corey LA & Eaves LJ, Childhood parental loss and alcoholism in women: a causal analysis using a twin-family design, Psychol Med, 26(1): 79–95, 1996.

131. Furukawa TA, Ogura A, Hirai T, Fujihara S, Kitamura T & Takahashi K, Early parental separation experiences among patients with bipolar disorder and major depression: a case-control study, J Affect Disord, 52(1–3): 85–91, 1999.

132. Dindo L & Coryell W, Comorbid major depression and panic disorder: significance of temporal sequencing to familial transmission, J Affect Disord, 82(1): 119–123, 2004.

133. Dannon P, Sason M, Shalgi B, Tusan L, Sapir Y & Kotler M, Comorbid psychiatric symptoms in pathological gamblers: anxiety, depression and substance abuse, Harefuah, 143(9): 643–646, 695, 2004.

134. James A, Lai FH & Dahl C, Attention Deficit hyperactivity disorder and suicide: a review of possible associations, Acta Psychiatr Scand, 110(6): 408–415, 2004.

135. Rounsavill BJ, Treatment of cocaine dependence and depression, Biol Psychiatry, 56(10): 803–809, 2004.

136. Speranza M, Corcos M, Levi G & Jeammet P, Obsessive-compulsive symptoms as a correlate of severity in the clinical presentation of eating disorders: measuring the effects of depression, Eat Weight Disord, 4(3): 121–127, 1999.

137. Serpell L, Livingstone A, Neiderman M & Lask B, Anorexia nervosa: obsessive-compulsive disorder, obsessive-compulsive personality disorder, or neither? Clin Psychol Rev, 22(5): 647–669, 2002.

138. Nagata T, Kawarada Y, Ohshima J, Iketani T & Kiriike N, Drug use disorders in Japanese eating disorder patients, Psychiatry Res, 109(2): 181–191, 2002.

139. Rudd MD, Dahm PF & Rajab MH, Diagnostic comorbidity in persons with suicidal ideation and behavior, Am J Psychiatry, 150(6): 928–934, 1993.

140. Bizeul C, Brun JM & Rigaud D, Depression influences the EDI scores in anorexia nervosa patients, Eur Psychiatry, 18(3): 119–123, 2003.

141. Kaye WH, Bulik CM, Thornton L, Barbarich N & Masters K, Comorbidity of anxiety disorders with anorexia and bulimia nervosa, Am J Psychiatry, 161(12): 2215–2221, 2004.

142. Riemann D, Hohagen F, Bahro M & Berger M, Sleep in depression: the influence of age, gender and diagnostic subtype on baseline sleep and the cholinergic REM induction test with RS 86, Eur Arch Psychiatry Clin Neurosci, 243: 279–290, 1994.

143. Soldatos CR, Insomnia in relation to depression and axiety epidemiologic considerations, J Psychosomatic Res, 38(1): 3–8, 1994.

144. Bourdet C & Goldenberg F, Insomnia in axiety: sleep EEG changes, J

Psychosomatic Res, 38(1): 93–104, 1994.

145. Torres AR, Dedomenico AM, Crepaldi AL & Miguel EC, Obsessive-compulsive symptoms in patients with panic disorder, Compr Psychiatry, 45(3): 219–224, 2004.

146. Klim YR, Park Q & Yu BH, Changes in lymphocyte subsets after short-term pharmacotherapy in patients with panic disorder, Psychitary Res, 128(2): 183–190, 2004.

147. Trifiletti RR & Packard AM, Immune mechanisms in pediatric neuropsychiatric disorders. Tourette's syndrome, OCD, and PANDAS, Child Adolesc Psychiatr Clin N Am, 8(4): 767–775, 1999.

148. Ravindran AV, Griffiths J, Merali Z & Anisman H, Circulating lymphocyte subsets in obsessive compulsive disorder, major depression and normal controls, J Affect Disord, 52(1–3): 1–10, 1999.

149. Monteleone P, Catapano F, Fabrazzo M, Tortorella A & Maj M, Decreased blood levels of tumor necrosis factor-alpha in patients with obsessive-compulsive disorder, Neuropsychobiology, 37(4): 182–185, 1998.

150. Andreoli AV, Keller SE, Rabaeus M, Marin P, Bartlett JA & Taban C, Depression and immunity: age, severity and clinical course, Brain Behav Immun, 7: 279–292, 1993.

151. Bartlett JA, Schleifer SJ, Demetrikopoulos MK & Keller SE, Immune differences in children with and without depression, Biol Psychiatry, 38: 771–774, 1995.

152. Andreoli A, Keller SE, Rabaeus M, Zaugg L, Garrone G & Taban C, Immunity, major depression, and panic disorder comorbidity, Biol Psychiatry, 31: 896–908, 1992.

153. Birmingham CL, Hodgson DM, Fung J, Brown R, Wakefield A, Bartrop R & Beumont P, Reduced febrile response to bacterial infection in anorexia nervosa patients, Int J Eat Disord, 34(2): 269–272, 2003.

154. Kahl KG, Hruse N, Rieckmann P & Schmidt MH, Cytokine mRNA expression patterns in the disease course of female adolescents with anorexia nervosa, Psychoneuroendocrinolog, 29(1): 13–20, 2004.

155. Nova E, Gomez-Martinez S, Morande G & Marcos A, Cytokine production by blood mononuclear cells from in-patients with anorexia nervosa, Br J Nutr, 88(2): 183–188, 2002.

156. Corcos M, Guilbaud O, Paterniti S, Moussa M, Chambry J, Chaouat G, Consoli SM & Jeammet P, Involvement of cytokines in eating disorders: a critical review of the human literature, Psychoneuroendocrinology, 28(3): 229–249, 2003.

157. Opdal SH, Opstad A, Vege A & Rognum TO, IL–10 gene polymorphisms are associated with infectious cause of sudden infant death, Hum Immunol, 64(12): 1183–1189, 2003.

158. Gleeson M & Cripps AW, Development of mucosal immunity in the first year of life and relationship to sudden infant death syndrome, FEMS Immunol Med Microbiol, 42(1): 21–33, 2004.

159. Harrison LM, Morris JA, Bishop LA, Lauder RM, Taylor CA & Telford DR, Detection of specific antibodies in cord blood, infant and maternal saliva and breast milk to staphylococcal toxins implicated in sudden infant death syndrome (SIDS), FEMS Immunol Med Microbiol, 42(1): 94–104, 2004.

160. Prandota J, Possible pathomechanisms of sudden infant death syndrome: key role of chronic hypoxia, infection/inflammation states, cytokine irregularities, and metabolic trauma in genetically predisposed infants, Am J Ther, 11(6): 517–546, 2004.

161. Alda M & Hrdina PD, Distribution of patelet 5-HT(2A) receptor densities in suicidal and non-suicidal depressives and control subject, Psychiatry Res, 94(3): 273–277, 2000.

162. Mendelson SD, The current status of the platelet 5-HT(2A) receptor in depression, J Affect Disord, 57(1–3): 13–24, 2000.

163. Audenaert K, Van Laere K, Dumont F, Vervaet M, Goethals I, Slegers G, Mertens J, Van Heeringen C & Dierckx RA, Decreased 5-HT(2A) receptor binding in patients with anorexia nervosa, J Nuclear Med, 44(2): 163–169, 2003.

164. Schruers K & Griez E, The effects of tianeptine or paroxetine on 35% CO2 provoked panic in panic disorder, J Psychopharmacol, 18(4): 553–558, 2004.

165. Bertani A, Perna G, Migliarese G, Di Pasquale D, Cucchi M, Caldirola D & Bellodi L, Comparison of the treatment with paroxetine and reboxetine in panic disorder: a randomized, single-blind study, Pharmacopsychiatry, 37(5): 206–210, 2004.

166. Wiegand MH, Galanakis P & Schreiner R, Nefazodone in primary insomnia: an open pilot study, Prog Neuropsychopharmacol Biol Psychiatry, 28(7): 1071–1078, 2004.

167. Mulrow CD, Williams JW Jr, Trivedi M, Chiquette E, Aguilar C, Cornell JE, Badget Noel PH, Lawrence V, Lee S, Luther M, Ramirez G, Richardson WS & Stamm K, Treatment of depression — newer pharmacotherapies, Psychopharmacol Bull, 34(4): 409–795, 1998.

168. Corman SL, Fedutes BA & Culley CM, Atomoxetine: the first nonstimulant for the management of attention-deficit/hyperactivity disorder, Am J Health Syst Pharm, 61(22): 2391–2399, 2004.

169.Oquendo MA, Kamali M, Ellis SP, Grunebaum MF, Malone KM, Brodsky BS, Sackeir HA & Mann JJ, Adequacy of antidepressant treatment after discharge and the occurrence of suicidal acts in major depression: a prospective study, Am J Psychiatry, 159(10): 1746–1751, 2002.

170. Sweet RA, Bergen SE, Sun Z, Sampson AR, Pierri JN & Lewis DA, Pyramidal cell size reduction in schizophrenia: evidence for involvement of auditory feedforward circuits, Biol Psychiatry, 55: 1128–1137, 2004.

171. Goldstein JM, Goodman JM, Seidman LJ, Kennedy DN, Makris N & Lee H, Cortical abnormalities in schizophrenia identified by structural magnetic resonance imaging, Arch Gen Psychiatry, 56: 537–547, 1999.

172. Hirayasu Y, Shenton ME, Salisbury DF, Dickey CC, Fischer IA & Mazzoni P, Lower left temporal lobe MRI volumes in patients with first-episode schizophrenia compared with psychotic patients with first-episode affective disorder and normal subjects, Am J Psychiatry, 155: 1384–1391, 1998.

173. Shergill SS, Brammer MJ, Amaro E, Williams SC, Murray RM & McGuire PK, Temporal course of auditory hallucinations, Br J Psychiatry, 185: 516–517, 2004.

174. Hayashi N, Igarashi Y, Suda K & Nakagawa S, Phenomenological features of auditory hallucinations and their symptomatological relevance, Psychiatry Clin Neurosci, 58(6): 651–659, 2004.

175. Dahmen N, Kasten M, Mittag K & Muller MJ, Narcoleptic and schizophrenic hallucinations Implications for differential diagnosis and pathophysiology, Eur J Health Econ, 3 Suppl 2: s94–98, 2002.

176. Martin JA & Penn DL, Attributional style in schizophrenia: an investigation in outpatients with and without persecutory delusions, Schizophr Bull, 28(1): 131–141, 2002.

177. Allen PP, Johns LC, Fu CH, Broome MR, Vythelingum GN & McGuire PK, Misattribution of external speech in patients with hallucinations and delusions, Schizophr Res, 69(2–3): 277–287, 2004.

178. Forte FS, Olfactory hallucinations as a proctologic manifestation of early schizophrenia, Am J Surg, 84(5): 620–622, 1952.

179. MedTerms, Hallucination, //www.MedicineNet.com, 2005.

180. American Psychiatric Association: Diagnostic and Statictical Manual of Mental Disorders, fourth Edition, Washington, DC, American Psychiatric Association , 1994.

181. Hansson LO, Waters N, Winblad B, Gottfries CG & Carlsson A, Evidence for biochemical heterogeneity in schizophrenia: a multivariate study of monoaminergic indices in human post-mortal brain tissue, J Neural Transm, 98: 217–235, 1994.

182. Jones HM & Pilowsky LS, Dopamine and antipsychotic drug action revisited, British J Psychiatry, 181: 271–275, 2002.

183. Jolliet P & Bourin M, Pharmacology of new antipsychotic drugs: Are they stabilizers of schizophrenic psychosis? Drugs News Perspect, 11(10): 625–630, 1998.

184. Llorca PM & Pere JJ, Clozapine, 10 years after – A clinical review, Encephale, 30(1): 474–491, 2004

185. Bai J, He F, Novikova SI, Undie AS, Dracheva S, Harouyunian V & Lidow MS, Abnormalities in the dopamine system in schizophrenia may lie in altered levels of dopamine receptor-interacting proteins, Biol Psychiatry, 56(6): 427–440, 2004.

186. Jeong SH, Joo EJ, Ahn YM & Kim YS, Association study of dopamine transporter gene and schizophrenia in Korean population using multiple single nucleotide polymorphism markers, Prog Neuropsychopharmacol Biol Psychiatry, 28(6): 975–983, 2004.

187. Lawford BR, Young RM, Swagell CD, Barnes M, Burton SC, Ward WK, Heslop KR, Shadforth S, van Daal A & Morris CP, The C/C genotype of the C957T polymorphism of the dopamine D2 receptor is associated with schizophrenia, Schizophr Res, 73(1): 31–37, 2005.

188. Goldman-Rakic PS, Castner SA, Svensson TH, Siever LJ & Williams GV, Targeting the dopamine D1 receptor in schizophrenia: insights for cognitive dysfunction, Psychopharmacology, 174(1): 3–16, 2004.

189. Bergson C, Levenson R, Goldman-Rakic PS & Lidow MS, Dopamine receptor-interacting proteins: the Ca(2+) connection in dopamine signaling, Trends Pharmacol Sci, 24(9): 486–492, 2003.

190. American Psychiatric Association: Diagnostic and Statictical Manual of Mental Disorders, fourth Edition. Washington, DC, American Psychiatric Association, 1994.

191. Bellino S, Rocca P, Patria L, Marchiaro L, Rasetti R, Di Lorenzo R, Paradiso E & Bogetti F, Relationships of age at onset with clinical features and cognitive functions in a sample of schizophrenia patients, J Clin Psychiatry, 65(7): 908–914, 2004.

192. Hafner H, Maurer K, Loffler W & Riecher-Rossler, The influence of age and sex on the onset and early course of schizophrenia, Brit J Psychiatry, 162: 80–86, 1993.

193. Schizophrenia Fellowship, Late Life. //www.sfnsm.org.au, 2005.

194. Goff DC & Evins AE, Negative symptoms in schizophrenia: neurobiological models and treatment response, Har Rev Psychiatry, 6(2): 59–77, 1998.

195. Malla AK, Takhar JJ, Norman RM, Manchanda R, Cortese L, Haricharan R, Verdi M & Ahmed R, Negative symptoms in first episode non-affective psychosis, Acta Psychiatr Scand, 105(6): 431–439, 2002.

196. Bogerts B, Zur Neuropathologie der Schizophrenien, Fortschr Neurol Psychiat, 52: 428–437, 1984.

197. Bogerts B, Schizophrenien als Erkrankungen des limbischen Systems. In Huber G ed., Basisstadien endogener Psychosen und das Borderline4Problem, Stuttgart: Schattauer : 163–179, 1985.

198. Bogerts B, David S, Falkai P & Tapernion-Franz U, Quantitative evaluation of astrocyte densities in schizophrenia, Presented at the 17th Congress of the Collegium Internationale Neuro-Psychopharmacologicum, Kyoto: Abst P-13 1–122, 1990.

199. Colter N, Battal S, Crow TJ, Johnstone EC, Brown R & Bruton CI, White matter reduction in the parahippocampal gyrus of patients withy schizophrenia, Arch Gen Psychiat, 44: 1023, 1987.

200. Gur RC, Schroeder L, Turner T, McGrath C, Chan RM, Turetsky BI, Alsop D, Maldji J & Gur RE, Brain activation during facial emotion processing, Neuroimage, 16(3 Pt 1): 651–662, 2002.

201. Phillips ML, Young AW, Scott SK, CaldeAJ, Andrew C, Giampietro V, Williams SC, Bullmore ET, Brammer M & Gray JA, Neural responses to facial and vocal expressions of fear and disgust, Proc R Soc Lond B Biol Sci, 265(1408): 1809–1817, 1998.

202. Phelps EA, O'Connor KJ, Gatenby JC, Gore JC, Grillon C & Davis M, Activation of the left amygdale to a cognitive representation of fear, Nat Neurosci, 4(4): 437–441, 2001.

203. Schneider F, Weiss U, Kessler C, Salloum JB, Posse S, Grodd W, Muller-Gartner HW, Differential amygdale activation in schizophrenia during sadness, Schizophr Res, 34(3): 133–142, 1998.

204. Phillips ML, Williams L, Senior C., Bullmore ET, Brammer MJ, Andrew C, Williams SC & David AS, A differential neural response to threatening and non-threatening negative facial expressions in paranoid and non-paranoid schizophrenics, Psychiatry Res, 92(1): 11–31, 1999.

205. Kucharska-Pietura K, Russell T & Masiak M, Perception of negative affect in schizophrenia - functional and structural changes in the amygdale. Review, Ann Univ Mariae Curie Sklodowska, 58(2): 453–458, 2003.

206. Jayakumar PN, Gangadhar BN, Subbakrishna DK, Janakiramaiah N, Srinivas JS & Keshavan MS, Membrane phospholipids abnormalities of basal ganglia in never-treated schizophrenia: a 31P magnetic resonance spectroscopy

study, Biol Psychiatry, 54(4): 491–494, 2003.

207. Bogerts B, Meertz E & Schonfeldt-Bausch R, Basal ganglia and limbic system pathology in schizophrenia. A morphometric study of brain volume and shrinkage, Arch Gen Psychiatry, 42(8): 784–791, 1985.

208. Gangadhar BN, Jayakumar PN, Subbakrishna DK, Janakiramaiah N & Keshavan MS, Basal ganglia high-energy phosphate metabolism in neuroleptic-naïve patients with schizophrenia: a 31-phosphorus magnetic resonance spectroscopic study, Am J Psychiatry, 161(7): 1304–1306, 1985.

209. Buckley P, O'Callaghan E, Mulvany F, Larkin C, Stack JP, Redmond O, Ennis JT, Thompson P & Waddington JL, Basal ganglia T2 relaxation times in schizophrenia: a quantitative magnetic resonance imaging study in relation to tardive dyskinesia, Psychiatry Res, 61(2): 95–102, 1995.

210. Dassa D, Sham PC, van Os J, Abel K, Jones P & Murray RM, Relationship of birth season to clinical features, family history, and obstetric complication in schizophrenia, Psychiatry Res, 64(1): 11–17, 1996.

211. Matsumoto H, Takei N, Saito F, Kachi K & Mori N, The association between obstetric complications and childhood-onset schizophrenia: a replication study, Psychol Med, 31(5): 907–914, 2001.

212. Preti A, Cardascia L, Zen T, Marchetti M., Favaretto G & Miotto P, Risk for obstetric complications and schizophrenia, Psychiatry Res, 96(2): 127–139, 2000.

213. Kirov G, Jones PB, Harvey I, Lewis SW, Toone BK, Rifkin L, Sham P & Murray RM, Do obstetric complications cause the earlier age at onset in male than female schizophrenics? Schizophr Res, 20(1–2): 117–124, 1996.

214. Kotlicka-Antczak M, Gmitrowicz A, Sobow TM & Rabe-Jablonska J, Obstetric complications and Apgar score in early-onset schizophrenic patients with prominent positive and prominent negative symptoms, J Psychiatr Res, 35(4): 249–257, 2001.

215. Rao ML & Möller HJ, Biochemical findings of negative symptoms in schizophrenia and their putative relevance to pharmacologic treatment, Neuropsychobiology, 30: 160–172, 1994.

216. Sandman CA, Glynn L, Wadhwa PD, Chicz-DeMet A, Porto M & Garite T, Maternal hypothalamic-pituitary-adrenal disregulation during the third trimester influences human fetal responses, Dev Neurosci, 25: 41–49, 2003.

217. Brown AS & Susser ES, In utero infection and adult schizophrenia, Ment Retard Dev Disabil Res Rev, 8(1): 51–57, 2002.

218. Izumoto Y, Inoue S & Yasuda N, Schizophrenia and the influenza epidemics of 1957 in Japan, Biol Psychiatry, 46(1): 119–124, 1999.

219. Limosin F, Rouillon F, Payan C, Cohen JM & Strub N, Prenatal exposure to influenza as a risk factor for adult schizophrenia, Acta Psychiatr Scand, 107(5): 331–335, 2003.

220. Wright P, Takei N, Rifkin L & Murray RM, Maternal influenza, obstetric complications, and schizophrenia, Am J Psychiatry, 152(12): 1714–1720, 1995.

221. Brown AS, Begg MD, Gravenstein S, Schaefer CA, Wyatt RJ, Bresnahan M, Babulas V & Susser ES, Serologic evidence of prenatal influenza in the etiology of schizophrenia, Arch Gen Psychiatry, 61(8): 774–780, 2004.

222. Gillmore JH, Jarskog LF, Vadlamudi S & Lauder JM, Prenatal infection and risk for schizophrenia: IL-I?, IL-6 and TNFx inhibit cortical neuron dendrite development, Neuropsychopharmacology, 29: 1221–1229, 2004.

223. Deidman LJ, Talbot NL, Kalinowski AG, McCarley RW, Faraone SV, Kremen WS, Pepple JR & Tsuang MT, Neuropsychological probes of fronto-limbic system dysfunction in schizophrenia, Schizophr Res, 6: 55–65, 1992.

224. Kopala L, Good K, Martzke J & Hurwitz T, Olfactory deficits in schizophrenia are not a function of task complexity, Schizophr Res, 17: 195–199, 1995.

225. Turetsky BI, Moberg PJ, Roalf DR, Arnold SE & Gur RE, Decrements in volume of anterior ventromedical temporal lobe and olfactory dysfunction in schizophrenia, Arch Gen Psychiatry, 60(12): 1193–1200, 2003.

226. Shergill SS, Brammer MJ, Amaro E, Williams SC, Murray RM & McGuire PK, Temporal course of auditory hallucinations, Br J Psychiatry, 185: 516–517, 2004.

227. Onitsuka T, Shenton ME, Salisbury DF, Dickey CC, Kasai K, Toner SK, Frumin M, Kikinis R, Jolesz FA & McCarley RW, Middle and inferior temporal gyrus gray matter volume abnormalities in chronic schizophrenia: an MRI study, Am J Psychiatry, 161: 1603–1611, 2004.

228. Harrison PJ, Freemantle N & Geddes JR, Meta-analysis of brain weight in schizophrenia, Schizophr Res, 64(1): 25–34, 2003.

229. Flashman LA, McAllister TW, Andreasen NC & Saykin AJ, Smaller brain size associated with unawareness of illness in patients with schizophrenia, Am J Psychiatry, 157(7): 1167–1169, 2000.

230. Ward KE, Friedman L, Wise A & Schulz SC, Meta-analysis of brain and cranial size in schizophrenia, Schizophr Res, 22(3): 197–213, 1996.

231. de Witte M, Working memory deficits in schizophrenia and the role of neuroticism, RuG, School of Behav and Cogn NeuroSci, 2004.

232. Talamini LM, Meeter M, Elvevaag B, Goldberg TE & Murre J, A

computational approach to memory deficit, Neuromod.org/ publications, 2000.

233. Pantelis C, Stuart GW, Nelson HE, Robbins TW & Barnes TR, Spatial working memory deficits in schizophrenia: relationship with tardive dyskinesia and negative symptoms, Am J Psychiatry, 158(8): 1276–1285, 2001.

234. Turner R. & Schiavetto A, The cerebellum in schizophrenia: a case of intermittent ataxia and psychosis-clinical, cognitive and neuroanatomical correlates, J Neuropsychiatry Clin Neurosci, 16(4): 400–408, 2004.

235. Martin P & Albers M, Cerebellum and schizophrenia: a selective review, Schizophr Bull, 21(2): 241–250, 1995.

236. Kleine JF, Guan Y, Kipiani E, Glonti M, Hoshi M & Büttner U, Trunk position influences vestibular responses of fastigial nucleus neurons in the alert monkey, J Neurophysiol, 91: 2090–2100, 2004.

237. Wang CS, Yang YK, Chen M, Chiu NT, Yeh TL & Lee IH, Negative symptoms and regional cerebral blood flow in patients with schizophrenia: a single photon emission computed tomography study, Kaohsiung J Med Sci, 19(9): 464–469, 2003.

238. Potkin SG, Alva G, Fleming K, Anand R, Keator D, Carreon D, Doo M, Jin Y, Wu JC & Fallon JH, A PET study of the pathophysiology of negative symptoms in schizophrenia, Am J Psychiatry, 159: 227–237, 2002.

239. Joseph AB, Anderson WH, O'Leary DH, Brainstem and vermis atrophy in catatonia, Am J Psychiatry, 142(3): 352–354, 1985.

240. Kinney DK, Yurgelun-Todd DA & Woods BT, Neurologic signs in patients with paranoid and nonparanoid schizophrenia, J Neuropsychiatry Clin Neurosci, 4: 447–449, 1992.

241. Flashman LA, Flaum M, Gupta S, Andreasen NC, Soft signs and neuropsychological performance in schizophrenia, Am J Psychiatry, 153: 526–532, 1996.

242. Dazzan P, Morgan KD, Orr KG, Hutchinson G, Chitnis X, Suckling J, Fearon P, Salvo J, McGuire PK, Mallett RM, Jones PB, Leff J & Murray RM, The structural brain correlates of neurological soft signs in AESOP first-episode psychoses study, Brain, 127(1): 143–153, 2004.

A-1. Lee M, Martin-Ruiz C, Graham A, Court J, Jaros E, Perry R, Iversen P, Bauman M & Perry E, Nicotine receptor abnormalities in the cerebellar cortex in autism, Brain, 125(Pt7): 1483–1495, 2002.

A-2. Deutsch SI & Campbell M, Status of cholinesterase activities in blood in neuropsychiatric disorders, Neurochem Res, 9(7): 863–869, 1984.

A-3. Chez MG, Aimonovitch M, Buchanan T, Mrazek S & Tremb RJ, Treating autistic spectrum disorders in children: utility of the cholinesterase inhibitor rivastigmine tartrate, J Child Neurol, 19(3): 165–169, 2004.

A-4. Perry EK, Lee MLW, Martin-Ruiz CM, Court JA, Volsen SG, Merrit J, Folly E, Iversen PE, Bauman ML, Perry RH & Wenk GL, Cholinergic activity in autism: abnormalities in the cerebral cortex and basal forebrain, Am J Psychiatry, 158: 1058–1010, 2001.

A-5. Miyazaki K, Narita N, Sakuta R, Miyahara T, Naruse H, Okado N & Narita M, Serum neurotrophin concentrations in autism and mental retardation: a pilot study, Brain Dev, 26(5): 292–295, 2004.

A-6. Perry R & Perry E, The cholinergic system in Alzheimer's disease, in biochemistry of dementia, John Wiley & Sons, pp 135–183, 1980.

A-7. Nelson KB, Grether JK, Croen LA, Dambrosia JM, Dickens BF, Hansen RL & Phillips TM, Neuropeptides and neurotrophins in neonatal blood of children with autism, mental retardation, or cerebral palsy, Neurology, 54(3): A247, 2000.

A-8. Crawford MA, Doyle W, Leaf A, Leighfield M, Ghebremeskel K & Phylactos A, Nutrition and neurodevelopmental disorders, Nutr Health, 9: 81–97, 1993.

A-9. Paumen M, Ishida Y, Muramatsu M, Yamamoto M & Honjo T, Inhibition of carnitine palmitoyltransferasel augments sphingolipid synthesis and palmitate-induced apoptosis, J Biol Chem, 272: 3324–3329, 1997.

A-10. Craciunescu CN, Brown EC, Mar MH, Albright CD, Nadeau MR & Zeisel SH, Folic Acid deficiency during late gestation decreases progenitor cell proliferation and increases apoptosis in fetal mouse brain, J Nutr, 134: 162–166, 2004.

A-11. Loy R, Heyer D, Williams CL & Meek WH, Choline-induced spatial memory facilitation correlates with altered distribution and morphology of septal neurons, Adv Exp Med Biol, 295: 373–382, 1991.

A-12. Meck W & Williams C, Perinatal choline supplementation increases the threshold for chunking in spatial memory, Neuroreport, 8: 3053–3059, 1997.

A-13. Fast D & Vance D, Nascent VLDL phospholipids composition is altered when phosphatidylcholine biosynthesis is inhibited: Evidence for a novel mechanism that regulates VLDL secretion, Biochim Biophys Acta, 1258: 159–168, 1995.

A-14. Cermak JM, Holler T, Jackson DA & Blusztajn JK, Prenatal availability of choline modifies development of the hippocampal cholinergic system, FASEB, 12: 349–357, 1998.

A-15. Williams CL, Meck WH, Heyer DD & Loy R, Hypertrophy of basal forebrain neurons and enhanced visuospatial memory in perinatally choline-supplemented rats, Brain Res, 794(2): 225–238, 1998.

A-16. Edited by Bauman ML & Kemper TL, The neurobiology of autism, John Hopkins University Press, 1994.

A-17. Albright CD, Tsai AY, Friedrich CB, Mar MH & Zeisel SH, Choline availability alters embryonic development of the hippocampus and septum in the rat, Brain Res Dev Brain Res, 113(1–2): 13–20, 1999.

A-18. Mellott TJ, Williams CJ, Meck WH & Blusztajn JK, Prenatal choline supplementation advances hippocampal development and enhances MAPK and CREB activation, FASEB, 18(3): 545–547, 2004.

A-19. Li Q, Guo-Ross S, Lewis DV, Turner D, White AM, Wilson WA & Swartzwelder HS, Dietary prenatal choline supplementation alters postnatal hippocampal structure and function, J Neurophysiol, 91(4): 1545–1555, 2004.

A-20. Meck WH & Williams CL, Choline supplementation during prenatal development reduces proactive interference in spatial memory, Brain Res Dev Brain, 118(1–2): 51–59, 1999.

A-21. Meck WH, Smith RA & Williams CL, Pre- and postnatal choline supplementation produces long-term facilitation of spatial memory, Dev Psychobiol, 21(4): 339–353, 1988.

A-22. Meck WH & Williams CL, Characterization of the facilitative effects of perinatal choline supplementation on timing and temporal memory, Neuroreport, 8(13): 2831–2835, 1997.

A-23. U.S. Food and Drug Administration, Folic acid fortification, FDA/CFSAN Folic Acid Fact Sheet, February 29, 1996.

A-24. California Department of Developmental Services, DDS Autism Report, 2003.

A-25. Wilson CA & Hanin I, Brain-derived neurotrophic factor induced stimulation of septal choline acetyltransferase activity in ethylcholine mustard aziridinium treated rats, Neurosci Lett, 229(3): 149–152, 1997.

A-26. Morse JK, Wiegand SJ, Anderson K, You Y, Cai N, Carnahan J, Miller J, DiStefano P, Altar CA & Lindsay RM, Brain-derived neurotrophic factor (BDNF) prevents the degeneration of medial septal cholinergic neurons following fimbria transaction, J Neurosci, 13(10): 4146–4156, 1993.

A-27. Gottschalk W, Pozzo-Miller LD, Figurov A & Lu B, Presynaptic modulation of synaptic transmission and plasticity by brain-derived neurotrophic factor in the developing hippocampus, J Neurosci, 18(17): 6830–6839, 1998.

A-28. Antony AC & Hansen DK, Hypothesis: folate-responsive neural tube defects and neurocristopathies, Teratology, 62(1): 42–50, 2000.

A-29. Daniel JM & Dohanich GP, Acetylcholine mediates the estrogens induced increase in NMDA receptor binding in CA1 of the hippocampus and the associated improvement in working memory, J Neurosci, 21(17): 6949–6956, 2001.

A-30. Mooney SB, Giudice LC, Endocrinology of pregnancy, Endotext.com, 2002.

A-31. Holmes A, Metal-metabolism and autism, //www.autisminfo.com/AmyHolmesMD.htm, 2005.

A-32. MoonDragon's Health & Wellness, Copper toxicity, //www.moondragon.org/health/disorders/coppertox.html, 2005.

A-33. Armitage A, Roffwarg HP, Rush AJ, Calhoun JS, Purdy DG & Giles DE, Digital period analysis of sleep EEG in depression, Biol Psychiatry, 31: 52-68, 1992.

A-34. Leopola U, Koponen H & Leinonen E, Sleep in panic disorders, J Psychosomatic Res, 18(1): 105-111, 1994.

A-35. Brake WG, Alves SE, Dunlop JC, Lee SJ, Bulloch K, Allen PB, Greengard P & McEwen BS, Novel target sites for estrogen action in the dorsal hippocampus: an examination of synaptic proteins, Endocrinology, 142(3): 1284–1289, 2001.